GREENSBORO
LUMBERJACK ELIMINATION MATCH
SUPER DESTROYER
& IVAN KOLOFF
Versus
PAUL JONES &
WAHOO McDANIEL
SIX MAN TAG TEAM MATCH
OLE ANDERSON
GENE ANDERSON
RIC FLAIR
Vs
SWEDE HANSON
SANDY SCOTT
TIGER CONWAY, JR.
BRUTE BERNARD Vs BOB BRUGGERS
KEVIN SULLIVAN Vs MR. HAYASHI
Vs FRANK MONTE ★ COWBOY PARKER Vs JOE FURR ★ TIO TIO Vs KEN DILLINGER
WORLD HEAVYW
WAHO
JACK BRISCO
WORLD TAG TEAM MATCH
OLE & GENE ANDERSON Versus PAUL JONES And TIGER CONWAY
DUSTY RHODES Versus RIC FLAIR
JERRY BRISCO Versus COWBOY
WRESTLING
GREENSBORO
WAR MEMORIAL COLISEUM
THUR. APR. 3
8:15 P.M.
DOUBLE MAIN EVENT
WORLD TAG TEAM MATCH
WAHOO McDANIEL
& PAUL JONES
Versus
OLE ANDERSON
& GENE ANDERSON
DUSTY RHODES Vs BLACKJACK MULLIGAN
RUFUS R. JONES & SONNY KING Versus MR. FUGI & ART NELSON
SUPER STAR BILL GRAHAM Versus ABE JACOBS
SANDY SCOTT Vs DOUG GILBERT ★ BOB BRUGGERS & TOMMY SEIGLER Vs KEN DILLENGER & COWBOY PARKER
WAR MEMORIAL
GREENSBORO
SAT. JULY
U. S. HEAVYWEIGHT CHAMPION
NNY VALENTI
Versus
HARLEY RAC
MID-ATLANTIC CHAMPION
RIC FLAIR Vs WA McD
MIXED-TAG TEAM MATCH
SHEPARD
MISSOURI MAULER
BORIS MALENKO
DOUG GILBERT Vs KLONDIKE BILL ★ TIM WOODS Vs MAN MT. BLACKWELL
RIAL COLISEUM
NSBORO
ULY 3
8:15
GIANT
ONES
DERSON
HARLEY RACE
SUN. SEPT. 7
DOUBLE MAIN EVENT
U. S. HEAVYWEIGHT TITLE MATCH
JOHNNY VALENTINE
CHAMPION
Versus
DUSTY RHODES
TEXAS TORNADO ELIMINATION MATCH
OLE & GENE ANDERSON
MID-ATLANTIC CHAMPIONSHIP
WRESTLING
GREENSBORO
SUN. NOV. 9
17 BIG MATCHES
U.S. CHAMPIONSHIP TOURNAM
WITH NAMES SUCH AS
RED BASTION
DUSTY RHODES
RUFUS R. JONES
OLE ANDERSON
RAY STEVENS
TERRY FUNK
GENE ANDERSON
STEVE STRONG
SUPER STAR BILLY GRAHAM
KEN PATERA
PAUL JONES
TIM WOODS
HARLEY RACE
BLACKJACK MULLIGAN
WAHOO McDANIEL
PROFESSOR MALENKO
TIGER CONWAY, JR.
CHAMPIONSHIP
WAR MEMORIAL COLISEUM
GREENSBORO
THANKSGIVING DAY
THURS. NOV. 27
8:15 P.M.
HEAVYWEIGHT TITLE MATCH
NO DISQUALIFICATIONS
WAHOO McDANIEL VS JACK BRISCO
HEAVYWEIGHT TITLE MATCH

Mid-Atlantic Championship Wrestling
1975 YEARBOOK

Dick Bourne & David Chappell
The Mid-Atlantic Gateway

Copyright © 2014 by Richmond W. Bourne. Independently published by the Mid-Atlantic Gateway.

Project concept, layout, and cover design by Dick Bourne.

The historical narratives and talent rosters were written and compiled by David Chappell. They were originally published as part of the "Mid-Atlantic Wrestling Almanac" on the Mid-Atlantic Gateway.

The special features and title histories written and researched by Dick Bourne. Some of this material was originally published on the Mid-Atlantic Gateway.

The retrospective of the 1975 United States Heavyweight Championship Tournament in Greensboro was written by Dick Bourne, with assistance of first-hand accounts from Dave Routh. The feature and includes contributions from Mark Eastridge, Carroll Hall, George South, Don Holbrook, John Hitchcock, Bill Janosik, John Pagan, and Scooter Lesley. Special thanks to Terry Funk and Paul Jones for their participation in this feature. Some of this material was previously published on the Mid-Atlantic Gateway in 2005, the 30th anniversary of the tournament.

Newspaper ads and results in the Newspaper Clippings section are from the vast collection of Mark Eastridge.

Editing assistance provided by Peggy Lathan.

Match results and listings in the Record Book chapter were compiled by Mark James from various sources. Mark's results collections can be found at MemphisWrestlingHistory.com. For more info, see the bottom of page 243.

Some event posters are from the collection of John Hitchcock at Parts Unknown Comic Store in Greensboro, NC.

Many photos within are from the copyrighted collection of Scooter Lesley of Ditchcat Photography and are used with permission. They were taken by the late Gene Gordon, one of the area's most famous wrestling photographers.

"Mid-Atlantic Wrestling Magazine" was the event program sold at the matches in 1975. No copyright was listed in these original publications. No copyright is claimed or inferred here in any way on this material. It is presented here for historical purposes only. A special thanks and salute to Les Thatcher who originally put those programs together for Jim Crockett Promotions.

For more information on Mid-Atlantic Wrestling and Jim Crockett Promotions history, visit the Mid-Atlantic Gateway at midatlanticgateway.com.

ISBN-13: 978-1502338426
ISBN-10: 1502338424
ACCAVER 75.CS.1.0.1.140918

TABLE OF CONTENTS

Introduction	4
Defining an Era	5
Title Histories	6
Talent Roster	9
History: January - March	12
Newspaper Clippings	22
Magazine: Vol. 1 Issue 1	52
History: April - June	70
Event Posters	82
Magazine: Vol. 1 Issue 2	88
History: July - September	105
Magazine: Vol. 1 Issue 3	116
The Tournament	134
History: October - December	150
Magazine: Vol. 1 Issue 4	160
The Record Book	194

"I can't make them believe wrestling is real, but I sure can make them believe I am real."

- Johnny Valentine

This book is dedicated to the memory of the legendary Johnny Valentine, seen here with the original Mid-Atlantic title belt.

Introduction

I had held a casual interest in professional wrestling since I was at least 8 or 9 years old, from around 1969. But it was in the early summer of 1975 that the wrestling-bug bit me, and I became a serious fan of the weekly adventures of the big wrestling stars that competed under the banner of Jim Crockett Promotions and the National Wrestling Alliance.

The angle that hooked me and turned me into a fan for life was the infamous "Supreme Sacrifice" match that Gene and Ole Anderson had with NWA world tag team champions Wahoo McDaniel and Paul Jones on television in June of 1975. It took place on the show "Mid-Atlantic Championship Wrestling" hosted by Bob Caudle and David Crockett. At that time it was extremely rare to see a title match of any kind on TV, much less for world titles. Wahoo and Paul had defeated the Anderson Brothers for those belts a few weeks earlier, and the Andersons were getting a rematch on television.

The two teams fought hard for over 20 minutes and Wahoo and Paul had gained the upper hand and looked to be closing in on the win. As Wahoo went into his famous war dance, which signified to fans that victory was near, a desperate Ole Anderson took Wahoo by the head and slammed him into the head of his brother Gene who was leaning in from their corner hoping for a tag. The collision knocked both wrestlers out; Gene fell to the floor and Wahoo fell unconscious to the mat, where Ole covered him for the three count. Ole Anderson had just sacrificed his own brother so that the team could regain their world tag team championship belts.

At 13 years old, and completely buying into this, I sat stunned in my living room floor. I was shocked that anyone would sacrifice their own brother just to win championships. This illustrated how important those tag team belts were to these guys who would apparently do anything to win them, and I was sure at that point that Wahoo McDaniel and Paul Jones would now do anything to get them back. I was hooked. Lots of other people were, too, as thousands of fans across the Carolinas and Virginia lined up at arenas to buy tickets to see the two teams battle for the world tag team titles that entire summer of 1975.

In the mid-1990s, I had just started exploring this new thing called the Internet and found a message board devoted to classic pro-wrestling from the 1970s. I posted a message asking if anyone remembered this famous wrestling angle as fondly as I did. A fellow from Richmond, VA, responded. Not only did he remember it, he still had an audio-cassette recording of the match the he made himself with a portable tape recorder and handheld microphone.

That fellow was David Chappell, and a great friendship was born from that message board exchange. David sent me a copy of the tape, and soon after we started talking over all the Mid-Atlantic Wrestling memorabilia we each had. In 2000 we decided to start The Mid-Atlantic Gateway, a website devoted to documenting the history of this area and that special time in pro-wrestling history.

When I decided to put together a series of yearbooks to collect some of this memorabilia and written history in printed form, it was an easy decision to select the year 1975 for the first book. That year got me hooked on Mid-Atlantic Wrestling and eventually lead to the partnership that began the Mid-Atlantic Gateway.

We hope you enjoy reliving some of these memories here with us.   - *Dick Bourne*

Defining the Mid-Atlantic Championship Wrestling Era

The "Mid-Atlantic" wrestling era by name did not have an official starting date, nor did it cease to exist on a certain official date. However, the time boundaries that mark the beginning and end of Mid-Atlantic Championship Wrestling (by name) line up nicely at 1973 and 1986 respectively, based on certain events that took place in those years.

The earliest official documented reference to "Mid-Atlantic" Wrestling was actually in March of 1972 when the designation started showing up in newspaper ads for shows in the Joe Murnick towns of Raleigh and Norfolk.

But in 1973, the branding became complete when the two TV shows taped in Raleigh ("Championship Wrestling" for the Raleigh market and "All-Star Wrestling" for all other markets) changed names to "Mid-Atlantic Championship Wrestling". During this same year, the Charlotte and High Point TV studio tapings were discontinued and all TV for the territory was consolidated to Raleigh.

In October of 1973, the Eastern Heavyweight Championship (the top singles title in the territory) was changed to the Mid-Atlantic Heavyweight Championship and a new belt presented to the reigning champion Jerry Brisco. In December, the Atlantic Coast tag team titles were changed to Mid-Atlantic tag team championships.

In the documentary "Jim Crockett Promotions: The Good Ol' Days", produced by Michael Elliot, David Crockett revealed that it was John Ringley (then Jim Sr.'s son-in-law) who actually came up with the name "Mid-Atlantic" Wrestling.

By January of 1974, the promotion now led by Jim Crockett, Jr. had effectively switched all references to the promotion to the name "Mid-Atlantic Championship Wrestling." The promotional materials, including event posters and newspaper ads, all said Mid-Atlantic Championship Wrestling.

In June of 1986, the "Mid-Atlantic Championship Wrestling" television show was renamed "NWA Pro Wrestling" and that December, the Mid-Atlantic heavyweight championship was vacated. Jim Crockett Promotions had begun expanding nationally and there was no longer a regional component or reference to the Mid-Atlantic region. The era known as "Mid-Atlantic Wrestling" had quietly come to an end.

TITLE HISTORIES
NATIONAL WRESTLING ALLIANCE AND JIM CROCKETT PROMOTIONS – 1975

NWA WORLD HEAVYWEIGHT CHAMPIONSHIP

Jack Brisco
Brisco entered the year 1975 the NWA world champion having defeated Shohei Baba on 12/9/74 in Toyoashi, Japan.

Terry Funk
Defeated Jack Brisco on 12/10/75 in Miami Beach, Florida

NWA WORLD TAG TEAM CHAMPIONSHIP

Gene & Ole Anderson
Announced January 29, 1975 in Raleigh, NC at WRAL TV Studios

The Anderson Brothers were announced on Mid-Atlantic television as having won a tournament in California to become the NWA World Tag Team Champions. They defeated Dino Bravo and Gino Brito in the finals of the tournament. This was a fictitious tournament to establish the championship. Broadcast date February 1, 1975.

Wahoo McDaniel and Paul Jones
5/15/75 Greensboro Coliseum, Greensboro, North Carolina

Gene and Ole Anderson (2)
6/11/75 at WRAL TV studios, Raleigh, North Carolina.

The famous "supreme sacrifice" angle where Ole Anderson sacrifices his brother Gene by throwing Wahoo McDaniel's head into the head of his brother Gene.

NOTE: Many published title histories list Tiger Conway, Jr. and Steve Keirn as winning the World Tag Team titles from the Andersons on 11/3/75 in Charlotte. Research has proven this not to be the case. Keirn and Conway never held the NWA World Tag Titles.

UNITED STATES HEAVYWEIGHT CHAMPIONSHIP

Harley Race
Race was brought into Greensboro by Jim Crockett Promotions as the U.S. Champion. Urban legend has it that a fictitious tournament was held in Florida for the title and that Race defeated Mid-Atlantic Wrestling legend Johnny Weaver in the finals of that tournament. This story was used to establish the championship in the area. There is a dispute as to whether or not this was actually ever mentioned on television.

Johnny Valentine, wearing the brand new United States heavyweight championship belt, leaves the ring after defeating Harley Race in Greensboro (Photo by Dave Routh)

Johnny Valentine
07/03/75 Greensboro Coliseum, Greensboro, NC

Title Vacated
Title is vacated following the 10/04/75 Wilmington, NC plane crash which ended the career of reigning champion Johnny Valentine. A tournament to fill the vacant title is scheduled for 11/9/75 in Greensboro.

Terry Funk
11/09/75 Greensboro Coliseum, Greensboro, NC

Funk defeats Paul Jones in the finals of the historic one-night U.S. Title tournament to fill the title vacated by Johnny Valentine.

Paul Jones
11/27/75 (Annual Thanksgiving Show) Greensboro Coliseum, Greensboro, NC

Jones defeats tournament winner Terry Funk who would go on to win the NWA world Championship from Jack Brisco three weeks later.

MID-ATLANTIC HEAVYWEIGHT CHAMPIONSHIP

Johnny Valentine
Valentine held the title coming into 1975 having been awarded the championship following an injury to champion Jerry Brisco in December of 1974.

Paul Jones
3/9/75 Park Center, Charlotte NC. Jones pins Valentine in a steel cage match.

Johnny Valentine
3/19/75. Announced at the TV taping in Raleigh (airing in most markets on 3/22/75) that Jones had been stripped of the title and the belt returned to Johnny Valentine by NWA President Sam Muchnick.

Mid-Atlantic Championship cont.

Wahoo McDaniel
06/29/75 Asheville Civic Center, Asheville NC

After a chase that went on for the better part of a year, Wahoo McDaniel finally defeated Johnny Valentine for the Mid-Atlantic title.

Ric Flair
09/20/75 Hampton Coliseum, Hampton, VA

Many title histories don't have Flair winning his first Mid-Atlantic title until spring of 1976, but it was actually on 9/20/75, two weeks before the Wilmington Plane Crash. Flair was allowed to maintain the title throughout his recovery and rehabilitation period, despite not defending the title during the NWA 30-day defense period. He returned to action in January, mostly in tag matches or six-man matches, and began defense of the title in February.

MID-ATLANTIC TAG TEAM CHAMPIONSHIP

Paul Jones & Tiger Conway, Jr.
The duo entered 1975 with the titles after having defeating Ric Flair and Brute Bernard for the titles on 12/6/74 at County Hall in Charleston, South Carolina. Brute Bernard substituted for Rip Hawk after Hawk had left the area for the IWA.

Gene & Ole Anderson
2/20/75 Greensboro Coliseum, Greensboro, NC

This was a World Tag Title vs. Mid-Atlantic Tag Title Match with Jones & Conway. After the Andersons unified the titles, the Mid-Atlantic Tag Titles were retired. They would be reinstated in September of 1976.

MID-ATLANTIC TELEVISION CHAMPIONSHIP

Paul Jones
12/26/74 Greensboro NC, Greensboro NC

Ric Flair
02/08/75 Memorial Coliseum, Winston Salem, North Carolina

Paul Jones
08/08/75 Richmond Arena, Richmond, VA

Title Vacated
12/3/75 - Title forfeited by Paul Jones after winning the U.S. championship on 11/27/75.
The title is vacant from 12/3/75 until 4/14/76. A tournament is conducted on Mid-Atlantic television.

TALENT ROSTER

The following pages contain a comprehensive list of all wrestlers, referees, TV ring announcers and broadcasters to appear on Mid-Atlantic Wrestling television and in the arenas. The main-roster wrestlers are divided up into three different categories: "main events", "mid card", and "lower card". Each category is sub-divided into "heels" and "babyfaces", which are insider terms for the bad guys and the good guys respectively. An asterisk (*) before the name indicates that the wrestler appeared in more than one category during the year.

MAIN EVENTS

BABYFACES
- *Avenger
- *Tiger Conway
- Paul Jones
- *Rufus R. Jones
- *Steve Keirn
- Sonny King
- Wahoo McDaniel
- *Ken Patera
- Tim Woods

HEELS
- Gene Anderson
- Ole Anderson
- Ric Flair
- *"Superstar" Billy Graham
- Ivan Koloff
- Angelo Mosca
- *Blackjack Mulligan
- *Spoiler #1
- Spoiler #2
- *Steve Strong
- Super Destroyer
- Johnny Valentine

MID-CARD

BABYFACES
- Tony Atlas
- *Avenger
- *Bob Bruggers
- *Tiger Conway
- *Charlie Cook
- Swede Hanson
- *Rufus R. Jones
- *Steve Keirn
- *Danny Miller
- *Ken Patera
- El Rayo
- Sandy Scott
- *Tommy Seigler
- *John "Wolfman" Smith
- *Roberto Soto
- *Ron Starr
- Johnny Weaver

HEELS
- Brute Bernard
- Jerry Blackwell
- Mike "The Judge" DuBois
- *Ken Dillinger
- Mr. Fuji
- *Doug Gilbert
- Boris Malenko
- Missouri Mauler
- *Blackjack Mulligan
- Art Nelson
- Chuck O'Connor
- *Cowboy Parker
- *Spoiler #1
- *Steve Strong

An asterisk (*) before the name indicates that the wrestler appeared in more than one category during the year.

LOWER CARD

BABYFACES
Billy Ashe
*Avenger
*Bob Bruggers
Bob Burns
*Charlie Cook
Joe Furr
*Johnny Heidman
Abe Jacobs
*Steve Keirn
Rick Kelly
Don Kernodle
Klondike Bill
L.D. Lewis
Pepe Lopez
Rick McGraw
*Danny Miller
Frank Monte
*Greg Peterson
Tony Rocca
Terry Sawyer
*Tommy Seigler
Don Serrano
*Roberto Soto
Mike Stallings
*Ron Starr
Kevin Sullivan
Tio Tio
Bobby Williams
Larry Zbyszko

HEELS
Blue Scorpion
Bill Crouch
*Ken Dillinger
*Jack Evans
Charlie Fulton
*El Gaucho
Pedro Godoy
George "Two Ton" Harris
Mr. Hayashi
Bill Howard
Frank Monte
Frank Morrell
Mike Paidousis
*Cowboy Parker
Buddy Porter
Larry Sharpe
*John "Wolfman" Smith
Doug Somers
Joe Soto
Joe Turner
Bill White

GUEST SHOTS

Andre the Giant
Bob Backlund
Ox Baker
Red Bastien
Jack Brisco
Jerry Brisco
Bobcat Brown
*Haystacks Calhoun
*El Gaucho
Jack Evans
Paul Figuaro
Terry Funk
*"Superstar" Billy Graham
*Johnny Heidman
Jose Lothario
*Blackjack Mulligan
Harley Race
Masked Raider
Johnny Rodz
Dusty Rhodes
Nelson Royal
Tom Stanton
Ray Stevens
Chris Taylor
Frank Valois
Bearcat Wright

WOMEN

Ann Casey
Donna Christianello
Dottie Downs
Joyce Grable
Susan Green
Leilani Kai
Paula Kay
Fabulous Moolah
Candy Rich
Sheila Shepherd
Belle Starr
Evelyn Stevens
Toni Rose
Vickie Williams

REFEREES

Walter Buckner
*Haystacks Calhoun (special)
Frank Dusek
Sonny Fargo
*El Gaucho
*Johnny Heidman
*Sonny King (special)
Bronco Lubich (one card)
Angelo Martinelli
*Greg Peterson
George Scott (special)
*Les Thatcher
Ron West
Tommy Young

Either Jim or David Crockett was a special referee for one card. The entry "Crockett" was listed in George Scott's Day Planner for referee.

MIDGET WRESTLERS

MEN
Sonny Boy Hayes
Haiti Kid
Cowboy Lang
Little John
Little Louie
Lord Littlebrook
Little Toyko

WOMEN
Darlin Dagmar
Diamond Lil

TELEVISION BROADCASTERS

Ed Capral
Bob Caudle
David Crockett
Sam Menaker
*Les Thatcher
*Johnny Weaver

Note: There were many wrestlers who appeared as special color commentators throughout the year.

TV PROMO ANNOUNCERS

Bob Caudle
Elliot Murnick
Billy Powell
Les Thatcher
Big Bill Ward

TV RING ANNOUNCERS

Carl Murnick
Elliot Murnick
Joe Murnick
David Crockett

Q1 HISTORY
by David Chappell

JANUARY

NWA World Tag Team Titles Come To The Mid-Atlantic Area

The month of January 1975 was dominated by the return of "The Minnesota Wrecking Crew" to the Mid-Atlantic area. Gene and Ole Anderson resurfaced in Jim Crockett Promotions at the tail end of 1974 after an eight-month hiatus, and immediately made their presence felt as the new year dawned. Johnny Valentine, Paul Jones, Wahoo McDaniel and the Super Destroyer also all had impressive months, but Gene and Ole Anderson stood out in January, as they brought the NWA World Tag Team Titles into the Mid-Atlantic area.

Gene and Ole Anderson hit the ground running upon their return to the Mid-Atlantic area, immediately targeting Mid-Atlantic Tag Team Champions Paul Jones and Tiger Conway, Jr. These four had some terrific bouts throughout the month, with Jones and Conway holding on to the Mid-Atlantic Tag Team Titles until nearly the end of February before the Anderson's finally prevailed. However, much bigger news would come about only days later regarding the Anderson Brothers.

On the January 29, 1975 television taping from the WRAL Studios in Raleigh, North Carolina, it was announced that Gene and Ole Anderson had competed in and won a tournament in California and were crowned the NWA World Tag Team Champions. The promotion stated that teams including Ray Stevens and Nick Bockwinkle, Eddie and Mike Graham, the Vachon brothers, Terry and Bobby Kay and the Funk brothers all participated in the tournament. Ole Anderson, ever modest, commented saying "could there be any doubt in anyone's mind that we would end up world champions? After all we are the greatest tag team in the history of wrestling. My brother and I know that the fans in this area are happy to have us back, and now that we are wearing the World Title belts, they will be even happier."

Despite the majority of fans in Jim Crockett Promotions disliking the Anderson's, there could be no doubt the elation of fans to have the World Tag Team Champs in their own backyard. There were challengers lining up immediately for Gene and Ole. In fact, during the month of January, the formidable duo of Wahoo McDaniel and Sonny King began teaming and were extremely impressive. These two spoke of teaming in the past, and felt their experience together would give them every chance to be successful. And in fact, the team of Wahoo and King would get the first shot at unseating the new champs as the calendar flipped over to February.

Mid-Atlantic Champion Johnny Valentine, Super Destroyer Have Good Months

Mid-Atlantic Heavyweight Champion Johnny "The Champ" Valentine continued to roll on in January of 1975, seemingly unbeatable. On Mid-Atlantic television in January, Johnny continued to put up his 2000 silver dollars frequently, steamrolling the competition. "The Champ" was especially brutal to a very young Kevin Sullivan during a match for his 2000 silver dollars that took place on January 22, 1975 in the Raleigh, NC WRAL studios. Valentine also defended his Mid-Atlantic title often in January, and had a memorable series of title bouts against Paul Jones in Charlotte, North Carolina this month. Jones, the 1974 Wrestler of the Year in the area and the reigning Mid-Atlantic Television Champion, battled valiantly during this series of title bouts but could not wrest the title from Valentine.

The month of January 1975 was also a successful one for the masked Super Destroyer. The Destroyer was having less interaction with Brute Bernard in January, after having purchased the Brute's contract in late 1974 and becoming almost a "manager" for Bernard. The two began to team infrequently in January, and instead the Super D. turned his attention to the other masked man that was in the area, the masked Avenger. While much smaller than the Destroyer, the Avenger was speedy and possessed a great deal of wrestling ability. The Avenger was on quite a hot streak, and he and the Super Destroyer started their memorable feud in earnest during the month of January to see who was the best masked man in the Mid-Atlantic area. This feud would last though the cold weather months of early 1975, but it was clear in January that this matchup of the masked men would be a significant test for the Super Destroyer.

Roster Movement

January of 1975 saw some significant movement in the talent roster of Jim Crockett Promotions. Long time mainstay Rip Hawk left the promotion for good at the end of December 1974. Rip's long time partner Swede Hanson stayed in the area, but January marked his slide into mid-card status. Veteran Johnny Weaver was also out of the area on extended leave, and would not return for many months. Tough main eventer Ivan Koloff left the area before the end of January, and would not return to Jim Crockett Promotions for over five years. Chuck O'Connor, a top mid-card performer, also left the area before the end of January and would not reemerge in the area again until late 1978, when he called himself John Studd. Despite these loses the talent-laden roster developed in 1974 remained significantly intact, and the continued rapid development of a young Ric Flair along with the Anderson's coming back on the scene and capturing the NWA World Tag Team Titles in short order, made the month of January 1975 one that would insure that the rest of the year held much promise and excitement.

WHO'S HOT

1. GENE & OLE ANDERSON---The Anderson's dominated all competition in January of 1975, and most importantly won and brought the NWA World Tag Team Titles to the Mid-Atlantic area this month.

2. JOHNNY VALENTINE---"The Champ" held onto his Mid-Atlantic Heavyweight Title, despite some classic battles against top challengers Paul Jones and Wahoo McDaniel.

3. SUPER DESTROYER---The Destroyer was as dominating as ever, and was entering a memorable "Feud of the Masked Men" with the masked Avenger where it was becoming clear that the loser would never be the same when the smoke cleared.

WHO'S NOT

1. SWEDE HANSON---The big Swede's ten-year run as a main event performer for Jim Crockett Promotions had reached its end, and January of 1975 began Swede's gradual but steady fall into mid-card status.

2. CHUCK O'CONNOR---O'Connor had been a solid mid-card wrestler for most of 1974, even headlining a few cards. But in January of 1975, the losses were frequent and O'Connor left the area entirely before the end of the month.

3. IVAN KOLOFF---The "Russian Bear" had a great run in the area for much of 1974, but began to be de-emphasized during January of 1975, and like O'Connor, left the Mid-Atlantic area before the month ended.

FEBRUARY

The month of February 1975 provided Mid-Atlantic Wrestling fans tons of hot action, despite the frigid weather. From the first days of February, where ice and snow played havoc with cards as far south as Columbia, South Carolina, to the last days of the month where there was the promise of spring in the air, February 1975 provided us with a wealth of fantastic memories.

Anderson Brothers Make First Defense of NWA World Tag Team Championships; also win Mid-Atlantic titles.

Early in the month of February, February 7th to be exact, Gene and Ole Anderson made the first defense of their recently won NWA World›s Tag Team Titles in Richmond, Virginia against the tandem of Wahoo McDaniel and Sonny King. In that match, as well as in the rest of their title defenses through the month, the Anderson›s successfully defended their titles. By the end of the month, the Anderson›s began facing the formidable duo of Paul Jones and Wahoo McDaniel, a team that would become a thorn in the sides of the Anderson›s through much of 1975.

The Andersons also won the Mid-Atlantic Tag Team Championships defeating the team of Paul Jones and Tiger Conway Jr. in Greensboro on February 20th.

History Made in Winston-Salem: Ric Flair wins his First Singles Championship

February of 1975 was a historic month for "Nature Boy" Ric Flair. On February 8, 1975, Flair took the measure of "Number One" Paul Jones by winning the Mid-Atlantic Television Title from Jones in Winston-Salem, North Carolina. Although widely reported as happening later in 1975, this was Ric Flair's first ever singles title in professional wrestling. After winning the TV title from Jones, Flair defended his new title successfully in a series of title bouts with Tiger Conway later during the month of February. Ric also wrestled Dusty Rhodes in Greensboro, North Carolina on February 20, 1975, starting a feud between the two that was confined primarily to Greensboro for the next few years, but one that would become much wider in scope in the years to come.

A major newcomer appeared on the scene in February of 1975, and his name was Ken Patera. Soft spoken and friendly, Ken made his first appearance on Mid-Atlantic television on February 12, 1975. The promotion hyped his Olympic weightlifting background, and promoted Patera as "The World's Strongest Wrestler." Before long, Patera would be performing feats of strength for fans in the area that were quite amazing. But in February, Patera wrestled primarily in mid-card matches and dominated them. The strongman from Oregon would take off in earnest in the month of March.

Johnny "The Champ" Valentine continued to maintain a stranglehold on the Mid-Atlantic Heavyweight Title during the month of February, despite a number of grueling defenses against Paul

Jones, Sonny King and Wahoo McDaniel. Valentine also maintained his 2,000 silver dollars in his continuing «challenge» matches on Mid-Atlantic Championship Wrestling television; however, the opponents in these TV matches were less than stellar. Johnny suffered a rare defeat in the month of February when he lost a brutal Indian Strap Match to Wahoo McDaniel in Hampton, Virginia on February 15th.

The battles between the Super Destroyer and the Avenger were as hot as ever, as this great feud between the masked wrestlers expanded into the month of February 1975. In fact, the matches between these two were never as even as they were in the month of February, as in several towns around the territory the two went to sixty-minute time limit draws. In many of these matches, the promotion made the Super D. post a cash bond to ensure that he would not run out of the ring when the action got too hot and heavy! While the bouts between these two in February were highly competitive, the upcoming month of March would prove to be a decisive turning point to this classic feud.

Feb. 20th An Interesting Night In Mid-Atlantic History

In addition to the Greensboro card mentioned previously, Thursday, February 20th was also a significant date for the promotion in both Norfolk, Virginia and Charlotte, North Carolina. In Norfolk, the promotion interestingly renewed an old feud that was rooted in 1974, and was over in almost everybody's mind. Bearcat Wright was brought back to the area to team with his brother Sonny King, to avenge Bearcat's 1974 injuries at the hands of the Super Destroyer and Johnny Valentine. In mid 1974, when Johnny Valentine put a bounty on Bearcat's head and the Super D. collected it, Sonny King came to the Mid-Atlantic area to get retribution for his brother. This angle was played out for a number of months in 1974, but had pretty much run its course by February of 1975. Thus, it was a big surprise to see Bearcat return for this "revenge" match, and for a couple of others in the month of March. The grudge matches between these four had inconclusive endings, and this 1974 angle finally expired for good in March of 1975.

February 20, 1975 was an amazing night in Charlotte, NC for Jim Crockett Promotions. On this night, the upstart International Wrestling Alliance (IWA) "invaded" the Charlotte Coliseum and put on a major card there in hopes of beginning a takeover of the Mid-Atlantic area. Starting in Charlotte so early, the hub of Mid-Atlantic Championship Wrestling, was an extremely bold and assertive move by the IWA. The IWA card on this night included stars like Ivan Koloff, Thunderbolt Patterson, Dino Bravo and the Mighty Igor, wrestlers who had made (or would subsequently make) major impacts in Jim Crockett Promotions.

Jim Crockett, Jr. took the threat of the IWA seriously, and decided to confront the threat head on. As a result, Crockett ALSO scheduled a major card on Thursday night, February 20, 1975 at Charlotte's Park Center to go directly up against the IWA, sandwiched between his normal Thursday Park Center cards that ran on February 17th and February 24th. And Jim Crockett made sure this February 20th card was not just another card! In addition to a main event of Gene and Ole Anderson against the "dream team" of Paul Jones and Wahoo McDaniel, Crockett brought in Dusty Rhodes, Harley Race and Haystacks Calhoun to bolster this line up. Yes, as of February 20, 1975, the battle between the IWA and Jim Crockett Promotions for control of the Mid-Atlantic area had been joined. It was equally clear that from this date and for about six months thereafter, Jim Crockett would do everything necessary to run the IWA out of his territory.

Even more amazing was the fact that Crockett held a card that same evening in Greensboro (mentioned earlier) where many of the wrestlers were double-booked, including the Anderson Brothers who had an amazing night. They defeated Paul Jones and Tiger Conway to win (and subsequently retire) the Mid-Atlantic Tag Team Titles and then quickly drove to Charlotte and successfully defended their NWA World Tag titles against Jones and McDaniel.)

February of 1975 was eventful for any number of reasons, and provided several historic "firsts" for the promotion and its wrestlers. But the upcoming month of March would not disappoint either, bringing in with it two of the biggest new stars in the history of Mid-Atlantic Championship Wrestling.

WHO'S HOT

1. RIC FLAIR---The Nature Boy notched what would be the first of many career singles titles this month. Ric showed in his subsequent successful title defenses against Tiger Conway, that his title victory was no fluke.

2. KEN PATERA---The "World's Strongest Wrestler" steamrolled through all of his opponents in the month of February. But could the newcomer keep this pace up as the opposition got stronger?

3. GENE AND OLE ANDERSON---The Minnesota Wrecking Crew were very impressive in their first full month as NWA World Tag Team Champs. By the end of the month, Gene and Ole were gearing up for the formidable challenge of Paul Jones and Wahoo McDaniel.

WHO'S NOT

1. BRUTE BERNARD---The "unpredictable one" no longer had the Super Destroyer behind him during the month of February. While still an entertaining character, the Brute was no longer logging victories in a regular fashion any more.

2. TIGER CONWAY---Losses were creeping in more frequently for Tiger in February, to the point that he was very close to slipping into mid-card status by the end of the month.

3. PAUL JONES---Reeling from his TV Title loss to Ric Flair, "Number One" began to focus more on a budding tag team with Wahoo McDaniel.

MARCH

The month of March 1975 saw significant changes and movement of wrestlers in Jim Crockett Promotions. Two of the biggest names in the history of Mid-Atlantic Championship Wrestling would enter the area in March, while two other big stars from 1974 and early 1975 would be de-emphasized. March also saw a blockbuster feud reach its conclusion, while perhaps the greatest tag team feud in Mid-Atlantic history got kicked into high gear later in the month. March of 1975 would in many ways shape the promotion for the remainder of this eventful year.

New Talent

New faces abounded in March, and immediately as March began fans in the area got their first glimpse of the big man from Eagle Pass, Texas, Blackjack Mulligan. Blackjack wrestled his first match in the area on March 3, 1975 in Greenville, South Carolina easily disposing of Charlie Cook, and Mulligan was first on Mid-Atlantic television for the TV tapings at the WRAL studios in Raleigh, North Carolina on March 5, 1975. Billed as being six feet nine inches tall and weighing over three hundred pounds, Mulligan brought a reputation just as large into the Mid-Atlantic area. Blackjack spent much of March beating up an assortment of the area's mid card "good guys" decisively, but much bigger things would soon be in store for the huge Texan.

At the end of March, another tremendous addition to Jim Crockett's talent roster entered the area. Rufus R. "Freight Train" Jones, hailing from Dillon, South Carolina, made his first appearance in the area in years when he wrestled in the WRAL TV studios on March 26, 1975, beating Cowboy Parker on the Mid-Atlantic Championship Wrestling show and later that Wednesday night teamed with Ken Patera to defeat Parker and Ken Dillinger on the "B" taping of the Mid-Atlantic Wrestling. Rufus had his first arena match in the area in Charlotte, North Carolina on March 31st, when he quickly dispatched Frank Morrell. While the "Freight Train" was just getting started in the month of March, it would not take Rufus long to establish himself as a main event performer, and one of the most popular wrestlers ever in the Mid-Atlantic area.

1974 NWA Rookie of the Year Steve Keirn also entered the Mid-Atlantic area in March of 1975. The promoters immediately booked Keirn against the area's toughest "bad guys" in televised matches, and while losing, the youngster held up surprisingly well. Steve also looked good in his early arena matches against a number of the territory's most experienced opening card wrestlers. Big things looked to be ahead on the horizon for this talented youngster from Florida.

March was not nearly so kind to Tiger Conway. After almost a year of headlining cards for the promotion, Conway dropped quickly into the mid card ranks during March. Unable to beat Ric Flair for the Mid-Atlantic Television Title, or to recover from losing the Mid-Atlantic Tag Team Titles to Gene and Ole Anderson, Tiger tried to get back on track and put everything on the line in a "Loser Leaves Town" match against Ole Anderson in Spartanburg, South Carolina on March 29, 1975. To the dismay of his many fans, the hated Anderson prevailed and sent Tiger packing. While Ole ran Tiger out of the area, when Conway finally came back to Mid-Atlantic Championship Wrestling later in 1975, he would give Ole and brother Gene some real "payback."

The captivating feud between the Avenger and the Super Destroyer played out to its thrilling conclusion during the month of March 1975. Throughout the month in the larger venues in the area, these two masked stars battled before packed houses in " No Disqualification—No Time Limit—There Must Be A Winner" climactic battles. The Super Destroyer used his superior size to finally wear down and subdue the game Avenger, who was unmasked as Reggie Parks. After these decisive matches in March, the masked Avenger continued to wrestle around the area for most of the remainder of 1975, but never wrestled higher than mid card matches after these devastating loses to the Super Destroyer. These March battles took their toll on the Super Destroyer as well, as the "Super D." could only muster one final mediocre program with Sonny King before leaving the area during the summer of 1975, actually leaving Jim Crockett Promotions before the Avenger did.

Ken Patera continued his rapid rise in Mid-Atlantic Championship Wrestling during the month of March. In his first full month in the area, Ken was firmly establishing himself as a main event performer as he was starting to meet and defeat the best and toughest the territory had to offer. Patera was showing the fans his amazing strength in amazing ways, and with his Olympic background and engaging personality, he was fast becoming an exceedingly popular star. During March another former Olympian, 1972 bronze medal wrestling winner, Chris Taylor made a brief pass through the area. At this point in their careers, though, both Taylor and Patera were "good guys," so there would be no battles between these Olympians.

Championships

Paul Jones defeated Johnny Valentine for the Mid-Atlantic title on March 9 in Charlotte. Jones began his defense of the title, but Valentine had other ideas and petitioned NWA president Sam Muchnick to review the film of the match which appeared to show Valentine's leg on the rope as the referee made the three count. Despite Jones removing the leg before the final count, Muchnick decided to strip Jones of the title and return it to Valentine weeks later. This was one of the more controversial decisions of the year.

Ric Flair defended his Mid-Atlantic Television Title impressively in March. The "Nature Boy" turned back the challenges of Tiger Conway, and was developing quite a rivalry with former champion Paul Jones over the TV Title. Hanging tough with the veteran Jones, the youngster Flair was growing up in a hurry and becoming a champion to be reckoned with.

The champion of all champions, Johnny "The Champ," Valentine, had a busy month. Maintaining his iron grip on the Mid-Atlantic Heavyweight Championship, Valentine defended his title in a number of spectacular bouts against Paul Jones during March. "The Champ" was also successful in several Mid-Atlantic Title bouts against top challenger Sonny King. Add to all this activity, Johnny also traveled to the St. Louis area in March for a series of great matches out there.

NWA World Tag Team Champions Gene and Ole Anderson were rapidly finding out in March how much pressure is associated with being the top tag team in the country. The Anderson's had their share of tough tussles in March with the teams of Wahoo McDaniel and Paul Jones, and also the formidable duo of Wahoo and Sonny King. In a rare main event caliber match that was wrestled on Mid-Atlantic Championship Wrestling television, Wahoo and Paul Jones battled Gene and Ole in a non-title bout on March 26, 1975 in the WRAL TV studios in Raleigh. This match would truly launch these two teams into violent competition over the NWA World Tag Team Titles that would last through nearly the rest of 1975. A tag team feud for the ages was just getting started.

Just as March is a transitional month between winter and spring, March of 1975 saw Jim Crockett Promotions transition out of one major feud featuring the Super Destroyer and the Avenger,

TELEVISION WRESTLING IN 1975
by Dick Bourne

As the year began, Jim Crockett Promotions taped two separate hours of TV both titled *Mid-Atlantic Championship Wrestling*.

The first hour was hosted by Bob Caudle and David Crockett and aired in every Crockett TV market in the Carolinas, Virginia, and a few selected markets outside of the territory.

The second hour was hosted by Les Thatcher and featured a different wrestler on color commentary each week. This second show aired in many, but not all, of the same markets that aired the main program hosted by Caudle and Crockett. It featured different matches, and usually aired on a different station within that market.

In October of 1975, the "B" show hosted by Thatcher was replaced by a new show called *Wide World Wrestling*. Veteran wrestling announcer Ed Capral was brought in to host the program. He kept Thatcher's tradition of having a different wrestler do color commentary each week.

Capral had been the long time voice of *Georgia Championship Wrestling* in the 1960s and early 1970s, preceding Gordon Solie.

The programs were taped every Wednesday night in the studios of WRAL-TV5 in Raleigh, NC.

and into a great new budding feud between Wahoo and Paul Jones against Gene and Ole Anderson. March also brought in with it two terrific stars of the future in Blackjack Mulligan and Rufus R. Jones, and effectively said goodbye to two major stars in Tiger Conway and the Avenger. Like the changing of the seasons, Mid-Atlantic Championship Wrestling was alive, vibrant and ever evolving, and the spring of 1975 brought forth the promise of even more excitement for all its many fans.

WHO'S HOT

1. SUPER DESTROYER---The "Super D." finally prevailed in his memorable program with fellow masked wrestler, the Avenger. This feud, perhaps because it was a rare mask versus mask confrontation, seemed to really captivate the Mid-Atlantic fans. Just when it seemed the Avenger had the Super Destroyer on the run, the Super D. came up with the final answer.

2. BLACKJACK MULLIGAN---The big man from Eagle Pass, Texas looked largely unstoppable as he roared into the territory in early March. His massive size along with a mean streak that just wouldn't quit was downright frightening. Everybody was waiting to see how the Texan would fare when he stepped up to tougher competition.

3. KEN PATERA---The strongman from Oregon proved to everybody that he was for real, as he faced tougher competition in March and continued to impress. Showing off his incredible strength, along with a sharp intellect, Patera looked to be a sure Mid-Atlantic area main event fixture for the foreseeable future.

WHO'S NOT

1. TIGER CONWAY---Tiger went from main event performer in early March to out of the area completely by the end of the month. Losing a "Loser Leaves Town" match to Ole Anderson on March 29th shocked Tiger and all of his many Mid-Atlantic fans. Everyone was asking, "How could he fall so fast?"

2. AVENGER---The masked man we learned was Reggie Parks gave it his all in a dynamic feud with the bigger and stronger Super Destroyer. This was a feud where it was a real shame either man had to lose. Unfortunately, the Avenger never fully recovered from the loss and slipped to mid card status almost immediately.

3. SWEDE HANSON---The big Swede continued to battle valiantly, but his slow but steady slide down the Mid-Atlantic Championship Wrestling totem pole continued. Victories that several months ago were plentiful were fast becoming more and more difficult to attain for the aging grappler.

Selected Newspaper Clippings

Edited by Dick Bourne

Mat Events Wednesday

The Mid-Atlantic wrestling night at Memorial Auditorium this week has been set for New Year's Night, at 8 o'clock p.m.

Highlighting the night will be a six-man tag team match, between the squads of Johnny Valentine, Ivan Koloff and The Super Destroyer, and Wahoo McDaniel, Sonny King and Paul Jones.

In a tag team match, Ole and Gene Anderson will take on Sandy Scott and Bob Brugers. Single matches will have Two-Ton Harris against Charlie Cook, and Frank Monti against Mike Stawlings.

Greenville, South Carolina 1/1/75
Ole Anderson pulls double duty on New Years night!

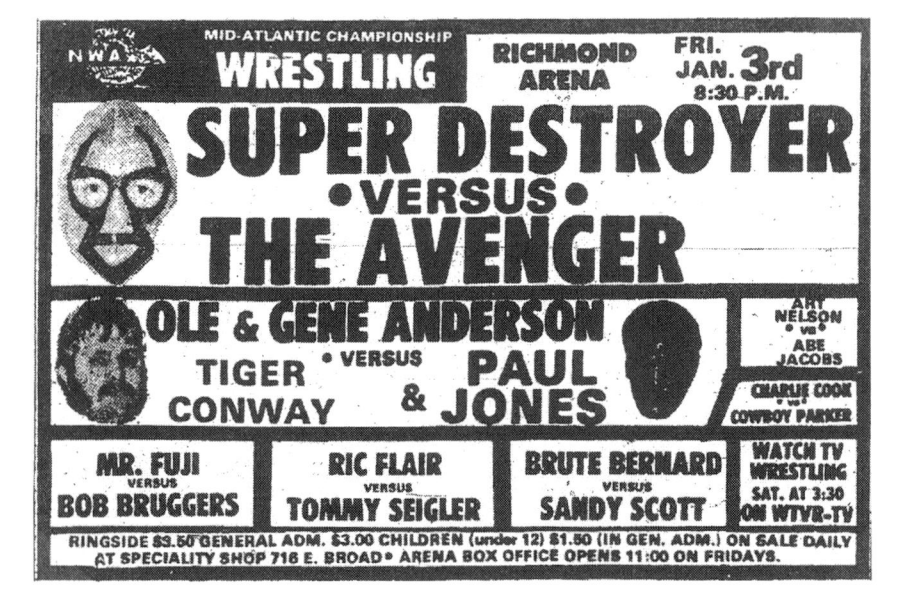

Jones, King, McDaniel Win Tag Match

Paul Jones, Sonny King and Wahoo McDaniel teamed Wednesday night to win a three-man tag match in wrestling action at Memorial Auditorium in Greenville.

The losing trio included Johnny Valentine, Ivan Koloff and Ole Anderson.

Anderson wrestled twice during the evening teaming with brother Gene in a two-man tag event, beating Sandy Scott and Bob Bruggers. The Super Destroyer missed a plane connection forcing Ole's double duty.

In other action Wednesday, newcomer Charlie Cook beat Two-Ton Harris and Frank Monte drew with Mike Stallings in the opening match.

There will be no further wrestling action until January 20.

NWA MID-ATLANTIC CHAMPIONSHIP WRESTLING
SCOPE EXHIBITION HALL — THURS. JAN. 2nd, 8:30 PM

FOR MID-ATLANTIC TAG TITLE
PAUL JONES AND TIGER CONWAY VERSUS RIC FLAIR AND IVAN KOLOFF

MR. FUJI vs SANDY SCOTT
BRUTE BERNARD AND ART NELSON v CHARLIE COOK AND TOMMY SIEGLER
ABE JACOBS vs COWBOY S. PARKER

WATCH TV WRESTLING SAT, 5 P.M. ON WAVY-TV

NWA MID-ATLANTIC CHAMPIONSHIP WRESTLING
RICHMOND ARENA — FRI. JAN. 3rd, 8:30 P.M.

SUPER DESTROYER VERSUS THE AVENGER

OLE & GENE ANDERSON VERSUS TIGER CONWAY & PAUL JONES

MR. FUJI VERSUS BOB BRUGGERS
RIC FLAIR VERSUS TOMMY SEIGLER
BRUTE BERNARD VERSUS SANDY SCOTT
ART NELSON vs ABE JACOBS
CHARLIE COOK vs COWBOY PARKER

WATCH TV WRESTLING SAT. AT 3:30 ON WTVR-TV

RINGSIDE $3.50 GENERAL ADM. $3.00 CHILDREN (under 12) $1.50 (IN GEN. ADM.) ON SALE DAILY AT SPECIALITY SHOP 716 E. BROAD • ARENA BOX OFFICE OPENS 11:00 ON FRIDAYS.

McDaniel Nabs Wrestling Win

Chief Wahoo McDaniel pinned Johnny Valentine in a non-title bout to capture the main event of Tuesday night's wrestling card at Township Auditorium.

In other matches, Gene and Ole Anderson defeated Sandy Scott and Bob Bruggers, Charlie Cook decisioned Cowboy Parker, Swede Hanson won by disqualification over Mr. Fuchi, Klondike Bill whipped Two-Ton Harris and Tio-Tio overcame Mike Paidouris.

Columbia, SC 1/7/75

Newspaper clippings from the collection of Mark Eastridge.

"NOTICE"

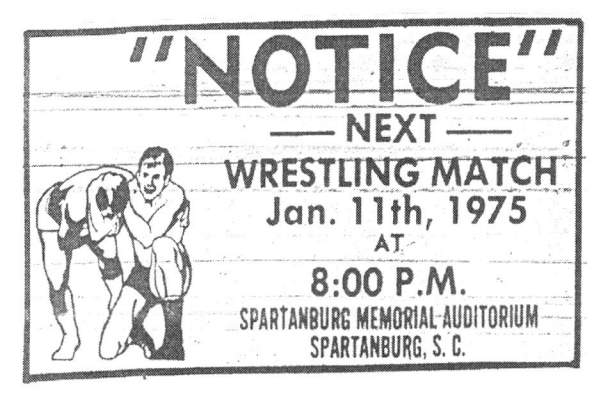

NEXT WRESTLING MATCH
Jan. 11th, 1975
AT
8:00 P.M.
SPARTANBURG MEMORIAL AUDITORIUM
SPARTANBURG, S.C.

McDaniels Takes $5,200 Purse

Wahoo McDaniels came out the winner in Monday night's 13-man Russian Roulette Battle Royal pro wrestling event held at Cumberland Memorial Arena.

McDaniels, who earned $5,200 for the win, was the last man in the ring after tossing Ole Anderson over the ropes.

1/13/75 Fayetteville

Conway, Jones Put Tag Title On Stake Friday

The Mid-Atlantic tag team champions, Tiger Conway Jr. and popular Paul Jones, will defend their title which they won recently against Rick Flair and Russia's Ivan Koloff in the main event of this coming Friday night's wrestling program at County Hall.

This is the first time that Conway and Jones have defended their title which they won from Flair and Rip Hawk a few weeks before Christmas, so Flair went out to get Koloff to team with him to try to get his title back.

In the semi-final match Cowboy Parker will take on Mike Stallings. In the No. 2 prelim Joe Furr will take on Frank Monte. Opening the show at 8:15 p.m. will be Johnny Heideman meeting Japan's Mr. Hayashi.

Charleston SC 1/17/75

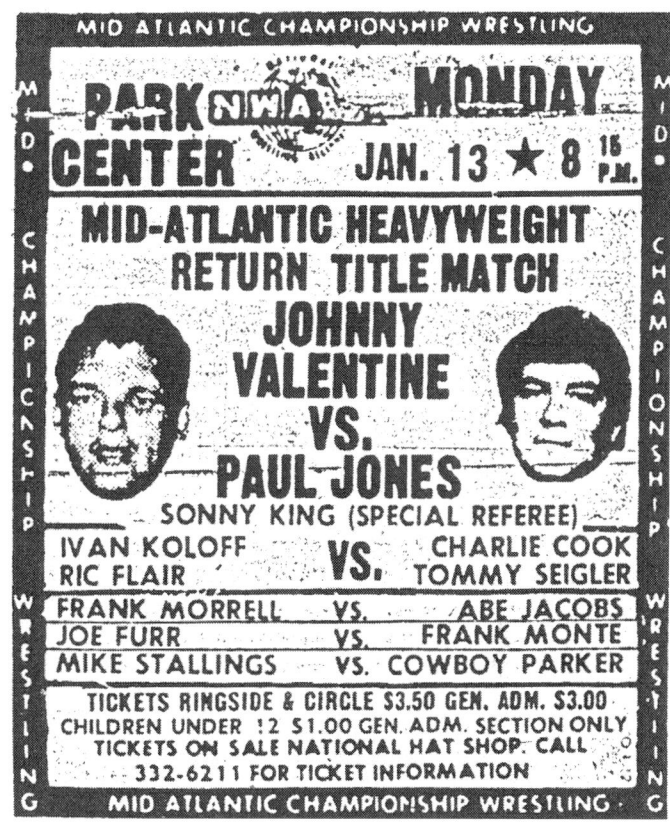

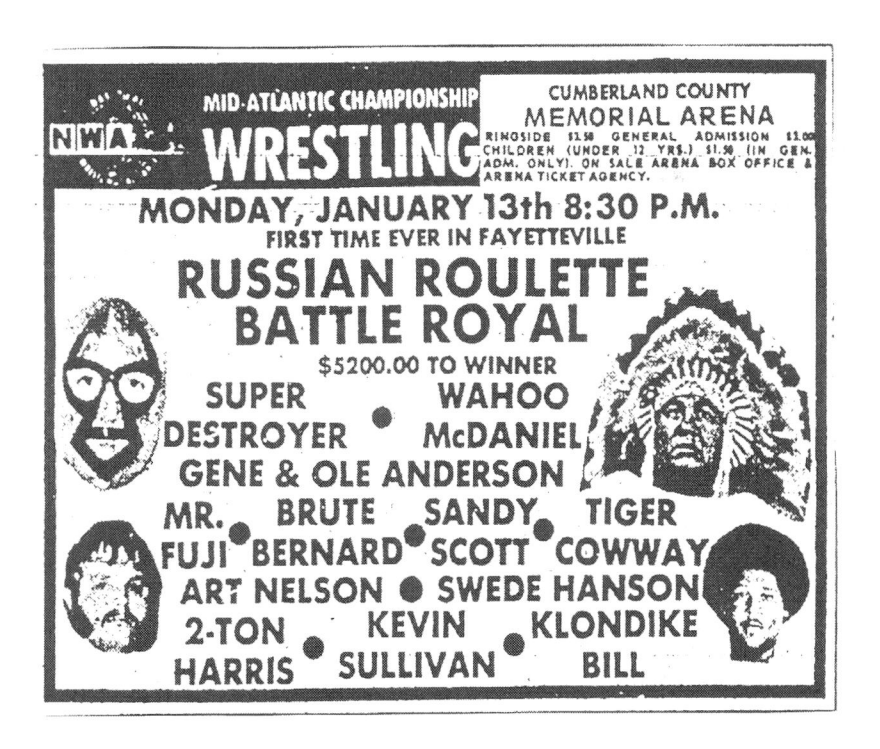

MID ATLANTIC CHAMPIONSHIP WRESTLING

PARK CENTER — MONDAY JAN. 13 ★ 8:15 P.M.

MID-ATLANTIC HEAVYWEIGHT RETURN TITLE MATCH

JOHNNY VALENTINE VS. PAUL JONES

SONNY KING (SPECIAL REFEREE)

IVAN KOLOFF / RIC FLAIR	VS.	CHARLIE COOK / TOMMY SEIGLER
FRANK MORRELL	VS.	ABE JACOBS
JOE FURR	VS.	FRANK MONTE
MIKE STALLINGS	VS.	COWBOY PARKER

TICKETS RINGSIDE & CIRCLE $3.50 GEN. ADM. $3.00
CHILDREN UNDER 12 $1.00 GEN. ADM. SECTION ONLY
TICKETS ON SALE NATIONAL HAT SHOP. CALL 332-6211 FOR TICKET INFORMATION

MID-ATLANTIC CHAMPIONSHIP WRESTLING

MID-ATLANTIC CHAMPIONSHIP WRESTLING

CUMBERLAND COUNTY MEMORIAL ARENA

RINGSIDE $2.50 GENERAL ADMISSION $2.00
CHILDREN (UNDER 12 YRS.) $1.50 (IN GEN. ADM. ONLY). ON SALE ARENA BOX OFFICE & ARENA TICKET AGENCY.

MONDAY, JANUARY 13th 8:30 P.M.

FIRST TIME EVER IN FAYETTEVILLE

RUSSIAN ROULETTE BATTLE ROYAL

$5200.00 TO WINNER

SUPER DESTROYER • WAHOO McDANIEL
GENE & OLE ANDERSON
MR. FUJI • BRUTE BERNARD • SANDY SCOTT • TIGER COWWAY
ART NELSON • SWEDE HANSON
2-TON HARRIS • KEVIN SULLIVAN • KLONDIKE BILL

An angered Brute Bernard gets warning from ref

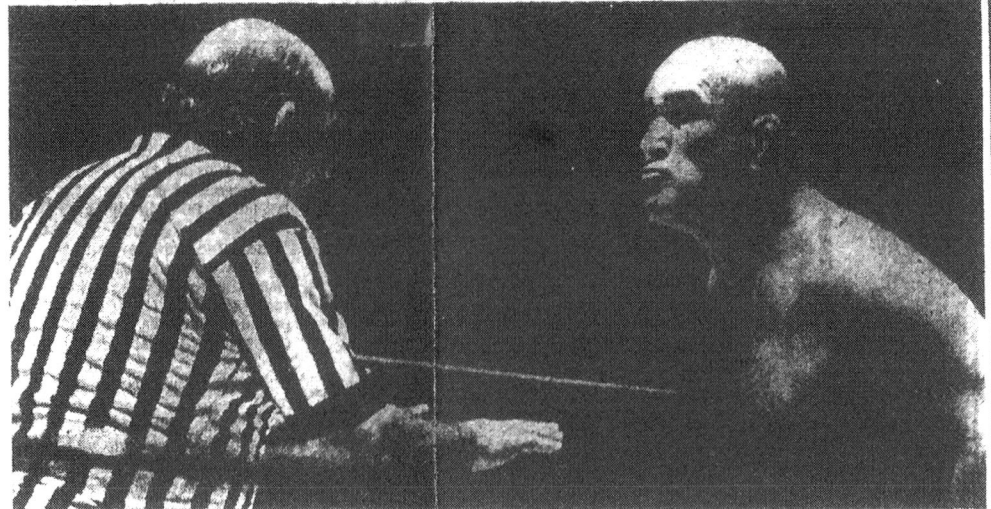

Staff Photo by Thomas Conway

Wahoo, Jones win on disqualification

The team of Wahoo McDaniel and Paul Jones defeated the Super Destroyer and Ivan Koloff in the tag-team main event of wrestling action in the Coliseum Thursday night.

It took the Destroyer 18 minutes to pin Jones in the first fall of the match. McDaniel downed Koloff after seven minutes in the second fall.

In the third and deciding fall of the match, the Destroyer was disqualified after six minutes to give his opponents the victory.

A six-man tag-team event saw the team of Ric Flair, Gene Anderson and Ole Anderson defeat Tiger Conway, Jr., Sandy Scott and Swede Hanson. Ole Anderson won the deciding fall over Hanson using a back drop.

In singles matches, Brute Bernard beat Tio Tio, Kevin Sullivan topped Mr. Hayashi, Mike Stallainges bested Franke Monte and Cowboy Parker won out over Joe Furr.

Conway, Jones To Again Fight Koluff, Flair

The sensational Mid-Atlantic tag team Champions Paul Jones and Tiger Conway Jr. will put their title on the line in a title rematch against their no. 1 rivals Rick Flair and Ivan Koloff in the main event of this coming Friday night's four event wrestling program at County Hall.

This past Friday night Jones and Conway won the match and retained their title but Flair and Koloff became so enraged that they beat up both Conway and Jones after the match. Conway and Jones then asked for a rematch.

The semifinal match will be between the Great Fugi and young Tommy Seigler.

The no. 2 prelim will have George (two-ton) Harris meeting Mike Stalling.

Opening the action at 8:15 PM will be Don Kernodle meeting Frank Monte.

Charleston SC 1/24/75

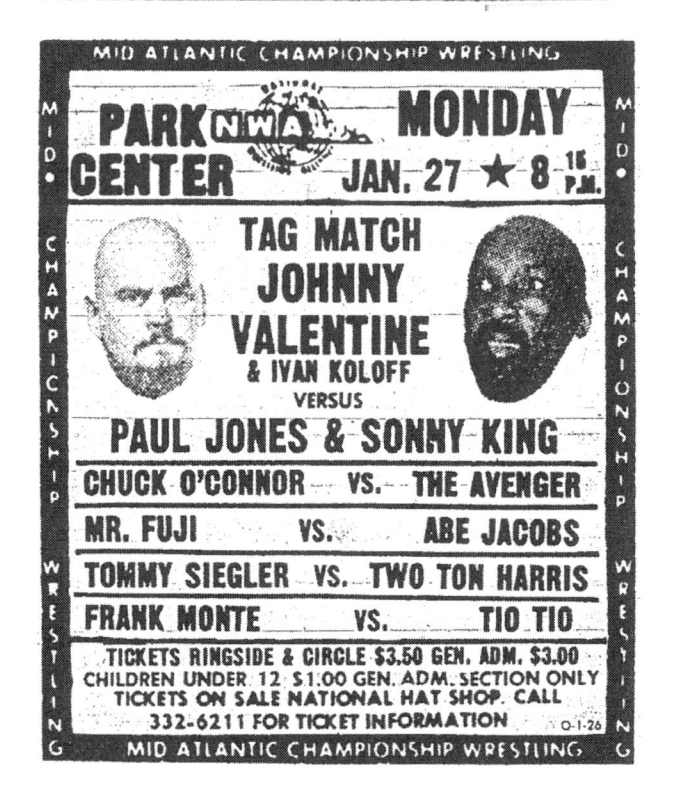

MID ATLANTIC CHAMPIONSHIP WRESTLING

PARK CENTER — NWA — **MONDAY JAN. 27 ★ 8:15 P.M.**

TAG MATCH
JOHNNY VALENTINE & IVAN KOLOFF
VERSUS
PAUL JONES & SONNY KING

CHUCK O'CONNOR — VS. — THE AVENGER
MR. FUJI — VS. — ABE JACOBS
TOMMY SIEGLER — VS. — TWO TON HARRIS
FRANK MONTE — VS. — TIO TIO

TICKETS RINGSIDE & CIRCLE $3.50 GEN. ADM. $3.00
CHILDREN UNDER 12 $1.00 GEN. ADM. SECTION ONLY
TICKETS ON SALE NATIONAL HAT SHOP. CALL
332-6211 FOR TICKET INFORMATION

MID ATLANTIC CHAMPIONSHIP WRESTLING

MID-ATLANTIC WRESTLING 1975 YEARBOOK

Brisco, Wahoo head wrestling

Jack Brisco is the world heavyweight wrestling champion and he intends to maintain the belt he has held form more then a year when he faces Wahoo McDaniel on the main event of tonight's wrestling card at the Greensboro Coliseum.

"This time the Indian will get the white man," says McDaniel in a rather whimsical tone. "No, I deeply respect Brisco. He has proven a real champion, but the crown is there for the best man and I think I rate that position right now."

Brisco and McDaniel have met before. McDaniel almost took a win — and a title which would mean at least $200,000 per year.

The all-star card, sponsored by the National Wrestling Alliance, has a number of matches.

The semi-final sends The Avenger against the Super Destroyer. Both are masked men. The Destroyer is arrogant, entirely unpredictable. The Avenger is the popular favorite.

Mike Paidousis, a former Tennessee football player, opens against Don Kernodle at 8:15.

Other matches include:

Mike Stallings against Ken Dillinger.

Art Nelson meeting clever Abe Jacobs.

Mr. Fuji against Klondike Bill.

Gene Anderson against Charlie Cook.

A team match which should draw its share of interests sends Ivan Koloff and Ric Flair against Tiger Conway Jr., and Paul Jones.

Greensboro, NC 1/30/75

Super Destroyer, Avenger Return To County Hall

After an absence of several weeks the two great masked men of Mid-Atlantic Championship wrestling will return to the local ring Friday night when the Super Destroyer meets The Avenger in the battle of the "Masks" in the main event of a four-event wrestling program at County Hall.

In this "battle of the masks," each masked man will be trying to unmask his opponent.

In the semifinal match the tag team of young Tommy Seigler and big Abe Jacobs will take on the team of Mr. Fugi and rowdy Art Nelson.

In the No. 2 prelim Klondike Bill will meet Mike Paidousis. Opening the show at 8:15 P.M. will be Mike Stallings meeting Ken Dillinger.

Charleston, SC 1/31/75

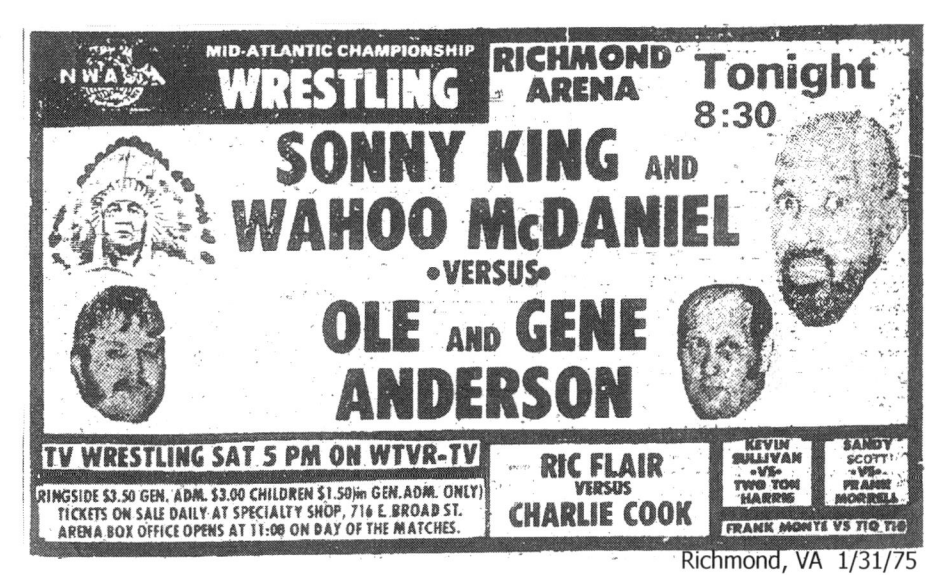

Richmond, VA 1/31/75

A busy Friday night in the Mid-Atlantic area, as most all nights were. There were often three shows a night within the territory.

Notice that Ric Flair was billed for Richmond against Charlie Cook, but was pulled from the show to replace Ivan Koloff in a Mid-Atlantic tag team title match in Lynchburg, VA. Flair teamed with frequent partner Johnny Valentine in a losing effort to defending champions Paul Jones and Tiger Conway, Jr.

Mat Team Keeps Title

Tiger Conway and Paul Jones kept their Atlantic Coast tag team wrestling championship here Friday night by defeating Johnny Valentine and Rick Flair in a wild match at City Armory.

In other matches, Swede Hanson defeated Cowboy Parker; Bobby Williams drew with Don Kernodle, and Mr. Hayashi defeated Joe Furr.

Lynchburg, VA 1/31/75

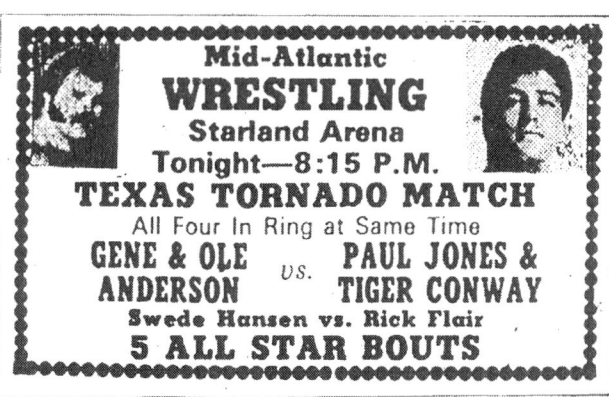

MID-ATLANTIC WRESTLING 1975 YEARBOOK

Mid-Atlantic WRESTLING
Starland Arena
Tonight—8:15 P.M.
TEXAS TORNADO MATCH
All Four In Ring at Same Time
GENE & OLE ANDERSON vs. PAUL JONES & TIGER CONWAY
Swede Hansen vs. Rick Flair
5 ALL STAR BOUTS

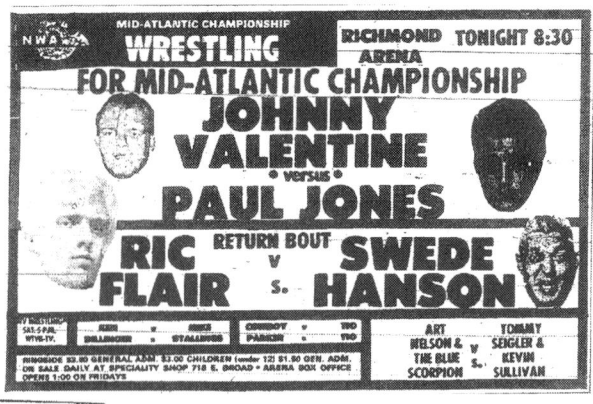

NWA MID-ATLANTIC CHAMPIONSHIP WRESTLING
RICHMOND ARENA TONIGHT 8:30
FOR MID-ATLANTIC CHAMPIONSHIP
JOHNNY VALENTINE versus PAUL JONES
RETURN BOUT
RIC FLAIR v. SWEDE HANSON

Art Nelson & The Blue Scorpion vs Tommy Seigler & Kevin Sullivan

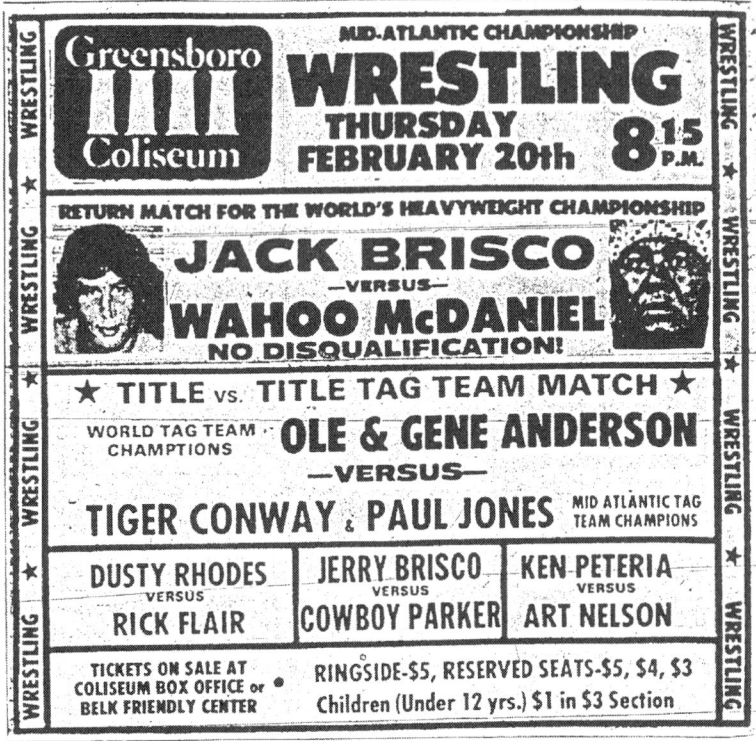

Greensboro Coliseum
MID-ATLANTIC CHAMPIONSHIP WRESTLING
THURSDAY FEBRUARY 20th 8:15 P.M.

RETURN MATCH FOR THE WORLD'S HEAVYWEIGHT CHAMPIONSHIP
JACK BRISCO versus WAHOO McDANIEL
NO DISQUALIFICATION!

★ TITLE vs. TITLE TAG TEAM MATCH ★
WORLD TAG TEAM CHAMPIONS **OLE & GENE ANDERSON**
—VERSUS—
TIGER CONWAY & PAUL JONES MID ATLANTIC TAG TEAM CHAMPIONS

| DUSTY RHODES versus RICK FLAIR | JERRY BRISCO versus COWBOY PARKER | KEN PETERIA versus ART NELSON |

TICKETS ON SALE AT COLISEUM BOX OFFICE or BELK FRIENDLY CENTER
RINGSIDE-$5, RESERVED SEATS-$5, $4, $3
Children (Under 12 yrs.) $1 in $3 Section

Brisco Still World Champ After Win

Jack Brisco still rules as the champion.

He needed 21 minutes to defeat Wahoo McDaniel in the feature wrestling match before a crowd of 7,812 at the Coliseum Thursday night.

The champ pinned McDaniel.

The Andersons, Ole and Gene, took both bouts. Gene settled the tag team affair while coming out ahead of Tiger Conway with a body slam in 19 minutes. Paul Jones was Conway's partner.

Dusty Rhodes and Rick Flair didn't decide anything. They were both out of the ring, and each was disqualified. Jerry Brisco employed a grape vine leg lock on Cowboy Parker to win.

A body press enabled Ken Peteria to beat Art Nelson. Kevin Sullivan and Tommy Seigler fought to a draw, and Sandy Scott and Tio Tio came out ahead of Frank Monte and Frank Morrell in another tag team affair. Scott whipped Morrell with drop kicks.

Greensboro, Feb. 20

Tuesday Night WRESTLING
CABLE TV
Channel 12
7:30 P.M.
For Free Installation
554-4100
Charleston SC

Jones Captures Wrestling Bout

Paul Jones scored seven falls to Johnny Valentine's four and claimed victory Monday night in a "Texas Death Match" at Park Center. Rick Flair was disqualified against Tiger Conway in another contest.

In other matches Mr. Fuji and Brute Bernard defeated Kevin Sullivan and Sandy Scott; Charlie Cook topped Two-Ton Harris, and Tio Tio whipped Mr. Hayashi.

Charlotte, Feb. 24

MID-ATLANTIC WRESTLING 1975 YEARBOOK

NWA Mid Atlantic Championship Wrestling

No bouts at Dorton Arena this week
Smithfield-Selma High School Gym
Sponsored by the Jaycees
TUES., FEB. 25TH — 8:15 P.M.

WAHOO McDANIEL & PAUL JONES
versus
JOHNNY VALENTINE & RIC FLAIR

Plus a big star-studded wrestling card

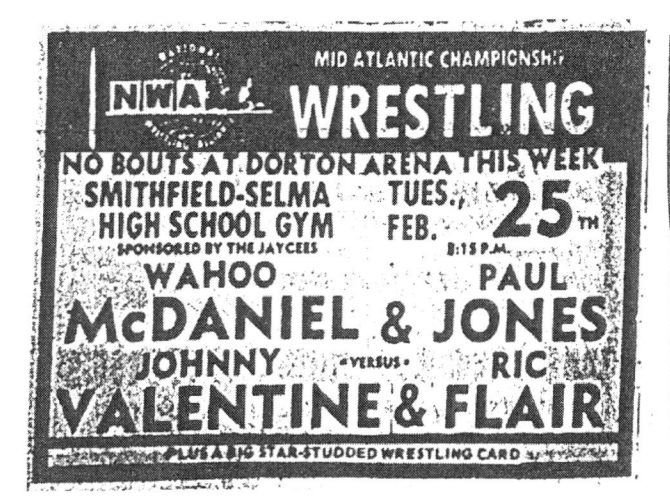

Mid-Atlantic Championship Wrestling

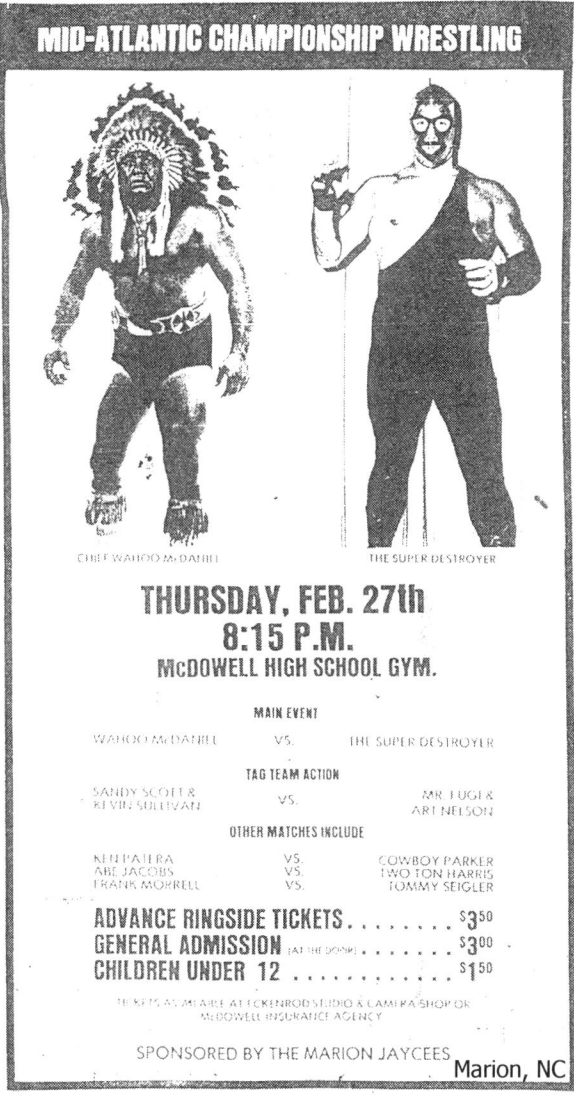

CHIEF WAHOO McDANIEL — THE SUPER DESTROYER

THURSDAY, FEB. 27th
8:15 P.M.
McDOWELL HIGH SCHOOL GYM.

MAIN EVENT
WAHOO McDANIEL vs. THE SUPER DESTROYER

TAG TEAM ACTION
SANDY SCOTT & KEVIN SULLIVAN vs. MR. FUGI & ART NELSON

OTHER MATCHES INCLUDE
KEN PATERA vs. COWBOY PARKER
ABE JACOBS vs. TWO TON HARRIS
FRANK MORRELL vs. TOMMY SEIGLER

ADVANCE RINGSIDE TICKETS $3.50
GENERAL ADMISSION (AT THE DOOR) $3.00
CHILDREN UNDER 12 . . . . $1.50

TICKETS AVAILABLE AT ECKENROD STUDIO & CAMERA SHOP OR McDOWELL INSURANCE AGENCY

SPONSORED BY THE MARION JAYCEES

Marion, NC

START BUS FUND — Members of the Rutherfordton Jaycees held a planning session at Carver Elementary School in Spindale last week in which plans were revealed to start a fund for an activity bus for Carver and New Hope elementary schools. Shown (l-r) are, Bruce Neal, Carver principal; Larry Ford, chairman of the drive; Pat Nanney, president of the Jaycees Club, and Tommy Porter, principal of New Hope school. (James Photo)

Spindale, NC March 8

NWA Mid Atlantic Championship Wrestling

PARK CENTER — SUNDAY MAR. 9 — $3.00

FENCE MATCH
JOHNNY VALENTINE vs. PAUL JONES

RIC FLAIR AND SUPER STAR BILLY GRAHAM VS. **WAHOO McDANIEL AND DUSTY RHODES**

GIRL MIDGETS
DARLIN DAGMAR vs. DIAMOND LIL

TIGER CONWAY, JR. AND SONNY KING vs. MR. FUGI AND BLUE SKORPION

BLACKJACK MULLIGAN vs. TIO TIO

TICKETS RINGSIDE & CIRCLE $5.00, GEN. ADM. $3.50
CHILDREN UNDER 12 $1.50, GEN. ADM. SECTION ONLY
TICKETS ON SALE NATIONAL HAT SHOP, CALL 527-0040 FOR TICKET INFORMATION

Mid Atlantic Wrestling Scheduled Here Again

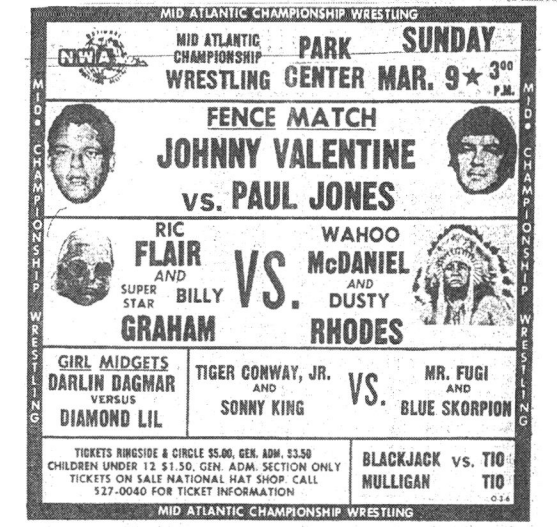

Mid-Atlantic Championship Wrestling will return to the Camden Arena this coming Saturday night, March 1, with the sensational Oklahoma Indian, Chief Wahoo McDaniel, meeting Ole Anderson in the main event of a colorful program starting at 8:15 p.m.

Wahoo, who used to play college football under Coach Bud Wilkinson at the University of Oklahoma and later in the pro ranks with both the Miami Dolphins and the New York Jets, is currently the most popular mat ace in Mid-Atlantic arenas.

However, as good as the Redskin is, popularity will mean nothing when he takes on rough and tumble Ole Anderson. Ole, one-half of the famed and feared "Minnesota Wrecking Crew", along with brother Gene, and together with his brother the newly crowned World Tag Team Champions is a big, bruising fellow with a nasty temper.

This is bound to be a popular match and since the Camden Arena was sold out the last time Mid-Atlantic Championship wrestling was held there, the Camden-Kershaw County Recreation Department has said that extra bleachers and chairs will be put into use to hold more fans on March 1.

Tiger Conway, Jr., and Rick Flair will meet in the semi-final.

Charlie Cook, former pro-footballer with the Pittsburg Steelers, will team with Big Swede Hanson to take on Japan's The Great Mr. Fuji and Art Nelson in a tag match. Mike Stallings and Ken Dillinger will meet in the opener.

Tickets are now on sale for this mat program at City Drug on DeKalb Street in downtown Camden, and the Camden Recreation Dept.

Camden, SC

Greensboro News & Record

Hatching A Plot At Pro-Am (Left To Right): Wahoo McDaniels, Evel Knievel, Bob Bruggers, Lee Trevino

Staff Photo By Jim Stratford

April 3, 1975

Wrestling tonight

Ole and Gene Anderson, known as the Minnesota Wrecking Crew for their disdain for law and order, place their World Tag Team title on line at the Coliseum here tonight.

The Andersons will be challenged by the popular twosome of Wahoo McDaniel and Paul Jones.

McDaniel is spending a good part of his week in Greensboro. He played in the pro-am event with Lee Trevino on Wednesday.

MID-ATLANTIC WRESTLING 1975 YEARBOOK

— MID-ATLANTIC CHAMPIONSHIP —
WRESTLING
THURSDAY APRIL 3rd — 8:15 P.M.

FOR THE WORLD'S TAG TEAM CHAMPIONSHIP

CHAMPIONS
OLE & GENE ANDERSON
— VERSUS —
WAHOO McDANIEL AND **PAUL JONES**

BLACK JACK MULLIGAN VS. **DUSTY RHODES**

SONNY KING AND RUFUS R. JONES VS. **MR. FUJI AND ART NELSON**

PLUS OTHER OUTSTANDING BOUTS

RINGSIDE—$5, RESERVED SEATS—$5, $4, $3
Children (Under 12 yrs.) $1.50 in $3 Section

TICKETS ON SALE AT COLISEUM BOX OFFICE,
BELK FRIENDLY CTR. & BELK FOUR SEASONS

GREENSBORO COLISEUM

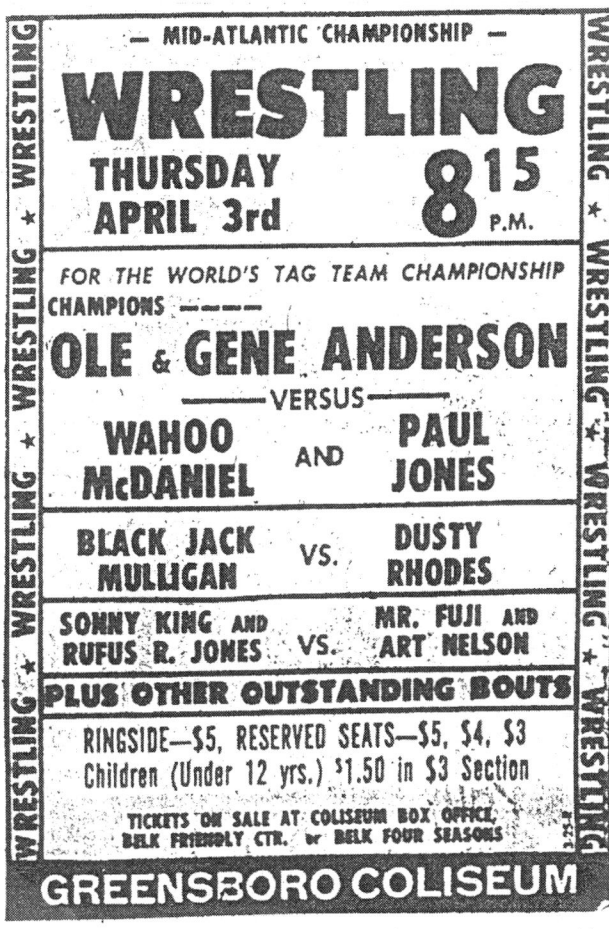

Wrestling tonight

Ole and Gene Anderson, known as the Minnesota Wrecking Crew for their disdain for law and order, place their World Tag Team title on line at the Coliseum here tonight.

The Andersons will be challenged by the popular twosome of Wahoo McDaniel and Paul Jones.

McDaniel is spending a good part of his week in Greensboro. He played in the pro-am event with Lee Trevino on Wednesday.

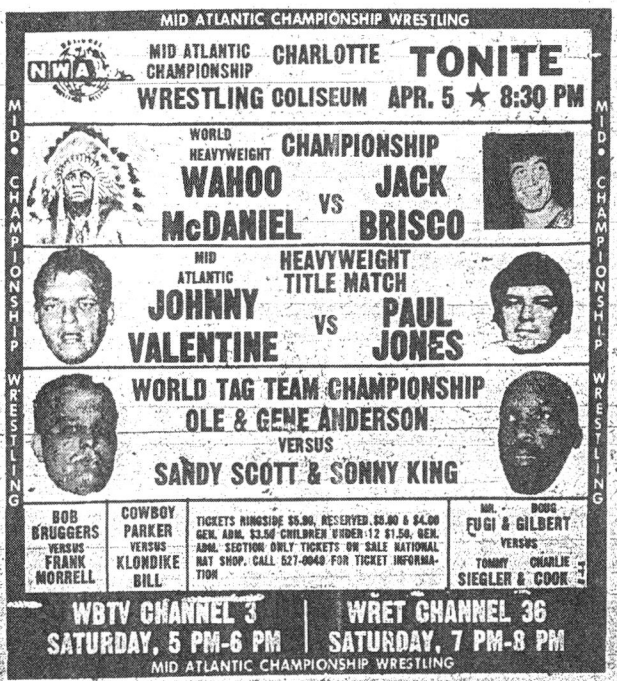

Jones is the current Mid-Atlantic Champion and he terms Wahoo "the best partner I could hope for."

In a challenge match, Blackjack Mulligan faces Dusty Rhodes. Mulligan is relentless in his pursuit of an opponent. He has more than 300 pounds to push aside any barriers. Rhodes has a vast following.

Rufus R. Jones and Sonny King, a black tandem with excellent qualifications, meet Mr. Fuji and Art Nelson in a team showdown.

Superstar Billy Graham opposes Abe Jacobs.

Sandy Scott is assured a spot on the card against a suitable opponent. Tommy Seigler and Bob Bruggars will also appear.

Greensboro, NC
April 3,

Wrestling Rematch Ordered

The National Wrestling Alliance, in one of its rare decisions, has ordered John Valentine, the Mid-Atlantic heavyweight champion, to defend his title against No. 1 challenger Texas Paul Jones in the main event of Tuesday night's five-match program at Columbia's Township Auditorium.

Valentine and Jones have been swapping the title for the past few weeks. However, when Jones won the belt back two weeks ago, Valentine went to the NWA with films of the match and the wrestling governing body ordered a return of the crown to Valentine and a rematch set up.

That rematch will come Tuesday as the main event of the five-card program. In other matches, Blackjack Mulligan will debut with Ric Flair against Swede Hanson and Tommy Seigler. Frank Monte meets Abe Jacobs. Klondike Bill tackles Cowboy Parker and in the 8:15 first bout Frank Morrell tests L. D. Lewis.

Columbia, SC
April 15

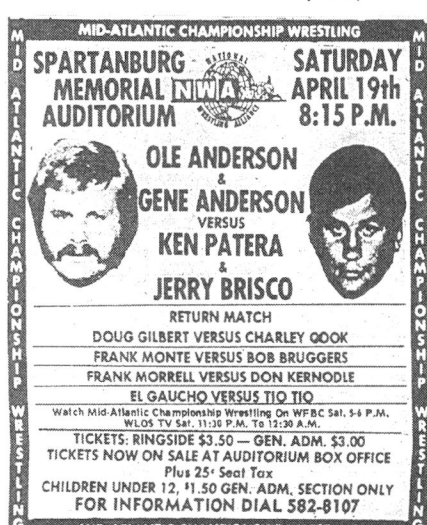

MID ATLANTIC CHAMPIONSHIP WRESTLING
CHARLOTTE COLISEUM — TONITE APR. 5 ★ 8:30 PM

WORLD HEAVYWEIGHT CHAMPIONSHIP
WAHOO McDANIEL VS **JACK BRISCO**

MID ATLANTIC HEAVYWEIGHT TITLE MATCH
JOHNNY VALENTINE VS **PAUL JONES**

WORLD TAG TEAM CHAMPIONSHIP
OLE & GENE ANDERSON VERSUS **SANDY SCOTT & SONNY KING**

BOB BRUGGERS VERSUS FRANK MORRELL
COWBOY PARKER VERSUS KLONDIKE BILL
MR. FUJI & DOUG GILBERT VERSUS TOMMY SEIGLER & CHARLIE COOK

TICKETS RINGSIDE $5.00, RESERVED $5.00 & $4.00 GEN. ADM. $3.50 CHILDREN UNDER 12 $1.50. GEN. ADM. SECTION ONLY TICKETS ON SALE AT NATIONAL HAT SHOP. CALL 527-0040 FOR TICKET INFORMATION.

WBTV CHANNEL 3 SATURDAY, 5 PM–6 PM
WRET CHANNEL 36 SATURDAY, 7 PM–8 PM
MID ATLANTIC CHAMPIONSHIP WRESTLING

MID-ATLANTIC CHAMPIONSHIP WRESTLING
SPARTANBURG MEMORIAL AUDITORIUM
SATURDAY APRIL 19th — 8:15 P.M.

OLE ANDERSON & GENE ANDERSON VERSUS **KEN PATERA & JERRY BRISCO**
RETURN MATCH

DOUG GILBERT VERSUS CHARLEY COOK
FRANK MONTE VERSUS BOB BRUGGERS
FRANK MORRELL VERSUS DON KERNODLE
EL GAUCHO VERSUS TIO TIO

Watch Mid-Atlantic Championship Wrestling On WFBC Sat. 5-6 P.M.
WLOS TV Sat. 11:30 A.M. To 12:30 A.M.

TICKETS: RINGSIDE $3.50 — GEN. ADM. $3.00
TICKETS NOW ON SALE AT AUDITORIUM BOX OFFICE
Plus 25¢ Seat Tax
CHILDREN UNDER 12, $1.50 GEN. ADM. SECTION ONLY
FOR INFORMATION DIAL 582-8107

MID-ATLANTIC CHAMPIONSHIP WRESTLING

MID-ATLANTIC WRESTLING 1975 YEARBOOK

Township Title Bout Scheduled

A return match for the Mid-Atlantic wrestling title between Johnny Valentine and challenger Paul Jones will headline Tuesday's five-event program at Township Auditorium.

The rules for the match have been relaxed by the National Wrestling Alliance. Valentine apparently had himself disqualified last week in order to save his title.

A pin or a disqualification will permit the title to change hands this week. Valentine had to agree to the rules or face suspension.

Rufus R. Jones and Sandy Scott will team to take on Ric Flair and Doug Gilbert in the semifinal, Art Nelson scraps Abe Jacobs, The Blue Scorpion meets Kelvin Sullivan and at 8:15 Larry Sharpe tests L. D. Lewis.

Columbia, SC
May 6

MID-ATLANTIC WRESTLING 1975 YEARBOOK

Wrestling matchup an edge for NWA

A wrestling battle turned from the mat to the boxoffice last night, and when the final results were tabulated it appeared the National Wrestling Alliance had a firm headlock on its opposition.

The NWA, which stages bouts regularly at Starland Arena, drew 2,199 to its card at the Salem-Roanoke Valley Civic Center. Meanwhile, the International Wrestling Association, holding its second show at the Roanoke Civic Center, attracted 1,450 customers.

But both groups appeared to have their own loyal followers. The NWA decided to stage its card last night in a head-to-head confrontation with the IWA after viewing the IWA's first offering in Roanoke two weeks ago.

Bob Hatch, the IWA President, said his group will return to Roanoke for another card on June 9. He also said the IWA could not operate in Roanoke on a regular basis if the shows took in only $5,400 each time.

In the NWA matches at Salem, Johnny Valentine retained his title belt by pinning Paul Jones, while Rick Flair kept his belt despite losing on a disqualification to Ken Patera. Swede Hansen and Charlie Cooke defeated Art Nelson and Mr. Fuji and while Honey Girl Paige and Vicki Williams stopped Paula Kay and Marie Lavieu in tag-team bouts.

In other matches, Ken Sullivan topped Frank Morell and Don Kernodle and the Blue Scorpion drew.

At Roanoke, Mil Mascaras kept his IWA title with a win over Eric The Red. Dino Bravo and Gino Brito won by disqualification over the Mongols while Rip Hawk beat Tex McKenzie. Beautifiul Bruce lost to Cowboy Bob Ellis.

The Ivan Koloff-Bulldog Brower vs. Ernie Ladd-Mighty Egor match ended in disqualification, while Dick Steinborn topped Joe Turko. Argentina Appolo beat Reginald Love and Hartford Love lost to Luis Martinez.

Wahoo, Jones Keep Tag Title

Wahoo McDaniels and Paul Jones defended their World Tag Team Championship by defeating Jack and Jerry Brisco at the Coliseum Thursday night.

3In another tag team match, Gene and Ole Anderson beat Swede Hanstn and Saney Scott.

Goes After Title
Chief Wahoo McDaniel, the former pro football linebacker, takes on Mid-Atlantic Heavyweight wrestling champion Johnny Valentine Friday night in a championship match at University Hall. Also on the card, sponsored by the Student Aid Foundation, is another feature match putting Ken Patera, the former Olympic weightlifter, against The Super Destroyer, a masked villain. Female wrestlers, a tag match and two other bouts are on the card which gets underway at 8 p.m.

Andersons Defend Title

Ole and Gene Anderson will defend their world tag team title against challengers Wahoo McDaniel and Paul Jones in the feature match of Mid-Atlantic Championship Wrestling at the Greensboro Coliseum at 8:15 tonight.

In a special return "bullstrap" match, Dusty Rhodes will face Black Jack Mulligan.

Also on the card will be Ken Patera meeting Rick Flair, Ox Baker testing Charlie Cook, Frank Monte meeting Sandy Scott and Bill Crouch testing Don Kernodle.

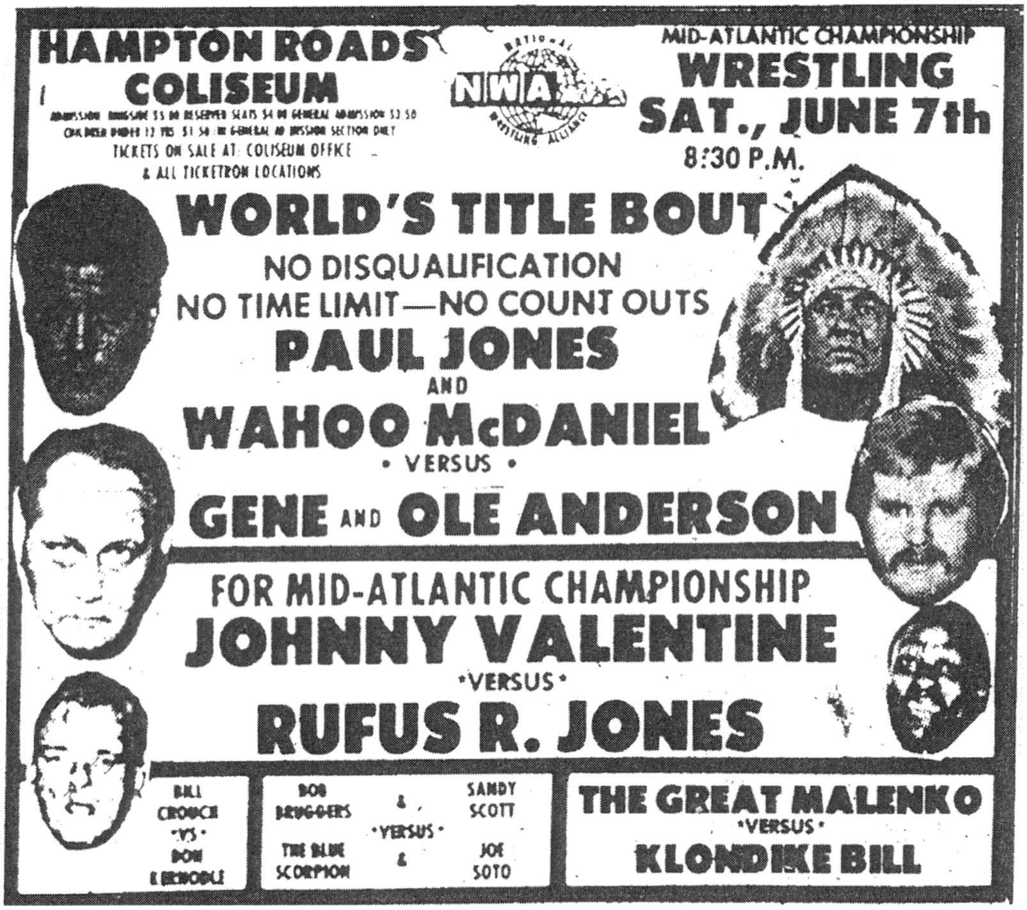
HAMPTON ROADS
COLISEUM
ADMISSION RINGSIDE $5.00 RESERVED SEATS $4.00 GENERAL ADMISSION $3.50
CHILDREN UNDER 12 YRS $1.50 IN GENERAL ADMISSION SECTION ONLY
TICKETS ON SALE AT: COLISEUM OFFICE
& ALL TICKETRON LOCATIONS
NWA
MID-ATLANTIC CHAMPIONSHIP
WRESTLING
SAT., JUNE 7th
8:30 P.M.
WORLD'S TITLE BOUT
NO DISQUALIFICATION
NO TIME LIMIT—NO COUNT OUTS
PAUL JONES
AND
WAHOO McDANIEL
• VERSUS •
GENE AND OLE ANDERSON
FOR MID-ATLANTIC CHAMPIONSHIP
JOHNNY VALENTINE
•VERSUS•
RUFUS R. JONES
BILL CROUCH •VS• DON KERNODLE
BOB BRUGGERS & SANDY SCOTT •VERSUS• THE BLUE SCORPION & JOE SOTO
THE GREAT MALENKO
•VERSUS•
KLONDIKE BILL

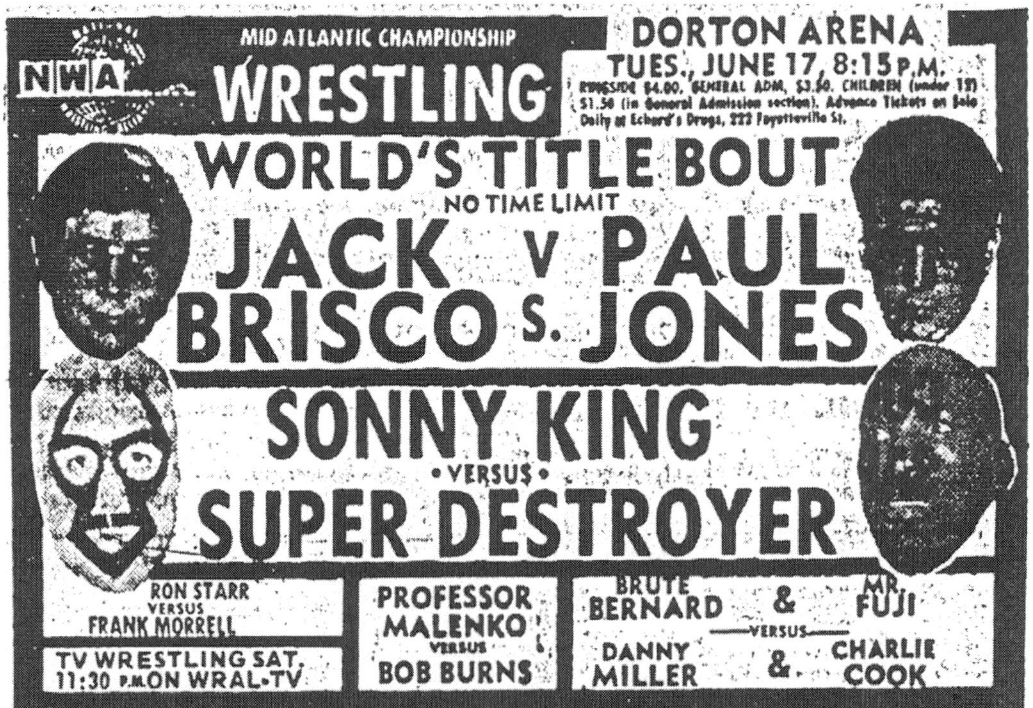
NWA
MID ATLANTIC CHAMPIONSHIP
WRESTLING
DORTON ARENA
TUES., JUNE 17, 8:15 P.M.
RINGSIDE $4.00, GENERAL ADM, $3.50, CHILDREN (under 12) $1.50 (in General Admission section). Advance Tickets on Sale Daily at Echerd's Drugs, 222 Fayetteville St.
WORLD'S TITLE BOUT
NO TIME LIMIT
JACK BRISCO VS. PAUL JONES
SONNY KING
•VERSUS•
SUPER DESTROYER
RON STARR
VERSUS
FRANK MORRELL
TV WRESTLING SAT. 11:30 P.M. ON WRAL-TV
PROFESSOR MALENKO
VERSUS
BOB BURNS
BRUTE BERNARD & MR. FUJI
—VERSUS—
DANNY MILLER & CHARLIE COOK

Pro Grapps at Elon Sunday

ELON COLLEGE — A battle for the World's Tag Team Championship highlights the return of outstanding Mid-Atlantic Championship Wrestling to the Elon College Gym on Sunday afternoon, June 22nd, at 3:00 p.m.

The main event will feature Gene and Ole Anderson putting their World's Tag Team Championship on the line against the former champions, Wahoo McDaniel and Paul Jones. These two teams are bitter enemies and when they square off in the ring with the titles at stake, anything could happen. The only thing that is certain about this championship match is that the fans will be treated to a wild and rugged battle for the titles.

This championship main event will be a one fall battle with an hour time limit.

Singles action has popular Swede Hanson going against the Mid-Atlantic TV Champion, Ric Flair. Hanson will have to be at his best in this bout as Flair has proven in the past that he will do anything he can to win his matches.

Ken Patera tangles with 400-pound Jerry Blackwell in another singles bout. Patera is considered to be the strongest wrestler in the world and he will need all of his strength when the clashes with the villianous Blackwell.

In another singles bout Professor Malenko, a rugged villian from Russia, goes against newcomer Ron Starr. There promises to be plenty of fireworks when these two wrestlers tangle in the ring.

In the opening bout Two-Ton Harris faces Don Kernodle, from Burlington and Elon College.

Advance tickets are on sale at the Burlington Sporting Goods.

WRECKING CREW — That's what they're called, the Minnesota Wrecking Crew. It's really Gene and Ole Anderson, the Anderson Brothers, who will pit their Mid-Atlantic tag team championship on the line in a program at Elon College Sunday afternoon (see story below).

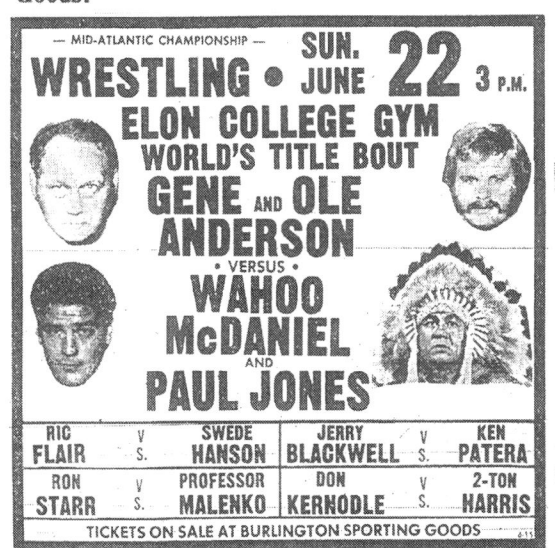

Wahoo McDaniel Ends the Long Reign of Johnny Valentine as Mid-Atlantic Champion

WRESTLING
MID-ATLANTIC HEAVYWEIGHT CHAMPIONSHIP

ASHEVILLE CIVIC CENTER
SUNDAY, JUNE 29, 3:00 P.M.

MAIN EVENT—TITLE MATCH
WAHOO McDANIELS—vs—JOHNNY WALENTINE
No Disqualification — No Time Limit — No Countdown
Special Referee — George Scott

NOTE: If Wahoo loses, he promises to stay out of Asheville for 6 months.

TAG TEAM—NON-TITLE MATCH
Ole & Gene Anderson — vs — Ken Patera and Rufus R. Jones

Art Nelson — vs — Bob Bruggers
Klondike Bill — vs — Jerry Blackwell
Sandy Scott — vs — Frank Monte
Ron Starr — vs — Larry Sharpe

BOX OFFICE OPENS SUNDAY 1:00 P.M.

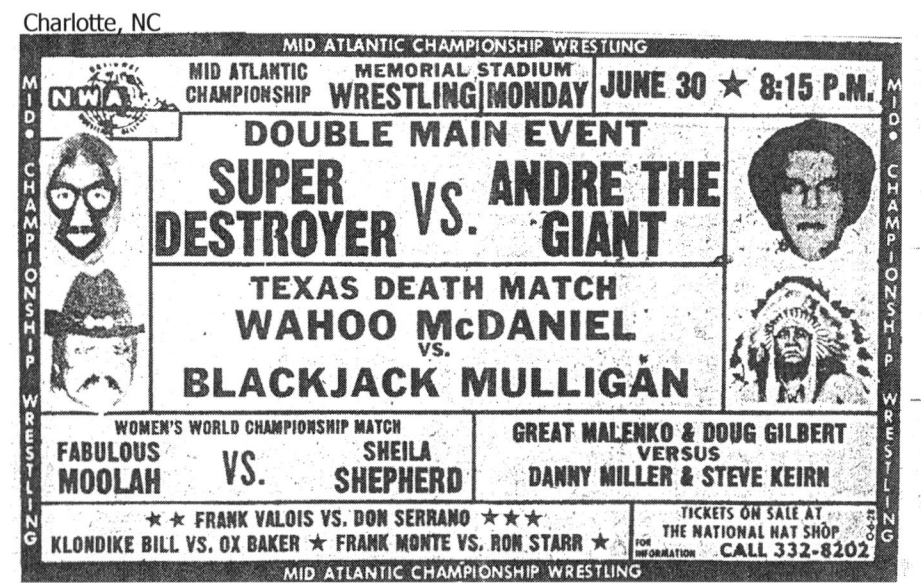

Charlotte, NC

MID ATLANTIC CHAMPIONSHIP WRESTLING
MEMORIAL STADIUM — MONDAY JUNE 30 ★ 8:15 P.M.

DOUBLE MAIN EVENT
SUPER DESTROYER vs. ANDRE THE GIANT

TEXAS DEATH MATCH
WAHOO McDANIEL vs. BLACKJACK MULLIGAN

WOMEN'S WORLD CHAMPIONSHIP MATCH
FABULOUS MOOLAH vs. SHEILA SHEPHERD

GREAT MALENKO & DOUG GILBERT VERSUS DANNY MILLER & STEVE KEIRN

★★ FRANK VALOIS VS. DON SERRANO ★★★
KLONDIKE BILL VS. OX BAKER ★ FRANK MONTE VS. RON STARR ★

TICKETS ON SALE AT THE NATIONAL HAT SHOP — CALL 332-8202

Flair Wins Main Event

Ric Flair defeated Wahoo McDaniel in the main event of Saturday night's weekly wrestling program at Spartanburg Memorial Auditorium.

In the other feature bout Ron Starr and Steve Kearn defeated Brute Bernard and Jerry Blackwell in a tag team match.

In other matches Charlie Cook won over Buddy Porter, Gregg Peterson and Charlie Fulton fought to a draw and Don Serrano topped Frank Morrell.

Spartanburg, SC June 28

Origin of the United States Championship in Jim Crockett Promotions

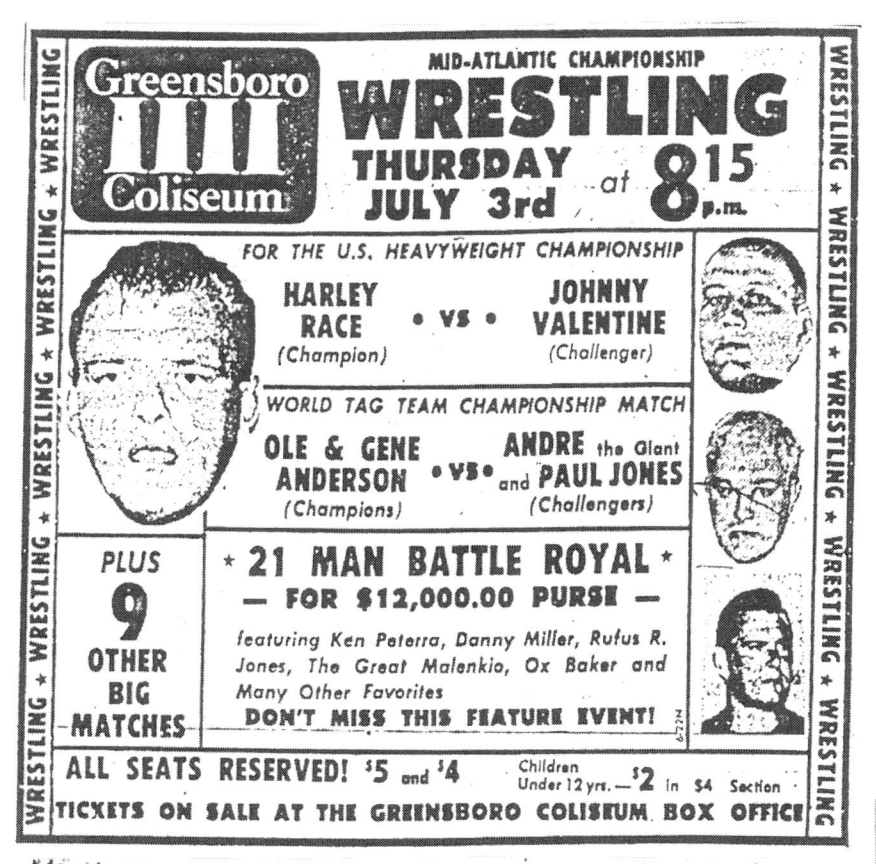

Greensboro Coliseum

MID-ATLANTIC CHAMPIONSHIP WRESTLING

THURSDAY JULY 3rd at 8:15 p.m.

FOR THE U.S. HEAVYWEIGHT CHAMPIONSHIP

HARLEY RACE (Champion) vs **JOHNNY VALENTINE** (Challenger)

WORLD TAG TEAM CHAMPIONSHIP MATCH

OLE & GENE ANDERSON (Champions) vs **ANDRE the Giant and PAUL JONES** (Challengers)

PLUS 9 OTHER BIG MATCHES

★ **21 MAN BATTLE ROYAL** ★
— FOR $12,000.00 PURSE —

featuring Ken Peterra, Danny Miller, Rufus R. Jones, The Great Malenkio, Ox Baker and Many Other Favorites

DON'T MISS THIS FEATURE EVENT!

ALL SEATS RESERVED! $5 and $4   Children Under 12 yrs. — $2 in $4 Section

TICKETS ON SALE AT THE GREENSBORO COLISEUM BOX OFFICE

Championship, 'Battle' In Coliseum Wrestling

Two NWA championships and a unique $12,000 purse will be up for grabs in tonight's holiday professional wrestling show at the Coliseum.

The action, which gets underway at 8:15, will be highlighted by a World Tag-Team match between title-holders Gene and Ole Anderson and challengers Andre the Giant and Paul Jones.

The reigning U.S. Heavyweight champion, Harley Race, will be in town to defend his title against the current Mid-Atlantic champion, Johnny Valentine. The latter's title will not be on the line.

And the main attraction is billed a massive battle royale with that $12,000 awaiting the lone survivor. Andre, the 7-foot-4, 400-plus-pound European, will be the center of attention in that one.

Valentine gets title

Johnny Valentine captured the U.S. Heavyweight professional wrestling championship by defeating Harley Race in the main event at the Coliseum Thursday night.

In other action, Gene and Ole Anderson defeated Paul Jones and Andre The Giant, Ken Patera won over Mr. Fuji, Rufus R. Jones defeated El Goucho, Morris Melinko won over Abe Jacobs and Ox Baker and Danny Miller fought to a 10 minute draw.

Other action saw Clondike Bill and Sandy Scott team to defeat George Harris and Frank Monte, Steve Keirns won over Joe Sopo and Ron Starrdef beat Don Ferrano.

Valentine Gets Championship

Johnny Valentine defeated Harley Race in the main event at the Coliseum Thursday night for the U.S. Heavyweight professional wrestling championship.

Other winners included Gene and Ole Anderson, Ken Patera, Rufus R. Jones, Morris Melinko and Steve Keirns.

Also winning were Clondike Bill and Sandy Scott and Ron Starr.

Rufus R. Jones captured the 20-man wrestling match at the end of the events, witnessed by an excess of 10,000 people.

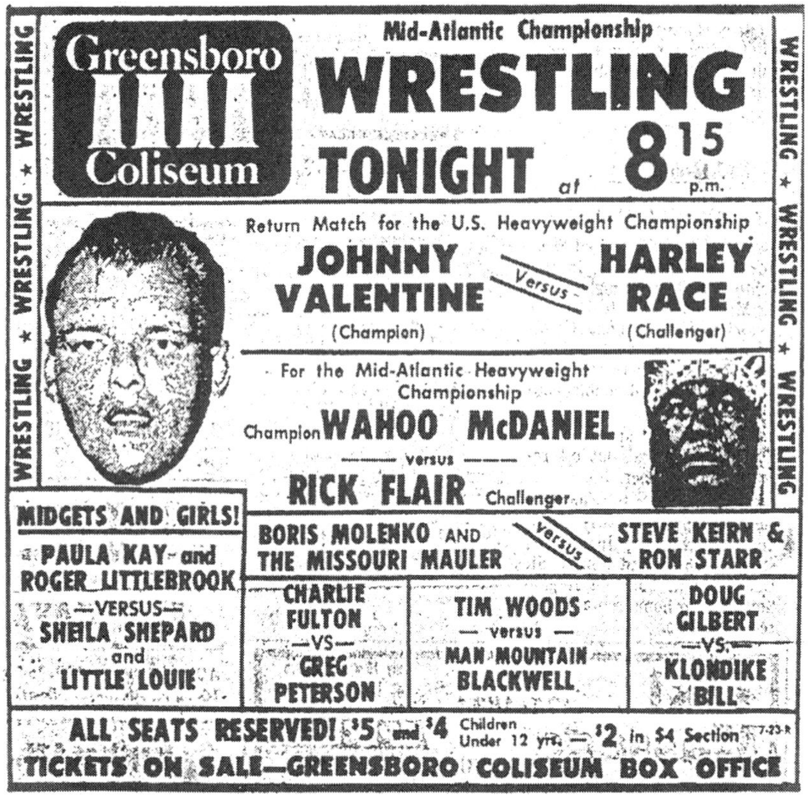
Greensboro Coliseum
Mid-Atlantic Championship
WRESTLING
TONIGHT at 8 15 p.m.
WRESTLING ★ WRESTLING ★ WRESTLING
Return Match for the U.S. Heavyweight Championship
JOHNNY VALENTINE (Champion)
Versus
HARLEY RACE (Challenger)
For the Mid-Atlantic Heavyweight Championship
Champion WAHOO McDANIEL
versus
RICK FLAIR Challenger
MIDGETS AND GIRLS!
PAULA KAY and ROGER LITTLEBROOK
—VERSUS—
SHEILA SHEPARD and LITTLE LOUIE
BORIS MOLENKO AND THE MISSOURI MAULER
Versus
STEVE KEIRN & RON STARR
CHARLIE FULTON —VS— GREG PETERSON
TIM WOODS — versus — MAN MOUNTAIN BLACKWELL
DOUG GILBERT —VS— KLONDIKE BILL
ALL SEATS RESERVED! $5 and $4 Children Under 12 yrs. — $2 in $4 Section
TICKETS ON SALE—GREENSBORO COLISEUM BOX OFFICE

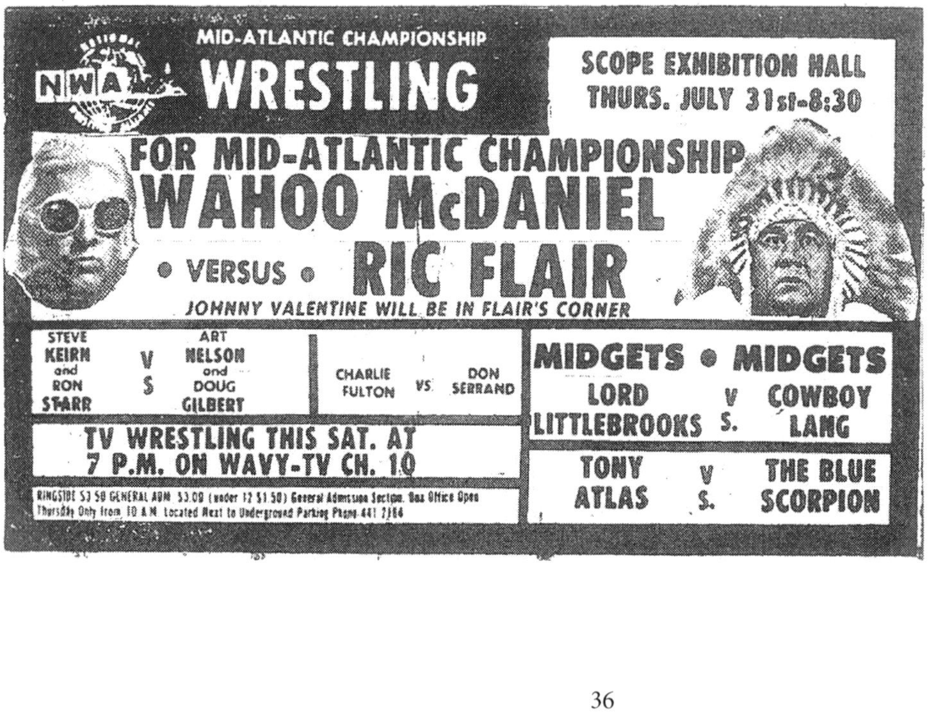
MID-ATLANTIC CHAMPIONSHIP
NWA
WRESTLING
SCOPE EXHIBITION HALL
THURS. JULY 31st-8:30
FOR MID-ATLANTIC CHAMPIONSHIP
WAHOO McDANIEL
• VERSUS •
RIC FLAIR
JOHNNY VALENTINE WILL BE IN FLAIR'S CORNER
STEVE KEIRN and RON STARR VS ART NELSON and DOUG GILBERT
CHARLIE FULTON VS DON SERRAND
MIDGETS • MIDGETS
LORD LITTLEBROOKS VS. COWBOY LANG
TONY ATLAS VS. THE BLUE SCORPION
TV WRESTLING THIS SAT. AT 7 P.M. ON WAVY-TV CH. 10

MID-ATLANTIC CHAMPIONSHIP
WRESTLING
THURS. JULY 31
ORANGEBURG
MIRMOW BALL PARK
- 8:15 P.M. -
TAG TEAM MATCH
RUFUS R. JONES
AND
KEN PATERA
— VS —
"THE WORLD'S TAG TEAM CHAMPIONS"
GENE, OLE
ANDERSON
MIDGET MEN!
LITTLE LOUIS
- VS -
LITTLE LOVE
Blackwell - vs - Hanson
Jacobs - vs. - Soto
Sullivan - vs. - Harris
TICKETS NOW ON SALE
WILLIAMS MUSIC CO.
RUSSELL STREET

Call White Tony Atlas

By DENNIS LATTA
Times Sports Writer

He looks like an Atlas. He lifts things like Atlas was supposed to have done, even if he can't carry the world. Atlas seems like a logical name for him.

So I guess, we'll call him Tony Atlas.

After three months of training, Roanoke's Tony White is ready to try his hand at professional wrestling. But he lost his last name when he lost his amateur status. Tony White is now Tony Atlas.

For years, Tony has been known as one of the strongest men in the Roanoke area. As a weightlifter and an arm wrestler, he is known around the state and this region of the country.

But there's no money to be made in weightlifting so Tony asked for a chance to become a professional wrestler. Even though Tony was an amateur wrestler in high school, the National Wrestling Alliance made him undergo three months of training. Graduation day is here.

Next Saturday night, Tony will make his debut in the Roanoke area. He had his first pro bout on July 10 but Saturday is the night he is looking forward to. For a rookie, he'll have a tough assignment in a masked veteran called the Scorpion.

"In the pros, I've found out that there are no children. These are all tough men. It's not like high school where you have someone's boy against you. This is a lot harder than amateur," Tony said from Charlotte where he is wrapping up his training.

"They teach more advanced stuff here. A lot of moves are legal in professional wrestling that aren't legal to amateurs. In the amateurs you can't apply pressure against a joint. You can do almost anything in the pros."

Becoming a professional wrestler isn't an easy task. Because the money is good, there's a long line of young men who want to try their hands at it.

"When I first started, I thought I was good. I found out in a hurry that there was a lot for me to learn. You've got to wrestle endlessly. It is important to be in top condition. I feel I'm in the best shape I've ever been," Tony said.

Tony had to beat out other hopefuls to be accepted by the NWA. "I had to wrestle the others who wanted to be wrestlers. I had to work."

Tony's strength hasn't been much help to the Roanoker. "Strength is really unimportant in the ring. You've got to know how to use it. Newcomers learn that quickly. You don't win on just strength."

But Tony White's name wasn't changed to Tony Atlas because he looks like a 90-pound weakling. "It was my idea. Tony Atlas was a name I use to use in weightlifting."

Now Tony is an unknown wrestler who is trying to get started and make a name. He's certain that will be a hard climb. "If anything is fake in wrestling, I wish they would tell me. I'm getting the hell beat out of me and I don't like that. But I'll learn."

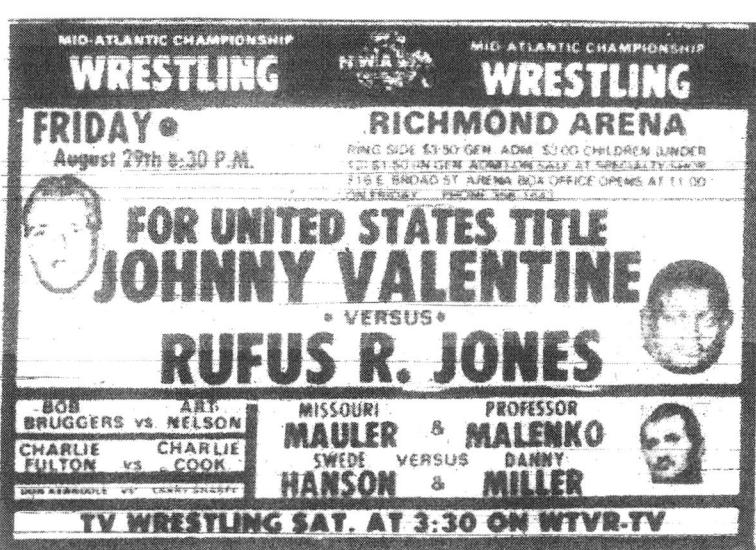

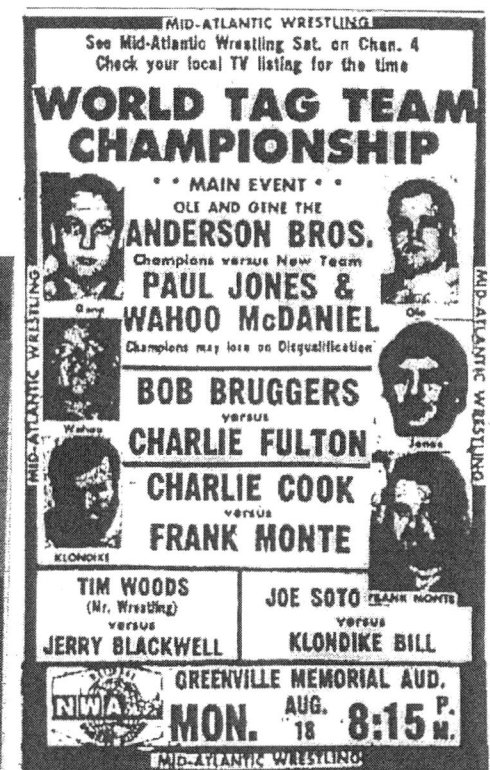

MID-ATLANTIC WRESTLING 1975 YEARBOOK

Classic Sunday Double Header

UNITED STATES HEAVY-WEIGHT CHAMPIONSHIP MATCH

★ ★ ★ ★ ★ ★ **MAIN EVENT** ★ ★ ★ ★ ★ ★

JOHNNY VALENTINE -vs- WAHOO McDANIELS

★ ★ ★ ★ ★ **OTHER EVENTS** ★ ★ ★ ★ ★

DUSTY RHODES AND PAUL JONES
—vs—
OLE AND GENE ANDERSON

★ ★ ★ ★ ★

KEN PATERA -vs- JERRY BLACKWELL

★ ★ ★ ★ ★ ★

TIM WOODS — VS — FRANK MONTE
STEVE KERN — VS — BOB BRUGGERS
JOE SOTO — VS — SANDY SCOTT

SUNDAY, AUG. 17 – 3:00 P.M.

Ringside $5.00 - General $4.00 - Children Under 12 $2.00
PLENTY OF FREE PARKING ON RANKIN STREET

ASHEVILLE CIVIC CENTER
Box Office Opens 1:00 Sunday
Regular Hours: Mon.-Fri. 10-5:30 P.M. — Sat. 11-4 P.M.

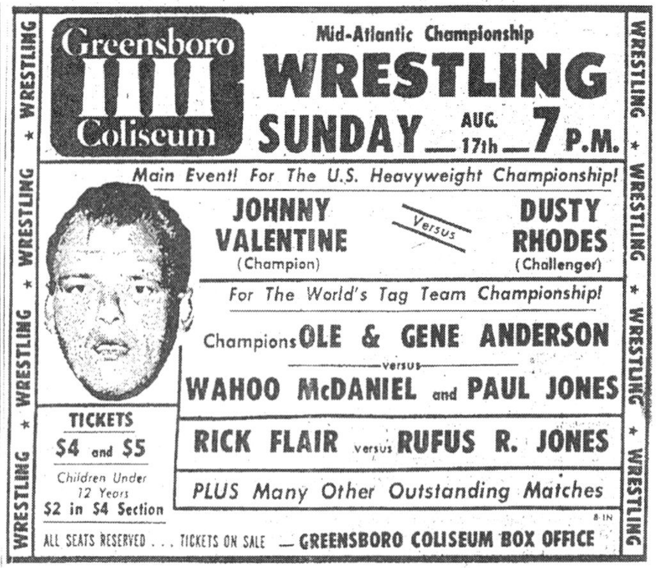

Greensboro Coliseum

Mid-Atlantic Championship WRESTLING

SUNDAY AUG. 17th 7 P.M.

Main Event! For The U.S. Heavyweight Championship!

JOHNNY VALENTINE (Champion) Versus **DUSTY RHODES** (Challenger)

For The World's Tag Team Championship!

Champions **OLE & GENE ANDERSON**
—versus—
WAHOO McDANIEL and PAUL JONES

RICK FLAIR versus **RUFUS R. JONES**

PLUS Many Other Outstanding Matches

TICKETS $4 and $5
Children Under 12 Years $2 in $4 Section

ALL SEATS RESERVED ... TICKETS ON SALE — GREENSBORO COLISEUM BOX OFFICE

MID-ATLANTIC CHAMPIONSHIP 8:15 P.M.

WRESTLING NWA

TUESDAY, AUG. 19

Columbia Township Auditorium

* 90 MINUTES *

WORLD'S TAG TEAM TITLE MATCH

THE CHAMPIONS

OLE AND GENE ANDERSON
-vs-
WAHOO McDANIEL AND PAUL JONES

3 OTHER MATCHES!

TICKETS NOW ON SALE TAYLOR ST. PHARMACY

ADMISSION
RESERVED RING SIDE $4
GENERAL ADMISSION $3.50
CHILDREN $1.50

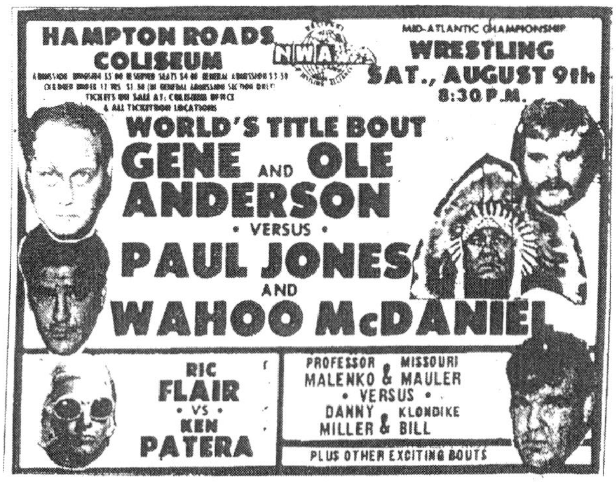

HAMPTON ROADS COLISEUM NWA

MID-ATLANTIC CHAMPIONSHIP WRESTLING

SAT., AUGUST 9th 8:30 P.M.

WORLD'S TITLE BOUT

GENE AND OLE ANDERSON
· VERSUS ·
PAUL JONES AND WAHOO McDANIEL

RIC FLAIR VS **KEN PATERA**

PROFESSOR MALENKO & MISSOURI MAULER
VERSUS
DANNY MILLER & KLONDIKE BILL

PLUS OTHER EXCITING BOUTS

MINNESOTA WRECKING CREW
Gene (Above) And Ole Anderson Ready

Tag Team Title On Line In Pro Wrestling Card

The world tag team championship will be on the line when Mid-Atlantic Championship Wrestling returns to Hampton Coliseum on Saturday for an 8:30 p.m. show.

The main event pits world champs Gene and Ole Anderson against Wahoo McDaniel and Paul Jones, the only team to defeat the brothers.

Ric Flair and Ken Patera tangle on the semifinal and in tag team action, The Missouri Mauler and Professor Boris Malenko oppose Danny Miller and Klondike Bill.

The singles matches are Tim Woods vs. Jerry Blackwell, Dan Kernodle vs. Bob Bruggers and Bob Burns vs. El Gaucho.

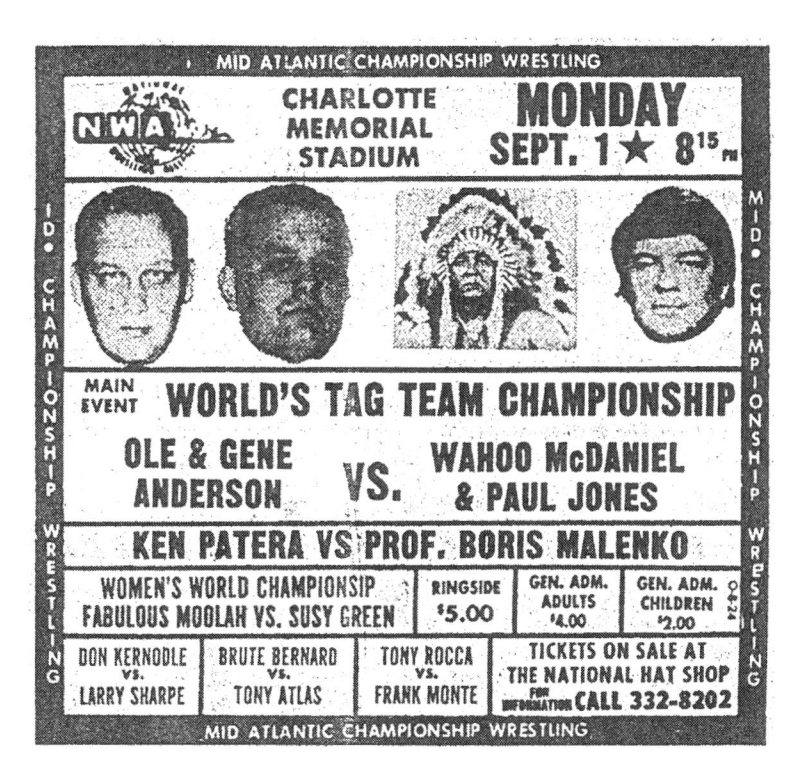

MID-ATLANTIC WRESTLING 1975 YEARBOOK

MID ATLANTIC CHAMPIONSHIP WRESTLING

NWA — **CHARLOTTE MEMORIAL STADIUM** — **MONDAY SEPT. 1 ★ 8:15 PM**

MAIN EVENT: WORLD'S TAG TEAM CHAMPIONSHIP

OLE & GENE ANDERSON VS. **WAHOO McDANIEL & PAUL JONES**

KEN PATERA VS PROF. BORIS MALENKO

WOMEN'S WORLD CHAMPIONSIP FABULOUS MOOLAH VS. SUSY GREEN

RINGSIDE $5.00 | GEN. ADM. ADULTS $4.00 | GEN. ADM. CHILDREN $2.00

- DON KERNODLE vs. LARRY SHARPE
- BRUTE BERNARD vs. TONY ATLAS
- TONY ROCCA vs. FRANK MONTE

TICKETS ON SALE AT THE NATIONAL HAT SHOP — FOR INFORMATION CALL 332-8202

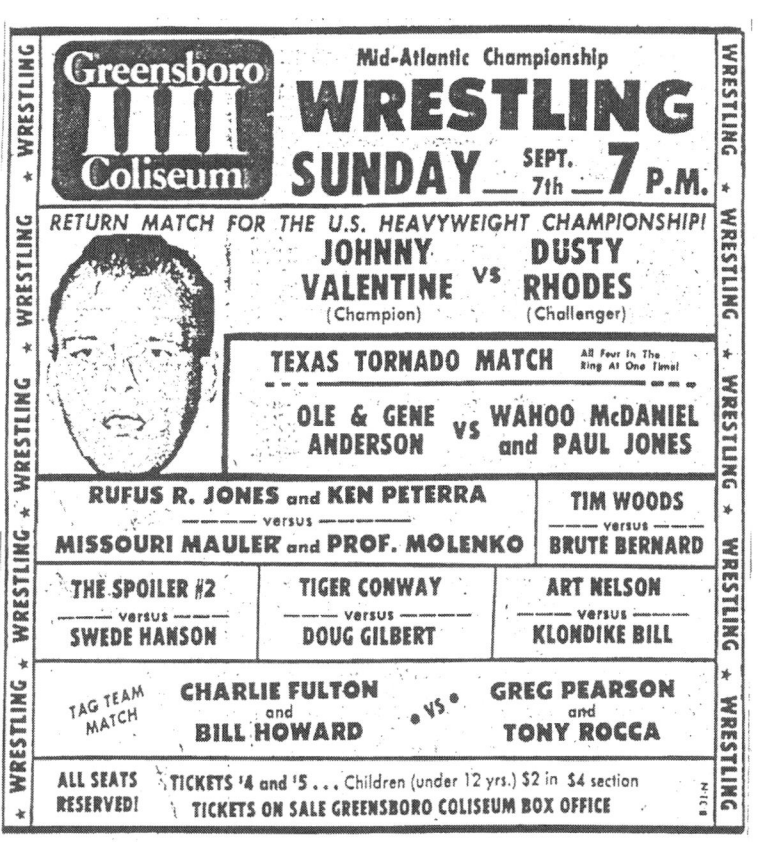

Greensboro Coliseum — Mid-Atlantic Championship WRESTLING

SUNDAY SEPT. 7th — 7 P.M.

RETURN MATCH FOR THE U.S. HEAVYWEIGHT CHAMPIONSHIP!

JOHNNY VALENTINE (Champion) VS **DUSTY RHODES** (Challenger)

TEXAS TORNADO MATCH — All Four In The Ring At One Time!

OLE & GENE ANDERSON vs **WAHOO McDANIEL and PAUL JONES**

RUFUS R. JONES and KEN PETERRA versus **MISSOURI MAULER and PROF. MOLENKO**

TIM WOODS versus **BRUTE BERNARD**

| THE SPOILER #2 versus SWEDE HANSON | TIGER CONWAY versus DOUG GILBERT | ART NELSON versus KLONDIKE BILL |

TAG TEAM MATCH: CHARLIE FULTON and BILL HOWARD vs **GREG PEARSON and TONY ROCCA**

ALL SEATS RESERVED! TICKETS $4 and $5 ... Children (under 12 yrs.) $2 in $4 section. TICKETS ON SALE GREENSBORO COLISEUM BOX OFFICE

MID-ATLANTIC CHAMPIONSHIP WRESTLING

COLUMBIA TOWNSHIP AUDITORIUM 8:15

TUESDAY SEPT. 9

WORLD'S TAG TEAM TITLE MATCH!

2 HOUR TIME LIMIT

TITLE CAN CHANGE HANDS BY DISQUALIFICATION

THE CHAMPIONS: GENE ANDERSON — OLE ANDERSON

-VS-

WAHOO McDANIEL — PAUL JONES

8 OTHER MATCHES!

CHAMPIONSHIP PRICES

- ADMISSION RESERVED RING SIDE — $4
- GENERAL ADMISSION — $3.50
- CHILDREN 3 YEARS TO 9 — $1.50

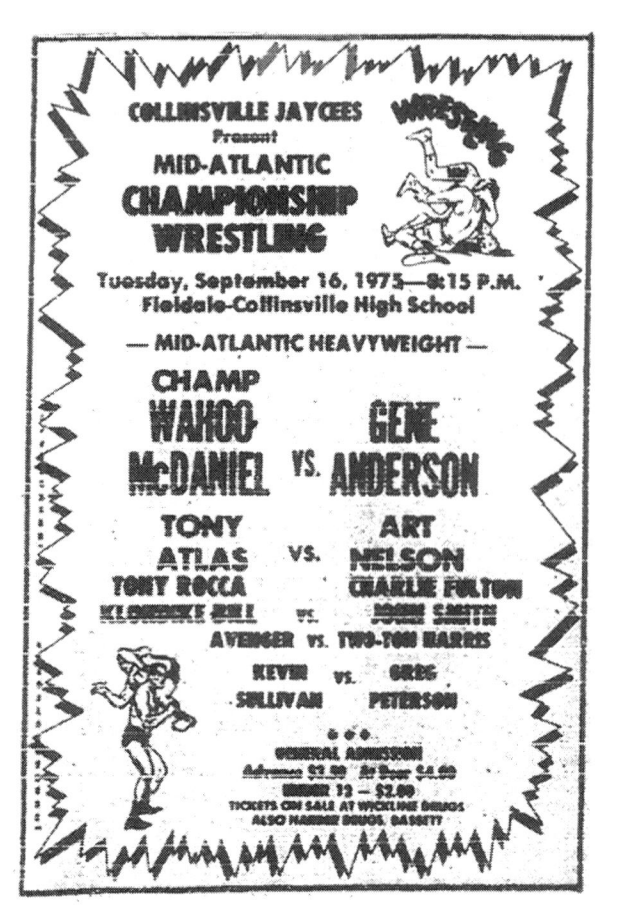

Ric Flair wins the Mid-Atlantic Championship

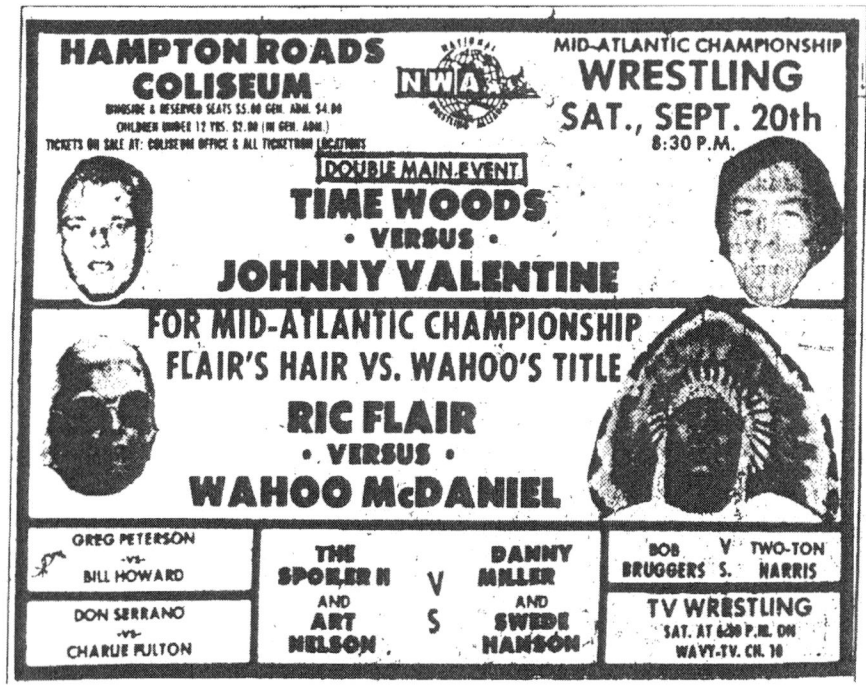

Mid-Atlantic Title Claimed by Flair

HAMPTON—Rick Flair, who had promised to shave his fleecy locks should he lose, Saturday night beat Wahoo McDaniel to win the Mid-Atlantic heavyweight wrestling championship.

In other matches, both Johnny Valentine and Tim Wood were disqualified in a no contest decision, Swede Hanson and Danny Miller won on a disqualification over Spoiler 2 and Art Nelson, Bob Brugers beat Two Ton Harris, Bill Howard drew with Greg Peterson and Charlie Fulton beat Don Serrano.

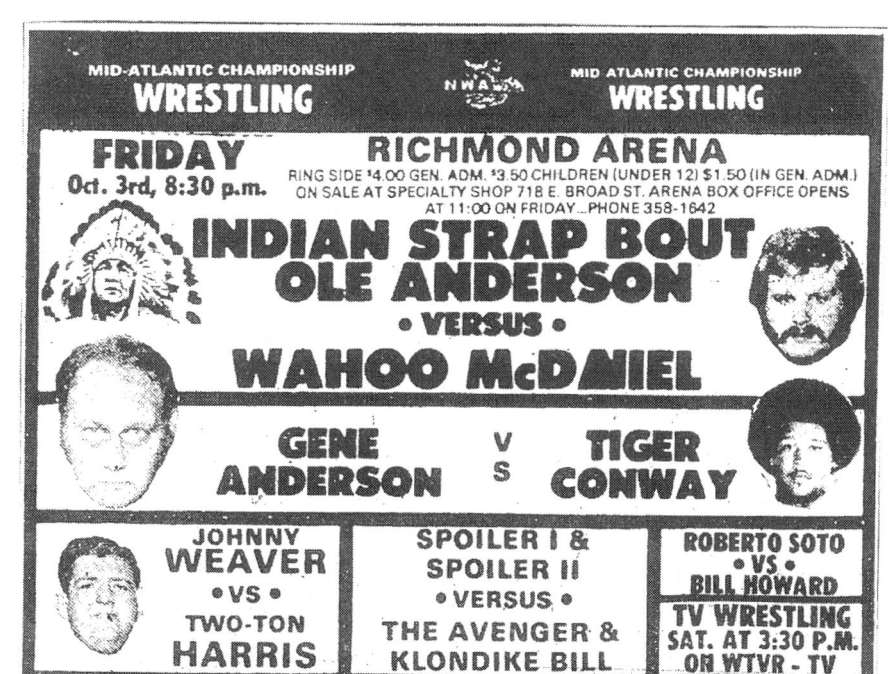

MID-ATLANTIC WRESTLING 1975 YEARBOOK

MID-ATLANTIC CHAMPIONSHIP WRESTLING — NWA — **MID ATLANTIC CHAMPIONSHIP WRESTLING**

RICHMOND ARENA
FRIDAY Oct. 3rd, 8:30 p.m.
RING SIDE $4.00 GEN. ADM. $3.50 CHILDREN (UNDER 12) $1.50 (IN GEN. ADM.)
ON SALE AT SPECIALTY SHOP 718 E. BROAD ST. ARENA BOX OFFICE OPENS AT 11:00 ON FRIDAY...PHONE 358-1642

INDIAN STRAP BOUT
OLE ANDERSON
· versus ·
WAHOO McDANIEL

GENE ANDERSON vs **TIGER CONWAY**

JOHNNY WEAVER · vs · **TWO-TON HARRIS**

SPOILER I & SPOILER II · versus · **THE AVENGER & KLONDIKE BILL**

ROBERTO SOTO · vs · **BILL HOWARD**

TV WRESTLING SAT. AT 3:30 P.M. ON WTVR - TV

Woods To Fight Valentine Friday Night

The former Mr. Wrestling, Tim Woods, will go against the U.S. Heavyweight champion, Johnnie Valentine, in a non-title match to headline this Friday night's Mid-Atlantic Championship Wrestling program at County Hall.

The no. 2 prelim will have Tonny Rocca meeting Ron Starr.

Advance tickets are on sale at Millers Drug Store, Reynolds Ave. and Central Drug Store, Meeting St. near George St.

Johnny Valentine wrestles what would be has last wrestling match in Charleston SC, 10/3/75, the night before the Wilmington, NC, plane crash.

Tag Title Bout Set at Coliseum

Tiger Conway and Steve Keirn will team up for a bid at the world tag team championship title held by Ole and Gene Anderson tonight (8:30 p.m.) at the Coliseum, heading a wrestling program that will also introduce two newcomers to the area.

Billy Graham will make his Richmond debut against Wahoo McDaniel, and Steve Strong will face Tim Woods, while preliminaries include a tag team bout of Spoiler I and II vs. Johnny Weaver and Swede Hanson, Mike Duois vs. Danny Miller, Klondike Bill vs. Bill Howard and Charlie Fulton vs. Tony Rocco.

Superstar Billy Graham makes his Richmond debut on 10/17/75, substituting for Ric Flair following Flair's injury in the Wilmington, NC, plane crash.

RICHMOND COLISEUM — NWA — **MID-ATLANTIC CHAMPIONSHIP WRESTLING**

NO MATCHES IN RICHMOND ON OCT. 10th
FRI. OCT. 17th 8:30 P.M.
RINGSIDE & RESERVED SEATS $6.00 GEN. ADM. $4.00. CHILDREN UNDER 12 YRS. $2.00 (IN GEN. ADM.) TAX INCLUDED. ON SALE AT COLISEUM BOX OFFICE.

OLE ANDERSON AND GENE ANDERSON v s. **STEVE KEIRN AND TIGER CONWAY**

GRUDGE MATCH
RIC FLAIR v s. **WAHOO McDANIEL**

PLUS OTHER BOUTS WATCH TV WRESTLING SAT. AT 3:30 P.M. ON WTVR-TV

RICHMOND COLISEUM
FRI. OCT. 17th 8:30 P.M.

WORLD ... **OLE & GENE** ... **STEVE KEIRN & TIGER CONWAY**

WAHOO McDANIEL · VERSUS · **SUPERSTAR BILLY GRAHAM**

STEVE STRONG v s. **TIM WOODS**

JOHNNY WEAVER & SWEDE HANSON · VERSUS · **SPOILERS I & II**

MILLER vs MIKE DUBOIS

KLONDIKE BILL vs BILL HOWARD

TONY ROCCO vs CHARLIE FULTON

DON'T MISS THE ACTION

TV WRESTLING SAT. AT 3:30 P.M. ON WTVR-TV

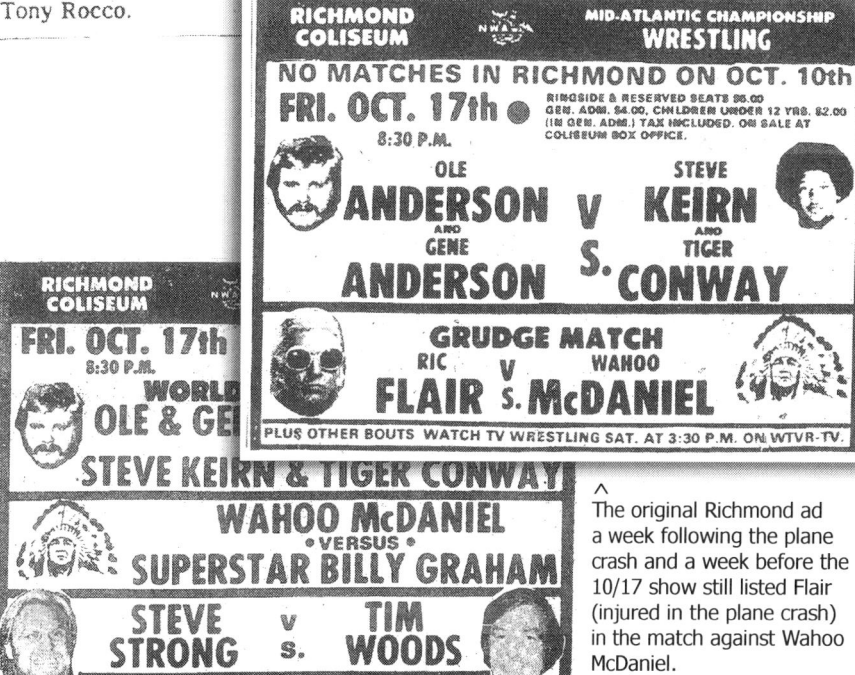

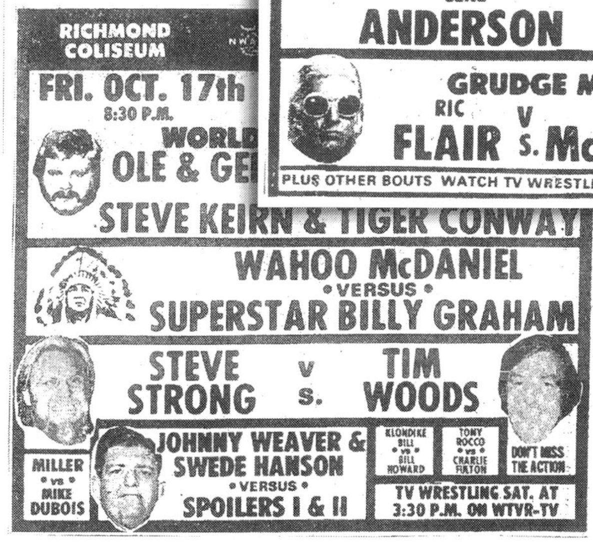

^ The original Richmond ad a week following the plane crash and a week before the 10/17 show still listed Flair (injured in the plane crash) in the match against Wahoo McDaniel.

< The corrected ad the week of the show listed Superstar Billy Graham as Wahoo's new opponent.

41

The Wilmington NC Plane Crash – Oct. 4, 1975

Promoter, 3 Wrestlers Injured In Plane Crash

By MARY BISHOP LACY and ROGER MIKEAL
Observer Staff Writers

Charlotte promoter David F. Crockett and three Charlotte-based professional wrestlers were among six persons injured Saturday evening when their plane crashed near Wilmington.

Crockett, 29, of 732 E. Park Ave., was reported in good condition late Saturday night at New Hanover Memorial Hospital in Wilmington. Also in good condition were wrestler Richard Flienr, 24, known professionally as Ric Flair, and George Burrell Woodin, 41, listed by the New Hanover County Sheriff's Department as a promoter.

Wrestlers Robert Bruggers, 31, and Johnny Valentine, 47, were reported by a hospital spokesman to be in serious condition.

THE PILOT of the plane, Joseph Michael Farkas, 29, was listed in critical condition and was undergoing surgery for head injuries at the hospital late Saturday night. The hospital spokesman said Farkas' identification bore addresses in Monroe, Charlotte and Connecticut.

Hospital officials refused to give details on the other men's injuries.

The six men reportedly left Charlotte in the yellow and white Cessna 310 at 5:30 p.m. for Saturday night wrestling matches at Wilmington's Legion Stadium. Who owned the plane and where it took off couldn't be learned immediately.

About 6:25 p.m., when the plane was about a mile west of the Wilmington airport and was approaching a runway, Farkas radioed the control tower that one of his engines had stopped, according to Deputy Sheriff E.D. Long.

Cutting across treetops and snagging a wing on a utility pole, the plane crashed about half a mile from the airport along a railroad embankment and near a state prison camp, according to sheriff's and state highway patrol reports.

SEVERAL of the crash victims were thrown from the plane, and one was pinned between seats inside, according to a spokesman for

See PROMOTER Page 8A, Col. 5

Promoter, 3 Wrestlers Injured In Air Crash

Continued from Page 1A

the Ogden Rescue Squad, which carried the men to the hospital.

Crockett is an official of Jim Crockett Promotions, a Charlotte-based enterprise that specializes in sports promotions.

Valentine, considered one of the top professional wrestlers in the country, has wrestled in a number of foreign countries, including Japan and Australia. Known as a lover of opera and fine cuisine, Valentine has been a professional wrestler for 25 years.

Flair is a flamboyant blond wrestler who has been wrestling in the Charlotte area about 2½ years. He is a native of Minnesota and had been scheduled to meet Ken Patera in a wrestling match at Charlotte's Park Center Monday night.

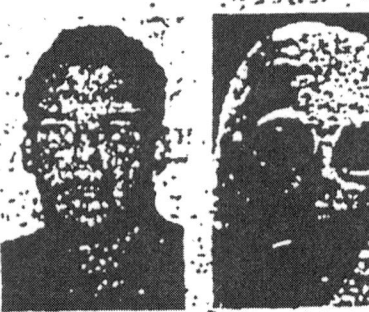

Bruggers, also from Minnesota, played with the Miami Dolphins football team as a linebacker for several years around 1970. He began wrestling in Charlotte about two years ago.

VALENTINE   FLAIR

You will note in the accompanying articles regarding the Wilmington plane crash there are references to a promoter named George Burrell Woodin. This was actually wrestler Tim Woods. The company was trying to avoid it getting out that Valentine and Woods, who were embroiled in the territory's top feud at the time, were actually travelling to the show together. So they identified Woods by his real name and identified him to the media as a promoter.

WILMINGTON MORNING STAR   FRIDAY, OCT. 3, 1975

MID ATLANTIC CHAMPIONSHIP
WRESTLING

TIM WOODS
VS
JOHNNY VALENTINE

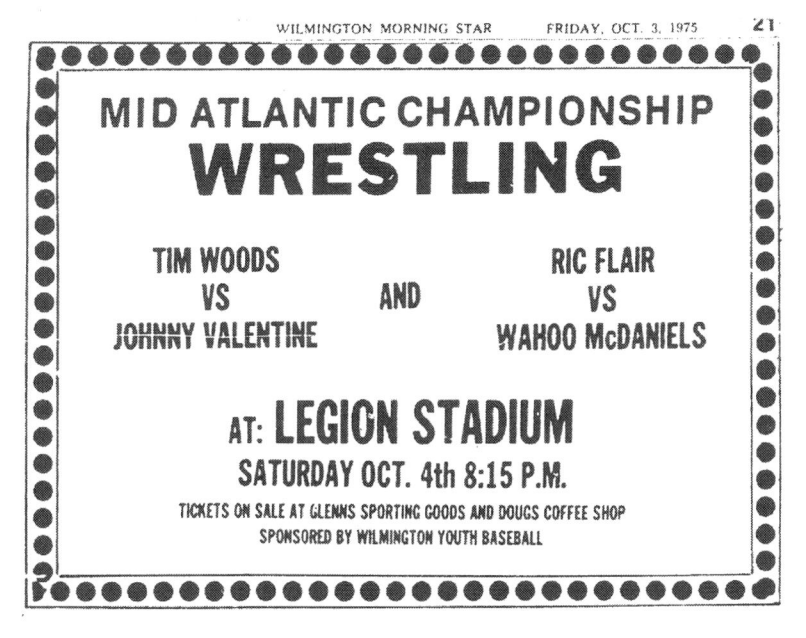

AND

RIC FLAIR
VS
WAHOO McDANIELS

AT: LEGION STADIUM
SATURDAY OCT. 4th 8:15 P.M.
TICKETS ON SALE AT GLENNS SPORTING GOODS AND DOUGS COFFEE SHOP
SPONSORED BY WILMINGTON YOUTH BASEBALL

FAA investigates plane crash here

Federal aviation officials are investigating the crash of a Cessna 310, which hit a railroad embankment near the New Hanover County airport Saturday, injuring all six passengers.

The New Hanover County Sheriff's Dept. confirmed representatives of the Federal Aviation Administration (FAA) and the National Transportation Board of Washington are investigating the crash.

Three of the persons injured in the 6:20 p.m. crash were professional wrestlers bound for matches at Legion Stadium.

A spokesman for New Hanover Memorial Hospital said its switchboard has been flooded with calls inquiring about the Wrestlers' conditions.

On Sunday, wrestlers Johnny Valentine, 47, and Bob Bruggers, were reported still in serious condition at the hospital.

Wrestler Rick Fliehr (Ric Flair), 24, was reported in satisfactory condition.

The pilot of the charter twin-engine plane, Joseph Michael Forkes, 28, of Monroe, was reported in critical condition in the hospital's intensive care unit.

Wrestling promoter David Crockett, 28, was reported in satisfactory condition, and promoter George Burrell Woodin was discharged from the hospital Sunday.

The plane had left Charlotte about 5:30 p.m. and, according to Sheriff's Dept. reports, was in radio contact with the airport's control tower when it began experiencing engine trouble about a mile west of the airport.

The plane had been orginally scheduled to land on runway five, but the pilot told the tower he would attempt a landing on old runway nine.

The plane crashed about a half mile from the runway, near the intersection of North 23rd Street and Gordon Road.

Danny Long, deputy sheriff, reported he talked to Woodin, who commented the plane's engines were sputtering and that the stall lights on its instrument panel had lit up.

The aircraft skimmed the top of some trees, narrowly missed a house, and a wing hit a utility pole as it fell to the ground just north of the county prison farm.

Between 3,500 and 4,000 spectators were at Legion Stadium following the accident.

Wrestlers at the stadium went on with their show, ending it with a free-for-all, in which the last man standing, Wahoo McDaniels, won $5,000.

3 Wrestlers Are Injured

WILMINGTON, N.C. (AP) — Three professional wrestlers and two promoters were hospitalized Sunday in satisfactory to serious condition after a plane bringing them to a match in Wilmington crashed just short of the runway Saturday night.

New Hanover County authorities identified the wrestlers as Richard Fliehr, 24, who uses the professional name Ric Flair; Robert Bruggers, 31, a onetime professional football player with the Miami Dolphins, and Johnny Valentine, 47.

Bruggers and Valentine were reported in serious condition Sunday at New Hanover Memorial Hospital.

Fliehr and promoters David F. Crockett and George Burrell Woodin, 41, were listed in satisfactory condition.

Joseph Michael Farkas, 28, pilot of the Cessna 310, was in critical condition after undergoing surgery for head injuries Saturday night.

The three wrestlers are based in Charlotte. They had been scheduled to participate in matches in Wilmington Saturday night.

Sheriff's Deputy E. D. Long said Farkas radioed about 6:25 p.m. that one of the Cessna's engines had gone as he was approaching the runway.

Long said the plane cut across sevral tree tops and snagged a wing on a utility pole before plunging to earth along a railroad embankment.

Victims of plane crash still in Port City hospital

Three professional wrestlers and their promoter, among six persons injured in the crash of a twin-engine charter plane near New Hanover County Airport Saturday evening, remain hospitalized.

John A. Westbrook, airport manager, said Tuesday, "All the officials investigating the accident departed Wilmington late Monday."

He said he had not been informed of any information gained by Federal Aviation Agency, Department of Transportation, and Cessna Aircraft personnel in their investigation of the wreckage of the Cessna 310 aircraft which crashed about 6:20 p.m. Saturday into a railroad embankment north of the intersection of Gordon Road and North 23rd Street.

"The investigators made no comment to me at all following their examination of the aircraft," Westbrook said, adding that he anticipates a report from the FAA on the airplane crash "in about forty to forty-five days."

Wrestlers Johnny Valentine, Ric Flair and Robert Bruggers, and promoter David Crockett are listed in good, satisfactory or stable conditions at New Hanover Memorial Hospital.

The pilot of the plane, Michael Farkas, remains in the hospital's intensive care unit and was listed in critical condition Tuesday afternoon.

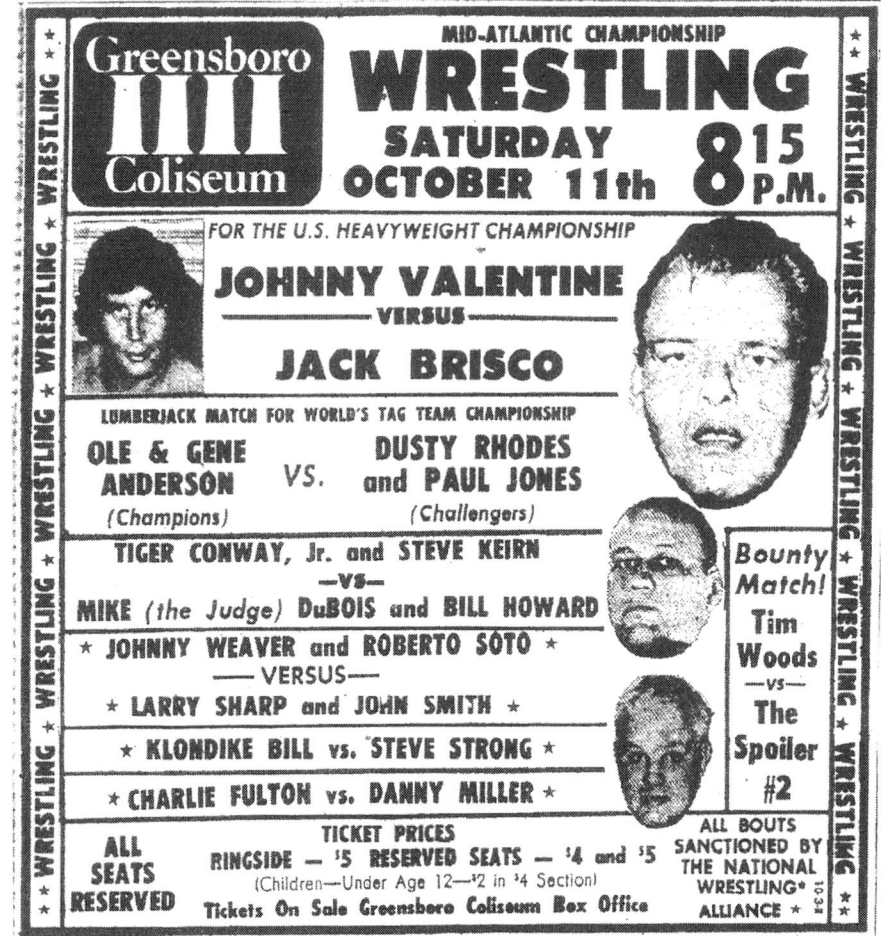

3 Wrestlers Remain In Hospital

WILMINGTON—Johnny Valentine, Ric Flair and Bob Bruggers, three professional wrestlers familiar to Carolinas and Virginia-area fans, remain hospitalized at New Hanover County Hospital following a Saturday evening plane crash near the Wilmington airport.

Valentine, 47, the reigning United States Heavyweight champion of the National Wrestling Alliance, and Bruggers, 31, were in serious condition Sunday according to a hospital spokesman. Flair, 24, whose legal name is Richard Fliehr, was reported in satisfactory condition.

Also in the twin-engine Cessna 310, which reportedly ran out of gas while trying to land, were pilot Michael Farkas of Monroe, who was in critical condition after undergoing surgery for head injuries and David Crockett and George Woodin, both of Charlotte, who were released from the hospital Sunday. Crockett and Woodin both are promoters.

The athletes involved wrestle for Jim Crockett Promotions of Charlotte and they were en route to a performance in Wilmington Saturday night.

"We understand all but the pilot were doing well this morning," a member of Crockett's family told the Daily News Sunday. "We understand a series of tests will be performed to determine the extent of the injuries."

Valentine was scheduled to wrestle in the main event of a Greensboro Coliseum card Saturday night, Oct. 11. Dory Funk will sub for Valentine in the match against Jack Brisco.

Greensboro Coliseum

MID-ATLANTIC CHAMPIONSHIP WRESTLING

SATURDAY OCTOBER 11th 8:15 P.M.

FOR THE U.S. HEAVYWEIGHT CHAMPIONSHIP

JOHNNY VALENTINE
— VERSUS —
JACK BRISCO

LUMBERJACK MATCH FOR WORLD'S TAG TEAM CHAMPIONSHIP

OLE & GENE ANDERSON VS. **DUSTY RHODES and PAUL JONES**
(Champions) (Challengers)

★ TIGER CONWAY, Jr. and STEVE KEIRN ★
— vs —
★ MIKE (the Judge) DuBOIS and BILL HOWARD ★

★ JOHNNY WEAVER and ROBERTO SOTO ★
— VERSUS —
★ LARRY SHARP and JOHN SMITH ★

★ KLONDIKE BILL vs. STEVE STRONG ★

★ CHARLIE FULTON vs. DANNY MILLER ★

Bounty Match! **Tim Woods** —vs— **The Spoiler #2**

ALL SEATS RESERVED
TICKET PRICES
RINGSIDE — $5   RESERVED SEATS — $4 and $5
(Children—Under Age 12—$2 in $4 Section)
Tickets On Sale Greensboro Coliseum Box Office

ALL BOUTS SANCTIONED BY THE NATIONAL WRESTLING ALLIANCE

Johnny Valentine had earned a shot at the NWA champion Jack Brisco by virtue of his win over Harley Race for the U.S. title. What an epic clash that would have been. Former NWA champion Dory Funk, Jr. substituted for Valentine on this huge Oct. 11 card in Greensboro, NC. Amazingly, Tim Woods was back in action a mere 7 days after being in the plane crash.

Crash victims still in hospital

By C. S. CRAWFORD
Staff Writer

Three professional wrestlers and their promoter, among six persons injured in the crash of a twin-engine charter plane near New Hanover County Airport Saturday evening, remain hospitalized.

John A. Westbrook, airport manager, said Tuesday, "All the officials investigating the accident departed Wilmington late Monday."

He said he had not been informed of any information gained by Federal Aviation Agency, Department of Transportation, and Cessna Aircraft personnel in their investigation of the wreckage of the Cessna 310 aircraft which crashed about 6:20 p.m. Saturday into a railroad embankment north of the intersection of Gordon Road and North 23rd Street.

"The investigators made no comment to me at all following their examination of the aircraft," Westbrook said, adding that he anticipates a report from the FAA on the airplane crash "in about forty to forty-five days."

Wrestlers Johnny Valentine, Ric Flair and Robert Bruggers, and promoter David Crockett are listed in good, satisfactory or stable conditions at New Hanover Memorial Hospital.

The pilot of the plane, Michael Farkas, remains in the hospital's intensive care unit and was listed in critical condition Tuesday afternoon.

Hospital authorities Tuesday released information concerning four of the injured persons, but said the Farkas family "has asked that no other information be released" concerning him, except that he is in "critical condition."

Valentine's attending physician reported that his patient had a severe fracture of the second lumbar vertebra.

He said as a result of the injury, Valentine has severe weakness in the lower limbs, but does have good sensation.

Valentine also has a contusion of the abdominal wall, but there is no evidence of internal injuries. He has a fractured ankle and superficial lacerations of the forehead and right hand. His condition was said to be stable.

The attending physician for Flair said he has fractures of three vertebrae, but has no nerve involvement. He has a fracture of one right rib, and has abdominal wall contusions with no evidence of internal injuries. His condition was reported as good.

Bruggers' attending physician reported he has a severe fracture of the first lumbar vertebra, but no nerve involvement. He has a fracture of the ankle and an abdominal wall contusion with no evidence of internal injuries. His condition was reported as good.

Crockett's attending physician reported his patient has an ankle fracture and a sprain of the shoulder, as well as multiple lacerations involving his right upper lip, his forehead, and his right ear.

R.J. Powell

Wrestling

Upholding the time-honored cliche, "the show must go on," a full wrestling program was presented by the Wilmington Youth Baseball Inc., in the open-air arena at Legion Stadium Saturday a week ago despite an earlier tragedy.

Professional wrestlers Johnny Valentine, Ric Flair and Robert Bruggers and promoter David Crockett were among six persons injured in the crash of a twin-engine Cessna 310 aircraft about 6:20 p.m. October 4 near the New Hanover County Airport.

Earlier this week, these four were reported in good, satisfactory or stable conditions at New Hanover Memorial Hospital.

"Being in fine physical condition before the accident was probably a big plus factor in the wrestlers' favor," Eddie Godwin, president of Wilmington Youth Baseball said of the matmen who were prevented from appearing on the stadium card because of the plane crash.

Godwin explained the show featuring eight other grapplers was staged in the open ring before the concrete stands in Legion Stadium with a crowd of "over 3600" watching the action.

"This, our sixth wrestling show, was one of the biggest events we have sponsored," said the Wilmington Youth prexy. "In addition to featuring a championship match, a trudge match was on the program."

"Our advance ticket sale was great, but the door sales were halted when we learned of the situation. Some 500-700 fans were turned away at the last show."

Helps baseball programs

The wrestling shows have been put on here by the baseball group to help finance the Babe Ruth Baseball program operated at Allsbrook Field on the Shipyard Blvd. each summer.

However, if plans announced by Godwin materialize, others will benefit by the grapplers appearing inside during the winter months.

"If a floor covering we have bought and ordered, arrives in time, the next wrestling show will be held in Brogden Hall at 13th and Market Streets," Godwin explains in revealing plans to move the monthly cards indoors until next spring.

"We hope everything can be worked out to stage the wrestling in Brogden Hall and if this is true, the matmen will return here November 1. Our plans are to donate one-half of the profit from the indoor shows to the athletic fund."

MID-ATLANTIC WRESTLING 1975 YEARBOOK

46

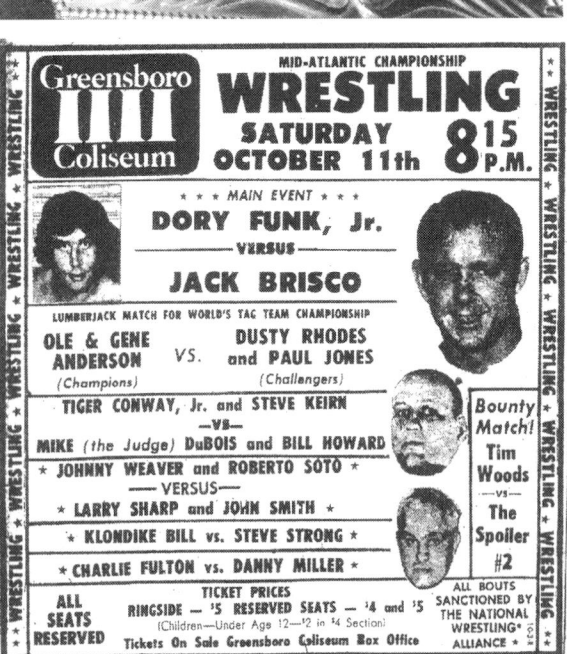

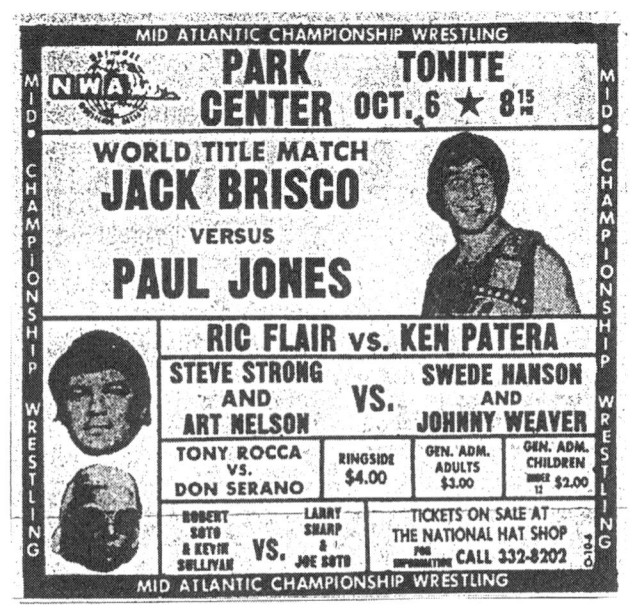

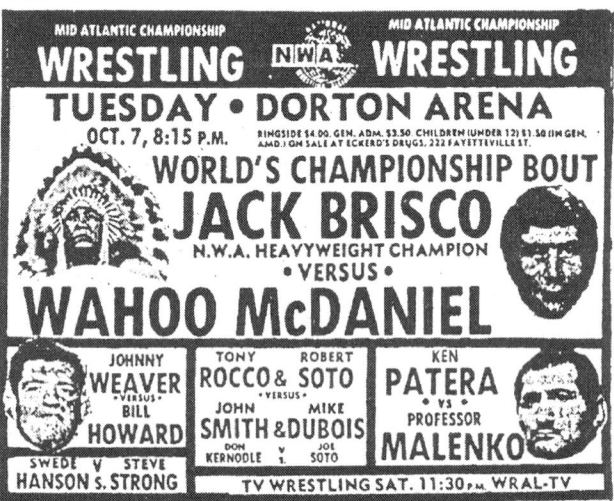

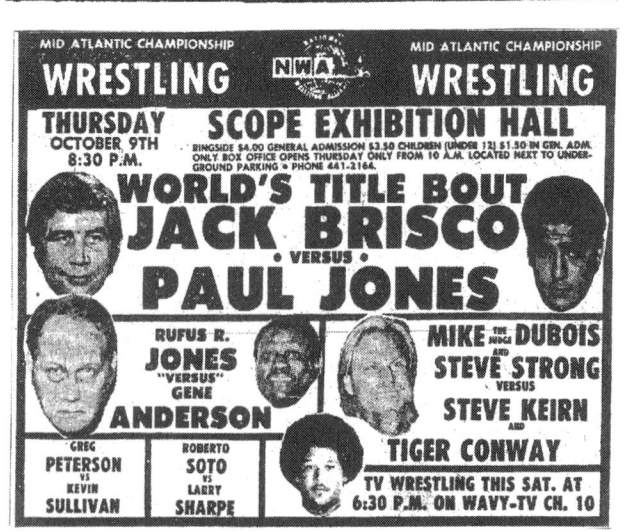

MID-ATLANTIC WRESTLING 1975 YEARBOOK

MID-ATLANTIC CHAMPIONSHIP WRESTLING
TUES. NOV. 4
COLUMBIA TOWNSHIP AUDITORIUM — 8:15 PM

★ WORLD'S TITLE MATCH ★

OLE ANDERSON
GENE ANDERSON
-vs-
RUFUS R. JONES
PAUL JONES

STEVE STRONG
-vs-
SWEDE HANSON

2 OTHER MATCHES

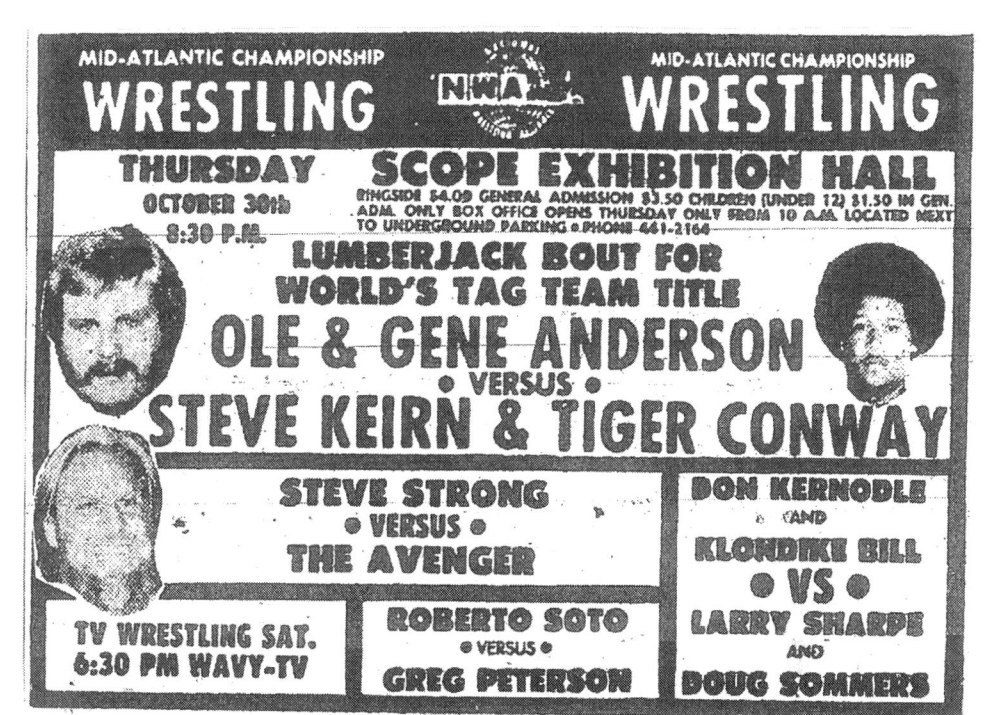

MID-ATLANTIC CHAMPIONSHIP WRESTLING — NWA

THURSDAY OCTOBER 30th 8:30 P.M.
SCOPE EXHIBITION HALL
RINGSIDE $4.00 GENERAL ADMISSION $3.50 CHILDREN (UNDER 12) $1.50 IN GEN. ADM. ONLY BOX OFFICE OPENS THURSDAY ONLY FROM 10 A.M. LOCATED NEXT TO UNDERGROUND PARKING • PHONE 441-2164

LUMBERJACK BOUT FOR WORLD'S TAG TEAM TITLE
OLE & GENE ANDERSON
• versus •
STEVE KEIRN & TIGER CONWAY

STEVE STRONG • versus • **THE AVENGER**

DON KERNODLE AND KLONDIKE BILL • VS • **LARRY SHARPE AND DOUG SOMMERS**

ROBERTO SOTO • versus • **GREG PETERSON**

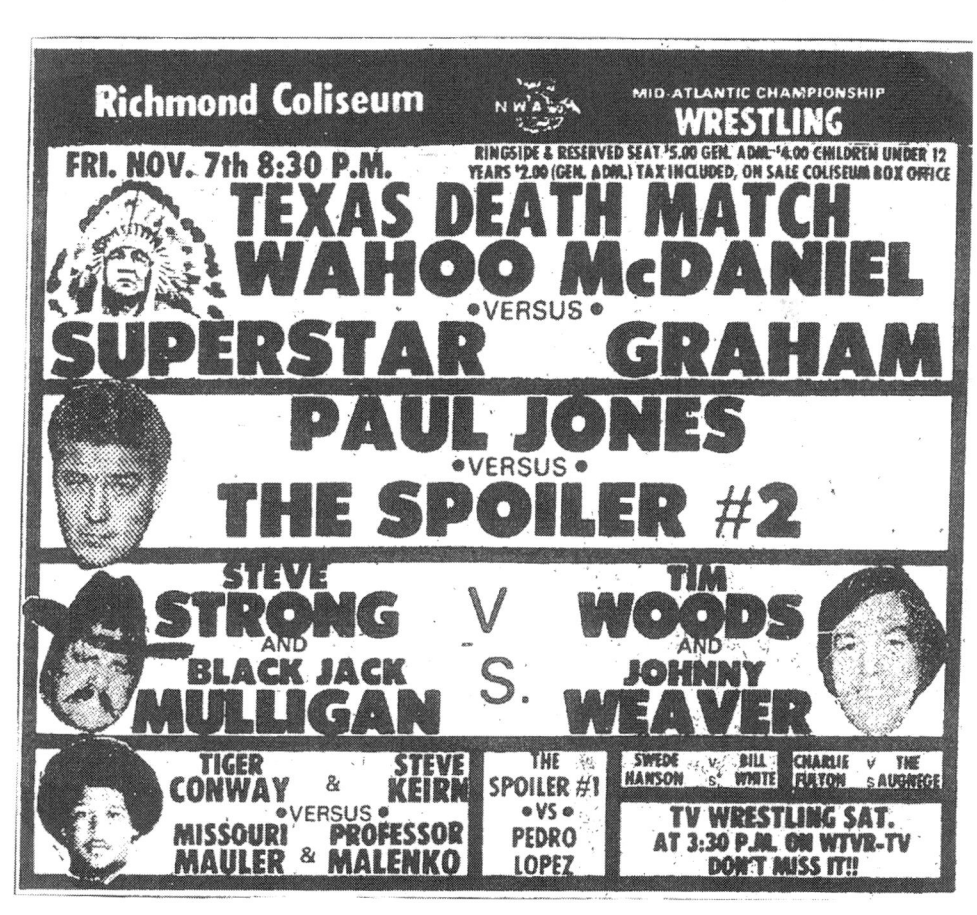

TV WRESTLING SAT. 6:30 PM WAVY-TV

Richmond Coliseum — NWA — MID-ATLANTIC CHAMPIONSHIP WRESTLING

FRI. NOV. 7th 8:30 P.M.
RINGSIDE & RESERVED SEAT $5.00 GEN. ADM. $4.00 CHILDREN UNDER 12 YEARS $2.00 (GEN. ADM.) TAX INCLUDED, ON SALE COLISEUM BOX OFFICE

TEXAS DEATH MATCH
WAHOO McDANIEL
• versus •
SUPERSTAR GRAHAM

PAUL JONES • versus • **THE SPOILER #2**

STEVE STRONG AND BLACK JACK MULLIGAN V.S. **TIM WOODS AND JOHNNY WEAVER**

TIGER CONWAY & STEVE KEIRN -vs- **MISSOURI MAULER & PROFESSOR MALENKO**

THE SPOILER #1 • vs • **PEDRO LOPEZ**

SWEDE HANSON v. BILL WHITE — CHARLIE FULTON v. THE SAVAGE

TV WRESTLING SAT. AT 3:30 P.M. ON WTVR-TV DON'T MISS IT!!

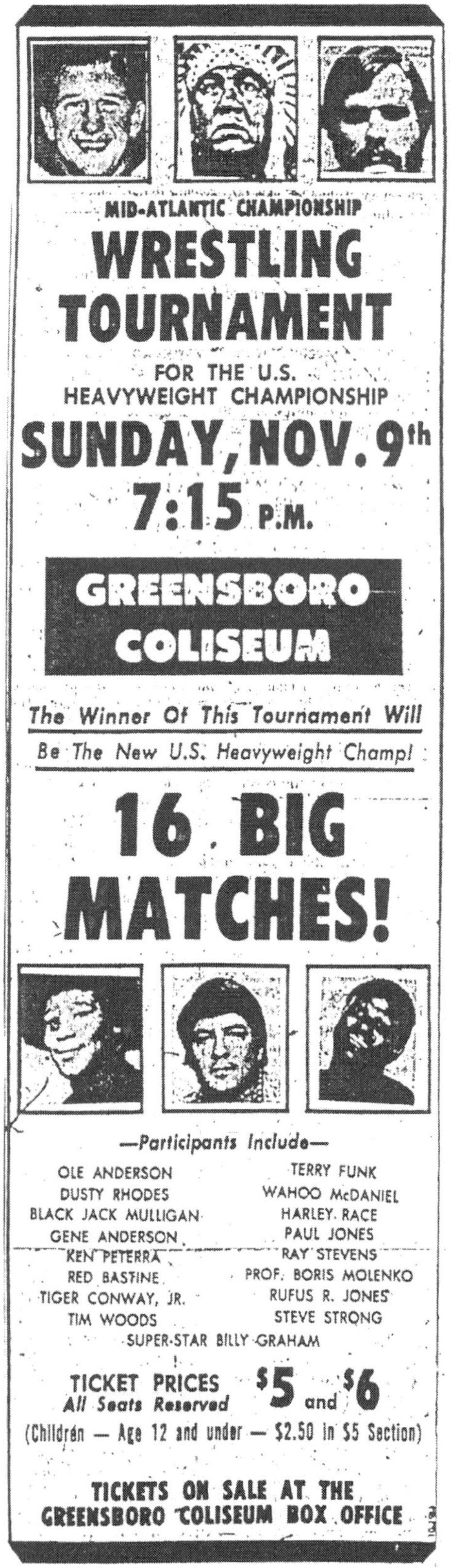

MID-ATLANTIC WRESTLING 1975 YEARBOOK

MID-ATLANTIC CHAMPIONSHIP WRESTLING TOURNAMENT

FOR THE U.S. HEAVYWEIGHT CHAMPIONSHIP

SUNDAY, NOV. 9th 7:15 P.M.

GREENSBORO COLISEUM

The Winner Of This Tournament Will Be The New U.S. Heavyweight Champ!

16 BIG MATCHES!

—Participants Include—

- OLE ANDERSON
- DUSTY RHODES
- BLACK JACK MULLIGAN
- GENE ANDERSON
- KEN PETERRA
- RED BASTINE
- TIGER CONWAY, JR.
- TIM WOODS
- SUPER-STAR BILLY GRAHAM
- TERRY FUNK
- WAHOO McDANIEL
- HARLEY RACE
- PAUL JONES
- RAY STEVENS
- PROF. BORIS MOLENKO
- RUFUS R. JONES
- STEVE STRONG

TICKET PRICES All Seats Reserved **$5 and $6**

(Children — Age 12 and under — $2.50 in $5 Section)

TICKETS ON SALE AT THE GREENSBORO COLISEUM BOX OFFICE

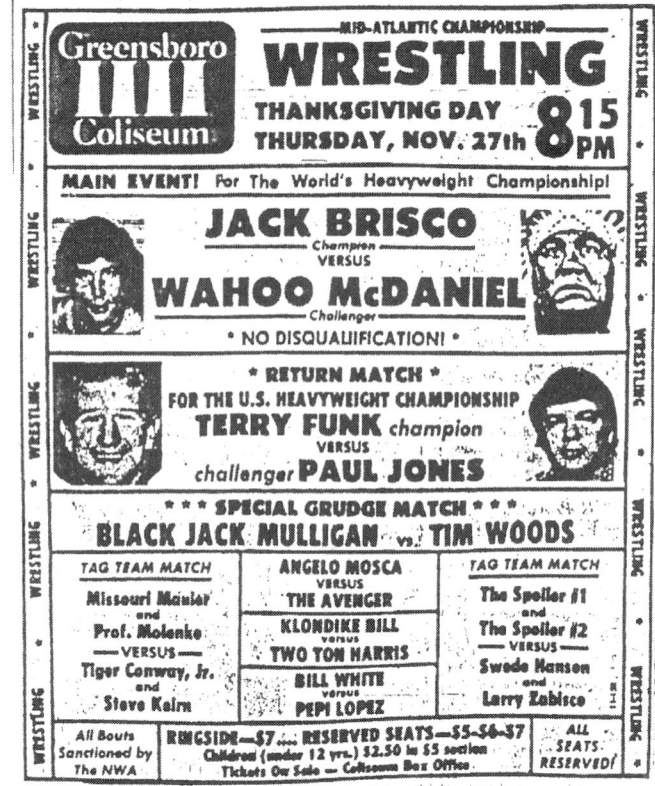

Greensboro Coliseum — MID-ATLANTIC CHAMPIONSHIP WRESTLING

THANKSGIVING DAY THURSDAY, NOV. 27th 8:15 PM

MAIN EVENT! For The World's Heavyweight Championship!

JACK BRISCO Champion **VERSUS** **WAHOO McDANIEL** Challenger

• NO DISQUALIFICATION! •

* RETURN MATCH *
FOR THE U.S. HEAVYWEIGHT CHAMPIONSHIP
TERRY FUNK champion VERSUS challenger **PAUL JONES**

* * * SPECIAL GRUDGE MATCH * * *
BLACK JACK MULLIGAN vs. TIM WOODS

TAG TEAM MATCH	ANGELO MOSCA versus THE AVENGER	TAG TEAM MATCH
Missouri Mauler and Prof. Molenko VERSUS Tiger Conway, Jr. and Steve Keirn	KLONDIKE BILL versus TWO TON HARRIS	The Spoiler #1 and The Spoiler #2 VERSUS Swede Hanson and Larry Zabisco
	BILL WHITE versus PEPI LOPEZ	

All Bouts Sanctioned by The NWA — RINGSIDE—$7 ... RESERVED SEATS—$5-$6-$7 — Children (under 12 yrs.) $2.50 in $5 section — Tickets On Sale — Coliseum Box Office — ALL SEATS RESERVED!

Paul Jones defeated Terry Funk for the U.S. title on this Greensboro card.

< See the special feature on the U.S. tournament elsewhere in this book.

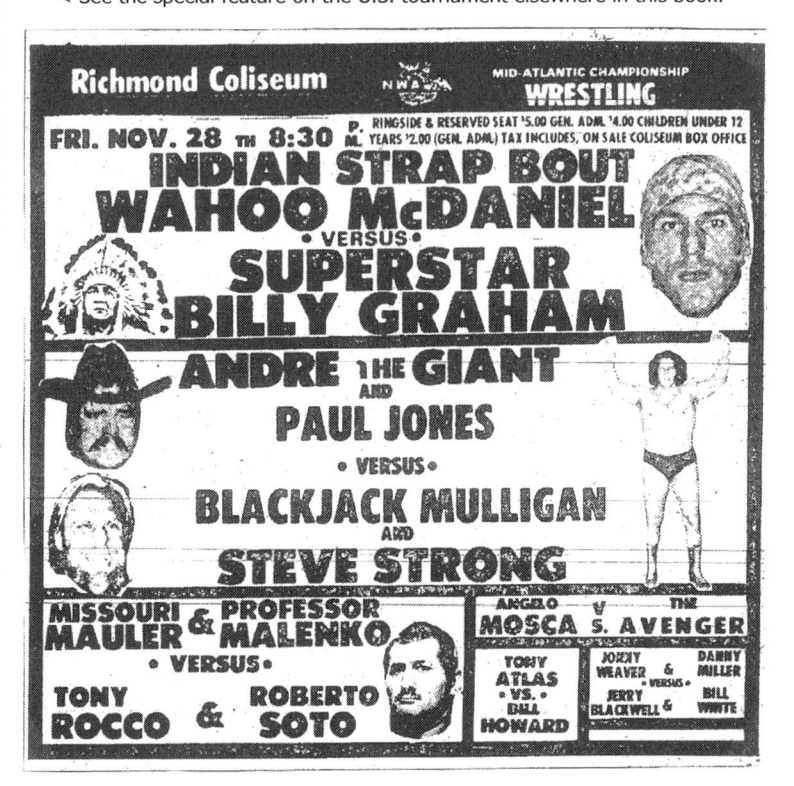

Richmond Coliseum — MID-ATLANTIC CHAMPIONSHIP WRESTLING

RINGSIDE & RESERVED SEAT $5.00 GEN. ADM. $4.00 CHILDREN UNDER 12 YEARS $2.00 (GEN. ADM.) TAX INCLUDES, ON SALE COLISEUM BOX OFFICE

FRI. NOV. 28 TH 8:30 P.M.

INDIAN STRAP BOUT
WAHOO McDANIEL • versus • **SUPERSTAR BILLY GRAHAM**

ANDRE THE GIANT AND PAUL JONES • versus • **BLACKJACK MULLIGAN AND STEVE STRONG**

MISSOURI MAULER & PROFESSOR MALENKO • VERSUS • **TONY ROCCO & ROBERTO SOTO**

ANGELO MOSCA vs. THE AVENGER

TONY ATLAS vs. BILL HOWARD

JOHNNY WEAVER & JERRY BLACKWELL vs. DANNY MILLER & BILL WHITE

Jack Brisco To Make Debut In Charleston

Two world championship title will be at stake this Friday night at County Hall.

Jack Brisco, the world's heavyweight champion, will make his first Charleston appearance defending his crown against Rufus R. Jones.

This will be big Rufus' biggest match of his career, and the first time the South Carolina native has wrestled for the world's title.

The other title up will be the world's tag team title. Gene and Ole Anderson defend their title against Tiger Conway Jr., and Steve Keirn.

The No. 3 prelim will have Swede Hansen meeting Joe Turner. The No. 2 prelim will have Peppe Lopez meeting Larry Sharpe.

Opening the show at 8:15 p.m. will be Don Kernodle meeting Charlie Fulton.

Advance tickets are on sale at Miller's Drug Store, Reynolds Ave. and Central Drug Store, Meeting St. near George St.

Briscoe Leaves Ring, But Maintains Title

Rufus Jones won his battle against Texan Jack Briscoe Friday night at County Hall, but failed to win the war.

Jones heaved his opponent over the top rope in a fast-paced climax to their world heavyweight championship match, effectively finishing Briscoe but disqualifying Jones from the title belt. A champion must be pinned or placed in a submission hold in order to relinquish his crown.

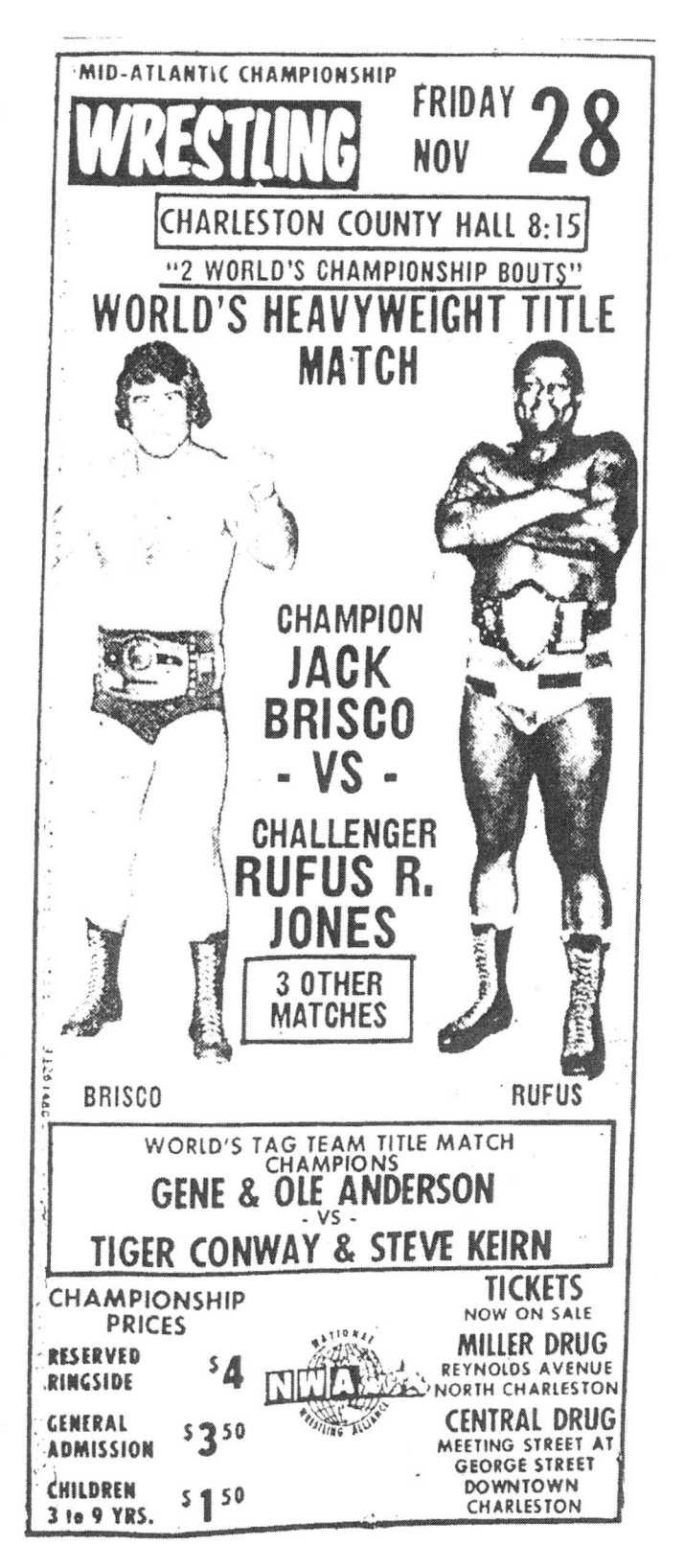

MID-ATLANTIC CHAMPIONSHIP WRESTLING

FRIDAY NOV 28

CHARLESTON COUNTY HALL 8:15

"2 WORLD'S CHAMPIONSHIP BOUTS"

WORLD'S HEAVYWEIGHT TITLE MATCH

CHAMPION **JACK BRISCO** - VS -
CHALLENGER **RUFUS R. JONES**

3 OTHER MATCHES

BRISCO — RUFUS

WORLD'S TAG TEAM TITLE MATCH
CHAMPIONS **GENE & OLE ANDERSON** - VS - **TIGER CONWAY & STEVE KEIRN**

CHAMPIONSHIP PRICES		TICKETS NOW ON SALE
RESERVED RINGSIDE	$4	MILLER DRUG REYNOLDS AVENUE NORTH CHARLESTON
GENERAL ADMISSION	$3.50	CENTRAL DRUG MEETING STREET AT GEORGE STREET DOWNTOWN CHARLESTON
CHILDREN 3 to 9 YRS.	$1.50	

NWA

MID-ATLANTIC WRESTLING 1975 YEARBOOK

WRESTLING TONIGHT 8:15
COLUMBIA TOWNSHIP AUDITORIUM

RUSSIAN CHAIN MATCH

THE 2 MEN WILL BE CHAINED TOGETHER WITH A 10 FOOT CHAIN WRIST TO WRIST

PROFESSOR BORIS MALINKO
-VS-
WAHOO McDANIEL

STEVE KEIRN & TIGER CONWAY
-VS-
MASKED SPOILERS 1 & 2

-3 OTHER MATCHES-

RINGSIDE $3.50
GENERAL ADMISSION $3.00
CHILD 3 YRS TO 9 $1.50

TICKETS NOW ON SALE TAYLOR ST PHARMACY

12/9/75 Columbia, SC

MID ATLANTIC CHAMPIONSHIP WRESTLING
NWA
TUESDAY • DORTON ARENA
DEC. 9, 8:15 P.M.

RINGSIDE $4.00 GEN. ADM. $3.50 CHILDREN (UNDER 12) $1.50
ADM. ON SALE AT ECKERD'S DRUGS, 222 FAYETTEVILLE ST.

FOR UNITED STATES TITLE
PAUL JONES
• VERSUS •
BLACKJACK MULLIGAN

STEVE STRONG AND MIKE "The Judge" DUBOIS
VS.
DANNY MILLER AND JOHNNY WEAVER

ANGELO MOSCA
• VERSUS •
SWEDE HANSON

JERRY BLACKWELL VS. TONY ATLAS

PEPE LOPEZ VERSUS CHARLIE FULTON

TV WRESTLING SAT. AT 11:30 P.M. ON WRAL-TV

12/9/75 Raleigh, NC

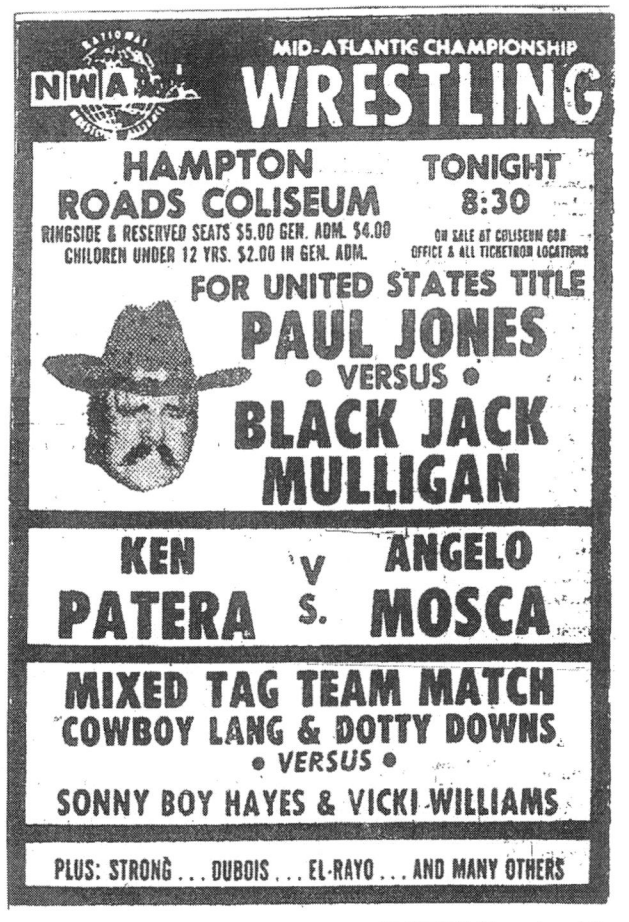

Wrestling Not Tonight

There is no professional wrestling scheduled for Greenville Memorial Auditorium Monday night. The next matches are set for Christmas night.

12/15/75 Greenville, SC

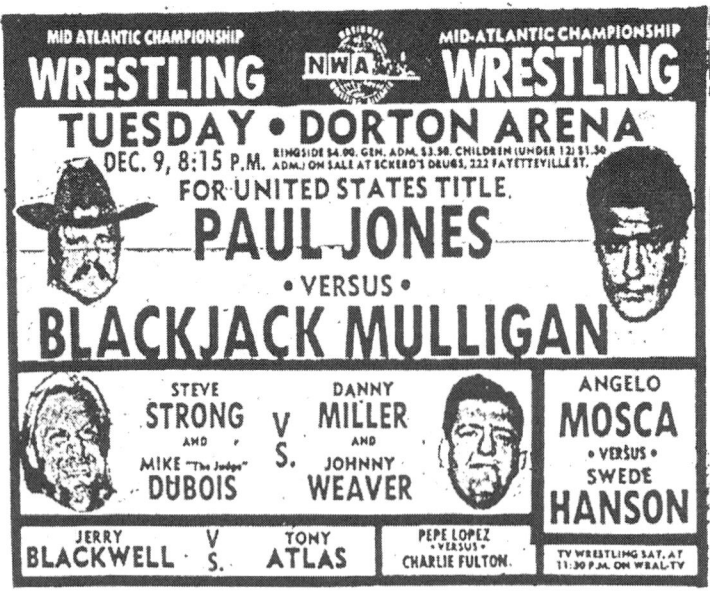

NWA MID-ATLANTIC CHAMPIONSHIP WRESTLING
HAMPTON ROADS COLISEUM
TONIGHT 8:30

RINGSIDE & RESERVED SEATS $5.00 GEN. ADM. $4.00
CHILDREN UNDER 12 YRS. $2.00 IN GEN. ADM.
ON SALE AT COLISEUM BOX OFFICE & ALL TICKETRON LOCATIONS

FOR UNITED STATES TITLE
PAUL JONES
• VERSUS •
BLACK JACK MULLIGAN

KEN PATERA VS. ANGELO MOSCA

MIXED TAG TEAM MATCH
COWBOY LANG & DOTTY DOWNS
• VERSUS •
SONNY BOY HAYES & VICKI WILLIAMS

PLUS: STRONG ... DUBOIS ... EL-RAYO ... AND MANY OTHERS

12/27/75 Hampton VA

MID-ATLANTIC WRESTLING

MID-ATLANTIC CHAMPIONSHIP WRESTLING
RICHMOND ARENA

RING SIDE $4.00 GEN. ADM. $3.50 CHILDREN (UNDER 12) $1.50 (IN GEN. ADM.)
ON SALE AT SPECIALTY SHOP 718 E. BROAD ST. ARENA BOX OFFICE OPENS AT 11:00 ON FRIDAY...PHONE 358-1642

FRIDAY December 12th, 8:30 p.m.

FOR UNITED STATES TITLE
PAUL JONES versus BLACKJACK MULLIGAN

SPOILERS #1 and #2 vs TIM WOODS and JOHNNY WEAVER

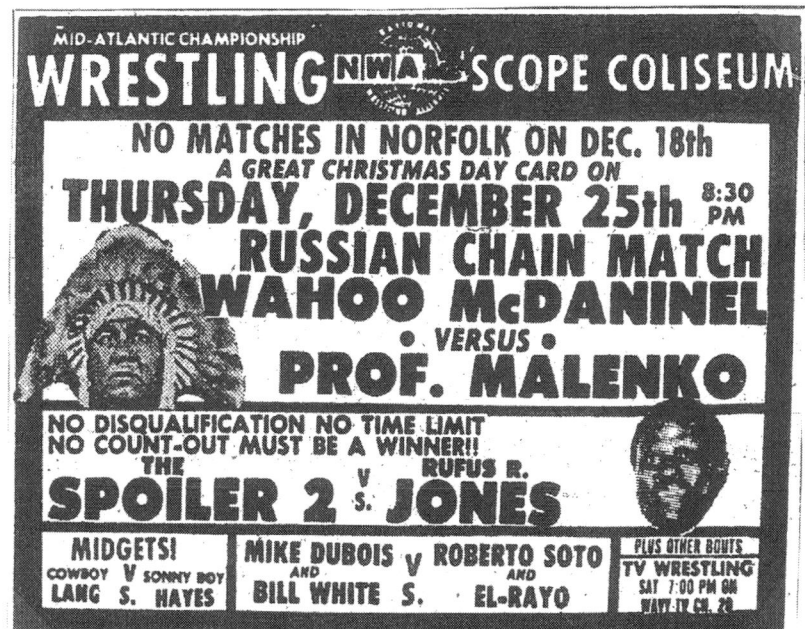

TONY ATLAS versus BILL WHITE

BILL HOWARD vs ROBERTO SOTO

PEPE LOPEZ vs 2-TON HARRIS

TV WRESTLING SAT. 2:00 P.M. WTVR-TV

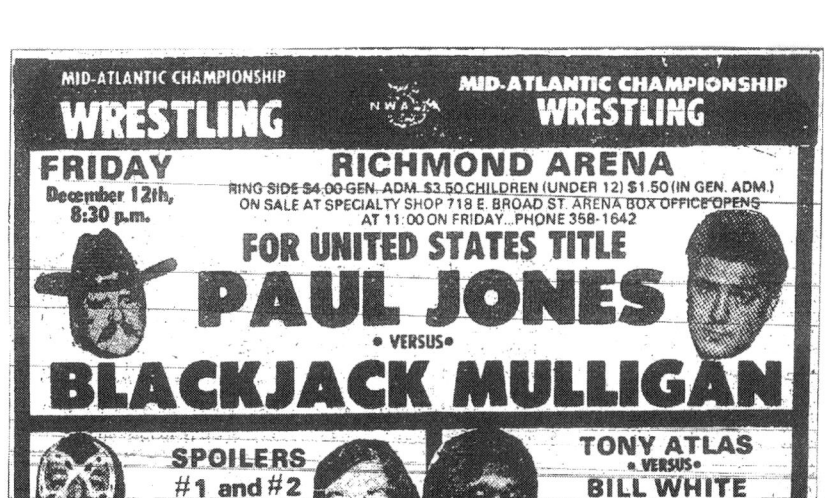

MID-ATLANTIC CHAMPIONSHIP WRESTLING — SCOPE COLISEUM

NO MATCHES IN NORFOLK ON DEC. 18th
A GREAT CHRISTMAS DAY CARD ON
THURSDAY, DECEMBER 25th 8:30 PM

RUSSIAN CHAIN MATCH
WAHOO McDANIEL versus PROF. MALENKO

NO DISQUALIFICATION NO TIME LIMIT NO COUNT-OUT MUST BE A WINNER!!

THE SPOILER 2 vs. RUFUS R. JONES

MIDGETS! COWBOY LANG V SONNY BOY HAYES

MIKE DUBOIS AND BILL WHITE V ROBERTO SOTO AND EL-RAYO

PLUS OTHER BOUTS
TV WRESTLING SAT 7:00 PM ON WAVY-TV CH. 20

WRESTLING
GREENVILLE MEMORIAL AUDITORIUM

SPECIAL CHRISTMAS NIGHT WRESTLING CARD
6 BIG MATCHES

MAIN EVENT—U.S. HEAVYWEIGHT CHAMPIONSHIP
Paul Jones vs. Black Jack Mulligan

TAG TEAM MATCH
Steve Strong and the Missouri Mauler
Vs.
Danny Miller and Sweede Hanson

GIRLS' MATCH
Sheila Shepherd Vs. Donna Christinello

OTHER MATCHES
Angelo Mosca Vs. Ken Paterna
Also: Bill Howard Vs. Tony Atlas
Charlie Fulton Vs. Don Serrano

CHRISTMAS NIGHT 8:00 p.m.

Mid-Atlantic Championship Wrestling Magazine

Volume One Issue One

MID-ATLANTIC CHAMPIONSHIP WRESTLING
magazine

JIM CROCKETT PROMOTIONS, INC.
CHARLOTTE, N. C.

THE HISTORY OF THE WORLD HEAVYWEIGHT TITLE

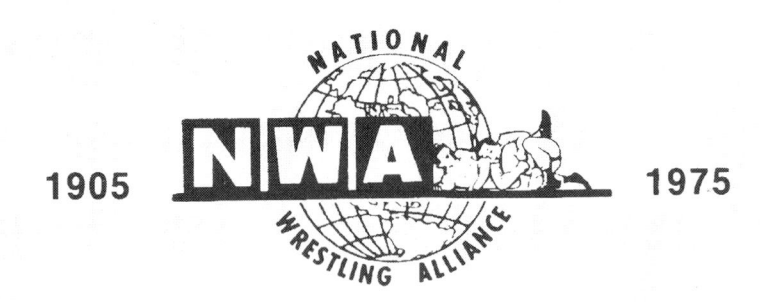

1905 NWA **1975**

1905—Frank Gotch defeated George Hackenschmidt

1906—Fred Beel defeated Gotch.

1906—Gotch defeated Beel.

1913—Gotch retired as world heavyweight champion.

1914—Charley Cutler defeated Henry Ordeman and Jesse Westegard in a tournament to fill the vacant title.

1915—Joe Stecher defeated Cutler.

1917—Earl Caddock defeated Stecher.

1920—Stecher defeated Caddock.

1921—Ed (Strangler) Lewis defeated Stecher.

1922—Stanislaus Zbyszko beat Lewis.

1922—Lewis defeated Zbyszko.

1925—Wayne Munn defeated Lewis.

1925—Zbyszko defeated Munn.

1925—Stecher defeated Zbyszko in a match at the old Federal League field in St. Louis, Missouri.

1928 (Feb. 20)—Lewis defeated Stecher at the Coliseum in St. Louis, Missouri.

1929—Gus Sonnenberg defeated Lewis in Boston, Massachusetts.

1931—Ed Don George defeated Sonnenberg in Boston, Massachusetts.

1931—Lewis defeated George in Los Angeles, California.

1931—Henry DeGlane defeated Lewis in Montreal, Canada.

1931—George defeated DeGlane in Boston, Massachusetts.

In the meantime, however, Dick Shikat had defeated Jim Londos in Pennsylvania in a 1929 bout and had claimed the title.

1930 (June 6)—Londos defeated Shikat in Philadelphia, Pennsylvania.

Then, in 1932, Lewis pinned Shikat in a match billed as the "world championship" in New York, New York.

1933—Jim Browning defeated Lewis in New York, New York.

1934—Londos defeated Browning in New York, New York.

1935 (June 27)—Danno O'Mahoney defeated Londos in Boston, Massachusetts.

1935 (June 30)—O'Mahoney defeated George in Boston, Massachusetts. The latter had been claiming the title since his 1931 defeat of DeGlane. By his victories, O'Mahoney became the undisputed champ.

1936—Shikat defeated O'Mahoney in New York, New York.

1936—Ali Baba defeated Shikat in Detroit, Michigan.

1936—Ali Baba was disqualified in a New Jersey bout against Dave Levin. The state athletic commission reversed the decision and allowed Ali Baba to keep title.

1936 (June 26)—Everett Marshall defeated Ali Baba in Columbus, Ohio.

1937 (Dec. 29)—Lou Thesz defeated Marshall in St. Louis, Missouri.

1938 (Feb. 11)—Steve (Crusher) Casey defeated Thesz in Boston, Massachusetts.

1938 (September)—The National Wrestling Association, at its convention in Montreal, recognized Marshall as champion for two reasons: Casey, the erstwhile champ, was out of the country, and Marshall had been disqualified in his bout with Casey because Casey had been thrown out of the ring. The decision was reversed as "the action was not deliberate."

1939 (Feb. 23)—Thesz defeated Marshall in St. Louis, Missouri.

1939 (June 23)—Bronko Nagurski defeated Thesz in Houston, Texas.

1940 (March 7)—Ray Steele defeated Nagurski in St. Louis, Missouri.

1941 (March 11)—Nagurski defeated Steele in Minneapolis, Minnesota.

1941 (June 5)—Sandor Szabo defeated Nagurski in St. Louis, Missouri.

1942 (Feb. 19)—Bill Longson defeated Szabo in St. Louis, Missouri.

1942 (Oct. 7)—Yvon Robert defeated Longson in Montreal, Canada.

1942 (Nov. 27)—Bobby Managoff defeated Robert in Houston, Texas.

1943 (Feb. 19)—Longson defeated Managoff in St. Louis, Missouri.

1947 (Feb. 21)—Whipper Billy Watson defeated Longson in St. Louis, Missouri.

1947 (Apr. 25)—Thesz defeated Watson in St. Louis, Missouri.

1947 (Nov. 21)—Longson defeated Thesz in St. Louis, Missouri.

1948 (July 20)—Thesz defeated Longson in Indianapolis, Indiana.

1949—The National Wrestling Alliance recognized Thesz as its world champion. Orville Brown, who had been recognized by the NWA since its organization in July, 1948, relinquished his claim because he was forced to retire from the ring due to injuries received in an automobile accident. He had been matched with Thesz in a title bout.

1956 (March 15)—Watson defeated Thesz in Toronto, Canada.

1956 (Nov. 9)—Thesz defeated Watson in St. Louis, Missouri.

1957 (Nov. 14)—Dick Hutton defeated Thesz in Toronto, Canada.

1959 (Jan. 9)—Pat O'Connor defeated Hutton in St. Louis, Missouri.

1961 (June 30)—Buddy Rogers defeated O'Connor in Chicago, Illinois.

1963 (Jan. 24)—Thesz defeated Rogers in Toronto, Canada.

1966 (Jan. 7)—Gene Kiniski defeated Thesz in St. Louis, Missouri.

1969 (Feb. 11)—Dory Funk, Jr., defeated Kiniski in Tampa, Florida.

1973 (May 24)—Harley Race defeated Funk, Jr., in Kansas City, Kansas.

1973 (July 20)—Jack Brisco defeated Race in Houston, Texas.

Jones Picked Wrestler Of The Year By Fans

As the joke goes, 1974 was a year of good news and bad news for Paul Jones. The good news was many-fold. At the very top of the list was the honor of being voted "Wrestler of the Year" by the fans in the Mid-Atlantic area. Paul was very pleased with the award, and it was indeed a good pick by the fans. They have seen Jones mature as a pro since his first appearance in this area in 1968. Paul has climbed the ladder and is now at the top of professional wrestling. His two most recent honors include being named Mid-Atlantic T.V. Champion and sharing the Mid-Atlantic tag-team title with Tiger Conway, Jr.

Paul is planning to do away with the bad news in the year 1975. He has been hassled by a couple of the sports roughousers and would like to square accounts with Johnny Valentine and The Super Destroyer. During 1975 Paul's major goal is winning the World Heavyweight Championship. Jones is rated by experts as the man most likely to unseat current title holder Jack Brisco. These two have met before, and their battles have become mat classics. Paul says, "I spend all of my spare time watching Brisco on film, and I feel that I'm drawing closer to wearing that N.W.A. Championship belt. Valentine and Destroyer are stepping stones to another shot at Brisco. I'll be putting up an all-out effort to get these men out of the way and looking forward to climbing in the ring with Brisco once again." Things look good for the Texan who is at the peak of his career. He has power, speed, and wrestling savvy to match that of the champion. The fans' pick as Wrestler of the Year in 1974 could very well end up as Champion of the Year in 1975!

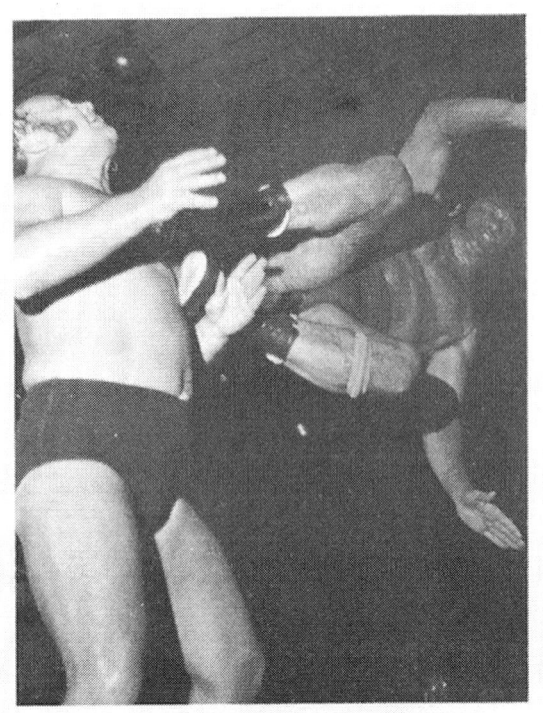

MID-ATLANTIC WRESTLING 1975 YEARBOOK

Jacobs hits Gene Anderson high, with a powerful dropkick

Referee tries to stop Valentine's attack on Jones

Super Star Billy Graham

Super Destroyer makes his move for his claw hold on Swede Hanson

The Pro Mat's Biggest Feud— Wahoo-Valentine

Everyone has heard of the historical battles between the Hatfields and the McCoys, the North and South, and Jesse James and the Railroad. Well, a feud to match those in scope is one that has raged for the last three years, and has been fought from coast to coast. It is between two giants of the wrestling world: Wahoo McDaniel and Johnny Valentine!

Wahoo McDaniel came to the squared circle of wrestling from the fields of professional football. If you look back over his life, you will see that this Indian gentleman is used to winning. His college days in Oklahoma were divided between wrestling and playing football on a team that won the Orange Bowl. He moved onto the pro gridiron and finished up his career with the Miami Dolphins as a linebacker. During that time he was wrestling in the off-season. Wahoo is a proud man, and gives 110 percent in everything he does; but above all, he is a sportsman. The first time he locked up with Johnny Valentine, the big blond tried to injure him, and the long battle was off and running. McDaniel would rather wrestle or fight Valentine than anything he can think of. His major goal is to rid wrestling of "Big John." "I'll sign a contract to meet him at anytime," states Wahoo. "He has repeatedly tried to ruin my wrestling career. He is the one man I would like to put out of business for good." Wahoo also ranks high on the list of men able to annex Jack Brisco's World Title in the near future.

Johnny Valentine is one of the meanest men in the mat sport. His plan is a simple one: to strike fear in the hearts of his opponents. He feels the best way to do that is to make them feel pain. The list of men he has put out of action is long, and it figures that in time it will all catch up with him. "I'll have to say that the Indian is tough, but maybe just a little dumb. Otherwise he wouldn't keep coming back for more punishment. But I'll give him what he's looking for." Just how long this feud will last is anyone's guess. It could end with both men in the hospital, and looking for another line of work. But one thing is for sure, anytime that Wahoo and Johnny step into a wrestling ring it will mean action for those watching."

MID-ATLANTIC WRESTLING 1975 YEARBOOK

Two rough grapplers go at it!
Johnny Valentine and Art Nelson

Ric Flair pitches Tiger Conway, Jr.
away in a high body-slam

The Super Destroyer drives Jerry Brisco
toward a turnbuckle

Former Pittsburgh Steeler Charlie Cook.
Keep an eye on him!

Super Destroyer Is Super Mad At Paul Jones

The Super Destroyer entered the Mid-Atlantic wrestling scene a little over a year ago, and since that time has a long list of victories to his credit. He will unmask if pinned or made to give up in a singles match. He is still wearing his beloved mask, and that speaks for itself. He is a talkative gentleman, and will be the first to tell you just how good he is, and whom he doesn't like. But it seems that he is yelling louder now than ever before. The subject of all his talk is Paul Jones, and the fact that Jones has dared to call him "Super Chicken"!

"I am a man or honor, and don't lower myself by calling other men names," says the Destroyer. "You have seen my crown and know that I am the King of wrestling. Kings should be spoken highly of and not lowered to name calling as in the case of Paul Jones. I back down from no man, and yet Jones has the nerve to call me chicken! If the promoters and the N.W.A. are going to allow this on television, then I must go forth and silence this fool myself. I am undefeated! Can Paul Jones say the same? No! All he can do is stand at a safe distance and call names like a little boy. When I have the chance, I would like to meet him one on one, man to man. Right now I am busy with other business interests as most successful men are. One thing that keeps me busy is handling the affairs of Brute Bernard whose contract I purchased."

The Super Destroyer's last statement brings up an interesting point. Will he settle this thing with Jones himself, or will he send Brute Bernard to do his work for him. Only time will tell. One things if for sure: Paul Jones is not a man to say something he can't back up. He wants the Super "D," and maybe the name calling will bring on the match much sooner. The meeting of these two will also prove whether the masked man is truly the Super Destroyer, or in fact "Super Chicken"!

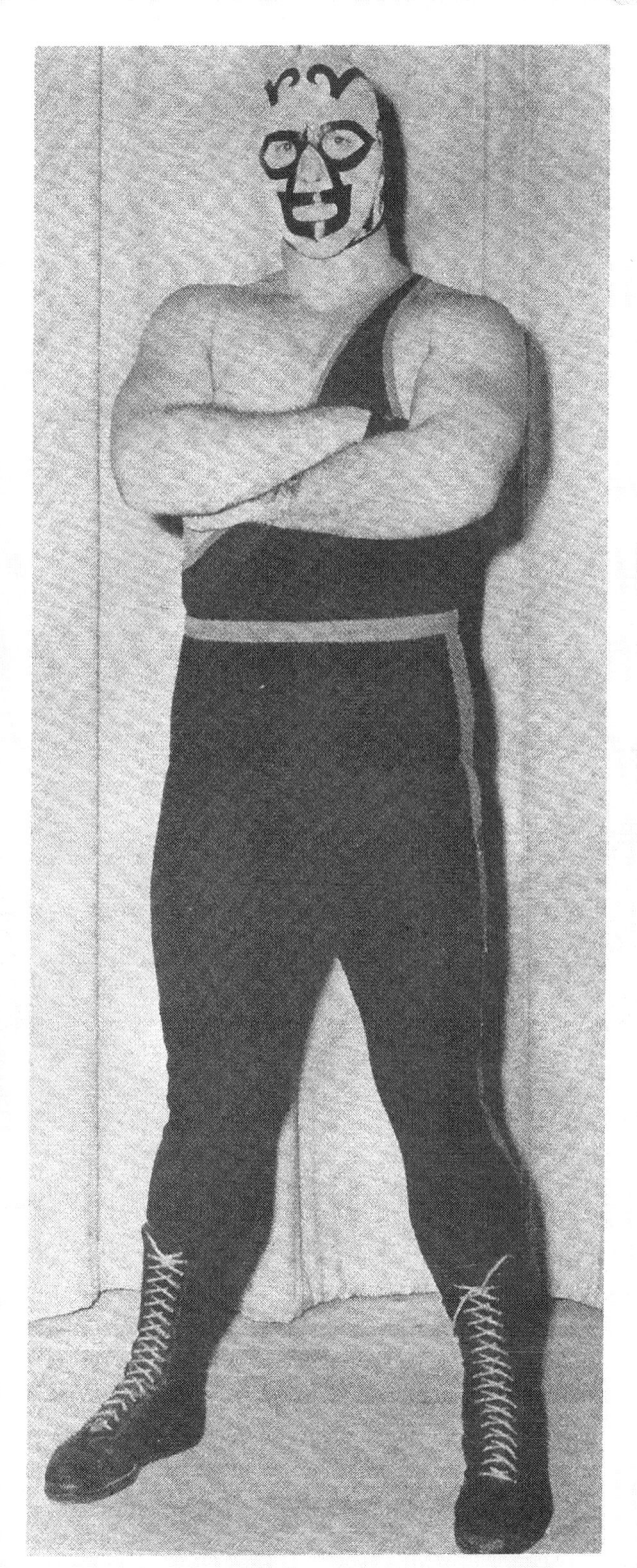

MID-ATLANTIC WRESTLING 1975 YEARBOOK

The American Dream Dusty Rhodes

Sonny King spins the head of Johnny Valentine with a right.

"The Super D" clamps a headlock on Wahoo McDaniel.

Wahoo is ready to take on the referee or anyone else!

Anderson Brothers
World Tag Team Champions

Ole and Gene Anderson now sit at the top of tag team wrestling. In a tournament held in California the Andersons aced out a long list of great tag combinations to wear the world belts. Entered in this event were the teams of Ray Stevens & Nick Bockwinkle, Eddie & Mike Graham, the Vachon Brothers, Terry & Bobby Kay, and the Funk Brothers, to name just a few. Ole and Gene came through the meet without a loss, and were awarded the title. They have just returned to the Mid-Atlantic area after an eight-month tour and winning the world title.

Ole, the speaker for the combo, had this to say: "Could there be any doubt in anyone's mind that we would end up world champions? After all we are the greatest tag team in the history of wrestling. My brother and I know that the fans in this area are happy to have us back, and now that we are wearing the World Title Belts, they will be even happier. Now it is up to the promoters to come up with some good wrestlers to meet us for the title. There are some "so so" wrestlers here now, but we are looking for top men. Class should only meet class. The chances are that we will retire with the title. It doesn't seem possible that any team could beat us."

The outspoken Andersons are without a doubt a great wrestling team, but no one is unbeatable. With men like Sonny King, Paul Jones, Wahoo McDaniel, Tiger Conway, Jr., the Avenger, and Ken Patera in this area, things will be close, and tough for the newly crowned tag team champions. "The Wrecking Crew" has its work cut out for it, and there is a chance they may lose their highly prized belts right here in the Mid-Atlantic area.

Johnny Valentine shows emotion. You don't see it often in this man.

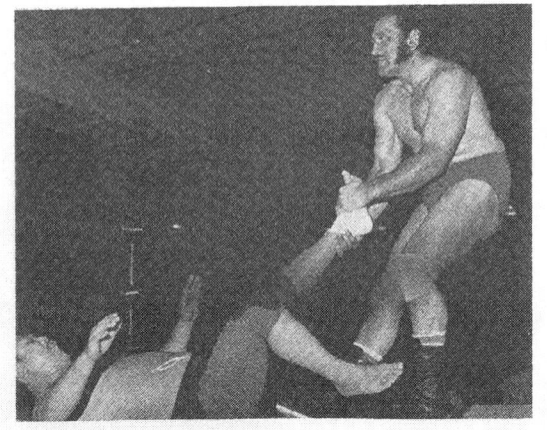

Abe Jacobs goes to work on the leg of Mr. Hyashi.

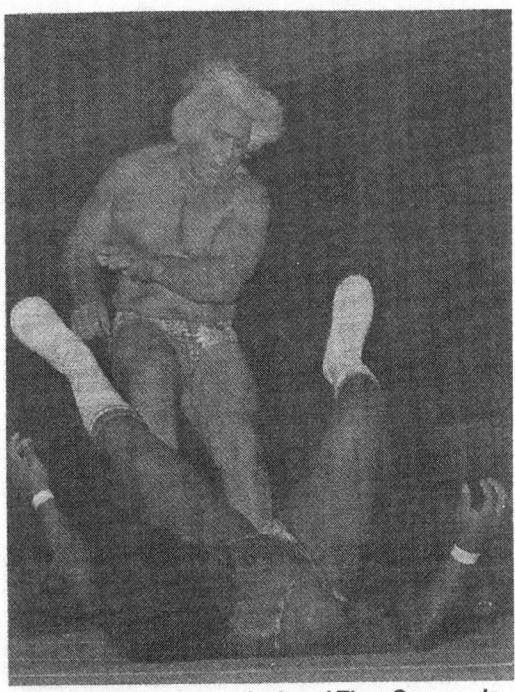

Ric Flair kicks away at the leg of Tiger Conway, Jr.

Ole Anderson and Paul Jones tangle.

Flair Has It All Together

Ric Flair has only been wrestling in the pro ranks for a little over two years. In that time he has taken giant steps toward the top. Ric is what the experts call a "natural." Even the people who don't like the way Flair goes about winning his matches will agree that he is good. But to really hear the story of Ric Flair, it has to be told by the man himself.

"Man, what can I tell you that doesn't show up each time I step into a wrestling ring?" was the way Flair opened up. "When you take a great mind, a great body, grace, skill, and good looks, you have a dude that is super bad. That dude is me! I am today, baby! Ric Flair is what's happenin'! Some of these old dudes will feel the power I project, and never want to wrestle me again. In my first year as a pro, I was picked as "Rookie of the Century," and it won't be long before I will be picked as "Wrestler of All Time." It's gotta happen, 'cause class shows. Can you dig that? I don't want to say that I'm a handsome guy, but what is my opinion against millions of women? They want a hero that can wrestle, and looks good, too. So it's no surprise that they pick me. I have it all together!"

Ric Flair thinks a lot of Ric Flair and doesn't try to keep it a secret. To be tops in any field you must believe in yourself, but maybe Flair overdoes it a little. The big man from the cold north country will hit the top very soon. His toughest tests will be right here in the Mid-Atlantic area. Men like Paul Jones, Wahoo McDaniel, Sonny King stand in his way. Ric may never become "Wrestler of All Time," but he is going to make it very rough on the grapplers that grace the top ranks of the sport. He is one young man who has the wrestling know-how to match his vocal cords.

MID-ATLANTIC WRESTLING 1975 YEARBOOK

Frank Morrell clamps on powerful headlock.

One of wrestling's top teams, Paul Jones and Wahoo McDaniel

Jack Brisco fights to get away from top challenger Wahoo McDaniel.

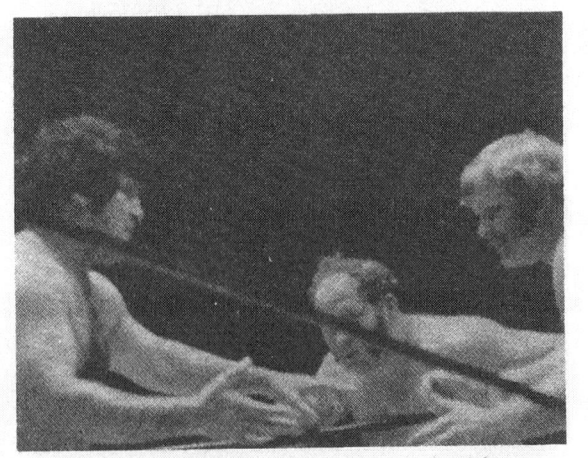

The Andersons try to corner opponent Paul Jones.

Ken Patera
America's Strongest Athlete

The strongest man in America has chosen professional wrestling as his new profession. Olympic weightlifter Ken Patera sent records toppling wherever he competed throughout his amateur career. It is certain that he will do the same during his career as a wrestler.

An all-around athlete in high school, Patera hurdled, high-jumped, wrestled, and was active in football, baseball and basketball. While in college at Brigham Young University, he broke dozens of records and became Western Athletic Conference champion in discus and shotput, and third in the world in the shotput. Later that year, he decided to concentrate his efforts on weightlifting. No one has ever dominated weighlifting as Ken Patera has during the four years he competed for the United States. In 1972 he won the Senior National Championships and the Olympic trials. He set six American records, which brought to 26 the number of American records Patera has set as a weightlifter. As a member of the U. S. Olympic team, he won a bronze medal in the press.

Ken has now entered the wrestling wars in the Mid-Atlantic area. He is showing just why he set all those weightlifting records. For such a big man, he has grace and speed to go along with his power. Many of wrestling's top names are based in this area, and it will be a tough test for this young man to face up to. "I want to face all the best," says Patera. "I won't turn down a chance to enter the ring with any of them."

Ken Patera dominated weightlifting while competing for the United States. He will dominate the world of professional wrestling before many years have passed. Keep your eye on this young man.

MID-ATLANTIC WRESTLING 1975 YEARBOOK

BLACK

JACK

MALLIGAN

One of texas' toughest arrives in the Mid-Atlantic area.

This man gets it on, in the squared circle, Rufus R. Jones.

Crowd favorite Tommy Siegler applies an armbar.

Wahoo & Jack square off to do battle in the title match.

Fuji, Master of Martial Arts

Mr. Fuji has been campaigning in the U.S. rings for a few years now. His list of big wins is very impressive, to say the least. His great knowledge of the martial arts has played a big part in his being a consistent winner. Karate, Judo and Kung-Fu were studied by the man from Japan from his childhood. He has added to this a solid working knowledge of our style of professional wrestling, to make him a very tough opponent for any man who steps in the squared circle with him.

His pet hold, "The Cobra," is the move to watch for. When he locks it on his man, you can start to put on your coat.

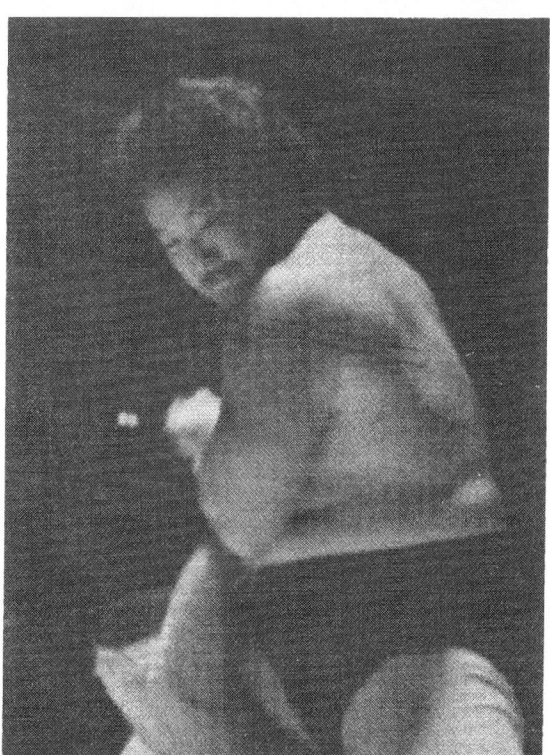

Mr. Fuji, a man of action.

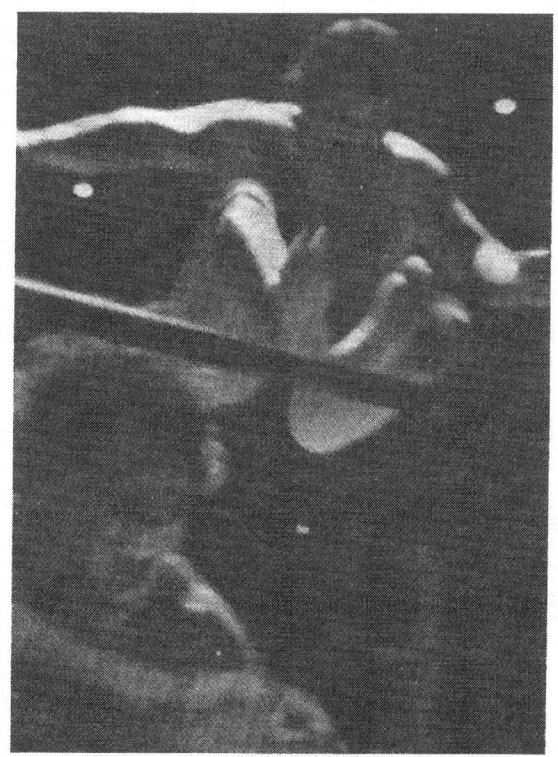

Mr. Fuji leaps high to end his match with Tommy Siegler.

KEN PATERA

Back Cover

SPOTLIGHT: Rufus R. "Freight Train" Jones

Dillon Native Enjoys Life As Pro Wrestler
By Phil Purvis, Morning News, May, 1975, Florence, SC

Mid-Atlantic Wrestling returned to Florence on Saturday night, May 10, and with it came about 5,000 screaming fans to watch their favorites compete in grueling matches pitting strength against strength, skill against skill. The favorites didn't always come out on top, but to the standing room crowd at Memorial Stadium, they were the true winners.

The big favorite of the night was featured in a tag team main event bout with the Mid-Atlantic Tag Team Championship Belt up for grabs. Gene and Ole Anderson, current belt holders, were meeting Chief Wahoo McDaniel and Dillon's own Rufus R. Jones. This is what the fans came to see, and what they saw, they liked.

Jones was born in the Little Rock section of Dillon County, the youngest of five girls and four boys, and later moved to New York where he played little league baseball, boxed and wrestled in amateur standings.

It was during this time that Jones had a chance to play baseball for the Brooklyn Dodgers. Instead, he chose professional wrestling. This, said the 6'1", 275 pound son of a sharecropper, was a decision he has always regretted. "I was a good ball player and feel like I could have made it in pro ball, but don't get me wrong, I love wrestling. That is one of the reasons I'm in it."

The other reason Jones is in it is the money. He said he made good money, but his lifestyle hasn't changed much since he first began to wrestle in Dillon County cotton fields as a youngster. "No, my style hasn't changed, but I live better than a sharecropper."

About his improved status, he said, "I worked hard to get where I am." Where he is today is right at the top of the wrestling profession, a place where the modest, but proud athlete would like to remain for some time to come.

When retirement comes, Jones will be prepared with a future in music. "I started music about a year ago and am working on an album now. I don't know when it will be ready because I am in no hurry. It will be something to do after I finish what I enjoy doing at the moment."

Professional wrestling attracts big crowds and is very popular on television. However, some believe the sport on the professional level is fake and a facet of the entertainment world using gimmicks to please the spectators rather than to really put on an exhibit of pure competition.

To this Jones replied, "The winner gets more money. Why should I let somebody beat me so he can get more money than I do? It is a rough sport and it is for real. It's not true that it's a fake. Where you have a lot of money involved, you are going to have people saying that."

It was homecoming for Jones, his first appearance in this area in about three years. "I just returned from Japan and it is good to be home again. I plan to be around for a while. Before, I was here for only four or five weeks, but now I'm going to stay around awhile."

"You know, I wrestled in a lot of places around the world, and before 25,000 people one time, but the greatest fans in the world are in South Carolina. It sure is good to be back home. I hated to leave before, but I'm planning on staying around awhile now."

Jones has two reasons for wanting to stay around his native territory. One is his step-mother, Mrs. James Lloyd, who still lives in the Little Rock community, and the second is the competition in the South. "The best competition in the world right now is in the South and the Midwest." According to the professional, "the money is where the competition is."

Jones and McDaniel lost their bid to capture the championship belt after the Anderson Brothers pulled an illegal switch when the referee's back was turned. McDaniel was in the ring with one brother when the other started to interfere. Jones came into the ring to prevent his partner from being double teamed, but was stopped by the official. During this time, the switch took place with the illegal partner making the pin on McDaniel.

After the bout, among the 100 or so well-wishes, autograph seekers, and renewed friendships, Jones said he felt cheated and disgusted about the tactics used to gain the victory.

Both Jones and McDaniel agreed to try to obtain a rematch with the Andersons in Florence. "If and when the rematch comes off, we will try to get two officials next time."

For Jones, the homecoming was a bittersweet thing. Bitter because of the way the defeat was handed to him and sweet because he was back home among old friends and childhood memories. ◆

Q2 HISTORY
by David Chappell

APRIL

April of 1975 saw Wahoo McDaniel have his strongest month yet as a member of Jim Crockett's roster. Despite not holding a championship belt, the Chief had a truly dominating month in April. The two singles champions of Mid-Atlantic Championship Wrestling, Johnny Valentine and Ric Flair, had unusual months during the month of April. Valentine traveled outside of the area for a good portion of the month, while Flair had an inordinate number of tag team matches in April. Gene and Ole Anderson, the NWA World Tag Team Champions, continued to have a busy schedule of tag matches in the area during the month of April.

Wahoo McDaniel's memorable month of April 1975 began with one of the Chief's other passions in life besides wrestling, as he played golf with his buddy Lee Trevino on April 2nd as part of the pro-am portion of the Greater Greensboro Open PGA event.

Wahoo had a memorable match in Charlotte, North Carolina on April 5, 1975 in the Charlotte Coliseum against NWA World's Heavyweight Champion Jack Brisco. Despite a large number of near falls by the Chief against the World Champion, Wahoo had to be content with a sixty minute draw against Brisco. This April 5th battle between Brisco and Wahoo was the World Champ's only title defense in the Mid-Atlantic area during the month of April.

The Chief was active in tag team matches this month, particularly against the NWA World Tag Team Champions Gene and Ole Anderson. Wahoo wrestled against the Andersons eight times in April, four times teaming with Sonny King and three times tagging with Paul Jones. In Norfolk, Virginia on April 10th, Wahoo teamed for the first time in the area with Rufus R. "Freight Train" Jones, as the new team had a classic battle against the "Minnesota Wrecking Crew."

McDaniel had a significant number of outright wins against Mid-Atlantic Heavyweight Champion Johnny "The Champ" Valentine during the month of April. While none of these victories was with the Mid-Atlantic Title on the line, Wahoo's performances did chip away somewhat at the aura of invincibility of Valentine. Certainly, Valentine had not had a month to this point in his Mid-Atlantic area stay where he had a more challenging series of bouts from his closest pursuers.

While Valentine had a tough month of April against the likes of Wahoo and Paul Jones, "The Champ" spent a significant part of the month campaigning outside of the Mid-Atlantic area. Early in April of 1975, Valentine wrestled in St. Louis, Dallas, San Antonio and Houston in addition to taking some days off. Valentine maintained the Mid-Atlantic Heavyweight Championship for the duration of the month of April, but he was not at his usual dominating best.

Mid-Atlantic Television Champion Ric Flair only defended his title five times during the month of April 1975. Two of those defenses were back to back defenses in Charleston, South Carolina on April 4th and 11th respectively against Paul Jones. Ken Patera got two title shots against the "Nature Boy," in the WRAL studios on April 16th and in Lynchburg, Virginia on April 18th. Abe Jacobs also tried unsuccessfully to wrest the TV Title from Flair in the WRAL TV studios on April 9th.

Rather than defending his TV Title, Flair was much more active in the tag team ranks during April. Ric was involved in a whopping twenty tag matches during the month of April, and ten of those were with new partner Blackjack Mulligan.

From April 16th to the end of the month, giant Haystacks Calhoun came into the area for a quick two week run, and was involved in a match of some sort nearly every night. In that span, Calhoun wrested ten times, including a wild match in Spartanburg, South Carolina on April 26, 1975 where Haystacks teamed with Rufus R. Jones against the Super Destroyer and big Blackjack Mulligan. Calhoun also served as a special referee twice in April, including being referee in a Mid-Atlantic Title match between Paul Jones and Johnny Valentine on April 29th in Columbia, South Carolina.

NWA World Tag Team Champions Gene and Ole Anderson wrestled almost exclusively as a tag team during the month of April, with both Gene and Ole having only two singles matches apiece during the month. On the tag team front, the Anderson's had their most title defenses in April against their budding nemeses Paul Jones and Wahoo McDaniel. But overall, the Anderson's faced the new team of Ken Patera and Sonny King the most during the month of April.

Rufus R. Jones made quite an impact in the Mid-Atlantic area during his first few weeks in the territory. The "Freight Train" was reintroduced to the area's fans during April of 1975 after being out of the area for two years, and he immediately became one of the territory's most popular fan favorites. His "head-butt" was an effective weapon against many of his early foes in Jim Crockett Promotions.

An example of Rufus' rapid rise on the cards can immediately be seen by looking to Charlotte, North Carolina on consecutive Park Center cards. On March 31st, Rufus started back in the territory with the second match against Frank Morrell. On the next Park Center card, which was held on April 14th, Rufus headlined the card, teaming with Wahoo against Ric Flair and Johnny Valentine. The "Freight Train" had quite an impressive month during April of 1975.

Like Rufus, another relative newcomer used the month of April as a major springboard. Blackjack Mulligan went from an early match against Charlie Cook on a March 31, 1975 Fayetteville, NC card, to headlining against Wahoo McDaniel on April 28th in Charlotte. This Charlotte match between Mulligan and McDaniel set in place a torrid "Cowboy versus Indian" feud that would rage throughout the month of May 1975, and which would feature a number of specialty matches. Mulligan also battled Dusty Rhodes in Greensboro, NC twice during the month of April, and both battles were rugged and bloody affairs.

While April of 1975 did not produce any title changes, its action was the precursor of major developments that would take place in May between the Anderson's and the team of Paul Jones and Wahoo McDaniel. April also set the table for a short bitter feud between Wahoo and Blackjack Mulligan that would erupt in May. But above all else, April 1975 was the month that Wahoo McDaniel's star shined the brightest in the Mid-Atlantic sky. Title or not, April of 1975 was undoubtedly Wahoo's month on top of the heap in Mid-Atlantic Championship Wrestling.

WHO'S HOT

1. WAHOO McDANIEL---During April, Wahoo closed in on both the NWA World Tag Team Titles, and also the Mid-Atlantic Heavyweight Title. The Chief also dished out some of the toughest whippings to Johnny Valentine that "The Champ" ever endured while wrestling for Jim Crockett Promotions.

2. RUFUS R. JONES---The "Freight Train" quickly moved from opening bouts to main events during the course of the month of April. The way the fans flocked to the Dillon, SC native was amazing. While wrestling mainly tag matches in April, Rufus would turn more to singles competition in the months to come.

3. BLACKJACK MULLIGAN---Mulligan formed a fearsome tag team with Ric Flair during April, and generally looked unstoppable in his bouts during the month. But would the "Cowboy" meet his match in the "Indian," Wahoo McDaniel. The month of May would tell the tale.

WHO'S NOT

1. THE AVENGER---The popular masked man who was headlining cards against the Super Destroyer just a month before, continued to slip down the cards during April. As an example of how far the Avenger's stock had fallen by the end of the month, on the April 30, 1975 television taping at the WRAL studios, the Avenger was teamed with Charlie Cook to wrestle the ferocious team of Johnny Valentine and the Super Destroyer. The "bad guys" prevailed with ease.

2. SWEDE HANSON---April continued the descent of this recent main event performer. The big Swede was quickly falling from the upper mid-card perch that he was occupying since the beginning of 1975. On the same April 30, 1975 TV taping referenced above, the promotion teamed Swede with Don Kernodle against Gene and Ole Anderson. The tag champs won convincingly.

3. BRUTE BERNARD---Brute was still entertaining with his antics in the ring, bit he was quickly becoming less than challenging for the younger and bigger "good guys" that were now operating in the territory.

MAY

May of 1975 saw the most significant title change of the year in Mid-Atlantic Championship Wrestling take place in mid month. After three and a half months of dominating the tag team division in the area as NWA World Tag Team Champions, Gene and Ole Anderson suffered a stunning defeat in the Greensboro Coliseum on May 15, 1975.

WAHOO McDANIEL & PAUL JONES vs. THE ANDERSON BROTHERS

The ultra popular duo of Paul Jones and Wahoo McDaniel became NWA World Tag Team Champions on the 15th, dethroning the seemingly invincible Anderson Brothers and making May a month to remember fondly by the fans of Jim Crockett Promotions.

At the 33 minute mark of the title bout, McDaniel caught Gene Anderson in a suplex and seconds later Paul Jones covered Gene for the three count, sending the Greensboro crowd into a frenzy, and the Anderson's into disbelief.

While Paul Jones and Wahoo were the Anderson's top challengers for the previous three months when Gene and Ole were World Tag Team Champions, interestingly the two teams did not wrestle each other at all in the month of May prior to the title change on May 15th. After Jones and Wahoo won the titles, they had two successful defenses against the Anderson's during the remainder of the month of May, in Ashville, NC on May 18th and in Norfolk, VA on May 29th.

JOHNNY VALENTINE

Mid-Atlantic Heavyweight Champion Johnny "The Champ" Valentine continued to travel some in the month of May, but to a lesser extent than he did in the month April. Valentine headed to St. Louis on May 2nd, and at the end of the month on May 31st headed to Houston. In between those two out of the area stints, Valentine got back to being his dominating best in the Mid-Atlantic area.

Valentine defended his Mid-Atlantic Title often in the month of May, with his most frequent challenger being Paul Jones. Chief Wahoo McDaniel also got a number of shots at Valentine's prestigious belt during the month. After Jones and McDaniel won the World Tag Team Titles, their focus shifted away from Valentine, though Jones nearly upended Valentine in a memorable title match in Charlotte's Memorial Stadium on May 16th, the night after Paul became one half of the World Tag Champs.

RIC FLAIR

May 3, 1975 was a date of some historical significance, as Ric Flair would defend a title against Wahoo McDaniel for the first time ever on that date. In Greenwood, SC, Flair defended his Mid-Atlantic Television Title against Wahoo, and Ric managed to barely emerge with his title still intact on May 3rd.

May was an unusually busy month for Flair defending his TV Title, as during the month the "Nature Boy" put the belt on the line a total of ten times, against Paul Jones, Ken Patera and Sonny King in addition to the title match against McDaniel in Greenwood

MID-ATLANTIC TELEVISION

Mid-Atlantic Championship Wrestling had an outstanding month in May as far as its television shows were concerned. In particular, the shows taped on May 7th and May 14th were excellent.

The May 7, 1975 television show had a main event caliber match between the Super Destroyer and Sonny King. The promotion followed up the next week with one of the best editions of Mid-Atlantic Championship Wrestling TV ever.

After running down the May 14th television card, David Crockett said, "The whole place is going to rock." And how right he was. There were three main event caliber matches on the Mid-Atlantic Championship Wrestling show, and the Wide World Wrestling show played a film of a great Wahoo McDaniel against NWA Champion Jack Brisco match.

The Mid-Atlantic show on May 14th started with a promoted "grudge match" between California star Jose Lothario and the Super Destroyer. David Crockett told the TV audience that Lothario had come in from California to get revenge against the Destroyer, because the Destroyer had hurt Lothario out in California. This angle was never followed up on any further after the TV match.

Two terrific tag team bouts rounded out the TV show on May 14th. In the first, Ken Patera and Rufus R. Jones dominated Gene and Ole Anderson, but without garnering a clean victory. Patera's strength was highlighted in this match, with the Anderson's having all kinds of problems dealing with the strongman from Oregon.

The May 14th TV show ended with an amazing match between Ric Flair and Johnny Valentine against Paul Jones and Wahoo McDaniel. Amazing in that this caliber matchup was almost never shown on TV, and in that there was never a feud between these four that was set up on the heels of this TV match. Nevertheless, what a great match to end one of the best TV programs in the promotion's history!

SUPER DESTROYER VS. SONNY KING

Two notable feuds were ongoing during the month of May 1975, but both proved to be short-lived. The first program involved the Super Destroyer against Sonny King. While these two had been wrestling sporadically against each other for the better part of a year, the promotion decided to start a pure program with these two in May.

To be sure, there was a history between the Destroyer and King. The Super D. had injured King's brother, Bearcat Wright, in mid 1974. But what got this program re-charged was a challenge by the Destroyer to King on Mid-Atlantic TV that aired on May 3, 1975, pitting their two finishing moves against each other-the claw versus the head-butt. On that same TV show, King had Ken Patera hit him over the head with a wooden chair to show the audience how hard his head was. The chair was shattered into a number of pieces.

On a subsequent TV show, the Super D. claimed he had outsmarted King, because the Destroyer could effectively put his claw on other parts of the body besides the head. To prove his point, the Super Destroyer beat preliminary wrester L.D. Lewis with a claw hold around Lewis' facial muscles rather than around his forehead. King responded that it didn't make any difference to him where the Destroyer applied the claw.

The Super Destroyer and King battled for several months around the circuit, in what would be the final program for each before both departed the Mid-Atlantic area in the summer of 1975.

BLACKJACK MULLIGAN VS. WAHOO MCDANIEL

The other major feud of May 1975 was a classic battle between Cowboy and Indian...Blackjack Mulligan versus Wahoo McDaniel. This program was far too short, and its life for the most part was confined to the month of May. The two never really feuded in an organized program after this, despite being major stars for JCP for many years after this time period.

During the month of May, these two progressed from straight singles matches, to bouts where Mulligan would be fined if he ran from the ring and finally moved to McDaniel's famed Indian Strap Matches.

McDaniel got the best of Mulligan throughout these contests, and effectively ran Mulligan out of the Mid-Atlantic area when he thrashed Blackjack in an Indian Strap Match in Richmond on May 30, 1975.

Mulligan immediately went to the WWWF where he quickly became one half of their World Tag Team Champs during the summer of 1975. However, Mulligan made several guest shot appearances back in the Mid-Atlantic area during the summer of 1975, challenging Wahoo to Texas Death Matches to try to avenge his defeats to McDaniel in the Indian Strap Matches during the spring. Included in those guest shots was a Texas Death Match in Richmond on July 18, 1975, where Wahoo again defeated Mulligan…this time at Blackjack's own specialty match.

Mulligan would not return to the Mid-Atlantic area in earnest until the autumn of 1975, when he would start his largely uninterrupted six year run for Jim Crockett Promotions that most fans remember him for.

May of 1975 had numerous big events as part of it, and would usher in June and the hot summer of 1975 with its own share of highlights. And at the very same time school was letting out in June, Mid-Atlantic Championship Wrestling would see the arrival of a "Professor," named Malenko.

WHO'S HOT

1. WAHOO MCDANIEL---During the month of May, Wahoo became one half of the NWA World Tag Team Champions, and also dispatched Blackjack Mulligan in a physical series of matches. The Chief was clearly on top of his game in May of 1975.

2. PAUL JONES---Jones also became one half of the NWA World Tag Team Champions in May, and in addition was the top challenger to both singles titles in the area. A terrific month for Mr. # 1.

3. JOHNNY VALENTINE---The "Champ" traveled less in the month of May, and had a number of memorable defenses of his Mid-Atlantic Heavyweight Title. With Paul Jones and Wahoo McDaniel becoming tag champions during the month, Valentine started seeing a singles challenge looming in the future from Olympic strongman Ken Patera.

WHO'S NOT

1. BLACKJACK MULLIGAN---The big Cowboy from Eagle Pass, Texas was thoroughly dominated in his feud during the month with Chief Wahoo McDaniel, to the point of his being run right out of the Mid-Atlantic area. However, as it turned out, fans would not have to wait long before seeing lots more of "Mully" in JCP.

2. GENE ANDERSON---Gene lost the fall that lost the World Tag Team belts to Jones and McDaniel in Greensboro. During bouts in May post May 15th, including some singles matches, Gene struggled as well.

3. OLE ANDERSON---Like his brother, Ole struggled to deal with the title loss on May 15th, and fought to get back on track in subsequent single and tag matches. However, June would be a much happier month for both Gene and Ole.

JUNE

One of the most memorable matches to ever occur in the history of Mid-Atlantic Championship Wrestling took place in the month of June 1975. What made this match even more memorable was because it was the first time that the NWA World Tag Team Titles had ever been defended on television.

THE SUPREME SACRIFICE

On June 11, 1975, Paul Jones and Wahoo McDaniel defended their NWA World Tag Team Titles against former champions Gene and Ole Anderson in the WRAL TV Channel 5 studios in Raleigh, North Carolina. This bout is remembered not only for its intensity, but also for an ending that nobody could have forecasted.

For much of the match, Gene and Ole were able to isolate Paul Jones in the ring and prevent Wahoo from becoming involved through use of their famous "Tag And Block" tactic. At one point, McDaniel appeared to be almost in tears as the Anderson's were slamming Jones repeatedly on his own arm and preventing Paul from making the tag. When Wahoo finally got in and he and Jones got the upper hand, the Anderson's shocked everyone by deliberately sacrificing a partner to win their title belts back. As Gene Anderson slumped over the ropes on the outside of the ring, Ole grabbed Wahoo and ran his head into Gene's, knocking both Gene and Wahoo senseless. As Wahoo was the legal man in the ring, Ole covered him and referee Sonny Fargo counted Wahoo out and the titles changed hands for all the TV viewers to see. The camera panned to the floor where Gene was laying prone, as announcer David Crockett yelled, "Gene Anderson…he's not moving…he's out cold! How could Ole Anderson sacrifice his brother like that?" Prior to the match, the Anderson's had said they would do anything and make any sacrifice to win the World Tag Team Titles back….and they lived up to their word by pulling off the "Supreme Sacrifice."

The "Supreme Sacrifice" match was not only significant in its own right, but it set off an unforgettable program that lasted through the summer of 1975 where Jones and Wahoo attempted to win the World Tag Team Titles back. These matches to come were some of the longest and greatest tag team matches in the history of professional wrestling.

NWA WORLD CHAMPION JACK BRISCO

NWA World Heavyweight Champion Jack Brisco was active in the area during the month of June. In Greensboro on June 5th, Jack teamed with his brother Jerry Brisco to go after then World Tag Team Champions Paul Jones and Wahoo McDaniel. While the Brisco's came up just short in that encounter, Jack was back in the area soon after that defending his singles World Heavyweight Title.

In Raleigh on June 17th, Jack defended his World Title against Paul Jones in a No Time Limit bout. Brisco turned around the next night and made a very rare appearance on the area's television shows, wrestling twice on TV from the WRAL studios. On the Mid-Atlantic Championship Wrestling program, Brisco wrestled a competitive match against the 1974 NWA Rookie of the Year, Steve Keirn. On the territory's Wide World Wrestling TV program, Brisco wrestled against the dangerous veteran Abe Jacobs. Brisco completed his mid-June sweep through the area the following night in Norfolk, Virginia, with a successful title defense against Sonny King.

THE MID-ATLANTIC CHAMPIONSHIP

The long reigning Mid-Atlantic Heavyweight Champion Johnny Valentine was finally dethroned on June 29th at the Civic Center in Asheville, North Carolina by the ultra popular Chief Wahoo McDaniel. As one would expect, Valentine did not go down without quite a fight! Wahoo snagged Valentine for a quick three count with only a couple of minutes left in the 60 minute time limit. Wahoo later said, he couldn't believe he had beaten the "Champ," and that he just wanted to get out of the ring and get gone! Wahoo didn't have much time to rest however, as he began title defenses against a young and hungry Ric Flair. This would begin a feud between Wahoo and Flair over the Mid-Atlantic belt that would last for a year and a half.

MID-ATLANTIC SUPERSTARS

Despite traveling to Tampa, Florida during the month of June, Mid-Atlantic Heavyweight Champion Johnny Valentine had a busy month of title defenses. Paul Jones and Rufus R, Jones were "The Champ's" featured opponents in June, though Johnny also wrestled Wahoo McDaniel and Ken Patera multiple times in singles action as well. June would be Valentine's last full month as Mid-Atlantic Heavyweight Champion, a title he had dominated for well over a year.

The area's other singles champion, "Nature Boy" Ric Flair continued to impress and hold the Mid-Atlantic Television Title during the month of June. While the largest number of Flair's title defenses came against old rival "Number 1" Paul Jones, Ric was also developing a healthy rivalry with former Olympian Ken Patera. Flair would make fun of Patera's 86 world weightlifting records, but nevertheless spent a good bit of time running away from Patera during their June title bouts.

The Super Destroyer and Sonny King wrestled each other almost non-stop during the month of June….and their many battles against each other would for all intents and purposes reach their end by the month's end. In June, these two wrestled in fence matches, lumberjack matches, matches with two referees and even matches where King would wear boxing gloves. While the Super Destroyer would win most of these climactic matches, both wrestlers would be leaving the area within a matter of several weeks.

A major addition to the area's roster in June was the arrival of "Professor" Boris Maximilianovich Malenko. "Professor" Malenko told the area's fans that he was from the Russian school "of hard knocks," that his school colors were "black and blue," and that his school yell was "Ouch." Malenko said he "was a human destruction machine, that would destroy everything in his path." During the month of June, the Professor lived up to his boastful words.

Using a devastating hold called the "Russian Sickle," Malenko racked up quite an impressive array of victories in the month of June. The Professor began his stint with Jim Crockett Promotions wrestling mainly single matches, though he would shortly form an impressive team with the Missouri Mauler and significantly later, in early 1976, begin his role as a manager that he is often remembered for by Mid-Atlantic fans.

June of 1975 ended with a bang with a spectacular card in Charlotte's Memorial Stadium on June 30, 1975. Highlighting that memorable summer outdoor show was a main event battle between the Super Destroyer and Andre the Giant. Blackjack Mulligan returned to the area for a guest shot appearance fresh from the WWWF, to battle old foe Wahoo McDaniel in a brutal Texas Death Match. Ox Baker even made a guest appearance on this end of the month summer spectacular.

June would give way to July, where there would be some major roster changes, and the heating up of the summer-long feud between the Anderson's and Paul Jones and Wahoo McDaniel. And before July was even three days old, there would be a major new title introduced into the area---and Johnny Valentine would not only then be the "Champ" of the Mid-Atlantic area….but the Champion of the whole United States!

Promotional Photographs of the Two NWA World Champions During 1975

N.W.A. CHAMPION JACK BRISCO

Terry Funk — WORLD HEAVYWEIGHT CHAMPION

WHO'S HOT

1. GENE & OLE ANDERSON---The "Minnesota Wrecking Crew" pulled out all the stops to regain the NWA World Tag Team Championship on June 11th for all to see on TV. And by the end of June they were embroiled in a red-hot feud with former champs Paul Jones and Wahoo McDaniel. The tag team feud between these two teams was like no other.

2. "PROFESSOR" BORIS MALENKO---The "Mad Russian" came into the area in June and made an immediate impact, dominating the competition with his devastating hold, the "Russian Sickle." Malenko was neither especially big nor quick, but he could think and boy could he ever wrestle!

3. JOHNNY VALENTINE---"The Champ" kept rolling along, despite dropping the Mid-Atlantic title to Wahoo McDaniel. So much so, in fact, that he was able to very soon shift his attention to a new, and even more prestigious, title belt.

WHO'S NOT

1. SONNY KING---After a strong year in the Mid-Atlantic area, King came out on the short end of his final series of matches against his big rival, the Super Destroyer. King only wrestled several dates for the promotion after the end of June.

2. SANDY SCOTT---An important player for Jim Crockett Promotions for many years, Scott's in-ring role began to be de-emphasized during the month of June. Sandy would only continue to be an active wrestler with the promotion for a couple of more months.

3. BOB BRUGGERS---Much like Sandy Scott, his frequent tag team partner, Bruggers continued to slide further down the mid-card ranks during the month of June. After so much promise during 1974, the middle of 1975 was not being overly kind to the former Miami Dolphins football player.

MID-ATLANTIC WRESTLING 1975 YEARBOOK

The Booker's Daily Planner

In this archive image of a page from George Scott's day planner, perspective is gained on what professional wrestlers could go through on an average day on the job.

Jim Crockett Promotions taped their weekly TV shows on Wednesday evenings at the television studios of WRAL-TV in Raleigh, NC. On June 11, 1975, the main event of the Mid-Atlantic Wrestling show (indicated here as "Raleigh TV A tape") was a NWA world tag team championship rematch featuring the Anderson Brothers vs. Wahoo McDaniel and Paul Jones. This was the match that ended with "Supreme Sacrifice" where brother sacrificed brother to regain the titles and the belts.

On many Wednesday nights during this time, Crockett also ran a spot-show in nearby Rocky Mount, NC at the local ball park. Many times, a wrestler would tape their TV match on the early tape that began around 7 PM and then dash to Rocky Mount in time to wrestle on the main event of that spot-show the same night.

Of particular note on this night, Wahoo McDaniel teamed with Paul Jones in a long brutal match against the Andersons for TV, and then made the 65-mile trip to the Rocky Mount Ball Park in time to wrestle in the main event against Mid-Atlantic heavyweight champion Johnny Valentine.

Rufus R. Jones also wrestled on that early TV tape and then made the trip in time for his semi-main event match against Ric Flair.

You know you've put in a full days work when you wrestle Gene and Ole Anderson, and then Johnny Valentine all within one evening. Wahoo was one tough individual!

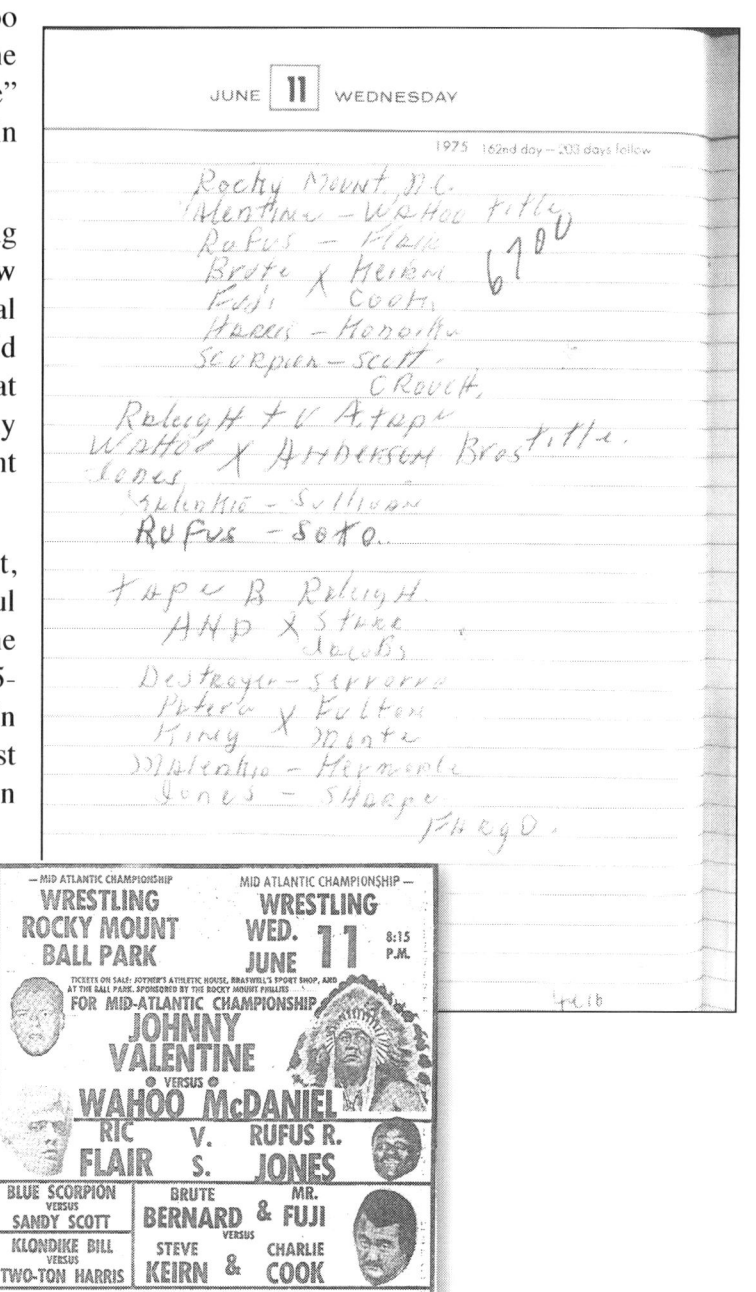

MID-ATLANTIC WRESTLING 1975 YEARBOOK

SPECIAL FEATURE
EVENT POSTERS
GREENSBORO, NORTH CAROLINA

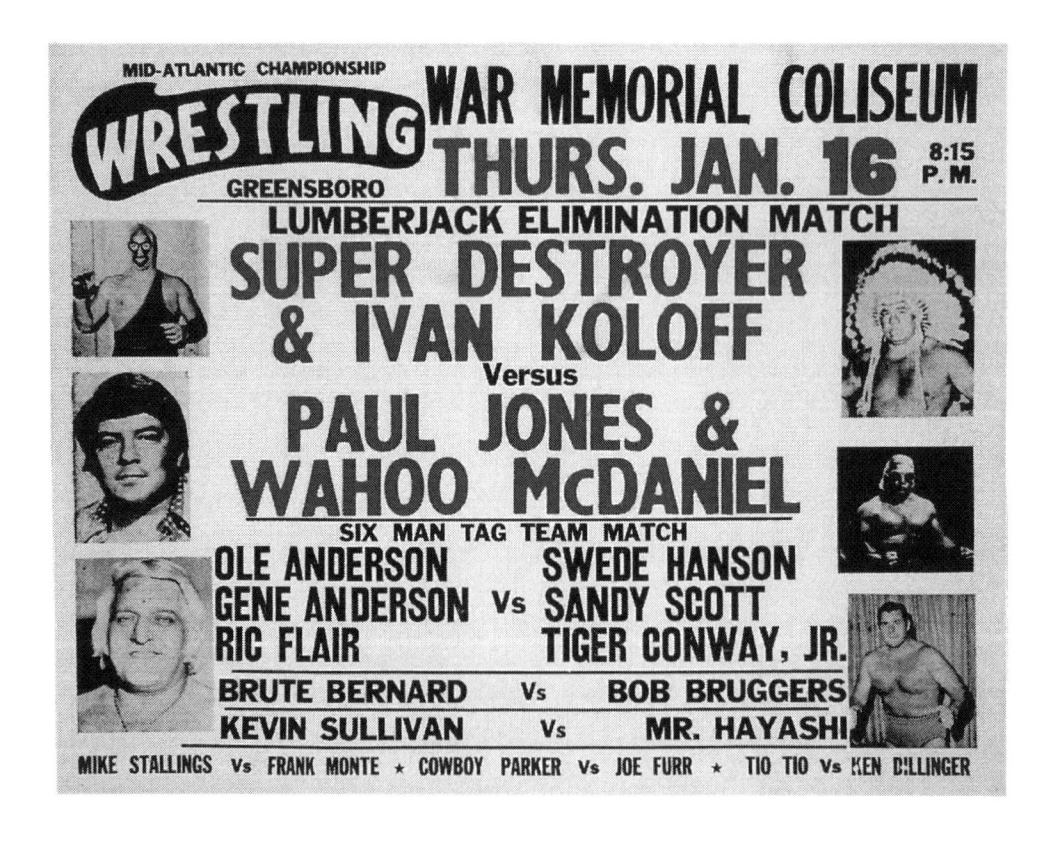

MID-ATLANTIC CHAMPIONSHIP WRESTLING
GREENSBORO

WAR MEMORIAL COLISEUM
THURS. JAN. 16 8:15 P.M.

LUMBERJACK ELIMINATION MATCH

SUPER DESTROYER & IVAN KOLOFF
Versus
PAUL JONES & WAHOO McDANIEL

SIX MAN TAG TEAM MATCH

OLE ANDERSON		SWEDE HANSON
GENE ANDERSON	Vs	SANDY SCOTT
RIC FLAIR		TIGER CONWAY, JR.

BRUTE BERNARD Vs BOB BRUGGERS
KEVIN SULLIVAN Vs MR. HAYASHI

MIKE STALLINGS Vs FRANK MONTE ★ COWBOY PARKER Vs JOE FURR ★ TIO TIO Vs KEN DILLINGER

MID-ATLANTIC WRESTLING 1975 YEARBOOK

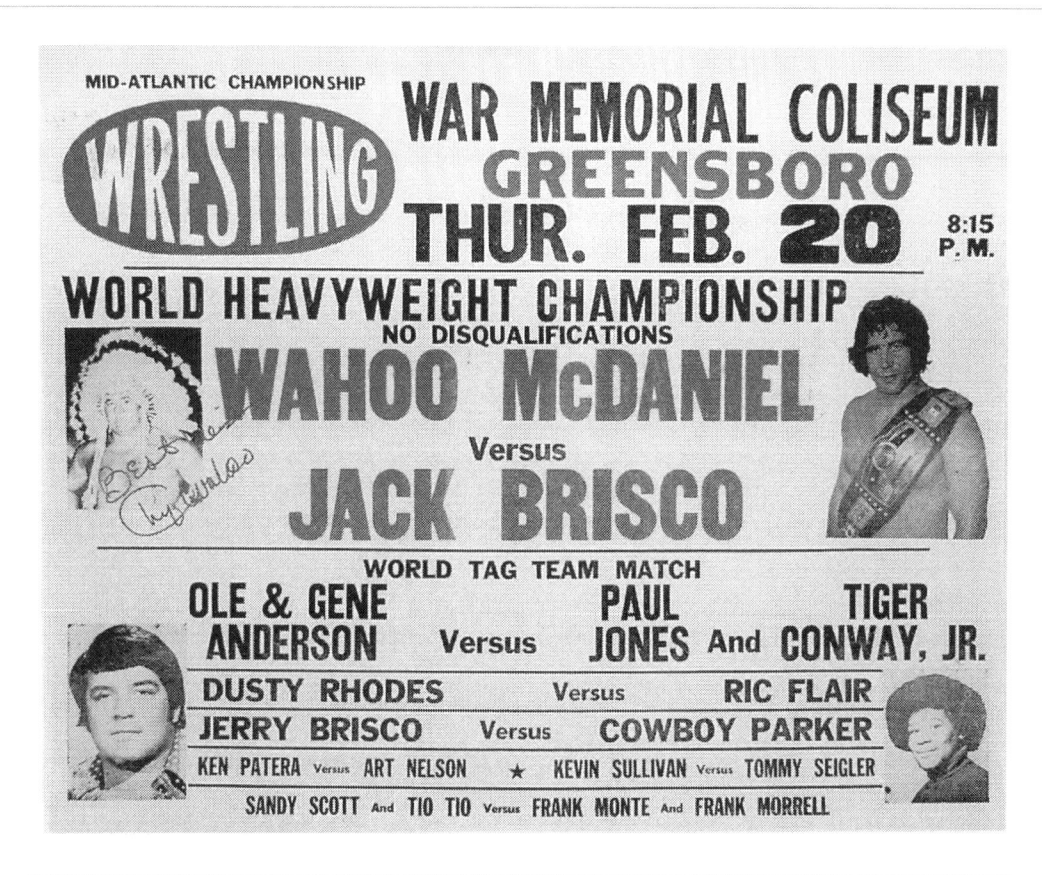

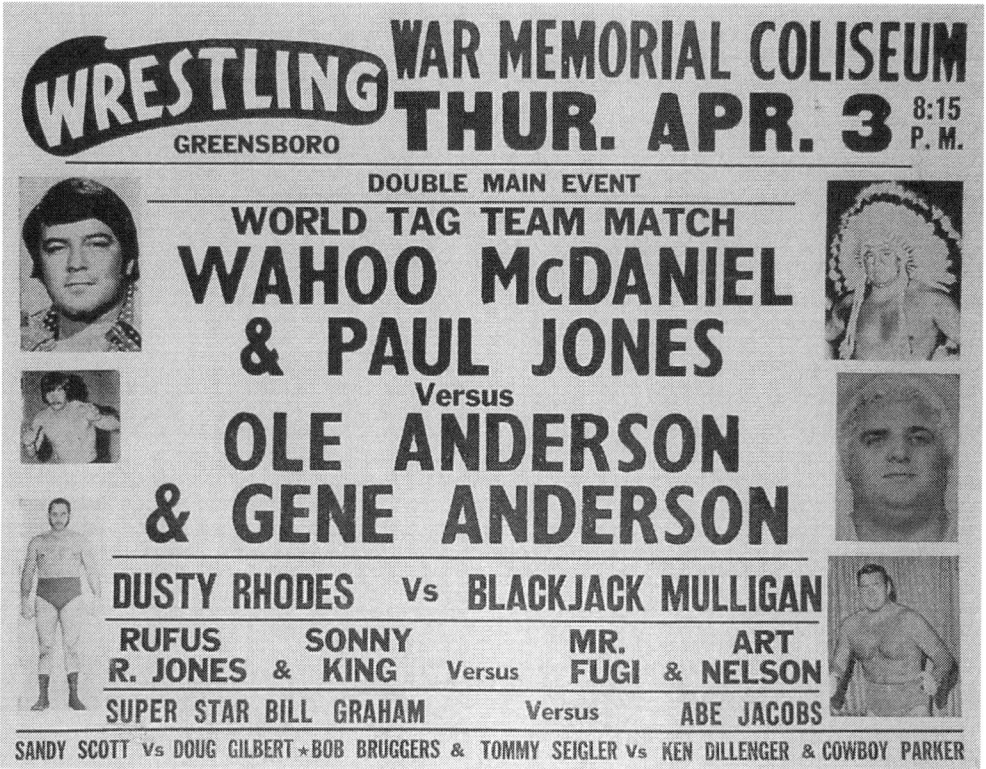

MID-ATLANTIC CHAMPIONSHIP WRESTLING

WAR MEMORIAL COLISEUM
GREENSBORO
THUR. FEB. 20 8:15 P.M.

WORLD HEAVYWEIGHT CHAMPIONSHIP
NO DISQUALIFICATIONS
WAHOO McDANIEL Versus **JACK BRISCO**

WORLD TAG TEAM MATCH
OLE & GENE ANDERSON Versus PAUL JONES And TIGER CONWAY, JR.

DUSTY RHODES Versus RIC FLAIR
JERRY BRISCO Versus COWBOY PARKER
KEN PATERA Versus ART NELSON ★ KEVIN SULLIVAN Versus TOMMY SEIGLER
SANDY SCOTT And TIO TIO Versus FRANK MONTE And FRANK MORRELL

WRESTLING – GREENSBORO
WAR MEMORIAL COLISEUM
THUR. APR. 3 8:15 P.M.

DOUBLE MAIN EVENT
WORLD TAG TEAM MATCH
WAHOO McDANIEL & PAUL JONES Versus **OLE ANDERSON & GENE ANDERSON**

DUSTY RHODES Vs BLACKJACK MULLIGAN
RUFUS R. JONES & SONNY KING Versus MR. FUGI & ART NELSON
SUPER STAR BILL GRAHAM Versus ABE JACOBS
SANDY SCOTT Vs DOUG GILBERT ★ BOB BRUGGERS & TOMMY SEIGLER Vs KEN DILLENGER & COWBOY PARKER

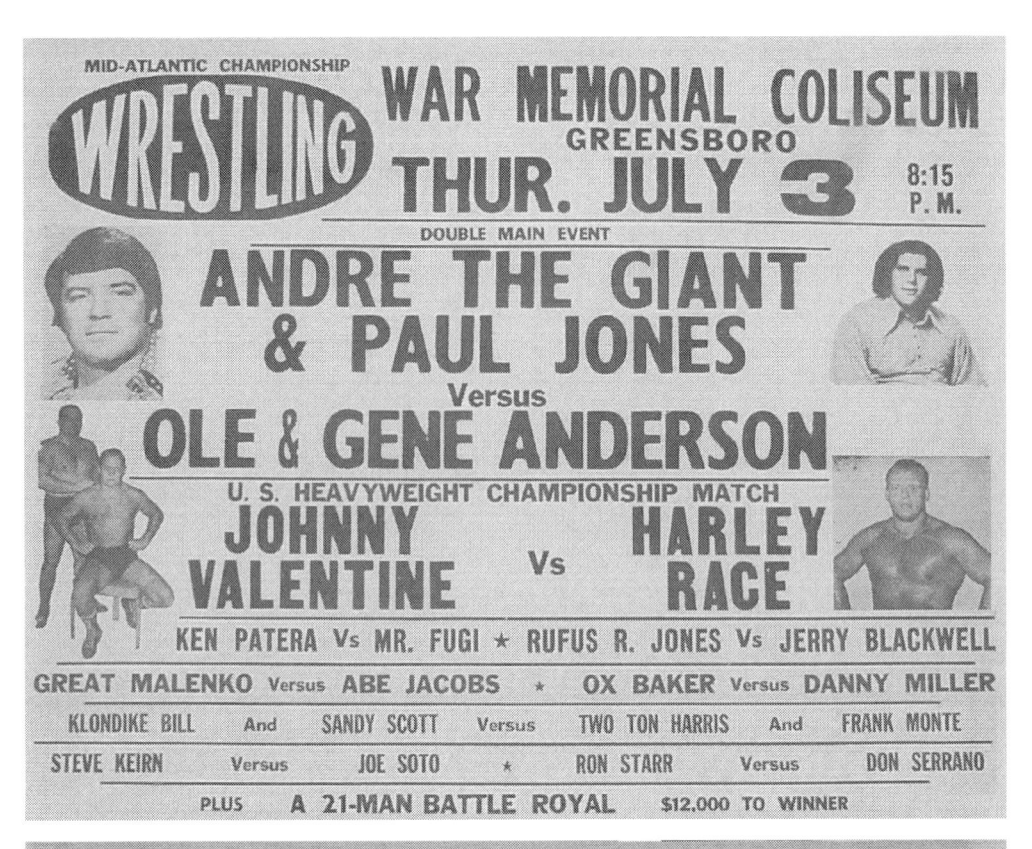

MID-ATLANTIC WRESTLING 1975 YEARBOOK

MID-ATLANTIC CHAMPIONSHIP WRESTLING
WAR MEMORIAL COLISEUM — GREENSBORO
THUR. JULY 3 — 8:15 P.M.

DOUBLE MAIN EVENT

ANDRE THE GIANT & PAUL JONES
Versus
OLE & GENE ANDERSON

U.S. HEAVYWEIGHT CHAMPIONSHIP MATCH
JOHNNY VALENTINE Vs **HARLEY RACE**

KEN PATERA Vs MR. FUGI ★ RUFUS R. JONES Vs JERRY BLACKWELL

GREAT MALENKO Versus ABE JACOBS ★ OX BAKER Versus DANNY MILLER

KLONDIKE BILL And SANDY SCOTT Versus TWO TON HARRIS And FRANK MONTE

STEVE KEIRN Versus JOE SOTO ★ RON STARR Versus DON SERRANO

PLUS A 21-MAN BATTLE ROYAL $12,000 TO WINNER

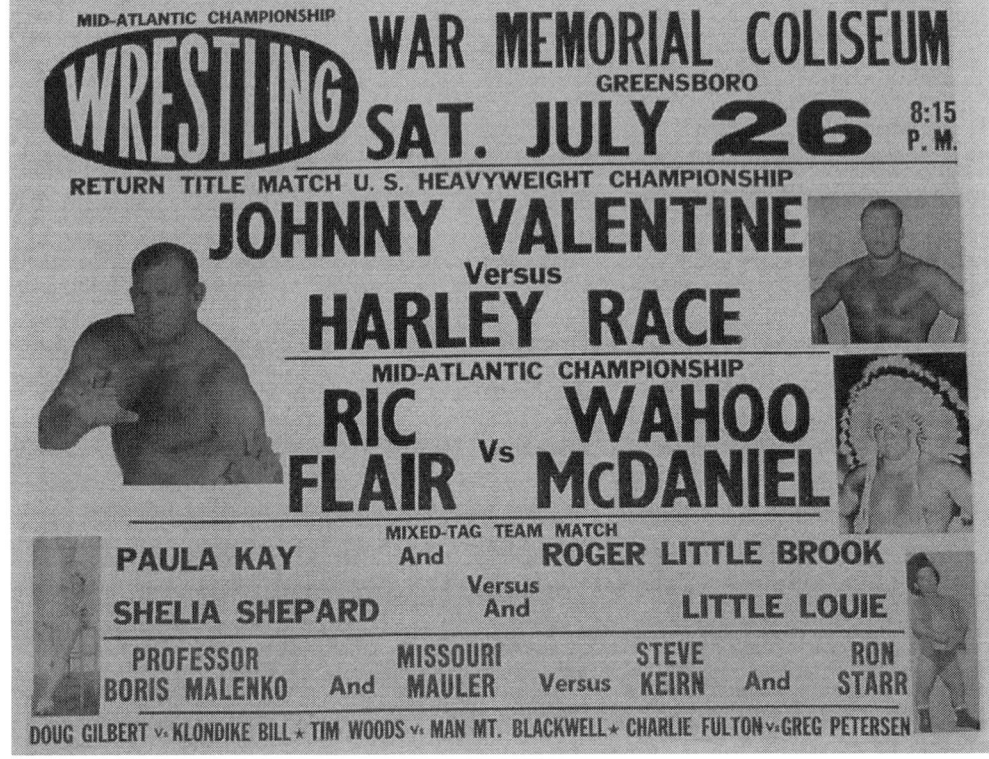

MID-ATLANTIC CHAMPIONSHIP WRESTLING
WAR MEMORIAL COLISEUM — GREENSBORO
SAT. JULY 26 — 8:15 P.M.

RETURN TITLE MATCH U.S. HEAVYWEIGHT CHAMPIONSHIP
JOHNNY VALENTINE Versus **HARLEY RACE**

MID-ATLANTIC CHAMPIONSHIP
RIC FLAIR Vs **WAHOO McDANIEL**

MIXED-TAG TEAM MATCH
PAULA KAY And ROGER LITTLE BROOK
Versus
SHELIA SHEPARD And LITTLE LOUIE

PROFESSOR BORIS MALENKO And MISSOURI MAULER Versus STEVE KEIRN And RON STARR

DOUG GILBERT Vs KLONDIKE BILL ★ TIM WOODS Vs MAN MT. BLACKWELL ★ CHARLIE FULTON Vs GREG PETERSEN

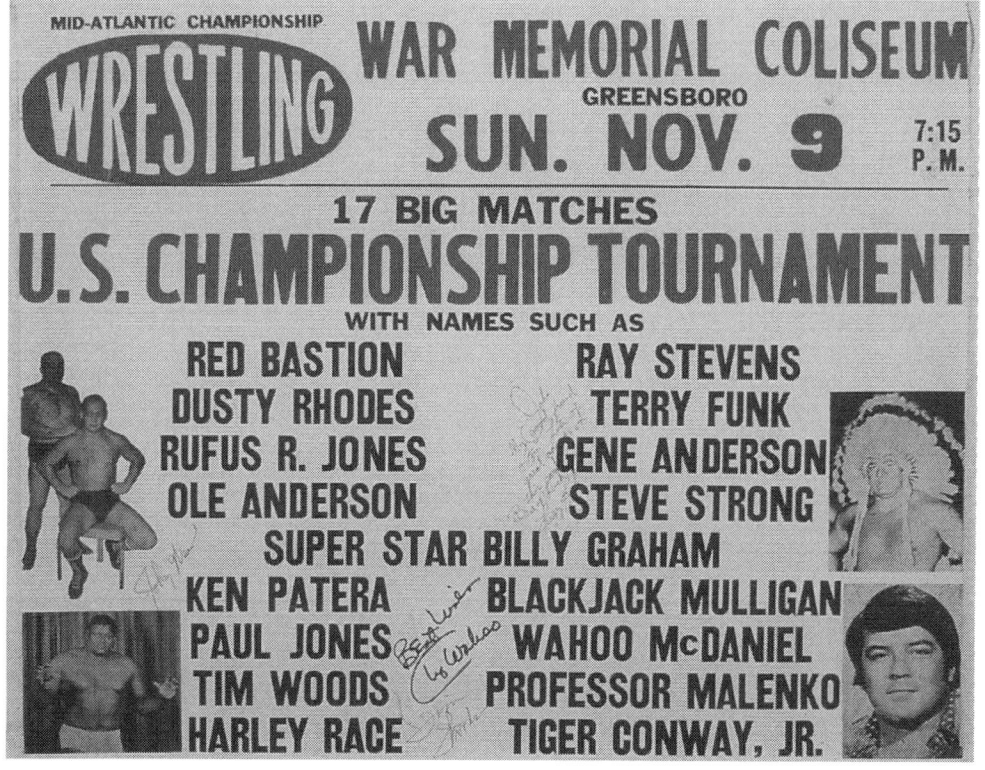

MID-ATLANTIC WRESTLING 1975 YEARBOOK

MID-ATLANTIC CHAMPIONSHIP WRESTLING
WAR MEMORIAL COLISEUM
GREENSBORO
SUN. SEPT. 7 — 7:00 P.M.

DOUBLE MAIN EVENT

U.S. HEAVYWEIGHT TITLE MATCH

JOHNNY VALENTINE
CHAMPION
Versus
DUSTY RHODES

TEXAS TORNADO ELIMINATION MATCH

OLE & GENE ANDERSON
Versus
PAUL JONES And WAHOO McDANIEL

KEN PATERA & RUFUS R. JONES Vs GREAT MALENKO & MISSOURI MAULER

TIM WOODS Versus BRUTE BERNARD ★ SWEDE HANSON Versus SPOILER NO. 2

TIGER CONWAY Versus DOUG GILBERT ★ ART NELSON Versus KLONDIKE BILL

CHARLIE FULTON And BILL HOWARD Versus GREG PETERSON And TONY ROCCA

MID-ATLANTIC CHAMPIONSHIP WRESTLING
WAR MEMORIAL COLISEUM
GREENSBORO
SUN. NOV. 9 — 7:15 P.M.

17 BIG MATCHES

U.S. CHAMPIONSHIP TOURNAMENT

WITH NAMES SUCH AS

RED BASTION — RAY STEVENS
DUSTY RHODES — TERRY FUNK
RUFUS R. JONES — GENE ANDERSON
OLE ANDERSON — STEVE STRONG
SUPER STAR BILLY GRAHAM
KEN PATERA — BLACKJACK MULLIGAN
PAUL JONES — WAHOO McDANIEL
TIM WOODS — PROFESSOR MALENKO
HARLEY RACE — TIGER CONWAY, JR.

85

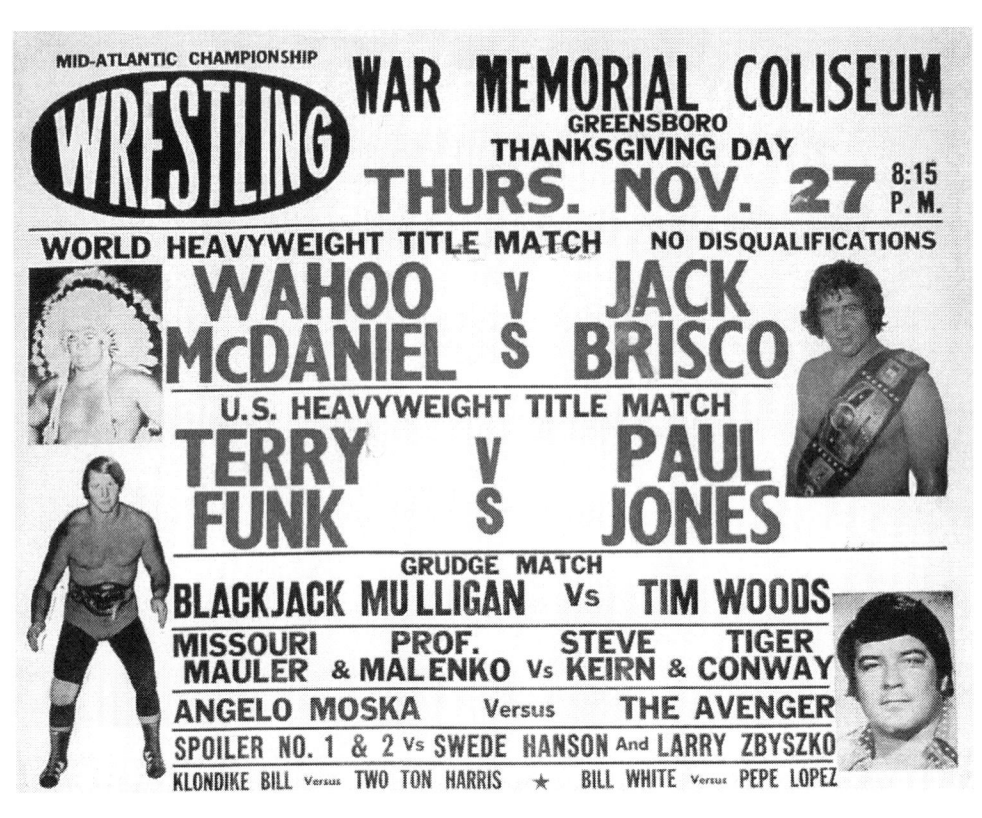

MID-ATLANTIC WRESTLING 1975 YEARBOOK

MID-ATLANTIC CHAMPIONSHIP WRESTLING
WAR MEMORIAL COLISEUM
GREENSBORO
THANKSGIVING DAY
THURS. NOV. 27 8:15 P.M.

WORLD HEAVYWEIGHT TITLE MATCH — NO DISQUALIFICATIONS
WAHOO McDANIEL vs JACK BRISCO

U.S. HEAVYWEIGHT TITLE MATCH
TERRY FUNK vs PAUL JONES

GRUDGE MATCH
BLACKJACK MULLIGAN vs TIM WOODS

MISSOURI MAULER & PROF. MALENKO vs STEVE KEIRN & TIGER CONWAY

ANGELO MOSKA versus THE AVENGER

SPOILER NO. 1 & 2 vs SWEDE HANSON and LARRY ZBYSZKO

KLONDIKE BILL versus TWO TON HARRIS ★ BILL WHITE versus PEPE LOPEZ

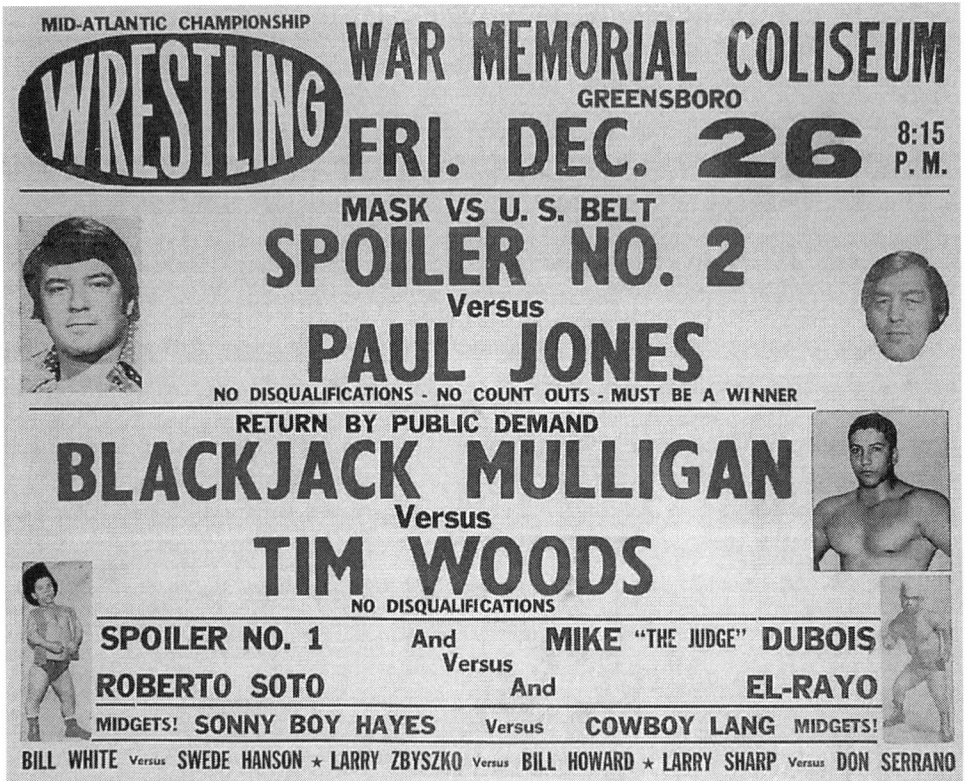

MID-ATLANTIC CHAMPIONSHIP WRESTLING
WAR MEMORIAL COLISEUM
GREENSBORO
FRI. DEC. 26 8:15 P.M.

MASK VS U.S. BELT
SPOILER NO. 2 versus PAUL JONES
NO DISQUALIFICATIONS - NO COUNT OUTS - MUST BE A WINNER

RETURN BY PUBLIC DEMAND
BLACKJACK MULLIGAN versus TIM WOODS
NO DISQUALIFICATIONS

SPOILER NO. 1 And MIKE "THE JUDGE" DUBOIS
Versus
ROBERTO SOTO And EL-RAYO

MIDGETS! SONNY BOY HAYES versus COWBOY LANG MIDGETS!

BILL WHITE versus SWEDE HANSON ★ LARRY ZBYSZKO versus BILL HOWARD ★ LARRY SHARP versus DON SERRANO

WRESTLING
GREENSBORO
THURS. JAN. 16
8:15 P.M.
LUMBERJACK ELIMINATION MATCH
SUPER DESTROYER & IVAN KOLOFF
Versus
PAUL JONES & WAHOO McDANIEL
SIX MAN TAG TEAM MATCH
OLE ANDERSON
GENE ANDERSON
RIC FLAIR
Vs
SWEDE HANSON
SANDY SCOTT
TIGER CONWAY, JR.
BRUTE BERNARD Vs BOB BRUGGERS
KEVIN SULLIVAN Vs MR. HAYASHI
STALLINGS Vs FRANK MONTE ★ COWBOY PARKER Vs JOE FURR ★ TIO TIO Vs KEN DILLINGER
WRESTLING
GREENSBORO
THUR. FEB. 20
WORLD HEAVYWEIGHT CHAMPIONSHIP
NO DISQUALIFICATIONS
WAHOO McDANIEL
Versus
JACK BRISCO
WORLD TAG TEAM MATCH
OLE & GENE ANDERSON
Versus
PAUL JONES And TIGER CONWAY, JR.
DUSTY RHODES Versus RIC FLAIR
JERRY BRISCO Versus COWBOY
KEN PATERA Versus ART NELSON
WRESTLING
WAR MEMORIAL COLISEUM
GREENSBORO
THUR. APR. 3
8:15 P.M.
DOUBLE MAIN EVENT
WORLD TAG TEAM MATCH
WAHOO McDANIEL & PAUL JONES
Versus
OLE ANDERSON & GENE ANDERSON
DUSTY RHODES Vs BLACKJACK MULLIGAN
RUFUS R. JONES & SONNY KING Versus MR. FUGI & ART NELSON
SUPER STAR BILL GRAHAM Versus ABE JACOBS
SANDY SCOTT Vs DOUG GILBERT ★ BOB BRUGGERS & TOMMY SEIGLER Vs KEN DILLENGER & COWBOY PARKER
MEMORIAL COLISEUM
GREENSBORO
JULY 3
8:15 P.M.
GIANT JONES
ANDERSON
CHAMPIONSHIP MATCH
HARLEY RACE
WAR MEMORIAL COLISEUM
GREENSBORO
SAT. JULY 2
U. S. HEAVYWEIGHT CHAMPIONSHIP
JOHNNY VALENTINE
Versus
HARLEY RACE
MID-ATLANTIC CHAMPIONSHIP
RIC FLAIR Vs WAHOO McDANIEL
MIXED-TAG TEAM MATCH
ROGER
SHEPARD
PROFESSOR BORIS MALENKO And MISSOURI MAULER
DOUG GILBERT Vs KLONDIKE BILL ★ TIM WOODS Vs MAN MT. BLACKWELL
MID-ATLANTIC CHAMPIONSHIP
WRESTLING
SUN. SEPT. 7
DOUBLE MAIN EVENT
U. S. HEAVYWEIGHT TITLE MATCH
JOHNNY VALENTINE
CHAMPION
Versus
DUSTY RHODES
TEXAS TORNADO ELIMINATION MATCH
OLE & GENE ANDERSON
WRESTLING
COLISEUM
GREENSBORO
SUN. NOV. 9
17 BIG MATCHES
U.S. CHAMPIONSHIP TOURNAMENT
WITH NAMES SUCH AS
RED BASTION
DUSTY RHODES
RUFUS R. JONES
OLE ANDERSON
RAY STEVENS
TERRY FUNK
GENE ANDERSON
STEVE STRONG
SUPER STAR BILLY GRAHAM
KEN PATERA
PAUL JONES
TIM WOODS
HARLEY RACE
BLACKJACK MULLIGAN
WAHOO McDANIEL
PROFESSOR MALENKO
TIGER CONWAY, JR.
MID-ATLANTIC CHAMPIONSHIP
WRESTLING
WAR MEMORIAL COLISEUM
GREENSBORO
THANKSGIVING DAY
THURS. NOV. 27
8:15 P.M.
WORLD HEAVYWEIGHT TITLE MATCH
NO DISQUALIFICATIONS
WAHOO McDANIEL VS JACK BRISCO
U.S. HEAVYWEIGHT TITLE MATCH
TERRY FUNK VS PAUL JONES
GRUDGE MATCH
BLACKJACK MULLIGAN Vs TIM WOODS
PAUL JONES
NO DISQUALIFICATIONS - NO COUNT OUTS - MUST BE A WINNER
RETURN BY PUBLIC DEMAND
BLACKJACK MULLIGAN
Versus

Mid-Atlantic Championship Wrestling Magazine

Volume One Issue Two

MAGAZINE

VOLUME NO. 1 **JIM CROCKETT PROMOTIONS, INC.** ISSUE NO. 2

MID-ATLANTIC WRESTLING 1975 YEARBOOK

SUPER DESTROYER

The Men In Jack Brisco's Life

When you think of a champion you may think of the glamour that goes with wearing the championship belt or perhaps the money that goes with each victory. But don't forget the pressure that is always present.

Jack Brisco is the N.W.A. Champion. For almost two years he has traveled around the globe putting his highly prized belt on the line against the world's best professional wrestlers. Each area offers at least one man who poses a serious threat to defeat the young champion from Oklahoma. No other section in the country however offers the challenge that looms in the Mid-Atlantic area. This area has three of the world's top "money wrestlers," and those are the hardest kind to beat. These three men loom as the world's top challengers. Their names are Wahoo McDaniel, Paul Jones, and Johnny Valentine and any one of them could turn Brisco's dream into a nightmare. These three men know the sweet taste of victory and have their eyes set on the championship crown. Brisco has become used to the life style of a winner and the fat paychecks that accompany each victory. He has no intention of losing his belt and will do anything to have his hand raised in victory. Some day Brisco's hold on the title belt will be broken and chances are it will happen right here in the Mid-Atlantic area.

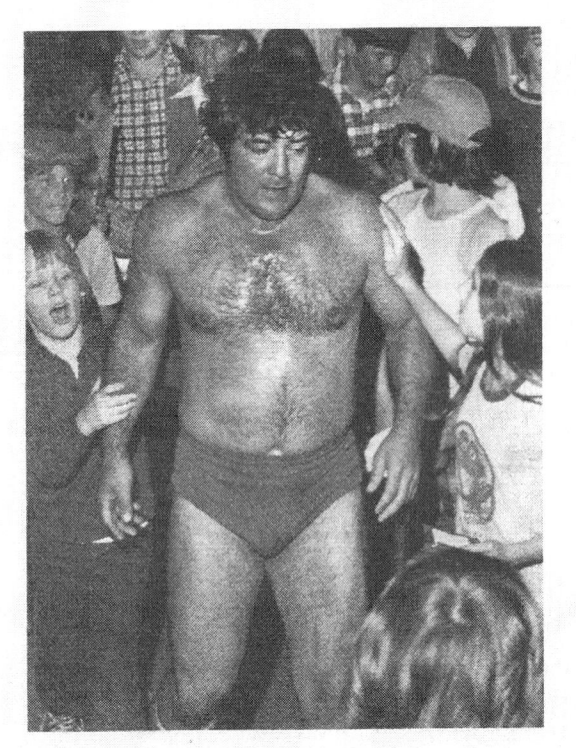

MID-ATLANTIC WRESTLING 1975 YEARBOOK

When you're Number 1, the fans flock to you

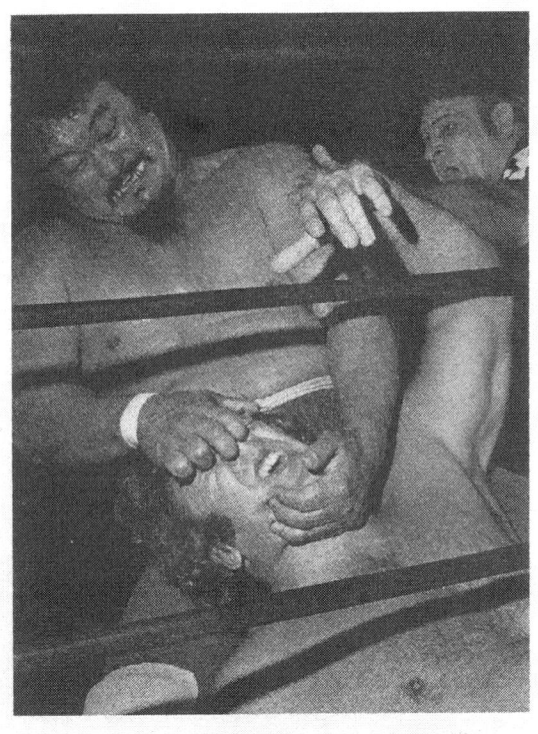

Mr. Fuji rips at the nose of his opponent

Destroyer and Patera carry their battle outside the ring

Doug Gilbert admires the arm of Ric Flair

Rufus R., He's a Star

"Rufus has come home to make some of those green bucks and plans on stayin' for a long while. This is my home and ain't nobody like Johnny Valentine or Destroyer going to run me away." Those were the remarks of the man from Dillon, S. C. who has come home after a whirlwind tour around the world. He plans to settle here for a while and enjoy his family.

The country boy from Dillon has come a long way since he left home seven years ago to enter professional wrestling. He started his career in Kansas City, Missouri and from there he has hit all the major wrestling cities in the world. Rufus has a win list over many of the top names in the sport. He is loved by fans wherever he travels. The city trappings are there. The big car, the fine suits, and the business interests outside wrestling. But through it all the "Good ole boy" still surfaces, and his down to earth approach to meeting people is a winner for him. As he says himself, "Baby, I loves to meet my fans, and rap with them. Those good folks are the ones that are cheerin' when I wrestles, and that sure makes me feel good." Jones may not be the smoothest grappler in the sport, but his style keeps his opponents off balance when they meet him in the ring. Since returning to this area he has picked up the nickname of "Freight Train" because of his train-like charge across the ring. Of course his head-butt is his number one weapon, and a lot of men have fallen before it.

Rufus R. Jones is a star, and to keep that rating in the Mid-Atlantic area he must stand up under some of the toughest wrestling the country has to offer. Men like the Anderson Brothers, The Super Destroyer, and Johnny Valentine will be out to knock him off, and in the process put another notch in their own gun. It will be a rough row to hoe, but if you've ever watched Jones before, then you know that he won't run from the challenge. He adds another star to the long list already in the area, and brings with him a flair for excitement.

MID-ATLANTIC WRESTLING 1975 YEARBOOK

SUPERSTAR Billy Graham poses for the fans

Kevin Sullivan drops on Steve Keirn

Blackjack Mulligan feels the Power of Wahoo's head lock

Jones tries to unmask the Super Destroyer

"Wrestler On The Rise"

When people talk about what it takes to be a top pro in any sport, they sometimes leave out the most important element. They mention size, ability, speed, and weight but they often forget desire.

Desire is what got Don Kernodle interested in amateur wrestling; desire is what made him good. Desire is what brought him to the attention of pro wrestling promoters, and desire will someday make him one of the top grapplers in the mat sport.

Don, at 5'11" and 230 pounds, had the raw material to be a wrestler when he entered Elon College in his home town of Burlington, North Carolina. The young fellow born under the sign of Taurus, was just that on the school wrestling mat. A bull! Upon ending an outstanding career in the college ranks, Kernodle was looking for a springboard into professional wrestling. He saw Bob Roop's two thousand dollar challenge on Raleigh's Mid-Atlantic Championship Wrestling and felt it would be a way to get some of the pros to take a look at him. If this was a fairytale, then we would tell you that Don defeated Roop, and pocketed the money, and went on to fame and fortune. But that was not the case. Don found out that it wasn't as easy as it looked, and lost to the ex-olympic star in five minutes. The promoters on hand for that TV program were impressed with this young man and talked to him about training for a pro career. Don will be the first to tell you that the next six months were the roughest in his life. Many times he wanted to call it quits, but that was where his desire came into play. Don Kernodle became a professional wrestler.

Now almost two years later he is moving steadily up the ladder toward the top. The victories are coming closer together, and as he meets tougher opponents the defeats are teaching him more. His idol is the World Champion, Jack Brisco, and he would like nothing better than to be the man to unseat the champ. The future is bright for Don, and as long as he keeps that all-important desire a star will someday hang on his door.

Wahoo puts the "STRETCH" on World Champion, Jack Brisco

BATTLE OF THE GIANTS—Black Jack Mulligan and Swede Hanson

Mr. Ota takes Bob Bruggers down by his arm

Brute Bernard and the "Super D" double-team Charlie Cook

I've Got A Lot Of Style!

The type of life style that Ric Flair represents goes back to Babe Ruth, Douglas Fairbanks, and maybe as far back as Don Juan. He lives in style, with each day another adventure. At twenty-six, when most young people are just getting started in their careers, Ric is already an established star. He drives a big black Caddy, eats the best foods, wears the finest clothes, and in general lives life to the fullest. He likes nothing better than to be recognized by a fan and if that fan happens to be a beautiful woman, then all the better. He is loud, brash, and a very colorful figure who is probably disliked by more fans than he cares to admit. But that doesn't seem to faze the big blond from Minneapolis. Many times the question comes up; *"Is Ric Flair all talk?"* The answer is, *"No, Ric Flair is for real!"*

If ever there was a natural at anything, it's Ric Flair at wrestling. Not only does he have all the tools of the trade, but they seem to flow together as one, and make this man a pure wrestling machine. "Nature Boy" has lined up a string of victories of the highest degree. Unless something unforseen stops him, this young man can go as far as he wants in professional wrestling. Ric likes to talk about Ric, and he has these comments to make: *"I am what every woman wants and every man wants to be. I am the main man! It's all together for me, and I'm headed to the top, nothing can stop me. I'm a child stealin', wheelin' dealin', Cadillac drivin' sonofagun. Line up the best at anything, and Ric can do it better. Do you know where I'm comin' from? I've got a lot of style. No, take that back, I am style!"*

Whether it's relaxing beside a swimming pool; riding a motorcycle; walking down the street; talking his talk; or flexing for the pretty ladies, Ric Flair does it in style. When he finally meets the World Champion, win or lose he'll do it in style!

MID-ATLANTIC WRESTLING 1975 YEARBOOK

Bob Bruggers has the advantage over Frank Monte

Tio-Tio tangles with Larry Sharpe

Jones and Valentine square off in one of their classic battles

Don Kernodle puts an end to his match with Frank Monte

TAG TEAM POWER!

Fans in the Mid-Atlantic area are cheering. It's not Christmas, so why all the racket? Well, two of their favorite people have done something big. Paul Jones and Wahoo McDaniel, "Number One" and "The Chief," call them what you want, are now wearing the belts that make them the World Tag Team Champions! They defeated the Anderson Brothers, Ole and Gene, in the Greensboro Coliseum. At this point in both their careers they are riding high. Jones and McDaniel have both been rated among the top contenders for the belt of World Heavyweight Champion, Jack Brisco. That alone would be enough for most men, but not this fearsome twosome.

For a lot of years these two have been at the top of singles wrestling. Both have long and impressive win records. They have wrestled in tag teams, but have never stayed with it for any length of time. Several months ago they formed a team and on their first outing together the experts saw the handwriting on the wall. They blended well together, knocking off some of the toughest tandems in the area. Paul and Wahoo were tuned into one another and when they entered the squared circle things began to happen. The biggest happening was that night in Greensboro when they aced the top tag team in the world for their title belts. What more could they want? Nothing, you say! Not true. They both still want a shot at Jack Brisco, and if one of them were to beat him, then they would have pulled off something that has never been done in professional wrestling. Holding two world titles at the same time!!! On the other hand they will have to work hard defending the tag title they now hold. Many great teams will be knocking at their door and the one knocking the hardest will be Ole and Gene Anderson. The "Wrecking Crew" doesn't give up easily. From this point on we'll see what Jones and McDaniel are made of. For now they are the tag team power. They wear the belts. But now the fight for Paul Jones and Wahoo McDaniel has just begun!

TV WRESTLING
"Behind The Scenes"

The most popular television programs in the southeast is Mid-Atlantic Championship Wrestling. So popular in fact, that now there are two Mid-Atlantic Wrestling programs! The matches are taped at the studios of WRAL-TV, Channel 5 in Raleigh North Carolina, and with the use of the WRAL mobile unit in some of the wrestling arenas in the Carolinas, and Virginia. Some of the photos on these two pages will give you an inside look at what goes on before the finished product is seen on your TV screen. That one-hour program is put together by the very capable production crew of Channel 5.

You see your favorites introduced in the ring by either David Crockett or Joe Murnick. You see them interviewed by Elliott Murnick, or David Crockett, and the hosts of these two great programs are either WRAL newsman Bob Caudle, or wrestler turned commentator Les Thatcher, who both double up on the interviews from time to time. From the team of men above you get great coverage of the best professional wrestling in the country. No matter which program you watch, Bob's or Les', you are seeing the major league of wrestling presented to you in a first-class manner.

Les Thatcher and Bob Caudle

David Crockett and Bob Caudle at their desk preparing to open their program

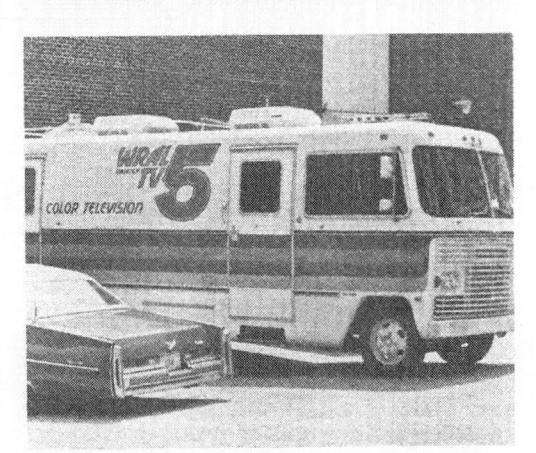

When you spot this mobile unit at a wrestling arena, WAVE! You'll be on TV!

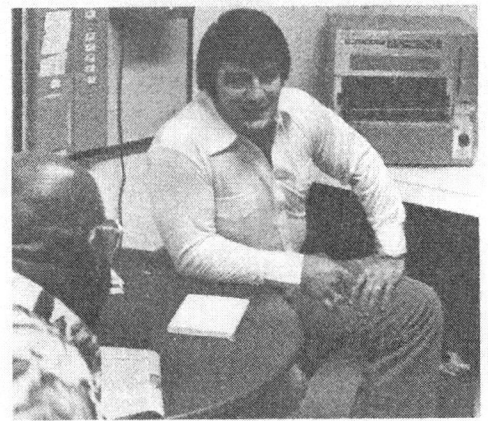

Paul Jones talks with Sonny King, while waiting to be interviewed

MID-ATLANTIC WRESTLING 1975 YEARBOOK

Wahoo listens in, and checks his fan mail, while waiting his turn at the microphone

In another part of the station Johnny Valentine looks over his FAN? MAIL

All systems are "GO" as Bob and David open the program

Joe Murnick introduces the wrestlers, and MID-ATLANTIC WRESTLING is on the air!

Ric Flair and Black Jack Mulligan watch the program from another studio

This is the type of action picked up by the Channel 5 Mobile Unit—a Wahoo-Brisco Title Match

MID-ATLANTIC WRESTLING 1975 YEARBOOK

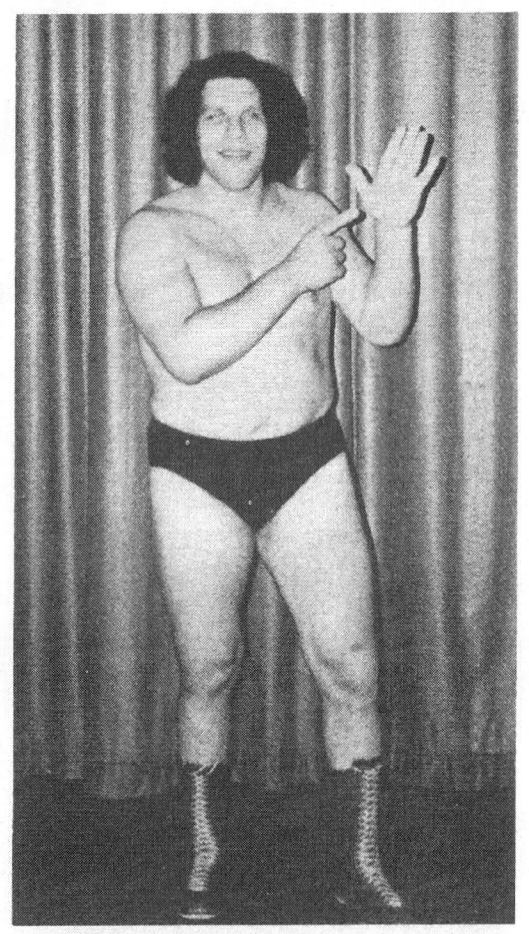

Andre the Giant—the biggest man in pro sports

Bill Crouch gives an elbow to Steve Keirn—Two of Wrestling's future STARS

One of the huge crowds to watch MID-ATLANTIC CHAMPIONSHIP WRESTLING—This one in Charlotte's Memorial Stadium

Parker holds Jacobs, as Nelson makes a crash landing

SPECIAL OFFER FROM BUTCH HARRIS LURES

The SENSATIONAL NEW FASBAK BASS PLUG

for only $2.25

This new plug runs deep where the big bass stay in 12'-15' of water. Fish the FASBAK in any of 4 ways:

1. The FASBAK is a deadly top water plug and can be pulled slowly across the surface.
2. Give the FASBAK a yank and several fast cranks to make it dive. Stop. Let it surface and do it again.
3. Reel it in at a constant speed either fast or slow and it runs at a depth that you can determine.
4. Troll it behind a boat and it runs deep, deeper, and deepest.

Send $2.00 plus 25¢ for shipping and handling to:
BUTCH HARRIS BASS LURES
421 Briarbend Drive, Charlotte, N. C. 28209

Enclosed is my check or money order for $ _____
Please send _____ Butch Harris Bass Lures
Name _____
Address _____
City _____ State _____ Zip _____

Offer Expires August 31, 1975

Check surface color desired
☐ Chad
☐ Blue
☐ Chartreuse
☐ Pike

MID-ATLANTIC WRESTLING 1975 YEARBOOK

RUFUS R. JONES

Q3 HISTORY
by David Chappell

JULY

July of 1975 was the most significant month of the year 1975 to date. July featured record crowds and gates in several Mid-Atlantic towns, a new title introduced to the area, significant roster movement and the blossoming of one of the greatest feuds in Mid-Atlantic Championship Wrestling history. All in all, July of 1975 was quite a month.

The month began with Andre the Giant continuing his swing through the area, which had begun in late June. The Giant's presence no doubt contributed to record gates in two of the area's most significant towns. Columbia, South Carolina set a record in its gate receipts for its July 1, 1975 card headlined by a spectacular bout between Andre and Wahoo McDaniel against Ric Flair and Johnny Valentine. Richmond, Virginia set a gate record as well from its super holiday card at the Richmond Coliseum on July 4, 1975 headlined by a 60 minute draw between NWA World Tag Team Champions Gene and Ole Anderson and challengers Wahoo McDaniel and Paul Jones, with a semi-final dream match-up of Andre The Giant against the Super Destroyer. Additionally, Greenville, South Carolina had a sellout crowd for its July 7, 1975 card featuring Andre, Paul Jones and Rufus R. Jones against the Anderson's and the Super Destroyer.

CHAMPIONSHIPS

Also early in July, a major new NWA Title found its home in the Mid-Atlantic area. On July 3, 1975, Harley Race defended the United States Heavyweight Championship against Mid-Atlantic Heavyweight Champion Johnny Valentine in the Greensboro Coliseum. After a titanic battle between these two legends, Valentine emerged victorious, and the U.S. Title would become and remain the territory's prized singles championship for the duration of the promotion.

Valentine would wrestle Race in a classic rematch in Greensboro for the U.S. Title on July 26, 1975. In another memorable bout, Valentine again prevailed and the United States Title stayed safely in the Crockett territory.

The "Nature Boy" Ric Flair continued to hold onto his Mid-Atlantic TV Title in July, but Paul Jones was starting to close in fast. On July 18th, Flair and Jones had a brutal Lumberjack Match in Richmond for Ric's TV Title, and Jones came so very close to winning the belt. This led to a climatic rematch in Richmond three weeks later between these two for the Mid-Atlantic TV Title.

That same July 18, 1975 card in Richmond saw the one-night return of Blackjack Mulligan for a brutal Texas Death Match against Wahoo McDaniel. Despite being a regular in the WWWF at the time, Blackjack came down I-95 South to try to avenge a beating he took from Wahoo in May in Richmond during an Indian Strap Match. Mulligan said an Indian Strap Match was thought up by savages, and that a Texas Death Match was where real men settled their differences. In his promo for the match, Blackjack asked if Wahoo was "man enough" to face him in a Texas Death Match. The answer was a resounding "Yes," as after quite a battle Wahoo defeated Mulligan once again.

The NWA World Heavyweight Championship was not actively defended in the area in July, as Champion Jack Brisco made only one defense during the month---that being against Wahoo McDaniel in Asheville, North Carolina on July 20, 1975.

But the NWA World Tag Team Titles could not have been more actively defended during the month of July. In addition to the Richmond 60 minute draw noted earlier, the champion Anderson Brothers wrestled Paul Jones and Wahoo McDaniel to several other 60 minute time-limit draws across the area in memorable matches during July. Then, in Raleigh on July 22nd, the time limit between these four was extended to 90 minutes! The 90 minute battles between these two amazing teams would soon spread around the territory like a summer wildfire out of control! And it was!

ROSTER CHANGES

July produced some significant roster movement in the area. Sonny King, who was a Main Event performer for the previous year, left the area in early July. King's last match in the area was against Mr. Fuji in Anderson, South Carolina on July 10, 1975.

Coincidentally, King's main rival for much of his Mid-Atlantic stay, the Super Destroyer, also saw the month of July spell the effective end of his stay in the Mid-Atlantic area after nearly two years.

United States Heavyweight Champion Harley Race (Original Art by John Pagan)

Unable to agree with the promotion on his role and direction in the Company, the Super D. and Mid-Atlantic Championship Wrestling parted ways forever on July 16, 1975. The Super Destroyer would finish out his remaining dates with the promotion through August 1, 1975.

Three noteworthy additions entered the area in July of 1975. Muscleman Tony White of Roanoke, Virginia made his debut on July 12, 1975 in Spartanburg, South Carolina. Called Tony Atlas by the promotion, Atlas amazed everyone with his tremendous bodybuilding physique at the outset, and settled into a solid mid card role for the rest of the year.

After a lengthy absence, the Missouri Mauler Larry Hamilton returned to the area on July 21st in Greenville. Almost immediately, the Mauler teamed up with Professor Boris Malenko---their first match together was on the Mid-Atlantic television taping on July 23rd from the WRAL TV studios in Raleigh. Malenko and Mauler would be a team to be reckoned with for the remainder of 1975.

Another veteran returning to the area in July was Tim Woods. Not wearing his "Mr. Wrestling" hood, Woods returned on July 26th in Greensboro against the mammoth Jerry Blackwell. Woods came back to Mid-Atlantic Wrestling because he was bent on revenge against Johnny Valentine for breaking his leg some time back. Woods was intent on paying Valentine back, and their feud against each other would begin in earnest during the upcoming month of August 1975. Mid-Atlantic Championship Wrestling in August of 1975 was shaping up to be as hot as the weather was outside!

WHO'S HOT

1. TONY ATLAS---The strongman from Roanoke, Virginia impressed everybody with his amazing physique and strength. But could the youngster stand up against all the experience and talent in the area?

2. MISSOURI MAULER---The Mauler came back to the territory with a vengeance, and looked better than ever. He quickly teamed with another recent returnee to the area, Professor Boris Malenko, to form an impressive tag team combination.

3. KEN PATERA---Patera continued his steady climb to the top of the Mid-Atlantic rankings. Combining amazing strength and growing experience, Patera rightfully received some of the first shots at Johnny Valentine's new United States Heavyweight Championship.

WHO'S NOT

1. SONNY KING---Sonny King wins this award two months running! After a strong stint in the area for a year, King left the territory for good in early July. King's best moments in the area were likely in the beginning of his run in 1974, rather than at the end of it in 1975.

2. SUPER DESTROYER---Unhappy over how he was being used, the Super D. and the promotion agreed to part ways in July. An inglorious way for such a great run to end. However,

strangely enough, it would get even worse for the Super Destroyer after he left the area!

    3.   ART NELSON---A big star with the promotion in the early 70s, Nelson's slide down the area's ladder continued in July. His solid tag team partnership with Mr. Fuji was also nearing its end.

AUGUST

The month of August 1975 started off in an eventful fashion in both the northern and southern ends of the Mid-Atlantic area. In the southernmost portion of the territory, the Super Destroyer wrestled his final match for Jim Crockett Promotions on August 1, 1975 in Charleston, South Carolina. By the end of the month of August, there would be an unusual television "unmasking" of the Super Destroyer by Rufus R. Jones, and mere days after that happened, a huge masked newcomer arrived in the area whose express purpose in coming to the area was to exact revenge on behalf of the departed and exposed Super Destroyer.

CHAMPIONSHIPS

At the other geographical end of the territory, August 1, 1975 saw a tremendous 90 minute draw between NWA World Tag Team Champions Gene and Ole Anderson and challengers Wahoo McDaniel and Paul Jones in Richmond, Virginia. A number of these 90 minute classics were repeated in early and mid August across the area. By the end of August, the time limit for championship bouts between these two teams had been extended at times to an amazing two hours, and matches with two hour time limits occurred in a number of the larger Mid-Atlantic venues, including Columbia, Greenville and Richmond. It's no stretch to say that these battles in August between the Anderson's and Jones and Wahoo were some of the greatest tag team bouts in wrestling history.

Richmond was not only the site of two classic tag team battles in August, but it was also the site of the area's only title change in the month of August. On August 8, 1975 in the Richmond Arena, Paul Jones defeated Ric Flair for the coveted Mid-Atlantic Television Title. The stipulation for this bout was that Jones would have his head shaved if he didn't win the title. To avoid that indignity, Jones had to wrestle a near perfect match---and he managed to pull it off. Jones' victory ended a six month back and forth battle over the TV Title with Flair. The Nature Boy proved to be a formidable holder of the TV belt---his first singles title. Jones' first defense of his newly won TV Title was on August 16th in Spartanburg, South Carolina against the Missouri Mauler.

United States Heavyweight Champion Johnny Valentine was active in the month of August, which was the first month that he defended his U.S. belt for an entire month's time. Valentine had a variety of opponents in August, but two opponents that gave him a difficult time were Ken Patera and

Rufus R. "Freight Train" Jones. Patera's strength gave Valentine some real fits early in the month of August. Later in the month of August, the unorthodox style of the "Freight Train" gave Valentine some anxious moments as well. But, through it all, Valentine would retain the U.S belt without interruption throughout August.

Wahoo McDaniel had perhaps the busiest month of anybody during the month of August. In addition to pursuing the World Tag Team Titles, the Chief had several superlative matches in August for the U.S. Title against old nemesis Johnny Valentine. During the month, the Chief also had a number of successful defenses of his newly captured Mid-Atlantic Heavyweight Title against the likes of Ric Flair and Ole Anderson.

While Gene and Ole Anderson had a number of classic bouts with Wahoo and Paul Jones during the month of August 1975, they also had some issues with the NWA arise over their in-ring behavior. In early August, the NWA fined both Gene and Ole $500 each for continually punishing an opponent after the final bell. As part of the NWA's sanction, the Anderson's were also prohibited from appearing on Mid-Atlantic Championship Wrestling television programming for two weeks. During this time, the Anderson's made a brief appearance in Florida before returning to Mid-Atlantic TV to denounce the NWA's penalty against them.

OTHER FEUDS

The new tag team of Professor Boris Malenko and the Missouri Mauler was extremely impressive during the month of August. With Malenko's "Russian Sickle" and the Mauler's "Missouri Knee Drop," it was clear that it would take a supreme effort from any of the area's best to knock this duo off. As the month was winding down, the Mauler and Malenko were beginning to face tougher competition. Malenko was also active in the singles ranks during August. On the August 20th taping of the Mid-Atlantic TV show, the "Professor" ripped and tore up Ken Patera's ear, causing a large gash requiring stitches. On August 23rd, Malenko had his patented "Russian Chain Match" against Rufus R. Jones, in Jones' backyard of Florence, South Carolina.

The top singles feud that played out in August was between "Mr. Wrestling" Tim Woods and U.S. Champion Johnny Valentine. Woods was seeking revenge for Valentine previously breaking his leg in a leg hold. Woods' challenge concerned Valentine so much that "The Champ" put a Bounty on Woods' head in August so he wouldn't have to get into the ring with the raging Woods. The primary bounty hunter early on was Valentine's good friend, Ric Flair.

In the middle of the month, it appeared that Woods was about to get his revenge against Valentine. In a match between the two, Woods had Valentine in the figure four leg lock in the middle of the ring with nowhere for Valentine to go. Woods was determined to keep the hold on Valentine until Valentine's leg was broken just the same way Johnny had done to Woods months earlier. But Ric Flair came to the ring to bail Valentine out, and then both of them were able to double team Woods. Woods called both Flair and Valentine cowards, and this feud was really heating up by month's end.

THE UNMASKING OF THE SUPER DESTROYER

While the Super Destroyer wrestled his last match in Mid-Atlantic Championship Wrestling on August 1st, he was back in the forefront of Mid-Atlantic Wrestling by the end of the month. And in an extremely unusual way. At the Mid-Atlantic Championship Wrestling television taping on August 20th, Rufus R. Jones came out and told the area's TV audience that he, Wahoo McDaniel and Paul Jones had unmasked the Super Destroyer. If that wasn't shocking enough, a large picture of the Super Destroyer without the mask on was put on the television screen. In a final indignity for the Super Destroyer, announcer Bob Caudle told the viewing audience that the Super Destroyer's real name was Don Jardine. Rufus Jones confirmed that, and laughingly told Caudle that the picture shown was the Super Destroyer, "the ol' cotton picker." Jones said the Super Destroyer was so embarrassed by being unmasked that he left the area and kept going.

It didn't take long for there to be repercussions from this TV "unmasking" of the Super Destroyer. On August 26, 1975, a mammoth masked newcomer named Spoiler # 2 made his Mid-Atlantic Championship Wrestling debut in Roanoke Rapids, North Carolina. On this night, Spoiler # 2 wrestled Rufus R. Jones, the man who had come on TV and made a mockery of the Super Destroyer.

We would soon learn that Spoiler # 2 came to the Mid-Atlantic area expressly to get revenge for his friend the Super Destroyer against the "good guys" led by Rufus R. Jones that had ended the Super Destroyer's Mid-Atlantic stint. Weighing 345 pounds but being amazingly agile with a devastating Stomach Claw as his finishing move, Spoiler # 2 presented a major threat to all the territory's fan favorites. Spoiler # 2 would soon bring in a masked partner, Spoiler # 1, and the tag teams in the area would not be safe either. Nobody knew who Spoiler # 2 was, but everybody knew that he was trouble. The new month of September would soon give us an idea of just how much havoc Spoiler # 2 could wreck.

WHO'S HOT

1. PAUL JONES---After months of chasing Ric Flair, Jones finally regaining his Mid-Atlantic TV Title from his young foe. "Number One" had to put his hair on the line to get the job done, but he rose to the occasion. Jones' victory on August 8th effectively ended this spirited feud between he and Flair over the Television Title.

2. TIM WOODS---"Mr. Wrestling" was unrelenting in his quest for revenge against Johnny Valentine for "The Champ" injuring him a number of months previously. Even a "Bounty" placed on his head by Valentine would not deter Woods. "Mr. Wrestling" vowed to go through any bounty hunters, and to eventually get Valentine. At this point, nobody was betting against Woods.

3. PROFESSOR BORIS MALENKO & MISSOURI MAULER---This team made steady strides throughout the month of August, and was becoming a force to be reckoned with in the tag team division. As the level of competition picked up for this duo, it remained to be seen how high their ascension would go.

WHO'S NOT

1. THE SUPER DESTROYER---After wrestling his last match for the promotion on August 1st, the Super Destroyer was later unceremoniously unmasked on TV by Rufus R. Jones by way of a photograph towards the end of the month. An embarrassing end for an outstanding competitor. But, by the end of the month, Spoiler # 2 had come on the Mid-Atlantic scene and was out for revenge for his fellow masked man, and friend, the Super Destroyer.

2. RIC FLAIR---The Nature Boy dropped the Mid-Atlantic TV Title to Paul Jones in early August, and was unsuccessful in his efforts to wrest the Mid-Atlantic Heavyweight Title from Wahoo McDaniel. Towards the end of the month, Ric became Johnny Valentine's chief bounty hunter against Tim Woods.

3. SWEDE HANSON---The big Swede continued his descent down cards through the month of August, which really had gradually been occurring throughout the year of 1975. While Swede was a formidable opponent for anyone, his victories were becoming less and less frequent.

SEPTEMBER

The month of September 1975 brought its share of thrills and upsets around the Mid-Atlantic area. And at the time, nobody would have ever guessed that this was the last full month that United States Heavyweight Champion Johnny Valentine would ever wrestle. September was also building for a number of terrific fall programs and angles in the territory. Unfortunately, the tragic airplane crash on October 4, 1975 in Wilmington, NC derailed many of those plans forever, while others were delayed while the promotion attempted to regroup in the aftermath of that fateful night in Wilmington.

September saw the return of two huge stars to the area, after prolonged absences. Both of these wrestlers were great main event stars from the past, but their returns would see them in reduced, though still important roles. Mike "The Judge" DuBois made his return to the Mid-Atlantic area after an absence of several years, on September 8, 1975 in Charlotte against the masked Avenger. Even better known to area fans, Johnny Weaver made his return to the area after being away the whole year of 1975, on Mid-Atlantic television taped in Raleigh on September 24, 1975 in a match against Joe Soto. Both these former main event stars settled into mid card roles, but it was still great to see these competitors back, and often times wrestling against each other again!

JOHNNY VALENTINE & THE BOUNTY ON TIM WOODS

There were few guest appearances in the area during September, but one big name who was headed to the area was that of Ray Stevens. On the September 10, 1975 taping of the Mid-Atlantic Championship Wrestling television show in Raleigh, a tape was shown to the area audience of the great Ray Stevens. And Stevens was put on a terrific card at the Greensboro Coliseum on September 28, 1975, where he was paired against Tim Woods in a Bounty Match.

Woods had to endure a number of Bounty Matches during the month of September, as the Bounty that Johnny Valentine had put on him was still in effect. The primary pursuer of the Bounty was "Nature Boy" Ric Flair, though Woods had to face other Bounty seekers during the month, including the rugged Gene Anderson. However, as the month wore on, there were more and more matches between Valentine himself and Woods, which were some of the fiercest that the territory had seen in a long while, as Woods was determined to exact revenge against Valentine for breaking his leg earlier. One can only speculate how torrid this feud between Woods and Valentine would have become, if not ended prematurely by Valentine's injury in the October 1975 plane crash.

In addition to holding off the enraged Woods, Valentine had a busy month of successful U.S. Title defenses in the month of September. Valentine turned back extremely tough challenges from Wahoo McDaniel, Paul Jones and Rufus R. Jones in September, maintaining his grip on the United States Title, and looking as determined as ever to keep it as long as he kept the Mid-Atlantic Heavyweight Title before.

FLAIR DEFEATS WAHOO FOR THE MID-ATLANTIC TITLE

Speaking of the Mid-Atlantic Heavyweight Championship, September of 1975 saw a major happening regarding this Title. Champion Wahoo McDaniel met Ric Flair at the Hampton Coliseum on September 20, 1975, putting his Title on the line against Flair's hair. Wahoo said he would send Ric home bald headed and make him "the laughing stock of the world," while Ric vowed Wahoo would have to kill him to take his "million dollar head of hair." Flair got the last laugh, defeating Wahoo with the aid of a pair of brass knucks, and walked out with the prestigious Mid-Atlantic Heavyweight Title. Ric didn't have long before his first title defense, facing Wahoo in a rematch for the title on September 22, 1975 in Conway, SC.

THE ANDERSON BROTHERS REMAIN DOMINANT

Paul Jones had a limited number of defenses of his Mid-Atlantic Television Title during the month of September, but they were all successful defenses. Paul battled his nemesis's Gene and Ole Anderson in several memorable singles encounters, with his TV Title at stake during the month. These bouts were every bit as brutal as his tag team battles with Wahoo as his partner against the Andersons.

September did mark the effective end of the monumental feud between Gene and Ole Anderson against Wahoo McDaniel and Paul Jones for the NWA World Tag Team Titles. Particularly early in September, there were continued epic battles between these four combatants around the territory, in two hour time limit, two referee and Texas Tornado specialty matches. The Anderson's slowly began to seize control of this program by mid month, but then a new and very surprising challenge presented itself to Gene and Ole!

On the September 17, 1975 taping of the Mid-Atlantic Championship Wrestling TV show, Gene and Ole Anderson wrestled the upstart duo of Tiger Conway and Steve Keirn. In one of the most stunning upsets in the history of Mid-Atlantic Wrestling on TV, and in front of one of the most raucous TV studio crowds ever, Keirn and Conway defeated the Anderson's cleanly to the shock of nearly everyone watching. The match was a non-title bout, and the Anderson's thus left WRAL still with the World Tag Team Titles…but the damage had been done. This amazing upset win propelled Keirn and Conway to a two month program against the Anderson's, where the youngsters gave the veteran duo all they could handle. The ascendance of Keirn and Conway also for all intents and purposes ended the Anderson's program with Wahoo and Paul Jones---one of the greatest tag team feuds anywhere at anytime.

The team of the Missouri Mauler and "Professor" Boris Malenko had another strong month in September. Malenko also continued to feud with Olympic strongman Ken Patera during the month in several tough matches, where Patera was trying to get even from the incident on TV earlier where Malenko bit his ear, leaving Patera "swimming in blood."

Spoiler # 2 continued to wreak havoc in the area during September, and lo and behold by the end of the month, he was joined by a tag team partner, Spoiler # 1. The masked Spoilers # 1 and # 2 had their debut match as a team in Spartanburg, SC on September 27, 1975 against Ken Patera and Bob Bruggers. There was no question that this new masked tandem meant business, and was trouble for any and everybody.

September of 1975 was an outstanding month for the Mid-Atlantic promotion, and October was looked forward to with much anticipation and excitement. No one in their worst nightmares could have predicted what October of 1975 held in store for Jim Crockett Promotions. The coming month would be the most chaotic in the promotion's history, with the territory's future in so many ways cloudy, murky and completely up in the air.

WHO'S HOT

Ric Flair---The "Nature Boy" beat Wahoo for the Mid-Atlantic Heavyweight Title in his biggest win to date. There may have been controversy in the way he did it, but there was no doubt that Ric Flair had made believers of everyone after taking the belt way from the great Wahoo…saving his hair in the process.

Steve Keirn & Tiger Conway---These guys beat the Anderson's on TV…cleanly! Even after it happened, nobody believed it. But Keirn and Conway were determined to prove that win on TV was no fluke.

Spoiler #2---The big masked man continued to dominate the competition in September. And now he gets a partner---Spoiler # 1!

WHO'S NOT

Wahoo McDaniel---Not often that we see the Big Chief in this position, but he lost his Mid-Atlantic Title during the month, and he and Paul Jones ultimately came out on the short end of the epic feud with Gene and Ole Anderson.

Gene and Ole Anderson---Not often are these two in this position either! BUT, they lost on TV to the upstarts Keirn and Conway! And neither could take the TV Title away from Paul Jones. The Anderson's definitely had better months than September of 1975.

Art Nelson---The former main event star for many years with Jim Crockett Promotions, dropped into the "opening card" category for the first time in September. In two more months, Nelson would leave the area for good.

Logos for the two television programs for Jim Crockett Promotions in 1975: *Mid-Atlantic Championship Wrestling* and *Wide World Wrestling*.

Wide World Wrestling debuted in October of 1975.

Mid-Atlantic Championship Wrestling Magazine

Volume One Issue Three

MID-ATLANTIC WRESTLING 1975 YEARBOOK

MAGAZINE

VOLUME NO. 1 — JIM CROCKETT PROMOTIONS, INC. — ISSUE NO. 3

1975 N.W.A.
OFFICIAL WRESTLING RULES
AS SANCTIONED BY
NATIONAL WRESTLING ALLIANCE

MAJOR RULE CHANGES

The count on the floor is no longer 20, but has been changed to a 10 count. The rule went into effect August 11, 1973. Intentional striking of referee will result in an automatic disqualification or suspension.

1. No hair pulling, eye gouging, strangle holds, or biting.
2. No pulling of trunks, masks, or any other equipment.
3. No straight punches or kicks with point of toe.

NOTE: Contestants who repeatedly violate any of the above rules will be disqualified. The following violations are automatic disqualification:

1. Throwing opponent over top rope.
2. Karate thrusts to the throat.
3. The piledriver hold.
4. Failing to break an illegal hold before the referee's FIVE COUNT.
5. The use of any foreign object.
6. Any interference with the duties of the referee.
7. Continuing to abuse a defeated opponent.
8. Any interference by managers, seconds, or corner men.
9. Tag team save rule: automatic disqualification when one team member saves another on any sure pinning or submission combination more than once.
10. No intentional punching or kicking in the groin or kidney area.

The following maneuvers are legal:

1. Judo chops, forearm blows, bolo punches, instep and flat-of-foot kicks.
2. The use of the ropes to gain leverage—contestants may spring against ropes as in tackles and other such maneuvers providing the contact with the rope is momentary.
3. It is legal to continue wrestling your opponent until he is clearly entangled in ropes and referee calls for a break (wrestlers cautioned to protect themselves on the break).

Contestants will get 10 counts on the apron of the ring and 10 on the floor.

Championships cannot change hands when the victory is gained by disqualification or count-out.

In any situation not covered by these rules, the N.W.A. will honor the judgment and discretion of the appointed referee.

NOTE: MATCHES SUBJECT TO CHANGE WITHOUT NOTICE DUE TO CONDITIONS BEYOND CONTROL, SUCH AS INJURIES, ILLNESS OR ACCIDENT.

REWARD
$50.00

For information leading to the arrest and conviction of persons throwing objects in the arena during wrestling matches.

MR. NICE GUY

So you haven't seen Andy Hardy since the last time you saw Mickey Rooney and Judy Garland do their thing on the late late show! Well, Andy is alive and well and wrestling in the Mid-Atlantic area. This Andy makes Mickey look like a midget, as he stands 6'4" and tips the scales at 260 lbs. None the less, he could fill the part.

Danny Miller was born and raised in a nice midwestern town and may have had some of the problems that the movie Andy had as a teenager. That is, if he had the time between excelling in high school football, baseball and wrestling. If he had any problems, they never stopped him from going on to Ohio State and playing football under the legendary Woody Hayes, and leading his wrestling team in Big Ten meets. "Woody taught me a lot and not just about football," Miller says. "He had a winning philosophy that just seemed to rub off." At the end of his college career it was only natural for Danny to turn to professional wrestling. His old brother, "Big Bill," had preceeded him to that profession a few years earlier. With the help and training of his brother the young man from Fremont, Ohio was on his way. It wasn't an easy road because everyone expected a great deal from "Bill's little brother." With the hard headed drive of his German ancestors Danny quickly made wrestling fans take notice. He aced the Texas State Championship to begin a brilliant career.

He has held the Florida State title and at one time shared the World Tag Team title with his brother. He entered the Mid-Atlantic wrestling area for the first time in 1971 and in short order won the Mid-Atlantic Heavyweight Championship. Danny has just completed a tour of the Western United States and Japan. He is now ready to jump into the thick of the toughest gathering of wrestlers in the world. The popular young man is a real hit with the fans. He is "Mr. Nice Guy" unless you are looking at him from across a wrestling ring!

MID-ATLANTIC WRESTLING 1975 YEARBOOK

The New Mid-Atlantic Heavyweight Champion, Wahoo McDaniel

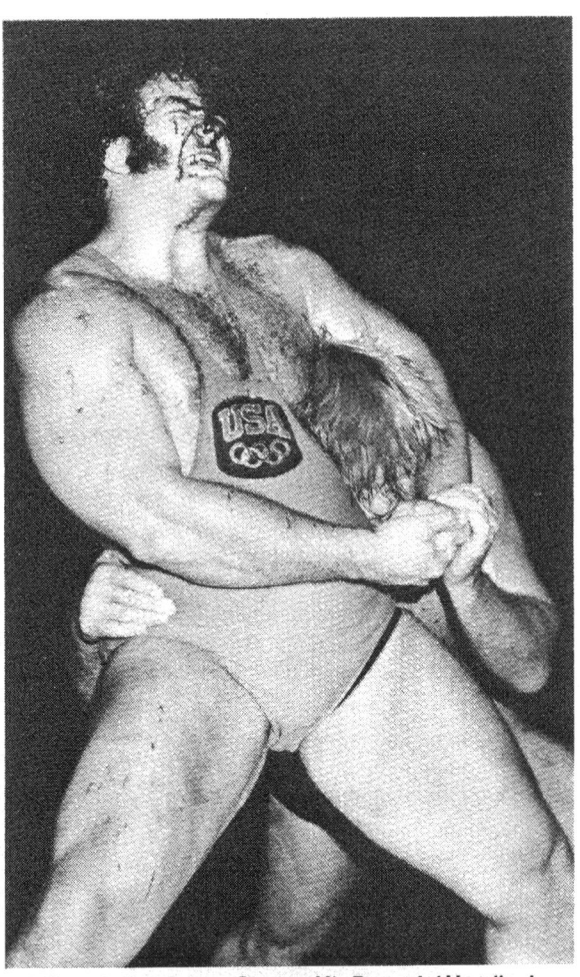

A Bloody Ken Patera Clamps His Powerful Headlock on Johnny Valentine

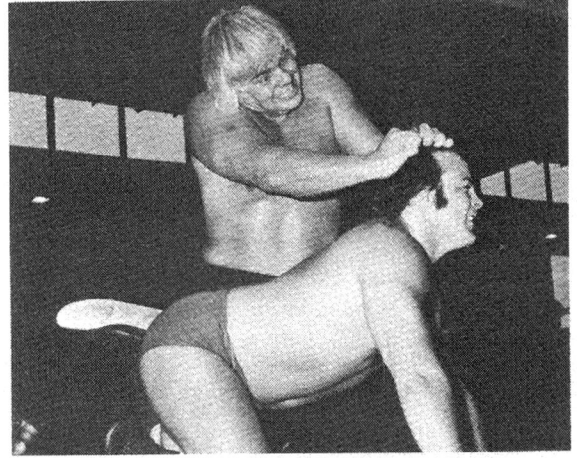

Larry Sharpe Yanks At the Hair of Kevin Sullivan

Wahoo Sends Ole Reeling With His Tomahawk Chop

NOT JUST ANOTHER PRETTY FACE

Professor Boris Malenko has returned to the wrestling wars in the Mid-Atlantic area. This man is no stranger to wars. They have been a part of his life since he was child growing up in war-torn Germany. It was tough growing up in Germany during the war, but even tougher if you were of Russian heritage. However, Malenko survived and returned to his native Russia to attend Leningrad University. During his teen years, while in college, Boris took up the sport of wrestling. He found the amateur sport very frustrating and so did the men who attempted to coach his early efforts. "This Malenko has all the skill and determination one could ask for," remarked an early trainer, "but he forfeits so many points on fouls and is so often disqualified that it reflects badly on the young man and his team."

Having acquired a basic knowledge of the wrestling science the young Russian decided to try the pro ranks. Shortly after arriving in the United States he began to mow down the toughest competitors. As a wrestler he is no "purist," but he certainly does have winning ways. Arriving on the scene just a few weeks after Malenko's return was his sidekick and former tag team partner, "The Missouri Mauler." They have teamed up once again and have plans to stand at the top of tag team wrestling. "My comrade and myself are the greatest wrestling machines in the sport," says The Professor. "We will rule tag team wrestling in the world before long. I am extremely well-read and pride myself on intellectual accomplishments as well as athletic achievements. I also enjoy classical music and other exotic pastimes. I dominate the most rugged game in professional sports, wrestling! You fans, clean yourselves up and come pay your respects to me in the wrestling arenas. You will watch me beat my opponents, then cheer me as I leave the ring. After all, I'm not just another pretty face!"

A STARR IS RISING!

Every year hundreds of young wrestling hopefuls try to make it into the pro ranks but only a handful make the grade and out of these only a few ever make it into the national spotlight. Most, however, are seen listed under the heading on wrestling ads around the country as "Plus Other Bouts." This will never be the fate of one young Georgia man if he has anything to say about it.

Ron Starr will make the wrestling world sit up and take notice. He is a young man in a hurry, brash, even bordering on cocky at times. If he were to be World Champion tomorrow, it wouldn't be soon enough for him. He has chosen a field and wants to get to the top in the fastest way possible. He began wrestling in high school and then moved on to the University of Georgia where he was a stand-out. Starr turned pro about three years ago. He stands 6'1" and weighs 228 lbs. The speed with which he wanted to climb to the top caused him some trouble in the early stages of his career. Doing things too quickly in a wrestling ring can cause you to make mistakes and Ron made his share. Soon he saw what he was doing and began to realize his mistakes. He gained control of his emotions and now is handling a grappling machine with speed in reserve. Once in a while Ron becomes over anxious, but over all, things keep getting better and better for Starr. "I've learned to handle my feelings and control my body," stated Ron. "I still have the same desire to reach the top, but now I'm in no hurry. I'm young and I'm going through a learning period. Things will fit together in time and when they do I'll be ready to gain the important wins that a wrestler needs to win titles. But, gosh, if I could cut down Valentine or Flair for one of their titles soon, it would be great!"

With all the natural talent that Ron has and a little bit of luck he will never be just another face in the crowd. Many years from now he'll be able to sit back and enjoy his hobbies of fishing and guns while looking back at his many accomplishments. Ron will be a brilliant star one day if he is only willing to be patient.

MID-ATLANTIC WRESTLING 1975 YEARBOOK

Danny Miller Hammerlocks Tough Doug Gilbert

Paul Jones Has Regained the Mid-Atlantic TV Title

Newcomer to Mid-Atlantic Wrestling, Tony Rocca

Steve Keirn Applies His Weight To Mr. Fuji's Head

A day with... RIC FLAIR

One of the hottest young grapplers in the pro sport today is Ric Flair. Our photographer spent a day with Ric and two of his lovely ladies. In the pictures on these two pages you will see that Flair does take time away from wrestling, and when he does he enjoys himself to the fullest. Everyone needs relaxation. When Ric relaxes, he does it in style. Move over, Joe Namath, here comes Ric Flair!

A Little Morning Sun, To Keep "Nature Boy" a Healthy Color

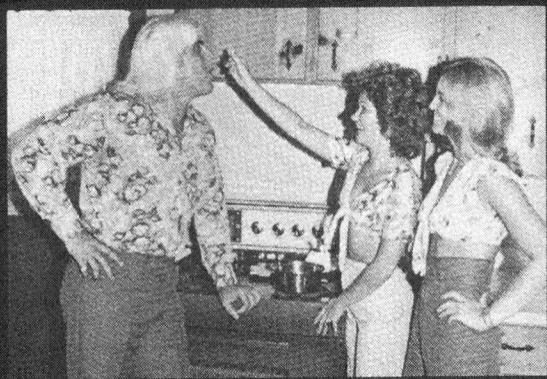

This Type of Weight Lifting Seems To Be Fun

After the Sun, A Light Lunch Before Going Shopping

Ric and the Ladies Get a Laugh Out Of His Joke

Our Trio Enters a Local Shopping Center

MID-ATLANTIC WRESTLING 1975 YEARBOOK

Flair Is Cornered By Teenage Fans

Time Out For an Ice Cream On a Park Bench

Window Shopping Draws a Laugh From Everyone. Do They Think It's Wahoo?

Ric Picks a Shirt, And The Lovelies Give It To Him As a Gift

When You're With the "Nature Boy" You're a Winner

MID-ATLANTIC WRESTLING 1975 YEARBOOK

The Andersons Individually

All wrestling fans are aware that Ole and Gene Anderson form the toughest tag team in professional wrestling and wear the World Championship belts. They think and wrestle as one when they are in the ring. Most people don't stop to think that when the battle is over the Andersons become two uniquely individual men, liking and disliking different things. Let's take a look at Ole and Gene Anderson as individuals.

Gene is the oldest of the two Andersons and was born in the chill of a Minnesota fall under the sign of Libra. Gene began wrestling in high school and from there went on to North Dakota State University for his college education and wrestling background. Gene is a dedicated family man and spends all his free time with wife and children. He doesn't have much to say and enjoys quiet, thoughtful activities when away from the wildness of the wrestling ring. Many Sunday afternoons in the fall are spent watching Pro Football on TV with the chess board in front of him and a friend. Gene feels that this mind game is a big help in the brothers' planning their ring strategy. His easy going manner is the stabilizing force for the "The Minnesota Wrecking Crew" when they enter the ring.

Ole, the wild, talkative member of this brother duo is the youngest and was born under the sign of Virgo. Like Gene he started wrestling in high school, but unlike his brother, went on to attend the University of Colorado on a football scholarship and wrestled in the off-season. Ole enjoys the outdoors when he can get away from the city, but his biggest joy is spending time redecorating his beautiful home. He does the largest share of the work himself. He enjoys working with his hands. Ole is the enforcer for the team and his weight-lifting keeps him in shape for that job. The younger Anderson is the drive that blends so well with his brother's stability to form a tag team that has been one of the very best since they joined forces some seven years ago.

MID-ATLANTIC WRESTLING 1975 YEARBOOK

Tim "Mr. Wrestling" Woods Returns To the Mid-Atlantic Wrestling Wars

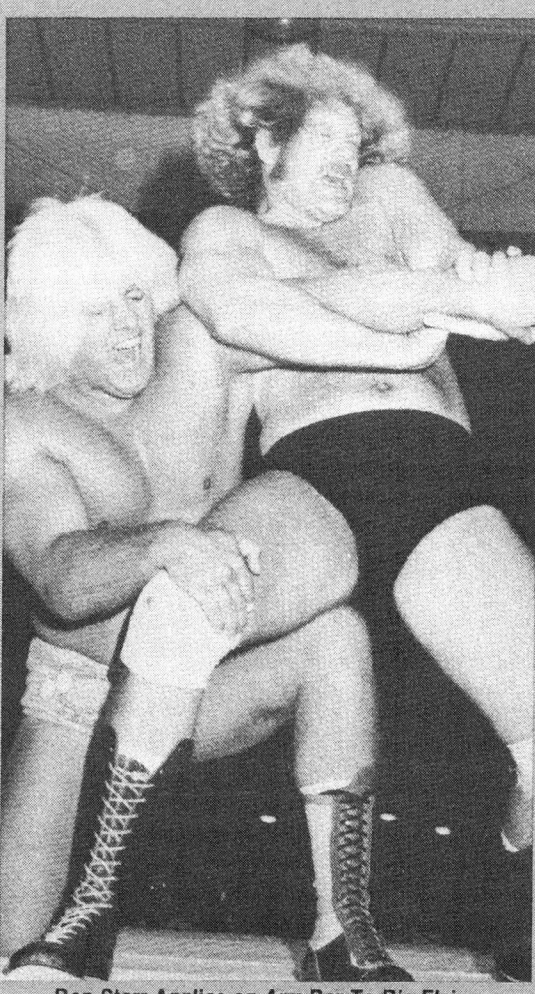

Ron Starr Applies an Arm Bar To Ric Flair

Malenko With a Short Arm Scissors On Starr

Mid-Atlantic Fans Enjoy the Action Of Midget Wrestlers

SO YOU WANT TO BECOME A WRESTLER?

Many young men would like to try their hand at professional wrestling but only a few ever make it. Just a few weeks ago, the young man you see pictured on these pages stepped into his first professional wrestling match. Tony White trained for many long hours over a seven month period to reach that point. But that's not where his wrestling career started. Tony has been involved in wrestling for nine of his twenty-one years. He had his first training in junior high school at age thirteen. From there he went on to wrestle for Roanoke Virginia's Patrick Henry High School, and won the state unlimited class title. At 6'2", 245 lbs., Tony has the size to make it big as a pro. He has the drive of a bull, and no wonder, as he was born under the sign of Taurus. Tony was tagged with the nickname of "Tony Atlas" by his fellow wrestlers. You only need to look at those granite carved muscles to see why. He has bench pressed a top weight of 580 lbs.! As his pro career progesses he won't find much time for his hobbies of drawing and hunting, but hopes to be able to carry on his work with children, as he was once a Vista volunteer. Things are looking good for Tony but it didn't come easy, and as you look at the pictures on these pages you'll see why. Do you still want to be a professional wrestler?

Tony Prepares For His Daily Workout

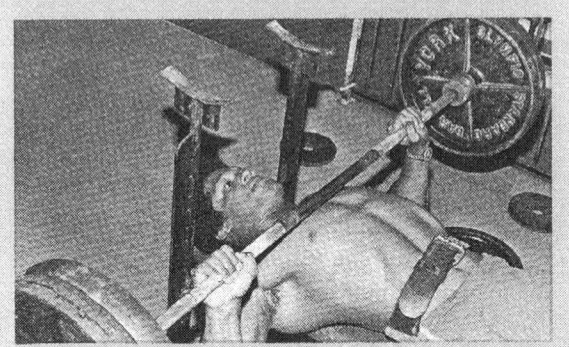

Next He Goes To the Weight Training Room

He Begins By Running the Indoor Track

Dips Help Develop the Upper Body

MID-ATLANTIC WRESTLING 1975 YEARBOOK

Bridges Develop the Neck, And Ready Him For a Workout On the Mat

Today's Workout Is With Widely Known Star, Sandy Scott

Tony Tries To "Sit Out" On Sandy

Tony and Sandy Tug For Position

Tony Tries a "Hiplock"

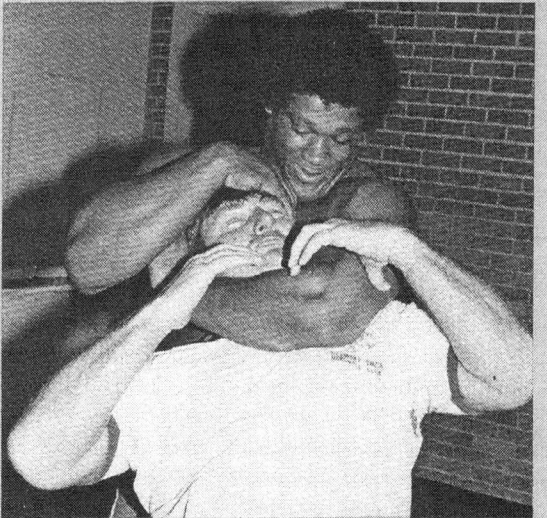

Atlas Hooks the Sleeper On Sandy

MID-ATLANTIC WRESTLING 1975 YEARBOOK

Bob Bruggers Cranks the Arm of Two-Ton Harris

Fast Moving Roberto Soto Has Arrived in the Mid-Atlantic Area

Miller Holds Frank Monte's Arm As Sandy Scott Lowers the Boom

Atlas Puts the Lights Out For the Blue Scorpion

ANY WAY YOU LOOK AT IT THE FASBAK IS A SENSATIONAL NEW BASS PLUG!

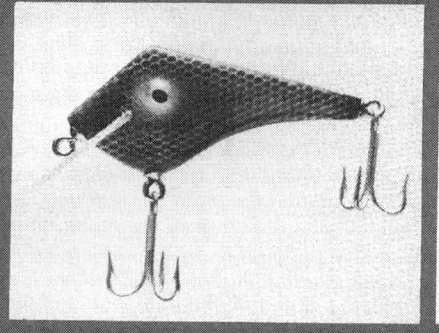

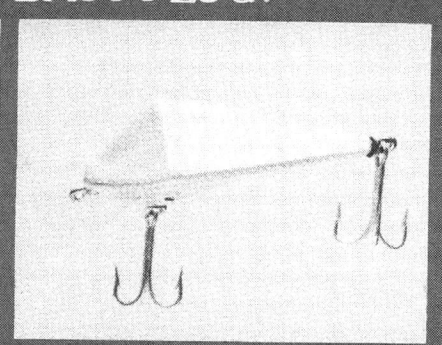

This new plug runs deep where the big bass stay in 12'-15' of water. Fish the FASBAK in any of 4 ways:

1. The FASBAK is a deadly top water plug and can be pulled slowly across the surface.
2. Give the FASBAK a yank and several fast cranks to make it dive. Stop. Let it surface and do it again.
3. Reel it in at a constant speed either fast or slow and it runs at a depth that you can determine.
4. Troll it behind a boat and it runs deep, deeper, and deepest.

BUTCH HARRIS BASS LURES
421 Briarbend Drive, Charlotte, N. C. 28209

SPECIAL INTRODUCTORY FIELD TEST OFFER
$8.00 RETAIL VALUE FOR ONLY $4.00

PATCH — BOAT DECAL

Enclosed is my check/money order for _____ for _____ Special Butch Harris Introductory Field Test Offer which includes 16 Butch Harris Worms, 36 Butterflies, plus a colorful boat decal and embroidered patch. All for ONLY $4.00.

Name _____
Address _____
City/State/Zip _____

The Butch Harris Worm with the patented spiral is available in 4 colors (Black, Blue, Green & Purple) and in 3 sizes (4½", 7¼" & 8¼"). This field test offer includes four worms in each of our four colors, or 16 worms.

The Butterfly has the same patented spiral and twin pulsating tails. It is available in 6 colors (Black, White, Purple, Blue, Chartreuse & Yellow). This field test offer includes 6 Butterflies in each of our 6 colors, or a total of 36 Butterflies.

"BUTCH" HARRIS
BUTCH HARRIS LURES
421 Briarbend Drive, Charlotte, North Carolina 28209

United States Champion
JOHNNY VALENTINE

133

THE TOURNAMENT

by Dick Bourne

This feature was originally published on the Mid-Atlantic Gateway during Thanksgiving week of 2005, celebrating the 30th anniversary of the events in Greensboro in November 1975. The plane crash in October and the U.S. tournament that followed it in November transformed the territory in profound ways from that day forward.

Project research by Dick Bourne. Contributions from Dave Routh, Mark Eastridge, Carroll Hall, George South, Don Holbrook, John Hitchcock, Bill Janosik, John Pagan, and Scooter Lesley.

Special thanks to Terry Funk and Paul Jones.

This photograph hung in Jim Crockett, Jr.'s office until the Charlotte offices of Jim Crockett promotions closed in the late 1980s. In the ring are Ole Anderson and Paul Jones. Local promoter Joe Murnick and ring announcer Tom Miller can be seen at sitting at ringside.

Tournament photos were taken by Bob McAlister and Gene Gordon. The copyrights on Mr. Gordon's photos are owned by Scooter Lesley.

REFLECTIONS

PAUL JONES

From telephone conversations with Paul Jones, November 2005.

Paul Jones was laughing as he remembered back to his recent reunion with Terry Funk.

"Terry was sitting there with a big grin on his face," Jones recently told me in a phone conversation from his home in Tampa, Florida. "He was looking at me and saying, 'Gee, it's good to see you Paul after so many years.' We were laughing and telling old stories. Terry was pretty lit after his Q&A (earlier that night at the Mid-Atlantic Legends Fanfest). Tommy Young kept bringing him beer and mixed drinks all during that thing. So later we're visiting in the hospitality room, and suddenly Terry got real serious and says "Paul, why in the hell did you hit me so hard?"

Funk was laughing as he and Paul reminisced in the VIP suite for wrestlers appearing at the NWA Wrestling Legends Fanfest in Charlotte this past August.

"He just kept asking me that. We were laughing, we had both had a few beers and were talking about that night in Greensboro."

Paul and Terry were remembering the famous US championship tournament held after that title had been vacated following Johnny Valentine's injury in the October 1975 Wilmington NC plane crash. Funk had won the tournament, defeating Jones in the finals. Both men wrestled four times that night, culminating in an 18 minute championship match.

"We were exhausted, yet we were both feeling great for that match. Everything had gone well that night. Everything was clicking."

Many of the details were forgotten about that night. Neither Funk nor Jones remembered exactly who they had wrestled that night 30 years ago, but Terry Funk remembered one detail very clearly.

"Paul, why did you hit me so hard?" Funk asked again. Funk was referring to a hard punch Jones landed above Funk's left eye that had opened him up and required 18 stitches to close later that night in a Greensboro hospital.

"Well Terry, *you* called it." Jones said.

"I know I called it, but why did you hit me *so hard*?" They were both laughing now, two old friends telling old war stories.

I asked Paul if the shot that opened Terry up was an accident (wrestlers call them "potatoes") or was it done to add something memorable to the match.

"I think Terry called that as a way to say thanks." Jones told me. "He never actually said so, but he was going over in my home territory, in my town. I had worked awfully hard all night and especially hard in that match. In those days, guys rarely came right out and said thanks. I've always thought it was Terry's way of saying thanks."

"I remember that show like it was yesterday," Jones said. "There was a lot of pressure on everyone during that time because the territory was in such a state of change after the plane crash. I was being set up as the top babyface. Ric Flair was getting ready to be given his first big break as one of the top heels, stepping into Valentine's shoes. Who knows if or when he would have had that break had the plane crash not happened. That's a tough way to look at it, but it's true. He certainly made the most of it."

The Tournament drew a record gate for the city of Greensboro and the entire southeastern United States at that time.

"Traffic was backed up all the way down High Point Road, out Holden road, all the way to I-85. Thousands were turned away. Everyone knew it was a special night and a big moment for the promotion. It's hard to believe it's been 30 years."

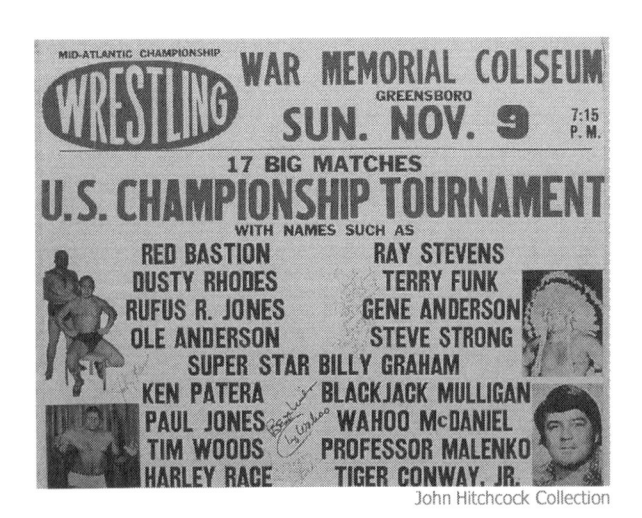

John Hitchcock Collection

TERRY FUNK

from telephone conversations with Terry Funk November 2005.

Wrestlers by and large don't remember too many specific things about specific cards or matches. Fans seem to remember these things a lot more clearly than the wrestlers do. But there are always landmark matches that are remembered clearly, big nights in their career. 1975 was a big year for Terry Funk, in a career that is still going strong today (as of this writing.)

One of those memorable matches for Terry Funk is obviously the night of December 10, 1975 when he defeated Jack Brisco to win the NWA World Heavyweight Championship. Another was one month earlier, for Jim Crockett Promotions in Greensboro NC.

On November 9, 1975, Terry Funk won the United States heavyweight championship in a one-night tournament that featured most of the top stars in the NWA at that time. When I spoke with Terry about that night, he didn't remember exactly who he had faced in the early rounds of the tournament , but he clearly remembered the final match, and man he faced across the ring.

"Paul Jones and I had a great match to end that tournament," Funk said. "My gosh, we wrestled something like 20 minutes, and this was after each of us had wrestled three other matches that night."

Funk was proud of how the whole thing came together, and how it all developed as the evening wore on. "This was a big night for the Charlotte territory. They were trying to move on after the plane crash. No one figured Johnny Valentine would ever wrestle again, and no one was sure about Ric Flair at that point either. They brought in guys from all over to be in that thing, it was a really big deal."

Funk was of course aware of the what was in store for him over the next weeks. "I was getting ready to win the NWA title from Jack. This tournament win helped establish me in the Crockett territory. When I came back a few months later with the NWA title, I had credibility with their fans because I had won that tournament. And of course, weeks after the tournament, I dropped the title to Paul, which then established him as the top guy there, and made him my natural opponent when I came into the territory to defend the title," Funk told me. "It was a brilliant plan by the booker there, George Scott. It kept the title strong. It kept Jones strong. It kept me strong. And we did big business for that thing as well as our matches later."

There was another little detail that Funk remembered about that night. "Paul opened me up, I mean really opened me up. I cut my eye pretty bad, and had to have 18 stitches later that night."

You could here the respect in Funk's voice as I reminded him of who he faced in the tournament's early rounds. Red Bastien, Rufus R. Jones, Dusty Rhodes. These were some of the biggest names in the business at the time. "All of those guys were so special, and so on top of their game during that time," Funk said.

Then there were the guys Paul Jones met along the way. Ole Anderson, Johnny Weaver, and Harley Race. And other names elsewhere in other parts of the bracket, including major stars like Wahoo McDaniel, Superstar Billy Graham, Blackjack Mulligan, and others.

"It was like a big pyramid," Funk said. "If Jones and I had just wrestled each other in a match for the vacant title, it wouldn't have meant as much. But the tournament built it up more, made it special. Our match was better because of the work that all those tremendous people did in their matches leading up to our match. It is important to realize that. Big names in our business put other big names over throughout that whole night. I have such respect for all of them."

"That night, wrestling all those different guys with all those different styles, helped prepare me to be NWA Champion," Funk said. "There is no doubt about that."

Photo by Bob McAlister

Wahoo McDaniel vs. Harley Race

Johnny Weaver vs. Paul Jones

TOURNAMENT JUDGES
Appointed by the National Wrestling Alliance

[Photographs taken that night in Greensboro by longtime fan and veteran referee Dave Routh.]

There were five judges appointed by the National Wrestling Alliance in case any of the tournament matches ended in a draw. They were (L-R) NWA president Jack Adkisson (aka Fritz Von Erich), promoter Joe Murnick, longtime Crockett associate and ring announcer Wally Dusek, wrestler and broadcaster Les Thatcher, and New Jersey State Athletic Commissioner (and father of wrestler Larry Sharpe) Augie Wilde (not pictured.)

MID-ATLANTIC WRESTLING 1975 YEARBOOK

Referee Greg Peterson and Wahoo McDaniel

Paul Jones vs. Terry Funk in the tournament finals.

MID-ATLANTIC WRESTLING 1975 YEARBOOK

TOURNAMENT BRAKETING

Original Brackets

SUNDAY NIGHT – NOVEMBER 9, 1975
7:15 P.M. – GREENSBORO COLISEUM

PARTICIPANTS:

- RED BASTIAN
- TERRY FUNK
- OLE ANDERSON
- GENE ANDERSON
- WAHOO McDANIEL
- PAUL JONES
- STEVE STRONG
- SUPERSTAR BILLY GRAHAM
- KEN PATERA
- DUSTY RHODES
- PROFESSOR MALENKO
- TIGER CONWAY
- HARLEY RACE
- RAY STEVENS
- BLACKJACK MULLIGAN
- TIM WOODS
- RUFUS R. JONES

Bracket pairings:
- STEVE STRONG vs RUFUS R. JONES
- TERRY FUNK vs RED BASTIAN
- KEN PATERA vs BLACKJACK MULLIGAN
- DUSTY RHODES vs PROFESSOR MALENKO
- WAHOO McDANIEL vs SUPERSTAR BILLY GRAHAM
- HARLEY RACE vs TIGER CONWAY
- PAUL JONES vs OLE ANDERSON
- RAY STEVENS vs TIM WOODS
- GENE ANDERSON

EXPLANATION:
The pairings were decided on a random drawing of the participants. All matches will be held Sunday, Nov. 9. A total of 16 matches. In case of a draw, judges at ringside will decide a winner.

TOURNAMENT FOR THE U.S. HEAVYWEIGHT CHAMPIONSHIP

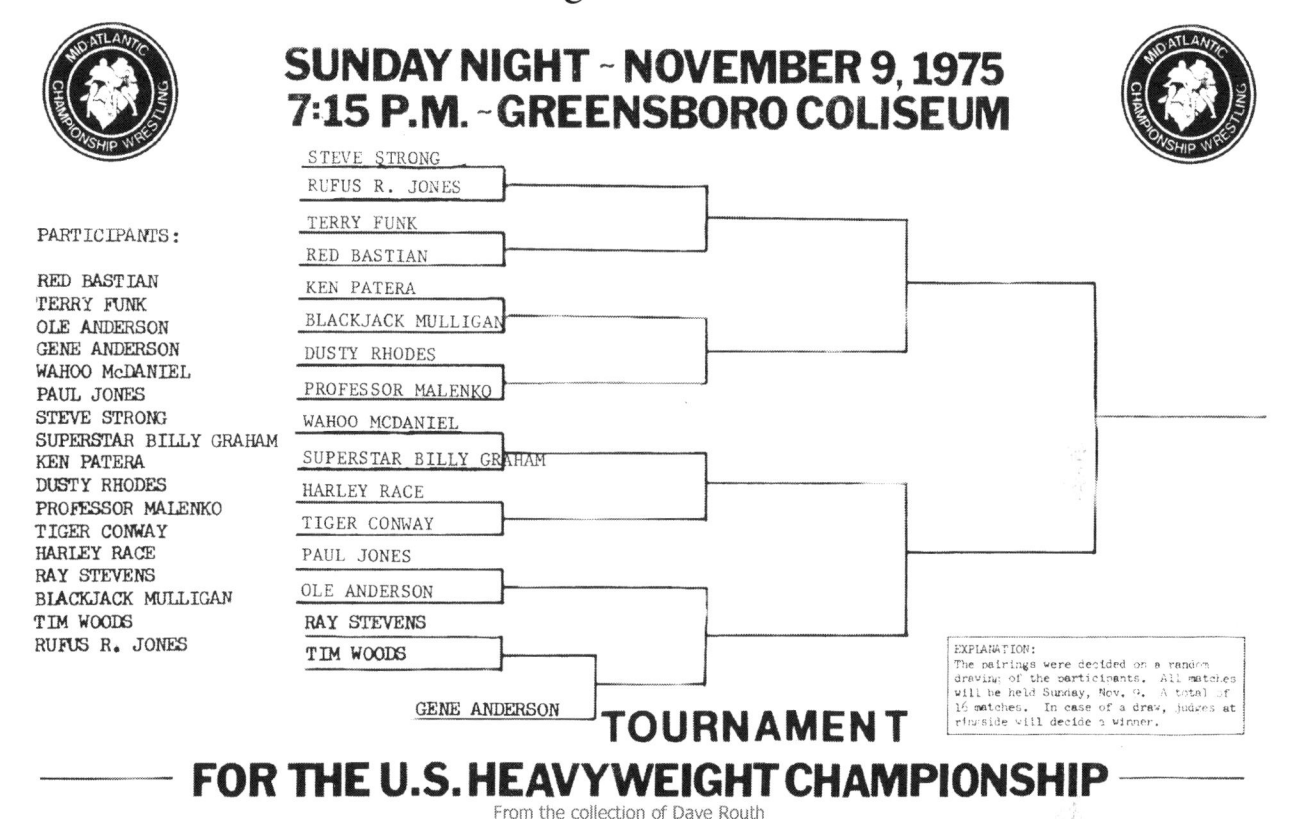

From the collection of Dave Routh

The above image features the original bracketing for the United States tournament. Bracket sheets like the one seen above were given out to fans before the event.

Several changes were made. Ray Stevens and Tim Woods were scheduled to meet each other in the opening round of the tournament. Stevens was announced as having "travel difficulties" and did not make the show. He was replaced by Johnny Weaver. Woods was injured prior to the tournament, but was not replaced. Instead, Weaver (replacing Stevens) met Gene Anderson in the first round. Anderson was originally scheduled for a bye in the original 19-man field. (These changes are shown in the revised bracket image on the next page.)

The revised brackets on the following pages were created by digitally modifying the original bracket sheet seen above. The original bracket sheet was provide by Dave Routh to the Mid-Atlantic Gateway,

MID-ATLANTIC WRESTLING 1975 YEARBOOK

REVISED BRACKETS

SUNDAY NIGHT – NOVEMBER 9, 1975
7:15 P.M. – GREENSBORO COLISEUM

PARTICIPANTS:

- RED BASTIAN
- TERRY FUNK
- OLE ANDERSON
- GENE ANDERSON
- WAHOO McDANIEL
- PAUL JONES
- STEVE STRONG
- SUPERSTAR BILLY GRAHAM
- KEN PATERA
- DUSTY RHODES
- PROFESSOR MALENKO
- TIGER CONWAY
- HARLEY RACE
- RAY STEVENS (WITHDRAWN)
- BLACKJACK MULLIGAN
- TIM WOODS (WITHDRAWN)
- RUFUS R. JONES
- JOHNNY WEAVER (SUBSTITUTE)

Bracket pairings:
- STEVE STRONG vs RUFUS R. JONES
- TERRY FUNK vs RED BASTIAN
- KEN PATERA vs BLACKJACK MULLIGAN
- DUSTY RHODES vs PROFESSOR MALENKO
- WAHOO McDANIEL vs SUPERSTAR BILLY GRAHAM
- HARLEY RACE vs TIGER CONWAY
- PAUL JONES vs OLE ANDERSON
- JOHNNY WEAVER vs GENE ANDERSON

EXPLANATION:
The pairings were decided on a random drawing of the participants. All matches will be held Sunday, Nov. 9. A total of 16 matches. In case of a draw, judges at ringside will decide a winner.

TOURNAMENT FOR THE U.S. HEAVYWEIGHT CHAMPIONSHIP

TOURNAMENT RESULTS

FIRST ROUND

Rufus R. Jones defeated Steve Strong by pinfall. Rufus pinned Strong with a backslide.

Terry Funk defeated Red Bastien by pinfall. Funk and Bastien wrestled clean until Funk turned, kicking Bastien until finally pinning him.

Blackjack Mulligan defeated Ken Patera by pinfall. Mulligan pinned Patera after coming off the top rope with a knee to Patera's throat.

Dusty Rhodes defeated Professor Boris Malenko by pinfall. Dusty pinned Malenko after delivering the bionic elbow drop.

Wahoo McDaniel defeated Superstar Billy Graham by pinfall. Graham had Wahoo in his full nelson when Wahoo kicked off the turn buckle. Both men fell to the mat with Graham maintaining the full nelson on Wahoo. Wahoo was on top of Graham and Graham's shoulders were to the mat, and the referee counted him out.

Harley Race defeated Tiger Conway Jr. by pinfall. Conway rolled Race into a reverse cradle out of the turnbuckle. Race continued the roll, and cradled Conway for the pin.

Paul Jones defeated Ole Anderson by pinfall. Anderson Irish-whipped Jones into the ropes and Jones caught him with body press coming out of the ropes for the pin.

Johnny Weaver defeated Gene Anderson by Judge's Decision following a 20 minute draw.

Weaver had Gene Anderson in the sleeper when time ran out. The panel of five judges voted Weaver the winner. The judges were (1) NWA President Jack Adkisson, (2) Raleigh promoter Joe Murnick, (3) wrestler and broadcaster Les Thatcher, (4) longtime Crockett Promotions associate and ring announcer Wally Dusek, and (5) New Jersey State Athletic Commissioner (and father of Larry Sharpe) Augie Wilde.

ROUND TWO - QUARTER FINALS

Terry Funk defeated Rufus R. Jones by pinfall. Terry Funk was re-entering the ring and Rufus picked him up for a slam. Funk held on to the ropes causing Rufus to lose his balance falling backwards with Funk on top of him. Funk held him for the three count.

Dusty Rhodes defeated Blackjack Mulligan by pinfall. Rhodes had Mulligan in a headlock when Mulligan shot him into the ropes. The two collided and Dusty fell to the ringside floor, landing on top of one of the official judges Augie Wilde. Blackjack fell to his back in the ring. The referee was distracted by Rhodes and Wilde, and began issuing the ten-count on Rhodes to return to the ring. While this was going on, Tim Woods, who had his hand broken by Mulligan some weeks earlier, entered the ring. Woods hit Mulligan with his cast, knocking Mulligan unconscious. Rhodes beat the ten count and returned to the ring, and then covered the unconscious Mulligan for the three count.

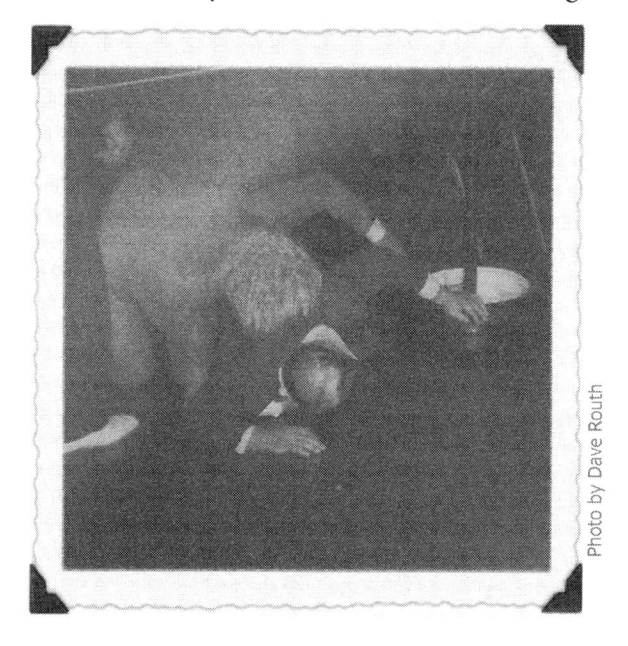

Harley Race defeated Wahoo McDaniel by disqualification. Wahoo threw Race into the ropes. Rather than bouncing off the ropes back toward Wahoo, Race jumped slightly, falling backward over the top rope to the floor, making it look as though Wahoo had thrown him over the top rope. The referee made the judgment that Wahoo had intentionally thrown Race over the top rope and disqualified McDaniel. An angry Wahoo brawled with Race outside of the ring, hitting him with a chair and also hitting referee Greg Peterson with a chair. Wahoo was later fined for these actions.

Paul Jones defeated Johnny Weaver by pinfall. Jones and Weaver wrestled a very scientific match with Jones pinning Weaver with an inside cradle.

ROUND THREE - SEMI-FINALS

Terry Funk defeated Dusty Rhodes by disqualification. This match was a brawl from the beginning, much of it taking place outside the ring until Rhodes was eventually disqualified.

Paul Jones defeated Harley Race by pinfall. Race held the advantage most of the match, using his trademark flying head butts and knee-drops. Jones caught him by surprise with the same maneuver he used earlier to defeat Ole Anderson, coming out of the ropes with a body press for the pinfall. A major advance for Jones as he defeats former United States champ and former NWA champ Race to advance to the finals.

FINAL BRACKET RESULTS

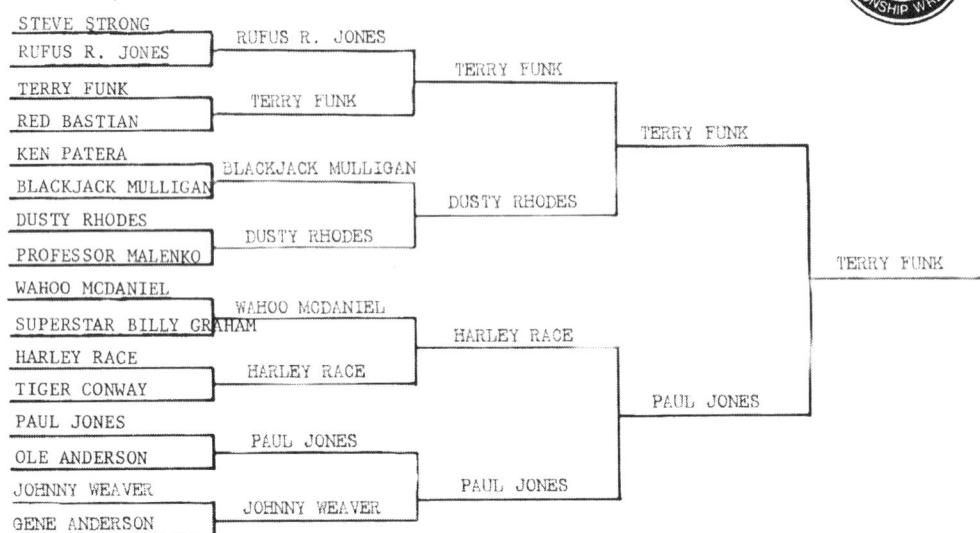

SUNDAY NIGHT - NOVEMBER 9, 1975
7:15 P.M. - GREENSBORO COLISEUM

PARTICIPANTS:

RED BASTIAN
TERRY FUNK
OLE ANDERSON
GENE ANDERSON
WAHOO McDANIEL
PAUL JONES
STEVE STRONG
SUPERSTAR BILLY GRAHAM
KEN PATERA
DUSTY RHODES
PROFESSOR MALENKO
TIGER CONWAY
HARLEY RACE
RAY STEVENS (WITHDRAWN)
BLACKJACK MULLIGAN
TIM WOODS (WITHDRAWN)
RUFUS R. JONES
JOHNNY WEAVER (SUBSTITUTE)

Bracket:
- STEVE STRONG vs RUFUS R. JONES → RUFUS R. JONES
- TERRY FUNK vs RED BASTIAN → TERRY FUNK
  - → TERRY FUNK
- KEN PATERA vs BLACKJACK MULLIGAN → BLACKJACK MULLIGAN
- DUSTY RHODES vs PROFESSOR MALENKO → DUSTY RHODES
  - → DUSTY RHODES
    - → TERRY FUNK
- WAHOO McDANIEL vs SUPERSTAR BILLY GRAHAM → WAHOO McDANIEL
- HARLEY RACE vs TIGER CONWAY → HARLEY RACE
  - → HARLEY RACE
- PAUL JONES vs OLE ANDERSON → PAUL JONES
- JOHNNY WEAVER vs GENE ANDERSON → JOHNNY WEAVER
  - → PAUL JONES
    - → PAUL JONES

FINAL: TERRY FUNK

(cont.)

FINAL ROUND - CHAMPIONSHIP FINAL

Terry Funk defeated Paul Jones by pinfall to win the United States Heavyweight Championship. Both wrestlers, exhausted from their earlier encounters, wrestled a methodical, scientific match early on. At the end, there were several back-and-forth near falls. Referee Greg Peterson was inadvertently knocked down, and while he was down, Jones was able to pin Funk for what seemed like a five or six count. Peterson, who was also physically involved earlier during the Wahoo/Race brawl, was unable to get into position to count the pin. Eventually, an exhausted Jones lifted Funk for a vertical suplex, but could not get Funk over. Funk quickly cradled Jones for a three count to win the match and the United States Heavyweight Championship.

United States Heavyweight Champion Terry Funk (Artwork by John Pagan)

Press Reports from the Tournament for the Vacant United States Heavyweight Championship

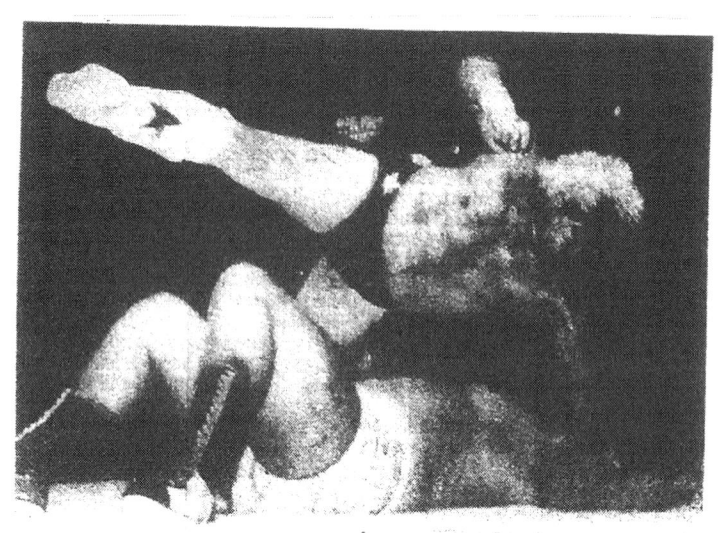

Bloodied Dusty Rhodes drives fist into foe

Wrestling talent draws fans

BY BOB HELLER
Staff Sports Writer

The greatest gathering of wrestling talent and the largest advance ticket sale in the Greensboro Coliseum's 17 years of housing professional wrestling cards are the principal ingredients in tomorrow night's battle for the National Wrestling Alliance's U.S. Heavyweight championship.

This unique one-night tournament concept was conceived by fallen title-holder Johnny Valentine and Charlotte promoter Jim Crockett in the wake of Valentine's severe injuries sustained in a Wilmington airplane crash some five weeks ago.

Valentine, currently in a rehabilitation center in Houston, may never wrestle again following that crash. Prior to that point, the 47-year old veteran had held the U.S. belt for several months, since defeating Harley Race in Greensboro last summer.

Race will be one of several nationally-known wrestlers who will be flying to Greensboro this weekend to join the eight or nine grapplers who call the Mid-Atlantic area their home.

In all, 17 pros will be competing for the money and prestige of the title in front of a possible record audience.

The current record house stands at just over 13,000, who paid their way to see a Thanksgiving night event two years ago.

As of Friday afternoon, the Coliseum reported that "over 5,000" tickets had already been sold, "by far the most we've sold in advance for a wrestling event," according to Louise Coble of the box office.

It will be a grueling night for all the participants, as four victories will be necessary to win the tournament and the championship belt.

Some very interesting matches are possible, as brothers and tag-team partners Gene and Ole Anderson are in the same bracket and they could meet in the quarterfinals. And partners Wahoo McDaniel and Paul Jones are also in that same lower bracket, though the possible clash wouldn't take place until the semifinal round.

There will be strict time-limits throughout the tournament, with the first-round bouts limited to either 15 or 20 minutes; second round, 30 minutes; semifinals, 45 minutes and the championship match, one hour.

Judges, including NWA President Jack Adkisson, will be at ringside to rule in matches in which neither wrestler records a clear pinfall.

Ric Flair, injured in the same accident which sidelined Valentine and another wrestler, Bob Bruggers, may be in the audience according the Promoter Crockett. Flair is the reigning Mid-Atlantic title-holder but he did not relinquish his crown because he is expected to return to ring action by the end of the year.

Ms. Coble reports that the Coliseum box office will open at 3 p.m. tomorrow in anticipation of the large gate sale for the 7:15 event.

Following are the tournament pairings:

UPPER BRACKET
Steve Strong vs. Rufus R. Jones
Terry Funk vs. Red Bastein
Ken Patera vs. Black Jack Mulligan
Dusty Rhodes vs. Professor Boris Malenko

LOWER BRACKET
Wahoo McDaniel vs. Superstar Billy Graham
Harley Race vs. Tiger Conway, Jr.
Paul Jones vs. Ole Anderson
Ray Stevens vs. Tim Woods
Gene Anderson, bye.

MID-ATLANTIC WRESTLING 1975 YEARBOOK

MID-ATLANTIC CHAMPIONSHIP WRESTLING TOURNAMENT

FOR THE U.S. HEAVYWEIGHT CHAMPIONSHIP

SUNDAY, NOV. 9th
7:15 P.M.

GREENSBORO COLISEUM

The Winner Of This Tournament Will Be The New U.S. Heavyweight Champ!

16 BIG MATCHES!

—Participants Include—

- OLE ANDERSON
- DUSTY RHODES
- BLACK JACK MULLIGAN
- GENE ANDERSON
- KEN PETERRA
- RED BASTINE
- TIGER CONWAY, JR.
- TIM WOODS
- TERRY FUNK
- WAHOO McDANIEL
- HARLEY RACE
- PAUL JONES
- RAY STEVENS
- PROF. BORIS MOLENKO
- RUFUS R. JONES
- STEVE STRONG
- SUPER-STAR BILLY GRAHAM

TICKET PRICES All Seats Reserved **$5 and $6**
(Children — Age 12 and under — $2.50 in $5 Section)

TICKETS ON SALE AT THE GREENSBORO COLISEUM BOX OFFICE

Wrestling Tourney: Survival Of Fittest

BY BOB HELLER
Staff Sports Writer

In what may boil down to the survival of the fittest, 17 professional wrestlers go after the vacated U.S. Heavyweight Championship of the National Wrestling Alliance tonight at the Coliseum.

Action gets underway at 7:15 in this unique, one-night tournament and a crowd of between 12,000 and 15,000 is expected to witness the unprecedented 16-bout program.

Steve Strong, a newcomer to this area from Arizona, will meet Rufus R. Jones, a regional favorite from Dillon, S.C., in the opening match. And two, three or perhaps four hours later, the new champion will be crowned.

The evening's events will be conducted in tournament fashion, and brackets are all set (see pairings at end of this article).

Johnny Valentine, title-holder since he defeated Harley Race last summer, was seriously injured in a Wilmington airplane crash five weeks ago. He has been forced into at least temporary retirement as a result, and tonight's tournament was conceived to fill the title vacancy.

• • •

CONDITIONING IS expected to be a key tonight, and the more aggressive wrestlers could possibly have an advantage, since four time-limit victories will be needed to secure the title.

First round matches will be limited to 15 or 20 minutes; quarterfinals, 30 minutes; semifinals, 45 minutes and the championship match, one hour.

Jack Adkisson, president of the National Wrestling Alliance, will head the crew of five judges, who will rule in the event of no pinfall or submission.

This is a single-elimination tournament, so a disqualification in one match would eliminate that wrestler from further competition.

• • •

WAHOO McDANIEL, an area favorite who has held the Mid-Atlantic and Tag-Team belt at one point, has perhaps the toughest draw.

He must meet the rugged Superstar Billy Graham of California in the first round. Should he advance, it would be Tiger Conway or Harley Race and then one of five in the semifinals—Paul Jones, Ole Anderson, Gene Anderson, Ray Stevens or Tim Woods.

The lower bracket appears to be the tougher of the two.

"Everyone is curious to see what's going to happen," McDaniel said Friday afternoon before a match in Richmond. "This is something that's never happened before. I think the most I've ever wrestled in one night has been two matches."

In preparation for tonight, McDaniel has tapered his schedule somewhat, with appearances Tuesday night in Raleigh and Friday in Richmond this past week. He wrestled one short match for television Wednesday evening.

"I've been doing additional road work for conditioning," said McDaniel, "and I ran eight or nine miles on each of my three days off this week."

• • •

COINCIDENTALLY, EACH of McDaniel's matches this past week were against Graham.

"I gave him some pretty bad cuts in an Indian strap match in Raleigh," he said, "and now I've got him again in Richmond. I would prefer not to have it this way, but these matches were signed before the draw for the tournament."

Graham, who appeared on NBC-TV's Tomorrow Show last week as part of a professional wrestling program, is only one formidable opponent Wahoo would have to face.

"Let's face it," he said, "there's going to be a lot of luck involved Sunday. And because many will be shorter matches than usual, it's going to be very hard to pin wrestlers of this caliber. If they punch me, I'm going to punch back."

McDaniel, former linebacker with the New York Jets and Miami Dolphins, concluded: "It's just like a big football game. Everyone will be keyed sky-high and the winner knows there'll be a lot of money involved."

Here are tonight's first-round pairings:

UPPER BRACKET
Steve Strong vs. Rufus R. Jones
Terry Funk vs. Red Bastien
Ken Patera vs. Black Jack Mulligan
Dusty Rhodes vs. Professor Boris Malenko

LOWER BRACKET
Wahoo McDaniel vs. Superstar Billy Graham
Harley Race vs. Tiger Conway, Jr.
Paul Jones vs. Ole Anderson
Ray Stevens vs. Tim Woods
Gene Anderson, bye.

Wahoo McDaniel...Toughest Draw

Newspaper Clippings from the collection of Mark Eastridge.

MID-ATLANTIC WRESTLING 1975 YEARBOOK

Belt by Dave Millican / Photo by Dick Bourne

Packed House Watches As Funk Wins Mat Title

BY BOB HELLER
Staff Sports Writer

The hot dogs had all disappeared. So had the pizza and the ice for the soft drinks.

But after 3½ hours and 14 professional wrestling matches, the crowd remained. A few youngsters no doubt had to make it home early, but when the new U.S. Heavyweight Champion of the National Wrestling Alliance was crowned Sunday night, most of the 15,076 fans remained.

They were less than thrilled with Terry Funk's 18-minute victory over Paul Jones in the final event, but such is life...

"It was like two weeks worth of wrestling in one night," the obviously drained Funk panted in the dressing room. "All the little injuries accumulate and there's no time to do anything about them.

"It was grueling, very grueling both physically and mentally. I imagine I lost close to 20 pounds in those four matches.

"I honestly don't know if I'd go through all this again. But I can tell you this is definitely the highlight of my wrestling career."

The 29-year-old Funk of Amarillo, Tex., is a member of the well-known wrestling family. His father Dory died in the ring two years ago and his brother, 32-year-old Dory Jr., once held the NWA's world title for over four years.

* * *

AS IS ALMOST always the case, there was action both in and around the blue-aproned ring. In fact, some of the fiercest brawling took place just a few feet in front of the ringside fans.

Financially, the evening was a huge success, both for the Coliseum management and for the wrestlers participating under the auspices of Jim Crockett Promotions of Charlotte.

There were a few kinks in the performance—like wrestler Tim Woods didn't dress due to a hand injury, combatant Ray Stevens was stranded in the Atlanta airport and the concession stands closed up shop less than two hours into the program—but otherwise, the show went on.

Sports purists would no doubt question the goings-on, but the throng which made it inside the Coliseum (well over 1,000 additional fans were turned away at the door) cheered with the partisan enthusiasm of an ACC basketball tournament audience.

* * *

AS FOR the matches themselves ... well, there were a few surprises.

The absence of Woods and Stevens created a shakeup in the lower bracket. Gene Anderson, originally given a first-round bye, was forced to meet Johnny Weaver, a last-minute substitute for Woods.

It was perhaps the most interesting match of the first round, and somewhat surprisingly, the aging Weaver decisioned Anderson in the only bout of the evening to go the full time limit.

The second round produced a pair of matches of main-event caliber.

In one, crowd-favorite Dusty Rhodes defeated Black Jack Mulligan with a little help from Woods.

In the other, Wahoo McDaniel was the victim of a dubious call when he was disqualified for throwing Harley Race over the top rope. It appeared, however, that Race arched himself over.

* * *

* * *

IN THE semifinal round the wrestlers began to show the strain of the long night's work. The pace slowed somewhat and the participants found it increasingly difficult to bounce back from absorbed punishment.

Funk and Rhodes were involved in a bloody, brawling semifinal event, in which the former was ruled the winner when referee Greg Petersen counted Rhodes out of the ring.

The other semi match pitted Jones against Race, who owned the U.S. title prior to his loss to Johnny Valentine last summer in Greensboro.

(Valentine's severe injuries suffered in a plane crash last month, of course, were responsible for Sunday's tournament in the first place.)

Jones survived a barrage of Race's favorite moves and head butts before finally springing off the ropes to pin his foe.

* * *

OBVIOUSLY, NEITHER Jones nor Funk was in top form for the championship match.

And unfortunately, a temporarily-dazed referee Petersen played a role in the outcome.

Jones apparently had Funk's shoulders pinned to the mat for four or five seconds, but Petersen couldn't get in position for the official count.

Moments later, Funk turned the tables on Jones by cradling him following an aborted suplex. Petersen was in position this time, he slammed the mat three times and the coveted belt and Heavyweight title were Funk's.

FIRST ROUND
Rufus R. Jones pin Steve Strong; Terry Funk pin Red Bastein; Black Jack Mulligan pin Ken Patera; Dusty Rhodes pin Professor Brork Malenco; Wahoo McDaniel pin Superstar Billy Graham; Harley Race pin Tiger Conway; Paul Jones pin Ole Anderson; Johnny Weaver decisioned Gene Anderson.

SECOND ROUND
Funk pin R. Jones; Rhodes pin Mulligan; Race over McDaniel on disqualify; P. Jones pin Weaver.

SEMIFINALS
Funk over Rhodes, counted out of ring; P. Jones pin Race.

CHAMPIONSHIP
Funk pin P. Jones in 18 minutes.

148

MID-ATLANTIC WRESTLING 1975 YEARBOOK

Funk to take belt with him to Texas

BY BOB HELLER
Staff Sports Writer

His face was bloody and his left eye was almost swollen shut. As soft-speaking Terry Funk sat in a Coliseum dressing room late Sunday night, he did not look like the newly-crowned U.S. Heavyweight champion of the National Wrestling Alliance.

But he was. And such an accomplishment was not easy.

"It was the most grueling thing I've ever been through," said the Amarillo, Tex., resident, "and frankly, I don't know that I'd go through it all again.

"But I won the title, and it's the highlight of my wrestling career," continued the 29-year-old Funk. "I just can't wait to tell my brother about it."

Funk's brother is Dory, Jr., who owned the NWA's World Title before Harley Race took it from him three years ago. Both are the sons of the well-known Dory Funk, Sr., who died in the wrestling ring two years ago.

"I trained very hard for this night," said Funk, "because I knew it would take a tremendous amount of time and muscle to win. Four matches and all that punishment... it's like two weeks of wrestling crammed into one night."

To win the title, Funk defeated Red Bastein, Rufus R. Jones, Dusty Rhodes and Paul Jones.

The Greensboro Record
SPORTS
Section B—Page 6 Mon., Nov. 10, 1975

"Each presented a different problem," said Funk, "and these were people I wasn't used to wrestling.

"Rufus used his strength and with Dusty, it's just like a big brawl. Paul Jones is probably the most dangerous, though, because of his scientific knowledge of wrestling. It's one constant worry against him to make sure you're not in a position where he can pin you with one quick move."

Funk hadn't wrestled Rufus Jones since a bout in St. Louis some three years ago, but he has had a running feud whith Rhodes, dating back to the days when the pair were teammates on West Texas State's football team.

"I was the starting offensive guard and Dusty was always No. 2," said Funk. "It really got to him and we've never seen eye to eye over much."

Funk last wrestled Paul Jones in Tampa, Fla., two or three years ago. "It was a tag-team match, and I didn't remember much about it," continued the new champion. "So the television station in Amarillo was nice enough to let me view some videotape of some of his recent matches."

A record wrestling crowd of 15,076 (with at least another 1,000 turned away) witnessed the four-hour affair. Judging by the response, Funk was not the most popular of winners.

"Don't worry about that," said Funk, "because nothing will get me back in this area as long as I hold the title. I'm going to take about a week off, sit back and enjoy myself and then worry about defending the title... in the Panhandle of Texas. They can all come to me, now."

Staff photo by Jim Stratford

Q4 HISTORY
by David Chappell

OCTOBER

THE PLANE CRASH

The month of October 1975 was a month like no other in the history of Mid-Atlantic Championship Wrestling. The landscape of Jim Crockett Promotions forever changed when a twin engine Cessna 310 plane crashed just short of its destination…the runway of the New Hanover County Airport in Wilmington, North Carolina during the early evening hours of October 4, 1975.

On that ill-fated plane were the promotion's top two singles wrestlers---the United States Heavyweight Champion Johnny Valentine and the Mid-Atlantic Heavyweight Champion Ric Flair. With them on the plane was Valentine's chief rival at the time, "Mr. Wrestling" Tim Woods, former Miami Dolphin football player Bob Bruggers and promoter/television announcer David Crockett.

The injuries sustained by Valentine and Bruggers were career ending. Ric Flair was put out of action for the remainder of 1975. Miraculously, Woods came back and wrestled the following Saturday night in Greensboro, North Carolina on a mega card. Crockett suffered only mild injuries. The pilot of the plane would later die from injuries he sustained in the crash.

The October 4th card in Legion Stadium in Wilmington was to feature matches between Valentine and Woods, and Flair versus Wahoo McDaniel. Bruggers was to team with Danny Miller against the Spoilers # 1 and # 2. Despite the calamity in the skies hours earlier, a make-shift card nevertheless was held in Wilmington before a large crowd.

Valentine's final match was the night before in Charleston, South Carolina, when he wrestled Woods. Bruggers' last match was Thursday October 2nd in Waynesville, North Carolina when he teamed with Tony Atlas against Art Nelson and Mike "The Judge" Dubois. Flair's last match for the year 1975 was on Friday October 3rd in Lynchburg, Virginia, when he escaped with his Mid-Atlantic Title on a double disqualification with Paul Jones.

THE AFTERMATH

Immediately after the plane crash there were changes in the promotion's talent roster. NWA World's Heavyweight Champion Jack Brisco appeared in the area for a calendar week, starting on October 5th putting his World Title up against Wahoo McDaniel in Asheville, North Carolina and wrapping up his stay with a successful defense against top challenger Dory Funk, Jr. in Greensboro, North Carolina. In the middle of his stay, Brisco successfully defended his title against Paul Jones in Charlotte, Wahoo in Raleigh, and Paul Jones again in Norfolk, Virginia.

Another newcomer that arrived right after the plane crash in Wilmington, was a young muscular grappler from Arizona named Steve Strong. This tanned muscleman made his Mid-Atlantic debut on October 6th at Charlotte's Park Center, teaming up with veteran Art Nelson against the popular duo of Swede Hanson and Johnny Weaver. Strong would become a major player with the promotion for the remainder of 1975.

A week after Strong burst on the scene, he was joined by the premiere muscleman in professional wrestling, "Superstar" Billy Graham. For the remainder of the month of October, and for a good bit during the rest of 1975, Graham took dates that were designated for the injured Ric Flair. Graham's first appearance in the area after the plane crash, was in Greenville, South Carolina on October 13th subbing for Flair against Wahoo McDaniel. During the remainder of October, Graham battled Wahoo in a number of memorable bouts. When Graham wasn't wrestling Wahoo in singles competition, he was teaming with his buddy Steve Strong in a formidable rulebreaking tag team that by any definition was dominating.

BLACKJACK RETURNS

The month of October 1975 also saw the reappearance in the area of a star that would be a mainstay in the Mid-Atlantic area for the rest of the decade of the 1970s, and into the early 1980s---Blackjack Mulligan. Seeking to find a performer that could somehow keep the promotion on track in the aftermath of the Wilmington plane crash, booker George Scott turned to the big man from Eagle Pass, Texas. And the big Texan would not disappoint. Appearing on both the Mid-Atlantic and Wide World Wrestling shows on October 15th and October 29th, Mulligan was set up to become the area's top heel as the calendar turned towards November. On the October 29th Mid-Atlantic Championship

Wrestling show, Mulligan participated in his first angle upon his return, joining with Steve Strong to injure Ken Patera in a TV weight-lifting contest. The prior week on Mid-Atlantic TV, Superstar Billy Graham and Strong were set to engage Patera in the weight-lifting showdown, but the television time ran short and the contest was put off to the following week.

TITLES & TAG TEAMS

Understandably, in the aftermath of Wilmington, the title situation in the territory was in shambles. With Johnny Valentine unable to wrestle and defend his United States Heavyweight Championship, the U.S. Title was scheduled to be put up for grabs in a one night tournament in Greensboro, North Carolina on November 9, 1975. Many of the greatest stars in the sport were set to be participating in this mega event.

While Ric Flair was also unable to defend his Mid-Atlantic Heavyweight Championship in the month of October, his Title was not vacated. With Flair's injuries not being as severe as Valentine's, the promotion hoped Flair could return in the not too distant future, and prevent another championship from having to be vacated and thrown up for grabs. As it would turn out, the promotion would be rewarded for its patience in the recovery of Ric Flair. Mid-Atlantic TV Titleholder Paul Jones was basically inactive for the month of October, as far as defending the TV Title.

Ironically, one of the positive things about the dark month of October 1975 was the strength of the tag team division. Of course, one of the reasons being that none of the wrestlers going down in the plane crash were tag team specialists. Gene and Ole Anderson had a busy month fending off the strong challenge of the youthful duo of Tiger Conway and Steve Keirn. These four battled in a number of specialty matches during October, including Lumberjack matches and Texas Tornado matches. While the battles between the Andersons and Keirn and Conway dominated the month of October, the month also saw impressive outings by a number of other teams, including the Spoiler # 1 and # 2, Professor Boris Malenko and the Missouri Mauler, in addition to the aforementioned duo of Steve Strong and Superstar Billy Graham. The "good guy" tandem of Paul Jones and Wahoo McDaniel was also re-energized, and had a number of strong matches against the "bad guy" tag teams mentioned above.

November of 1975 would see the continuation of the plane crash aftermath, with the one night United States Heavyweight Championship tournament looming on November 9, 1975 in the Greensboro Coliseum. That one night in and of itself, would make next month yet another historic month in the history of Mid-Atlantic Championship Wrestling.

WHO'S HOT

SUPERSTAR BILLY GRAHAM---The muscle bound and charismatic Graham was a very different character than what the Mid-Atlantic area had seen previously. His bouts with Wahoo were truly a stark contrast in styles.

STEVE STRONG---Graham's running mate from Arizona was the perfect compliment to the "Superstar." Young and brash with lots of muscles, Strong lived up to his name.

BLACKJACK MULLIGAN---Despite appearing only on TV during the month of October, the big Texan was back! November would be the month where Mulligan's presence would fully be felt.

WHO'S NOT

JOHNNY VALENTINE---The Wilmington plane crash would tragically end the U.S. Champion's illustrious in-ring career.

BOB BRUGGERS---While wrestling primarily preliminary matches at the time of the plane crash, Bruggers was nevertheless a talent who had his career cut far too short by that tragic October 4th evening in Wilmington.

RIC FLAIR---The plane crash appeared to have claimed the career of Ric Flair as well, but the "Nature Boy" had other ideas!

NOVEMBER

November of 1975 began with the departure of a stalwart performer that had been a mainstay in Jim Crockett Promotions for many years. Art Nelson wrestled his last match in the Mid-Atlantic area on November 1, 1975, battling long-time foe Sandy Scott in Spartanburg, South Carolina. While being de-emphasized by the promotion for much of 1974 and all of 1975, Nelson left a lasting impact on fans in the Carolinas and Virginia.

The early part of November also produced an unusual evening for announcer Les Thatcher. On November 4, 1975, Thatcher was pressed into service as a referee for a card in Danville, Virginia! Active in the promotion's office in addition to his announcing duties, Thatcher added the position of "Referee" to his already long list of credentials.

On the subject of "Referees" in Mid-Atlantic Championship Wrestling, the month of November 1975 showcased the debut of the greatest of them all...Tommy Young. On November 22, 1975 in Roanoke, Virginia, Tommy Young refereed his first Mid-Atlantic card in what would be a career without parallel for anyone who donned the striped shirt. Tommy's unique style was an immediate hit with Mid-Atlantic fans

The early days of November 1975 saw the arena debut of the big man from Eagle Pass, Texas--- Blackjack Mulligan. After returning to the area to only television appearances in the month of October,

Mulligan reappeared in the area's arenas in early November. Blackjack's first arena match back was in the Richmond Coliseum on November 7th, teaming with Steve Strong to defeat Johnny Weaver and Tim Woods. The big Texan was off and running in a big way all through the month of November.

THE U.S. TITLE TOURNAMENT

There may have been no more important date or memorable card in Mid-Atlantic history than November 9, 1975. On that Sunday night in Greensboro, North Carolina a record capacity crowd of 15,076, with thousands of others being turned away, saw Texas sensation Terry Funk emerge victorious in a 16 man Tournament for Johnny Valentine's vacated United States Heavyweight Championship. Funk took the measure of Paul Jones in 18 grueling minutes in the final match of the Tournament, to take the United States Title back to Amarillo, Texas with him.

In addition to top flight Mid-Atlantic stars such as Wahoo McDaniel, Rufus R. Jones and Ken Patera participating in the Tournament, other big name stars such as Harley Race, Red Bastien and Dusty Rhodes from the NWA played significant roles in this mega Tournament. (See the special feature "The Tournament" elsewhere in this book.)

For those that were unable to see the U.S. Title Tournament live, or who wanted to relive the magical moments from that night, the November 19th Wide World Wrestling television program showed film highlights of Paul Jones beating Harley Race in the Tournament semi-finals, and Dusty Rhodes defeating Blackjack Mulligan in the second round of the Tournament. The Rhodes victory over Mulligan was accomplished with the help of interference by Tim Woods, who got revenge against Blackjack in a big way for the breaking of his hand on television several weeks earlier. The Woods-Mulligan feud would take off from this point, and last into early 1976.

ARRIVALS AND RIVALRIES

A major new star entered the territory in November of 1975, and he was none other than "Big Nasty" Angelo Mosca. With a stellar football background at Notre Dame and in the Canadian Football League, Mosca brought both impressive size and athleticism into the squared circle. Angelo's initial match for Jim Crockett Promotions was a win over Klondike Bill on November 10th at Charlotte's Park Center.

Mosca quickly earned his Mid-Atlantic stripes in November by battling, and getting the best of , big Swede Hanson. And on the November 26th taping of the Mid-Atlantic Championship Wrestling TV show at the WRAL Studios, Mosca came out along with Steve Strong and interrupted the interviews of good-guys Rufus R. Jones and Johnny Weaver...setting the stage for a tag team battle the next week on television. Mosca also had less than complementary things to say about another former pro football player, Chief Wahoo McDaniel. A collision course between these two ex-footballers seemed inevitable as November neared its end.

Another newcomer to the area, arriving during the month of November, was youngster Larry Zbyszko. While taking his lumps during his early Mid-Atlantic matches, Zbyszko showed real potential, and battled some of the area's fiercest bad guys tooth and nail.

Gene and Ole Anderson had another very successful month in November, holding onto their NWA World Tag Team Titles with a large number of Title defenses. As was the case in the month of October, the top challengers to the "Minnesota Wrecking Crew" was the young duo of Steve Keirn and Tiger Conway. However, as the month of November progressed, the champs began to take firm control of the game challengers. By the end of November, the Anderson's had taken Keirn's and Conway's best shot…and were looking for new teams to challenge them.

A highly entertaining feud broke out during November between Professor Boris Malenko and the big Chief Wahoo McDaniel. This would continue into December, including Wahoo's Indian Strap Match and Boris' famed Russian Chain Match. The bad blood came about when Wahoo broke Boris' teeth, though the two had issues back to Wahoo's football career when Malenko broke McDaniel's hand and Wahoo had to go to football camp one year with a cast on that hand. During the November 1975 wars, Malenko would often team with the Missouri Mauler against Wahoo and his fine partner, Paul Jones.

THE NWA WORLD CHAMPIONSHIP

NWA World Heavyweight Champion Jack Brisco visited the area over Thanksgiving week, and had a memorable series of Title defenses again the territory's top talent. Wahoo McDaniel, Paul Jones and Rufus R. Jones all had shots at the World Title during the last week in November, and all three came up just a bit short. Brisco's disqualification win over Rufus R. Jones in Charleston, South Carolina on November 28th would be Jack's last Title defense in the Mid-Atlantic area as NWA World's Heavyweight Champion.

The end of the month of November 1975 saw another historic Mid-Atlantic card of epic proportions. And again the event took place in the Greensboro Coliseum. On Thursday night November 27th, Paul Jones got revenge against Terry Funk, winning the U.S. Title and bringing it back to the Mid-Atlantic area! A wild crowd of 12,102 fans saw "Mr. # 1" send Funk back to Texas empty handed, after 22 minutes of incredible brawling. As the month of November ended, Paul held both the U.S. Title and the Mid-Atlantic Television Title. With Ric Flair still not physically able to defend his Mid-Atlantic Heavyweight Title, Paul Jones was THE singles titleholder in the Mid-Atlantic area!

The month of November 1975 proved without a doubt that the territory was not only going to survive after the Wilmington plane crash…but that Mid-Atlantic Championship Wrestling was going to thrive. And the best was yet to come!

WHO'S HOT

1. PAUL JONES---Jones made the finals of the November 9th U.S. Title Tournament, beating Harley Race to reach that final match. And then came back on November 27th to take the U.S. belt away from Terry Funk. At this juncture, no one would have bet against Jones becoming NWA World Champion, and in short order!

2. BLACKJACK MULLIGAN---The big Cowboy from Eagle Pass, Texas began hitting his stride in November. Dominating foe after foe, Mulligan would soon turn his attention to Paul Jones. As great as Jones was going, could anybody stop the steamroller known as Blackjack Mulligan?

3. ANGELO MOSCA---A truly impressive newcomer to the area, with a great athletic background and an ornery attitude to match. This "Madman" from Boston had "Superstar" written all over him from the outset.

WHO'S NOT

1. ART NELSON---The great Jim Crockett Promotions veteran wrestled his last match for the territory on November 1st. A tremendous career for this tough guy in the Carolinas and Virginia, which unfortunately stalled out for most of 1975 as the promotion went with younger talent.

2. SWEDE HANSON---Another veteran with Jim Crockett Promotions that started his descent down the cards during the year of 1975. While coming out on the short end against a talent like Angelo Mosca in November was no disgrace, it signaled that Swede's days in Main Events were over for good.

3. STEVE KEIRN/TIGER CONWAY---This dynamic team gave the Anderson's all they could handle, but by the end of November 1975 it appeared clear that they weren't going to take the "Wrecking Crew's" belts. After this fine run, neither Keirn nor Conway would sniff Main Events in the Mid-Atlantic area again. But they certainly fought the good fight against Gene and Ole.

DECEMBER

December of 1975 saw a limited amount of in-ring action, as Jim Crockett Promotions gave its wrestlers a ten day break from December 14th through December 24th. As the territory had been in upheaval since the Wilmington, North Carolina plane crash in early October of 1975, everybody without a doubt deserved a holiday break. Nevertheless, December 1975 was an eventful month in the history of Mid-Atlantic Championship Wrestling.

NEW NWA CHAMPIONS

Paul Jones was announced on Mid-Atlantic Championship Wrestling television as the new United States Heavyweight Champion on December 3, 1975 from the WRAL studios. Paul stated that due to the travel associated with defending the U.S. Title, he was relinquishing his Mid-Atlantic Television Title as he couldn't properly hold and defend both belts at the same time. David Crockett told the viewing audience that a tournament was being set up to crown a new Mid-Atlantic Television Champion. This tournament would be front and center during the early months of 1976.

The man who Paul Jones defeated for the U.S. Heavyweight Title, Terry Funk, pulled a major upset and unseated Jack Brisco for the NWA World Heavyweight Championship on December 10, 1975. However, due to the time the promotion took off during the month of December, Mid-Atlantic fans were not told of the change on TV until a number of weeks later. In fact, on the Mid-Atlantic Championship Wrestling 1975 Year In Review show that ran in most Jim Crockett Promotions cities on Saturday, December 27th and featured Funk against Wahoo McDaniel and Paul Jones in great matches from the year 1975, Terry Funk was not introduced as the new NWA World Champion! On the Mid-Atlantic Championship Wrestling TV show featuring Bob Caudle and David Crockett, this would not happen until the show that ran during the first week of 1976.

DECEMBER RIVALRIES

Tim Woods was announced during the month of December as having won a major tournament in Japan. Woods was getting ready to become embroiled in a major feud with Blackjack Mulligan, that would run through the early months of 1976. One of the first major bouts between Woods and Mulligan took place in the Greensboro Coliseum on December 26, 1975, with "Mr. Wrestling" winning, but having to be taken to the hospital after the bout. Things between these two combatants were just beginning to heat up as 1975 came to an end.

Blackjack Mulligan's battles in December of 1975 were not confined to those with Tim Woods. Mulligan's push for Paul Jones' United States Heavyweight Championship began with his first U.S. Title match against Jones, on December 9, 1975 at the Dorton Arena in Raleigh, North Carolina. These two would battle over the U.S. Title throughout 1976, and into the early months of 1977. Despite the vast difference in physical size between Jones and Mulligan, their budding feud would be among the most memorable in Mid-Atlantic history.

Two other rivals that went at each other hot and heavy during the month were Wahoo McDaniel and "Professor" Boris Malenko. The "Professor," still smarting from having his teeth broken by the big "Chief," engaged McDaniel in a series of Russian Chain matches. These bouts were Boris' favorite specialty matches, and were held in a number of the territory's big cities during December. Despite Malenko's advantage in these bouts, Wahoo came out the victor in all of these brutal encounters. Wahoo would then turn his attention to a building rivalry between former pro football players, with "Big Nasty" Angelo Mosca. Wahoo's program with Professor Malenko would spell the end of Malenko's full time in-ring career for Jim Crockett Promotions. Thereafter, the "Professor" wrestled sparingly,

MID-ATLANTIC WRESTLING 1975 YEARBOOK

New NWA World Champion Terry Funk moments after defeating Jack Brisco for the honors in the Miami Beach Convention Center on 12/10/75. (Original art by John Pagan.)

and focused his attention on managing, where he would excel as well.

Gene and Ole Anderson continued their tight grip on the NWA World Tag Team Titles during the month of December. The Anderson's finished their program with the young upstarts, Steve Keirn and Tiger Conway, defeating the youngsters in the last matches of the feud during December. For the rest of the month, the Anderson's took on duos made up from the area's finest good guys...Paul Jones, Wahoo McDaniel, Rufus R. Jones and Ken Patera. But the results were always the same---the Anderson's retained their Titles.

The last week of 1975 saw several "No DQ, There Must Be A Winner" matches involving Spoiler # 2 and the area's top good guys. When Paul Jones was involved, the matches were "Mask versus U.S. Title" bouts. These matches stretched into the first two weeks of 1976, and went around to all the big towns in the area. The results were all the same regardless of the town...Spoiler # 2 was defeated and was unmasked, effectively ending the big man's stint in the Mid-Atlantic area.

Another top flight star who concluded his time in the Mid-Atlantic area during the final days of 1975 was Superstar Billy Graham. After primarily battling Wahoo McDaniel during his Mid-Atlantic run, Graham teamed with Blackjack Mulligan to wrestle Tim Woods and Rufus R. Jones in Columbia, South Carolina on December 30, 1975. Despite having Ric Flair in his corner to interfere, Graham was pinned by Woods. The "Superstar" would soon head back to the WWWF full-time, and achieve his greatest fame there over the next two to three years.

"NATURE BOY" RIC FLAIR RETURNS TO TELEVISION

December of 1975 also saw the re-emergence of Mid-Atlantic Heavyweight Champion "Nature Boy" Ric Flair. While not wrestling, Flair was guest commentator on a number of the area's TV wrestling programs. One thing became very clear, the plane crash had in no way affected Ric's ability to talk! Flair also seemed to be building up alliances with two of the area's most feared rule breakers, Blackjack Mulligan and Angelo Mosca. By the end of the month, Flair began his transition back to active duty, seconding several of his wrestling friends in the area's arenas.

WRESTLER OF THE YEAR

As the month of December, and the year of 1975, reached its last week, several notable occurrences took place. One, the promotion reminded us that the 1975 "Wrestler of the Year" contest was nearing its end, and for fans to get their ballots in. While the winner's name, Wahoo McDaniel, would not be released until early 1976, Wahoo's eventual victory would not come without controversy. Ric Flair was the top vote-getter, but was disqualified for sending in hundreds of ballots voting for himself, making Wahoo the winner!

Despite December of 1975 being a short month in terms of in-ring action, it set the table nicely for a number of huge programs that would boil over into the beginnings of the bi-centennial year of

1976. And December gave us pause to remember the year of 1975 as a whole, a year that was truly unforgettable in the annals of Mid-Atlantic Championship Wrestling history!

WHO'S HOT

PAUL JONES---"Mr. # 1" held onto his newly won United States Heavyweight Championship, and at this time was widely considered a top contender for the NWA World Heavyweight Championship. Jones was probably at the zenith of his Mid-Atlantic career this month.

BLACKJACK MULLIGAN---The big Cowboy from Eagle Pass, Texas was already right on Paul Jones' heels, setting his sights on becoming the new United States Champion. Mulligan was destroying everything in his path, and appeared nearly invincible.

ANGELO MOSCA---The "Madman" from Boston was tearing through the competition, and was zeroing in on Wahoo McDaniel. As tough as the "Big Chief" was, Mosca seemed to have all of the attributes needed to give Wahoo a real run for his money.

WHO'S NOT

SPOILER # 2---After coming into the area in the late summer of 1975 to avenge the unmasking of his friend, the Super Destroyer, December saw Spoiler # 2 suffer the same fate and exit from the territory!

SUPERSTAR BILLY GRAHAM---Coming into the area after the plane crash to help fill the void created by Ric Flair's injury, Graham exited the area just as Flair was returning. No coincidence!

STEVE STRONG---Graham's running mate, Strong began to slide down the cards just as "Superstar" was leaving the territory. Again, no coincidence!

Back in 1975, long before VHS home-video recording, David Chappell started recording Mid-Atlantic Wrestling on audio cassettes using a portable cassette tape recorder with a hand-held microphone plugged into the side. It was from these tapes that David was able to piece together the week-to-week television history of Mid-Atlantic Wrestling.

At left is an actual audio cassette tape David recorded in 1975.

MID-ATLANTIC WRESTLING 1975 YEARBOOK

The Booker's Daily Planner

The day before and the day of the Willmington NC plane crash that changed the face of the Mid-Atlantic territory forever.

A Raleigh TV taping for Mid-Atlantic and Wide World Wrestling. Plus the two annual Thanksgiving shows for 1975 in Greensboro, NC, and Norfolk, VA.

Mid-Atlantic Championship Wrestling Magazine

Volume One Issue Four

MID-ATLANTIC WRESTLING 1975 YEARBOOK

MID-ATLANTIC WRESTLING 1975 YEARBOOK

Chief Wahoo McDaniel

MR. WRESTLING

AAU CHAMPION **NWA CHAMPION**

You would almost have to say that Tim Woods is a man with a split personality because it is difficult to believe that the man you have just seen in the ring and the man you are now talking with is the same. Well, as difficult as it may seem, he is indeed the same man. Outwardly Tim is a well-scrubbed all-American businessman with a very successful air about him. Crammed inside however is perhaps professional wrestling's most talented and successful competitor.

Tim is a man who has done it all. His amateur background includes high school and college National AAU Championships and the Southern, Florida and Georgia State professional titles. He has not only excelled as a wrestler but in auto drag racing, motorcycle racing, photography and as a capable and shrewd businessman.

There are two things that keep him from being happy. Tim wants to be the World Heavyweight Champion. He has defeated six World Champions but never in a championship match. Is he jinxed? Some people think so. Once in a championship match, Tim was thrown from the ring when a turnbuckle broke and knocked unconscious. Things were going his way in a second championship match when stitches broke in an injured hand and the referee stopped the bout. Woods is a champion in quest of a World Title.

The second problem stems from a broken leg he received at the hands of Johnny Valentine. Woods is back with vengence in his eyes to pay back that score.

Woods will never quit; he will face all comers; he will once again wear a Championship belt. That is why he is called "Mr. Wrestling."

MID-ATLANTIC WRESTLING 1975 YEARBOOK

Gene & Ole Anderson
World Tag Team Champions

MID-ATLANTIC WRESTLING 1975 YEARBOOK

Don Kernodle Makes a Move on Don Serrano

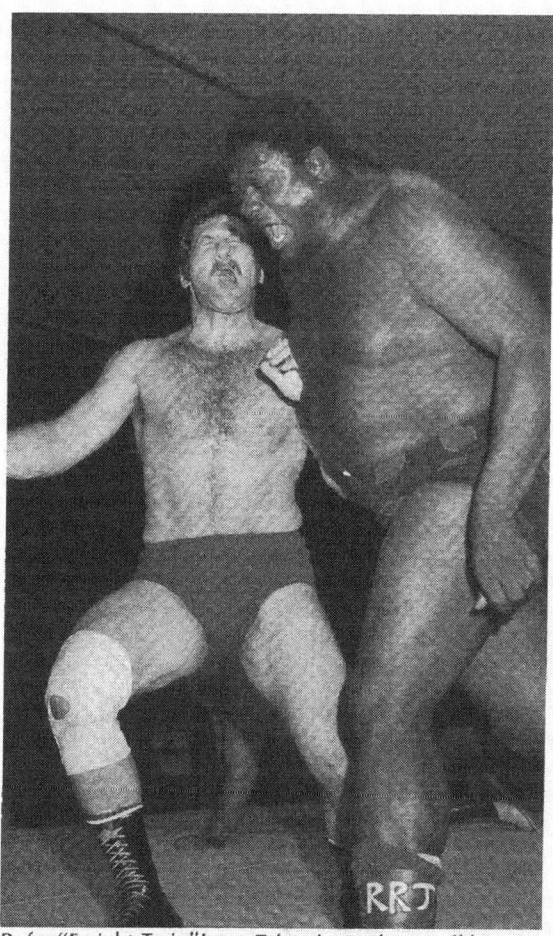

Rufus "Freight Train" Jones Takes the Professor off his Feet

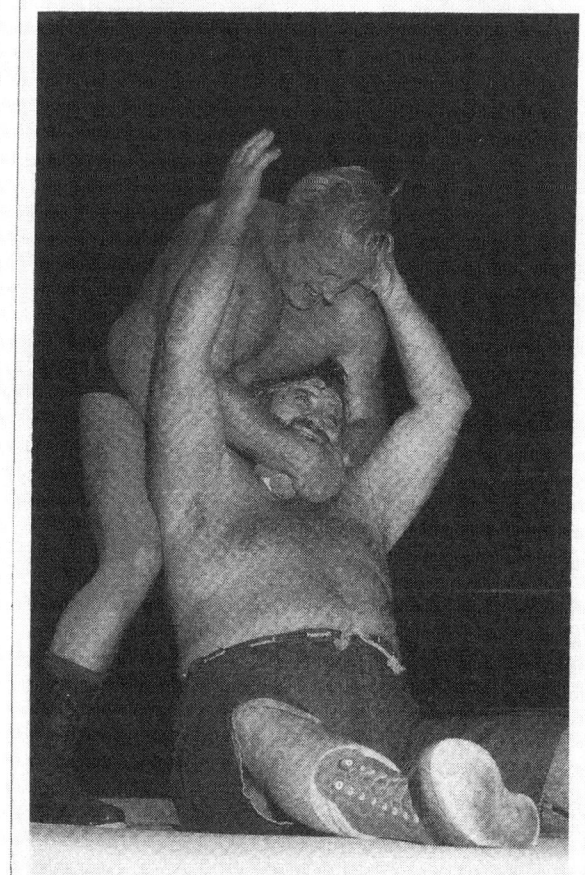

Art Nelson with a Chin-Lock on Klondike Bill

Valentine Stands Over Harley Race in their Battle for U.S. Crown

THE MAN FROM EAGLE PASS

"I have returned!" The voice that rumbled from deep within the huge man was as rugged as his face was stern. "This hick town needs some cleaning up and I aim to handle that chore. The ladies will be happy and the little fat men will shake in their shoes when they hear that Blackjack is back in town. I was sittin' on my ranch down in Eagle Pass, Texas, enjoyin' myself when I got word what some of your sissy rasslers was sayin' about Jack. Imagine ol' Jack laying low to keep from gettin' whipped. I wasn't plannin' on leaving my spread but my foreman "Spider" Grip said, Jack boy, go on up there and straighten that mess out. Well, I'm here and I aim to start taking names and whippin' tails. I plan on starting with that fat Indian boy (Wahoo McDaniel) and those pretty faces, Tim Woods and Steve Keirn. I'm not forgettin' about those boys Paul Jones and Kitty Cat Conway. Those boys keep saying they are from Texas. Shucks, we whip children with a razor strap for lying. I'm gonna teach these younguns a real lesson in manners."

Blackjack Mulligan is indeed a huge hulk of a man at 6'7" and over 300 lbs. He has damaged many wrestlers with a vicious blow from his giant fist or a kick from his boot. He plans to "clean up this mess" and perhaps he will. But if he left the safety of his ranch to come to the Mid-Atlantic area for a cake walk, he better not unpack his bags. There are plenty of men here who will button his loud lip.

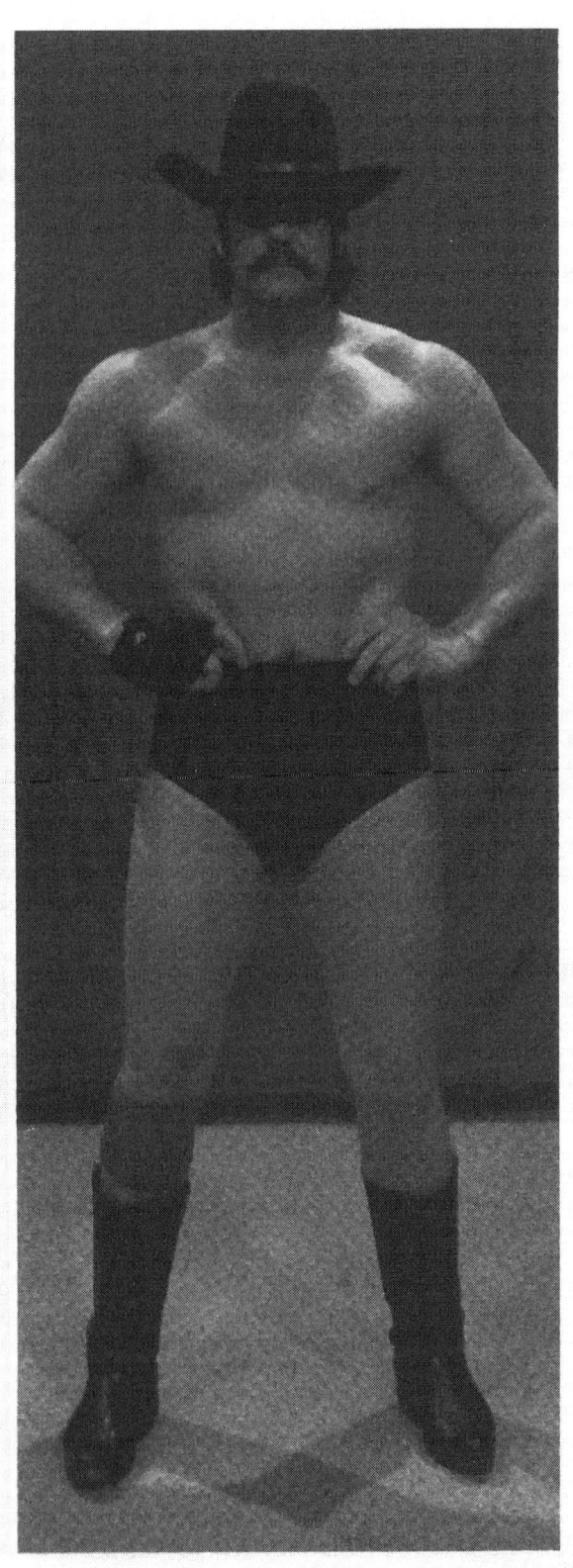

MID-ATLANTIC WRESTLING 1975 YEARBOOK

Paul Jones

MID-ATLANTIC WRESTLING 1975 YEARBOOK

Spoiler II Finds the Only Way to Hold Swede Down is to Stand on Him

Ole Ready to Drive a Foot into Wahoo's Chest

The Greensboro Coliseum Packed with Wrestling Fans

"The Champ" Leaps from the Ropes on to "The American Dream"

PAUL JONES THE MAN

One of the best known and most popular people in the Mid-Atlantic area is Paul Jones. His dark, square cut, handsome features are the heartbeat of a thousand ladies and the nightmare of every man who must face him in the ring. The current Mid-Atlantic TV Champion, Paul is a rugged and capable competitor. How would you like to know more about the Paul outside of the ring? I spent the day at home with "PJ" and here is my report. Paul always has a kind word for children and enjoys mingling and signing autographs. Youngsters who know where Paul lives drop by to say "hello" or ask advice or just to see "the famous man who lives up the street." He enjoys his private time and spends as much as possible with his family. His mother still lives in his hometown of Port Arthur, Texas where Paul returns for some of her good home cooking. Paul and his mom both enjoy country music.

Paul is an intense young man who is now getting involved in real estate and the stock market. He is keeping his eye on the future when he will be able to use another skill to earn his living. Unlike the violence of the wrestling wars my day with Paul was calm. We enjoyed some good food and good company; even a little football on television. It was almost a perfect day ... almost ... I saw his eyes squint into small slits; his mouth became a fine, tight line; he lost his temper and kicked his lawnmower because it wouldn't start. After all, Paul Jones is only human.

MID-ATLANTIC WRESTLING 1975 YEARBOOK

Rufus R. Jones

MID-ATLANTIC WRESTLING 1975 YEARBOOK

Tony Rocco Uses a Headlock to take Two Ton to the Mat

Doug Gilbert Opens Up On Tiger Conway

Serrano Takes the Judge Up and Over with a Hiplock

Wahoo Locks Ole in a Stretch

I HAVE A MISSION

Huge... Imposing... Scary... Words that fittingly describe the masked giant in the black outfit. This awesome veteran of many wrestling wars punishes his opponent again for the three count; dusts off his hands and stalks from the ring.

In the dressing room he sits puffing on a big cigar while his partner, Spoiler I, sits quietly and looks on.

He is a man with a mission which is almost an obsession. "I have a job to do," says the Spoiler II. "My friend, the Super Destroyer, Don Jardine, wrestled in this area for almost two years. He smashed all of his competition until a few of your local wrestlers ganged up on him and took his mask off. They know who they are so I won't call names. What I want to tell you and your readers is that I am here on a mission. I have come to avenge the defeat of my friend and pay back those wrongdoers. I will meet all comers and if I, The Spoiler II, ever lose I will take off my mask for all to see. My partner and I, The Spoiler I and The Spoiler II will meet all of your tag teams and (as he dusts his hands) smash them all." He is grim and positive in the way he talks. He is confident that he will get those men who he is after. No one knows who he is or where he came from but one thing is sure... during his brief stay he has punished many area grapplers and has his eyes set on "His Mission."

MID-ATLANTIC WRESTLING 1975 YEARBOOK

Johnny Weaver

Klondike Bill Readies Art Nelson for a Trip Across the Ring

Jerry Blackwell Makes a Grab for the Avenger

Mr. Wrestling Forgets the Rules and Turns to the Anderson's Tactics

This is the Kind of Action You See When the World Title is at Stake

LOOK AT ME!

I work hard to search out stories of interest for your fans but the other night while I was at home at my typewriter a story came to me. The door swung open and in he marched, Ric Flair, a man of a million words. As usual there was a beautiful woman on each arm and he was talking a mile a minute. Before he could get out the words Mid-Atlantic Heavyweight Champion, I saw the belt around his waist. "Hey my man I know how hard you work so I'm bringing you a $$$$$$ million dollar story. I AM the new Mid-Atlantic Champion. Was there ever any doubt; I am the greatest wrestler in the world today. I am the Champion! Raquel and Joey flew in when they heard the news and we are going to Vegas for a party." Before I could get a word in he sat down in an easy chair and pulled the two girls on his lap. "One punch—with one punch I knocked that squawman McDaniel out cold. He has been running from me because he knew that I would take his belt. And you know what is next? That's right. Jack Brisco is next and the World Heavyweight Championship. I am the next World Champion. No one can stand in my way. When you are as great as I am nobody can compare. Now I can take all of this money and buy a new car and a mink coat for each of my babies."

I sat taking all of this in knowing that Ric Flair, the new Mid-Atlantic Heavyweight Champion, may be telling the truth. He is in fact a great wrestler. How great? Well no one knows yet. But one thing is sure, he is headed for the top and along the way he will leave behind big cars, broken hearts and dozens of aching grapplers who got in his way.

"Let's go, girls. We don't want to miss our Vegas connection. What a party this will be. Maybe Joe Namath can join us." As quickly as he interrupted my evening he was off again. Flair will have to defend his title while he looks for a shot at Brisco, and, you can bet that Wahoo McDaniel will be hot on his trail.

MID-ATLANTIC WRESTLING 1975 YEARBOOK

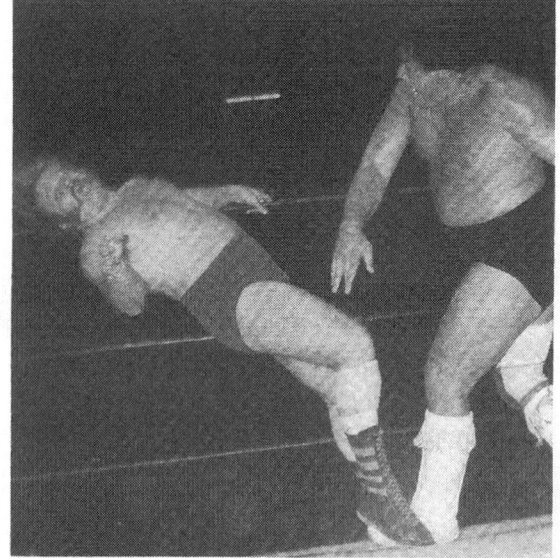

Wahoo's Chop Sends Ole Crashing to the Canvas

The Mauler Chokes Rufus With the Tag Rope

The Spoiler II Lands with all his Weight on Klondike Bill

Tim Woods Hooks Gene Anderson in Mid Ring

THIS MAN DOESN'T RUN

Everyone knows by now that Ric Flair beat Wahoo McDaniel for his Mid-Atlantic Heavyweight Championship belt in Hampton, Virginia. Wahoo is visably shaken by this turn of events but has been very quiet. He doesn't make excuses; Wahoo isn't like that. He was beaten.

"I don't cry over spilled milk. Flair is tough; rugged; one good wrestler. But he hit me with something. The fans who were there saw him hit me with something and knock me out cold with one punch. I still can't believe it; Flair ran out of the ring with my Championship belt. I fought the hardest battle in my life to get that belt and no one is going to take it away with a cheap shot."

As McDaniels talks he becomes more upset, more annoyed at the idea of a defeat, any defeat. "I've tried to be cool about this but he hit me with something. I've signed a contract to meet him again and if he can beat me fair and square then I will take my hat off to him. He is cocky enough to think that he can beat me; well let him prove it. I'll give him a wrestling lesson that he won't soon forget: I have never been scared of anyone. I don't back up for anybody. When I get hit I come back and hit a little harder. If Flair wants to be hit again and again, well tell him I'll wrestle him a hundred times. Valentine knows that I don't run. I took the wind out of his sails when I won his belt and I'll take a couple of pegs out of Flair. I'll not sit and cry; I'll fight back. Flair will be sorry."

Wahoo is certainly a man of his word so be prepared.

MID-ATLANTIC WRESTLING 1975 YEARBOOK

Mike "The Judge" Dubois

Ray Stevens has earned the name "The Crippler."

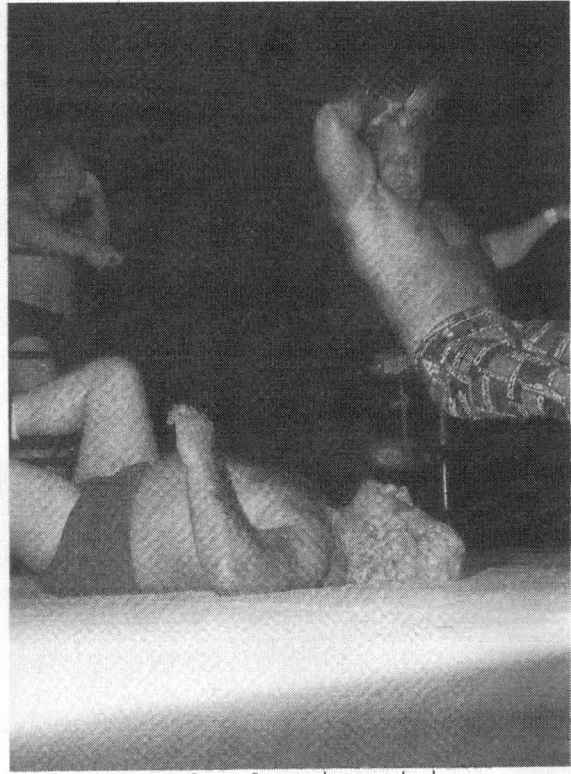

Newcomer Steve Strong lowers the boom on Swede Hanson

Rugged Tag Duo Professor Malenko and The Missouri Mauler

THEY COME OUT SMOKIN'

It was a beautiful day for traveling, and we were heading north on I-85 in a custom van. I was relaxed in a sprawling bean bag chair and listening to rock music pounding out of the stereo. My partners in the van kept time to the music with bobbing heads and clapping hands. We were worlds away from the crowds and the lights of professional wrestling with two of the sport's most promising stars. Their lives are not always so easy and carefree; especially when your names are Steve Keirn and Tiger Conway.

Just a short time ago they teamed up to enter the wrestling wars of the Mid-Atlantic area. They need the escape of music and relaxation; because when they enter the ring, their shoulders are heavy under the pressure to win and to keep their string alive. Reach the top . . . in some people's eyes they have already reached the top. On a television show taped in Raleigh recently, fans could not believe their eyes when the young stars took on The World Tag Team Champions, Ole and Gene Anderson and scored a stunning upset. Was it an upset? Perhaps. "Hey Bro, we knew we had our thing together when we stepped into the ring. Looky here, I wanna tell you the Andersons are tough, but their time is comin'! They will lose their belts, and I jus' hope it's us in the ring. We will be pressin' those dudes; and every time they look back, we will be gaining on them." Conway's comments were cut short by Keirn's interruption. "He's right, man. Our time is now. If everything goes right for us, we will be the champs. We work hard together, and the more we work, the better we get."

"Hey man, you can tell your readers that Steve and TC have it all together and are lookin' for a chance to get it on with the Andersons."

Actions certainly speak louder than words, and Steve Keirn and Tiger Conway are two action-packed men headed for the top.

MID-ATLANTIC WRESTLING 1975 YEARBOOK

Paul Jones Bridges his Way Out of Gene Anderson's Head Scissors

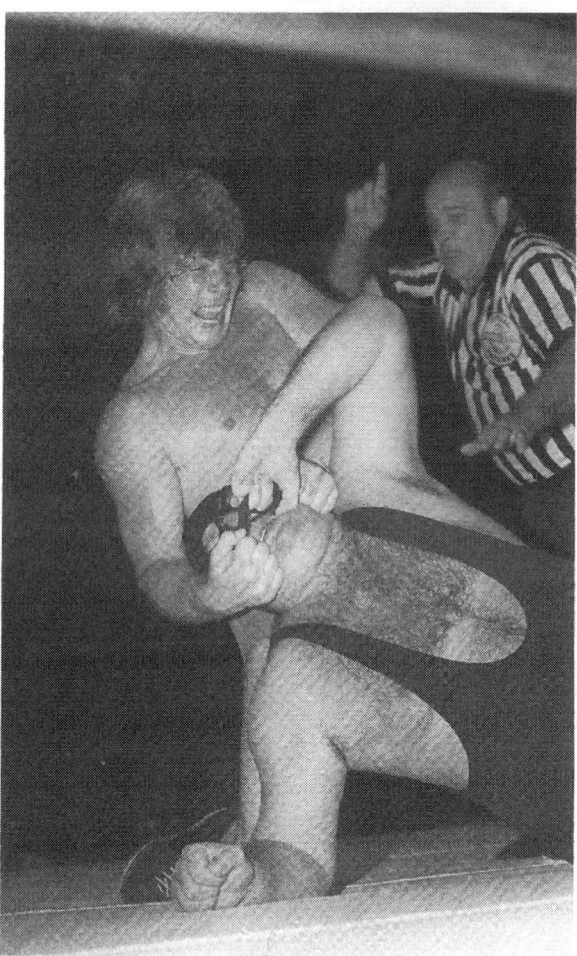

Bob Bruggers Attempts to Unmask Spoiler II

Roberto Soto Blocks Doug Sommer's Attempt at a Front Face Lock.

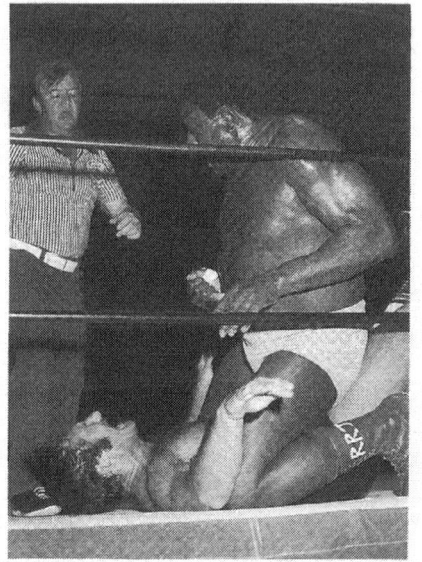

Rufus R. Has Malenko Down and in Trouble

"Super Star" Billy Graham

THE PEOPLE'S CHOICE

"Life can be a drag or life can be a bust, but you gotta keep on keepin' on." So is the code of one of professional wrestling's true super stars. The man they call "The American Dream" and "The Big Dust," Dusty Rhodes. The big blond has a rap for everyone; the young and the old, and people of all colors. Wrestling arenas fill when his name is on the billboard and his lifestyle is the envy of thousands of young men all around the country. If you see his name listed to appear at your local arena, don't miss it. Because he will keep on keepin' on!

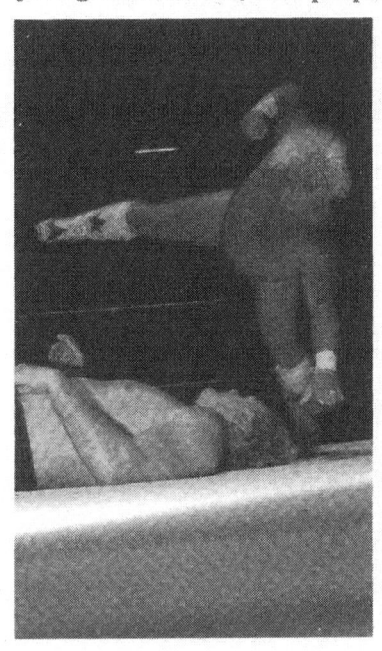

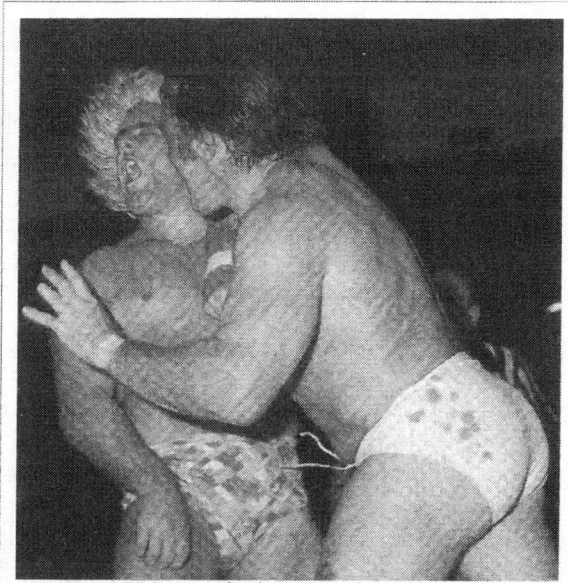

MID-ATLANTIC WRESTLING 1975 YEARBOOK

Woods' Blast to Flair's Jaw Rocks Him in One of their Bloody Matches

Wahoo on the War Path Throws a Chop to Valentine's Head

Strong Man Ken Patera Lifts the Professor by his Hair

Don Kernodle Bears Down on Two Ton Harris

MID-ATLANTIC WRESTLING 1975 YEARBOOK

Ken Patera

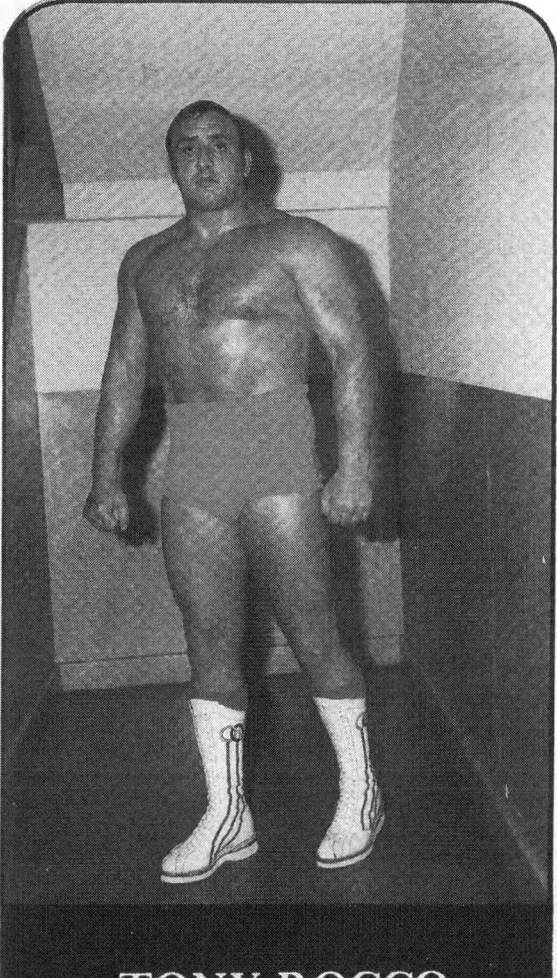

TONY ROCCO

The NWA is a world-wide organization attracting the world's greatest athletes to compete in this challenging profession. Italy certainly has contributed a long list of impressive participants, but none are more knowledgeable and skillful than Tony Rocco. Tony has all of the tools to head this list and continues to impress fans and opponents with his ring savvy. One needs only to watch this agile athlete to appreciate his ability. Tony enjoys swimming and auto racing in his free time.

Keep an eye on this young battler, but don't be fooled by his handsome Italian smile; Tony Rocco can mix it up when the time comes.

STEVE STRONG

"Muscles on top of muscles, and muscles where other people have none." Those are comments that can truthfully be made about young Steve Strong from Arizona. He has entered the wrestling wars of the Mid-Atlantic area and is making big waves. The two-year pro out of Phoenix University has been trained under the watchful eye of "Superstar Billy Graham." Before turning professional, Steve piled up honors in both basketball and weightlifting. He was two time college All-American and Arizona powerlifting champion. Muscles don't make a wrestler; Steve will have to prove just how tough he really is.

MID-ATLANTIC WRESTLING 1975 YEARBOOK

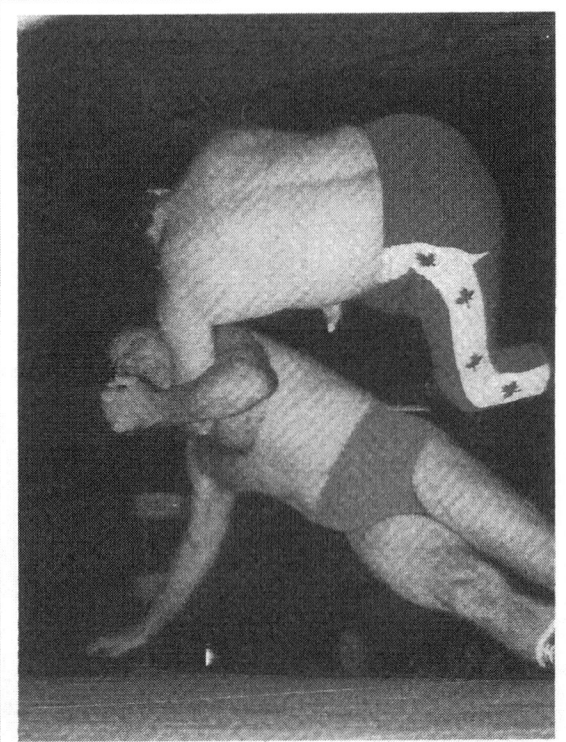

Weaver Hooks the Judge with an Arm Drag

Tony Rocco Takes Larry Sharpe High on his Way to the Canvas

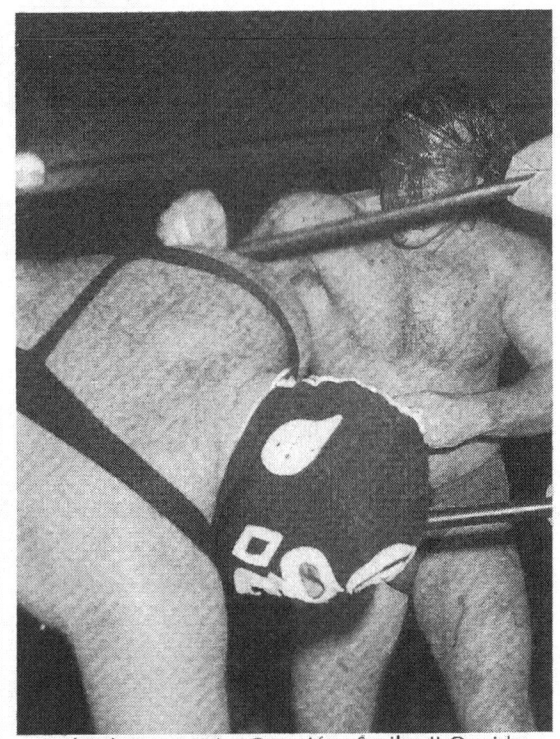

A Bloody Steve Keirn Goes After Spoiler II Outside the Ring

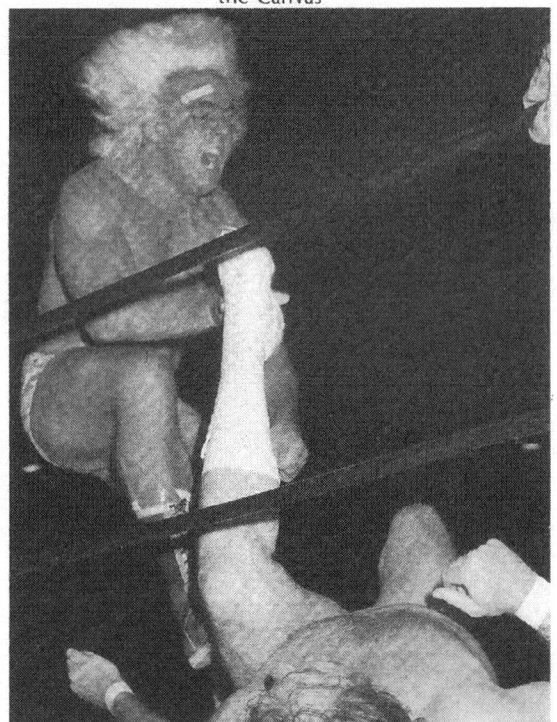

Flair Has His Work Cut Out for Him When He Takes On Tim Woods

28

MID-ATLANTIC WRESTLING 1975 YEARBOOK

Steve Keirn & Tiger Conway

MID-ATLANTIC WRESTLING 1975 YEARBOOK

TONY ATLAS

In our last issue you saw a story and pictures on how Tony Atlas trained and began his professional wrestling career. Now some five months later what has happened to this rookie? Oh, not very much, he's just looked like a four-year veteran against the likes of such great stars as Johnny Valentine, The Andersons, Ric Flair and others. Tony is stardom bound and unless something unforseen happens he will be a regional champion somewhere in these United States before too much longer. His future is being shaped by such men as George Scott, Wahoo McDaniel, Paul Jones, and others. With this type of training and guidance how can he go wrong! As you watch this young fellow move about a wrestling ring, keep in mind that he may someday be the champion wrestler of the world.

JOHNNY WEAVER

What can be told to the professional wrestling fans of the southeast about Johnny Weaver that they don't know already? This gentleman from Indiana has left his mark on wrestling rings all over the area. Several times singles champion and many times tag team champion "Mr. Defense" has done it all. Weaver went on tour for almost a year. In that time he covered most of the U.S.A. and parts of Canada. While he was gone, the always rich in wrestling talent Mid-Atlantic region became the center of top grappling talent for the country. This never say quit guy has his work cut out for him and he's looking forward to it! He says he'll battle his way back to the top of the heap and when he gets there, he plans to stay.

MID-ATLANTIC WRESTLING 1975 YEARBOOK

Ric Flair

MID-ATLANTIC WRESTLING 1975 YEARBOOK

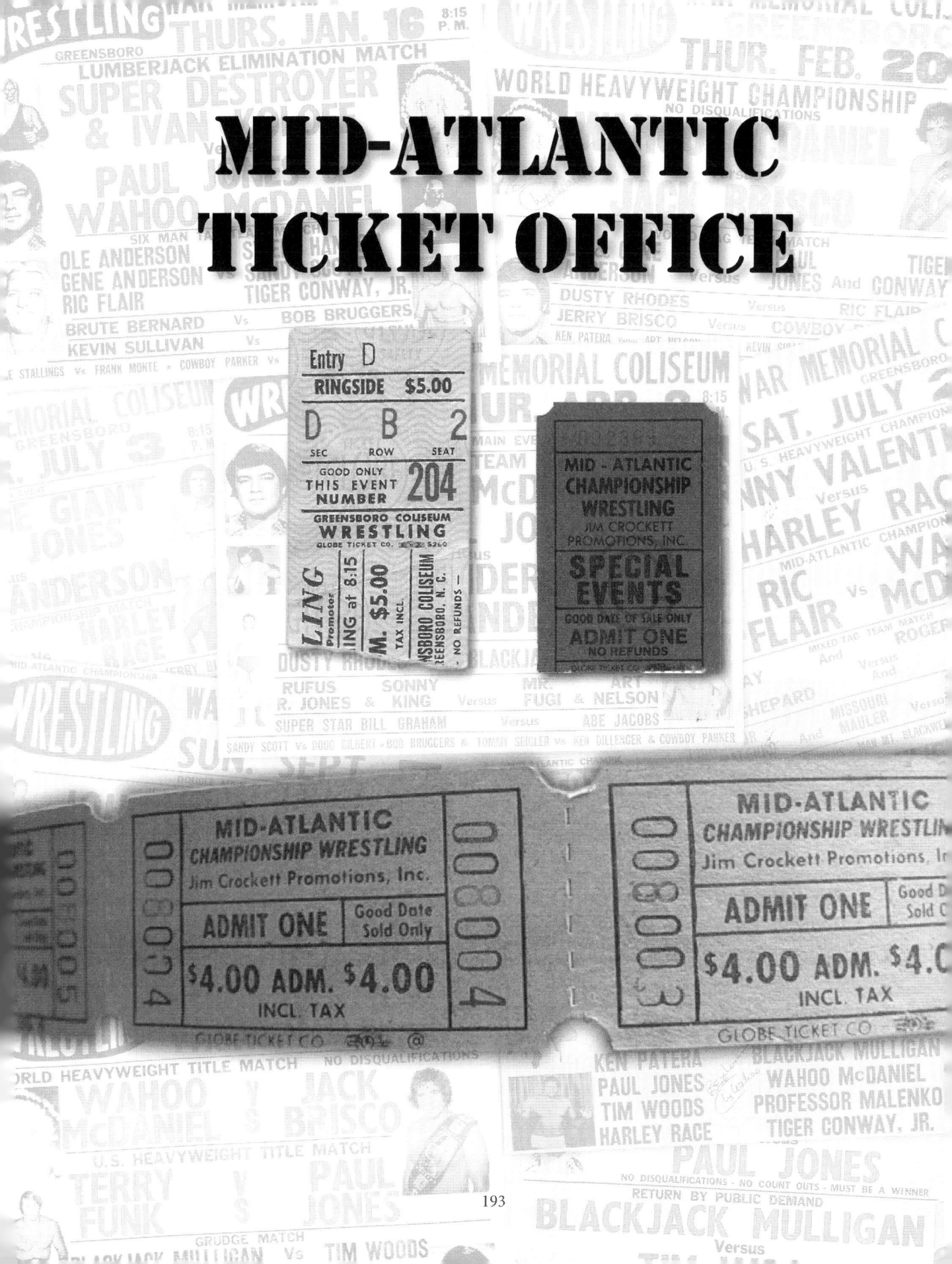

MID-ATLANTIC TICKET OFFICE

193

RECORD BOOK

Match Listings and Results compiled by Mark James from his collection "Wrestling Record Book: Jim Crockett Promotions 1970-1979"

JANUARY

1/1/75: Greenville, SC @ Memorial Auditorium
Paul Jones, Sonny King & Wahoo McDaniel beat Ivan Koloff, Johnny Valentine & Ole Anderson (sub for Super Destroyer)
Gene & Ole Anderson beat Sandy Scott & Bob Bruggers
Charlie Cook beat George Harris
Frank Monte draw Mike Stallings

1/1/75: Raleigh, NC @ WRAL Studios (TV)

1/2/75: Norfolk, VA @ Scope
Paul Jones & Tiger Conway, Jr. beat Ivan Koloff & Ric Flair
Mr. Fuji beat Sandy Scott
Charlie Cook & Tommy Seigler beat Brute Bernard & Art Neilson
Abe Jacobs draw Cowboy Parker

1/3/75: Richmond, VA @ Coliseum
The Avenger beat Super Destroyer by DQ
Gene & Ole Anderson beat Paul Jones & Tiger Conway, Jr.
Ric Flair beat Tommy Seigler
Mr. Fuji beat Bob Bruggers
Sandy Scott beat Brute Bernard
Abe Jacobs draw Art Neilson
Charlie Cook beat Cowboy Parker

1/3/75: Charleston, SC @ County Hall
Wahoo McDaniel & Sonny King beat Johnny Valentine & Ivan Koloff
Swede Hanson beat Chuck O'Connor
Klondike Bill & Tio Tio beat Frank Morrell & George Harris
Joe Furr beat Ken Dillinger

1/4/75: Roanoke, VA @ Starland Arena
The Avenger beat Super Destroyer by reverse decision
Tiger Conway, Jr. beat George Harris
Abe Jacobs & Tommy Seigler beat Mr. Fuji & Art Neilson
Cowboy Parker beat Tio Tio
Joe Furr beat Pedro Godoy

1/4/75: Winston-Salem, NC @ Memorial Coliseum
Paul Jones, Wahoo McDaniel & Sonny King vs. Ric Flair, Johnny Valentine & Ivan Koloff
Gene & Ole Anderson vs. Sandy Scott & Bob Bruggers
Chuck O'Connor vs. Charlie Cook
Don Kernodle vs. Frank Morrell
Mr. Hayashi vs. Mike Stallings

1/5/75: Asheville, NC @ Civic Center
Wahoo McDaniel beat Johnny Valentine by DQ
Paul Jones & Tiger Conway, Jr. beat Ivan Koloff & Ric Flair
Ole Anderson beat Tommy Seigler
Klondike Bill beat George Harris
Frank Monte beat Mr. Hayashi
Mike Paidousis draw Don Kernodle

1/6/75: Charlotte, NC @ Park Center
Johnny Valentine beat Paul Jones by CO
Swede Hanson & Tiger Conway, Jr. beat Gene & Ole Anderson by DQ
Ric Flair beat Bob Bruggers
Mr. Fuji beat Don Kernodle
Frank Morrell beat Joe Furr

1/7/75: Columbia, SC @ Township Auditorium
Wahoo McDaniel beat Johnny Valentine via pinfall
Gene & Ole Anderson beat Sandy Scott & Bob Bruggers
Charlie Cook beat Cowboy Parker
Swede Hanson beat Mr. Fuji by DQ
Klondike Bill beat George Harris
Tio Tio beat Mike Paidousis

MID-ATLANTIC WRESTLING 1975 YEARBOOK

1/7/75: Raleigh, NC @ Dorton Arena
Ric Flair, Ivan Koloff & Super Destroyer DDQ Paul Jones, Tiger Conway, Jr. & Sonny King
Tommy Seigler beat Brute Bernard by DQ
The Avenger beat Frank Monte
Art Neilson draw Abe Jacobs
Mike Stallings beat Mr. Hayashi

1/8/75: Raleigh, NC @ WRAL Studios (TV)

1/9/75: Norfolk, VA @ Scope
Paul Jones & Tiger Conway, Jr. beat Ivan Koloff & Ric Flair
Swede Hanson beat Mr. Fuji by DQ
Cowboy Parker beat Bob Bruggers
Mike Stallings beat Ken Dillinger
Frank Monte draw Tio Tio

1/10/75: Charleston, SC @ County Hall
Sonny King beat Johnny Valentine by CO
Tommy Seigler beat Art Neilson
Abe Jacobs beat Mike Paidousis
Joe Furr & Don Kernodle beat Mr. Hayashi & Roberto Soto

1/10/75: Lynchburg, VA @ City Armory
Super Destroyer & Ivan Koloff beat Wahoo McDaniel & The Avenger by DQ
Charlie Cook beat Cowboy Parker
Bobby Williams beat Ken Dillinger
Bob Bruggers beat Frank Monte
Tio Tio beat Johnny Heidman

1/10/75: Richmond, VA @ Coliseum
Paul Jones & Tiger Conway, Jr. DDQ Gene & Ole Anderson
Swede Hanson beat Ric Flair
Klondike Bill beat Mr. Fuji
Sandy Scott beat George Harris
Mike Stallings draw Frank Monte

1/11/75: Spartanburg, SC @ Memorial Auditorium
Paul Jones beat Ivan Koloff
Sonny King beat Ric Flair by DQ
Cowboy Parker & Art Neilson beat Abe Jacobs & Bob Bruggers
Tio Tio beat Mr. Hayashi
Mike Paidousis draw Don Kernodle (20:00)

1/11/75: Conway, SC @ Williams-Brice Building
Wahoo McDaniel vs. Johnny Valentine
Plus other matches

1/11/75: Roanoke, VA @ Starland Arena
Tiger Conway, Jr. & The Avenger beat Super Destroyer & Mr. Fuji via pinfall
Charlie Cook beat Frank Monte
Bobby Williams beat Frank Morrell
Mike Stallings beat Joe Furr

1/13/75: Greenville, SC @ Memorial Auditorium

1/13/75: Charlotte, NC @ Park Center
Johnny Valentine DCO with Paul Jones (37:00) in a match with Sonny King as special referee
Ivan Koloff & Ric Flair beat Charlie Cook & Tommy Seigler
Abe Jacobs beat Frank Morrell
Frank Monte beat Joe Furr
Cowboy Parker beat Mike Stallings

1/13/75: Fayetteville, NC @ Cumberland County Memorial Auditorium
Wahoo McDaniel won a $5200 battle royal by throwing Ole Anderson over the top rope
Also in Battle Royal: Super Destroyer, Gene Anderson, Mr. Fuji, Brute Bernard, Tiger Conway, Jr., Sandy Scott, Art Neilson, Swede Hanson, George Harris, Kevin Sullivan & Klondike Bill

1/14/75: Columbia, SC @ Township Auditorium
Johnny Valentine vs. Wahoo McDaniel
Gene & Ole Anderson vs. Tommy Seigler & Charlie Cook
Brute Bernard vs. Swede Hanson
Frank Morrell vs. George Harris
Mr. Hayashi vs. Mike Stallings

1/14/75: Raleigh, NC @ Dorton Arena
Paul Jones, Tiger Conway, Jr. & Sonny King beat Ric Flair, Ivan Koloff & Super Destroyer in a Texas tornado match
Abe Jacobs beat Art Neilson by DQ
Sandy Scott beat Mike Paidousis
Kevin Sullivan beat Ken Dillinger

1/15/75: Raleigh, NC @ WRAL Studios (TV)

1/16/75: Greensboro, NC @ Coliseum
Paul Jones & Wahoo McDaniel beat Super Destroyer & Ivan Koloff by DQ in a 2 of 3 falls, lumberjack elimination match
Gene & Ole Anderson & Ric Flair beat Tiger Conway, Jr., Swede Hanson & Sandy Scott (18:00)
Brute Bernard beat Tio Tio
Kevin Sullivan beat Mr. Hayashi
Mike Stallings beat Frank Monte

195

MID-ATLANTIC WRESTLING 1975 YEARBOOK

Cowboy Parker beat Joe Furr

1/16/75: Norfolk, VA @ Scope
Johnny Valentine vs. Sonny King
Charlie Cook & Tommy Seigler vs. Art Neilson & Mr. Fuji
Also included Abe Jacobs, Klondike Bill and others

1/17/75: Goldsboro, NC @ Wayne County Boys Club
Gene & Ole Anderson vs. Sonny King & Sandy Scott
Plus other matches

1/17/75: Richmond, VA @ Coliseum
Super Destroyer & Johnny Valentine beat Wahoo McDaniel & Swede Hanson
Charlie Cook & Tommy Seigler beat Mr. Fuji & Brute Bernard
Kevin Sullivan beat Ken Dillinger
Tio Tio draw George Harris

1/17/75: Charleston, SC @ County Hall
Paul Jones & Tiger Conway, Jr. beat Ivan Koloff & Ric Flair
Cowboy Parker vs. Mike Stallings
Joe Furr vs. Frank Monte
Mr. Hayashi vs. Johnny Heidman

1/18/75: Roanoke, VA @ Starland Arena
Tiger Conway, Jr. & Sandy Scott beat Gene & Ole Anderson
Abe Jacobs beat Art Neilson
Mike Stallings draw Frank Monte
Johnny Heidman draw Joe Soto

1/18/75: Spartanburg, SC @ Memorial Auditorium
Ric Flair & Ivan Koloff beat Sonny King & Swede Hanson
Klondike Bill beat Cowboy Parker
Kevin Sullivan beat Mr. Hayashi
Mike Paidousis beat Joe Furr

1/18/75: Hampton, VA @ Coliseum
Wahoo McDaniel draw Johnny Valentine in a match with George Scott special ref
Super Destroyer beat Paul Jones by DQ
Charlie Cook beat Brute Bernard
Tommy Seigler beat Mr. Fuji
Don Kernodle & Tio Tio beat Ken Dillinger & George Harris
Charlie Cook beat Frank Morrell

1/20/75: Charlotte, NC @ Park Center
Johnny Valentine beat Paul Jones (45:00) in a lumberjack match
Sonny King beat Ivan Koloff by DQ

Ric Flair & Mr. Fuji beat Abe Jacobs & Tiger Conway, Jr.
Sandy Scott draw Art Neilson
Kevin Sullivan beat Ken Dillinger

1/20/75: Greenville, SC @ Memorial Auditorium
The Avenger & Wahoo McDaniel beat Super Destroyer & Brute Bernard
Gene & Ole Anderson beat Charlie Cook & Swede Hanson
Cowboy Parker beat Mike Stallings
Tommy Seigler beat Frank Monte

1/21/75: Columbia, SC @ Township Auditorium
Ric Flair, Ivan Koloff & Super Destroyer beat Paul Jones, Tiger Conway, Jr. & Sonny King
The Avenger beat Art Neilson
Joe Furr draw Mr. Hayashi (20:00)
George Harris draw Mike Stallings (20:00)

1/21/75: Raleigh, NC @ Dorton Arena
Johnny Valentine beat Wahoo McDaniel by DQ
Gene & Ole Anderson beat Charlie Cook & Sandy Scott
Abe Jacobs beat Brute Bernard by DQ
Mr. Fuji beat Klondike Bill
Frank Monte draw Tio Tio

1/22/75: Raleigh, NC @ WRAL Studios (TV)

1/23/75: Norfolk, VA @ Scope
Wahoo McDaniel & Sonny King beat Gene & Ole Anderson
The Avenger beat Art Neilson
Kevin Sullivan & Sandy Scott beat The Outlaws (Cowboy Parker & Ken Dillinger)
Tio Tio beat Brute Bernard by DQ

1/24/75: Charleston, SC @ County Hall
Paul Jones & Tiger Conway, Jr. vs. Ric Flair & Ivan Koloff
Mr. Fuji vs. Tommy Seigler
George Harris vs. Mike Stallings
Don Kernodle vs. Frank Monte

1/24/75: Lumberton, NC @ Recreation Center
Wahoo McDaniel vs. Johnny Valentine

1/24/75: Richmond, VA @ Coliseum
The Avenger DDQ Super Destroyer
Gene & Ole Anderson beat Sonny King & Sandy Scott
Abe Jacobs beat Brute Bernard by DQ
Kevin Sullivan beat Mr. Hayashi
Joe Furr beat Ken Dillinger

196

MID-ATLANTIC WRESTLING 1975 YEARBOOK

1/25/75: Roanoke, VA @ Starland Arena
Paul Jones & Tiger Conway, Jr. beat Gene & Ole Anderson by DQ
Abe Jacobs beat Cowboy Parker
Sonny King beat George Harris
Ken Dillinger draw Joe Furr

1/25/75: Spartanburg, SC @ Memorial Auditorium
Wahoo McDaniel & Charlie Cook beat Ric Flair & Johnny Valentine
Tommy Seigler beat Mr. Fuji by DQ
Art Neilson beat Don Kernodle
Kevin Sullivan beat Frank Monte
Mike Paidousis draw Tio Tio (20:00)

1/26/75: Marion, NC @ McDowell High School
Paul Jones & Tiger Conway, Jr. vs. Gene & Ole Anderson
Ric Flair vs. Swede Hanson
Art Neilson vs. Sandy Scott
Mr. Fuji vs. Klondike Bill
Frank Morrell vs. Tio Tio

1/26/75: Greenville, SC @ Memorial Auditorium (Special Sunday Card)
Johnny Valentine beat Sonny King
Super Destroyer beat Wahoo McDaniel in a lumberjack match
Charlie Cook & The Avenger beat Chuck O'Connor & Brute Bernard
Tommy Seigler draw Kevin Sullivan
Cowboy Parker draw Abe Jacobs
Joe Furr beat Mike Paidousis

1/27/75: Charlotte, NC @ Park Center
Paul Jones & Sonny King beat Ivan Koloff & Johnny Valentine
The Avenger beat Chuck O'Connor
Abe Jacobs beat Mr. Fuji by DQ
Tommy Seigler beat George Harris
Frank Monte draw Tio Tio

1/27/75: Fayetteville, NC @ Cumberland County Memorial Auditorium
Wahoo McDaniel & Tiger Conway, Jr. vs. Gene & Ole Anderson
Swede Hanson vs. Art Neilson
Ric Flair vs. Charlie Cook
Kevin Sullivan vs. Mr. Hayashi
Sandy Scott vs. Frank Morrell

1/28/75: Columbia, SC @ Township Auditorium

Paul Jones, Tiger Conway, Jr. & Sonny King vs. Super Destroyer, Ivan Koloff & Ric Flair in a Texas tornado match
The Avenger vs. Chuck O'Connor
plus other matches

1/28/75: Raleigh, NC @ Dorton Arena
Wahoo McDaniel beat Johnny Valentine by DQ
Charlie Cook & Tommy Seigler beat Art Neilson & Mr. Fuji
Klondike Bill beat Frank Monte
Don Kernodle draw George Harris
Frank Morrell beat Joe Furr

1/29/75: Raleigh, NC @ WRAL Studios (TV)
Gene & Ole Anderson were announced as winning a tournament in California to become NWA World Tag Team Champions

1/30/75: Greensboro, NC @ Coliseum
NWA World Champion Jack Brisco beat Wahoo McDaniel (32:00) by DQ
The Avenger beat Super Destroyer (17:00) by DQ
Tiger Conway, Jr. & Paul Jones beat Ric Flair & Mr. Fuji (sub for Ivan Koloff)
Art Neilson draw Abe Jacobs (20:00)
Gene Anderson beat Charlie Cook
Mr. Fuji beat Klondike Bill
Mike Stallings beat Ken Dillinger
Don Kernodle beat Mike Paidousis

1/30/75: Norfolk, VA @ Scope
Johnny Valentine beat Swede Hanson
Ole Anderson DDQ Sonny King
Kevin Sullivan & Sandy Scott beat Frank Morrell & Frank Monte
Tio Tio beat George Harris
Mr. Hayashi beat Joe Furr

1/31/75: Charleston, SC @ County Hall
The Avenger beat Super Destroyer
Tommy Seigler & Abe Jacobs beat Mr. Fuji & Art Neilson
Klondike Bill beat Mike Paidousis
Ken Dillinger draw Mike Stallings

1/31/75: Lynchburg, VA @ City Armory
Paul Jones & Tiger Conway, Jr. beat Ric Flair & Johnny Valentine (sub for Ivan Koloff)
Swede Hanson beat Cowboy Parker (sub for Chuck O'Connor)
Bobby Williams draw Don Kernodle
Mr. Hayashi beat Joe Furr

MID-ATLANTIC WRESTLING 1975 YEARBOOK

1/31/75: Richmond, VA @ Coliseum
Sonny King & Wahoo McDaniel beat Gene & Ole Anderson
Charlie Cook beat Frank Monte (sub for Ric Flair)
Sandy Scott beat Frank Morrell
Frank Monte beat Tio Tio
Kevin Sullivan beat George Harris

FEBRUARY

2/1/75: Conway, SC @ Williams-Brice Building
Wahoo McDaniel vs. Johnny Valentine
Ivan Koloff vs. Charlie Cook
The Avenger & Sandy Scott vs. Chuck O'Connor & Cowboy Parker
Frank Monte vs. Joe Furr

2/1/75: Roanoke, VA @ Starland Arena
Paul Jones & Tiger Conway, Jr. beat Gene & Ole Anderson Texas tornado match
Ric Flair beat Swede Hanson
Don Kernodle beat Frank Monte
Tio Tio beat Johnny Heidman
Mike Stallings beat Mr. Hayashi

2/1/75: Spartanburg, SC @ Memorial Auditorium
Sonny King beat Super Destroyer by DQ
Tommy Seigler & Kevin Sullivan beat Art Neilson & Man Mountain Blackwell
Abe Jacobs beat George Harris
Klondike Bill beat Mike Paidousis

2/3/75: Charlotte, NC @ Park Center
Super Destroyer beat Swede Hanson to win the 13-man battle royal and $5,400
Ric Flair beat Klondike Bill
Tiger Conway beat Frank Morrell
The Avenger beat Frank Monte
Tio Tio beat Ken Dillinger
Charlie Cook draw Francisco Flores

2/3/75: Greenville, SC @ Memorial Auditorium
13-man $5400 Russian Roulette battle royal
Paul Jones beat Ole Anderson
Wahoo McDaniel beat Johnny Valentine
Sonny King beat Gene Anderson
Kevin Sullivan beat Cowboy Parker
Mr. Fuji draw Tommy Seigler
Abe Jacobs draw Art Neilson
Note: Sandy Scott was first man eliminated thus had no singles match

2/4/75: Columbia, SC @ Township Auditorium
Paul Jones, Tiger Conway, Jr. & Sonny King beat Super Destroyer, Ric Flair & Blue Scorpion (sub for Ivan Koloff)
The Avenger beat Mr. Fuji
Frank Monte beat Mike Stallings
Kevin Sullivan beat Mr. Hayashi

2/4/75: Raleigh, NC @ Dorton Arena
Johnny Valentine beat Wahoo McDaniel
Gene & Ole Anderson beat Charlie Cook & Tommy Seigler
Swede Hanson beat Cowboy Parker
Don Kernodle beat Mike Paidousis
Joe Furr draw Ken Dillinger

2/5/75: Raleigh, NC @ WRAL Studios (TV)

2/6/75: Elizabeth City, NC @ Northeastern High School
Ric Flair, Gene & Ole Anderson vs. Wahoo McDaniel, The Avenger & Sonny King
Plus other matches

2/6/75: Norfolk, VA @ Scope

2/7/75: Charleston, SC @ County Hall
Johnny Valentine DCO with Paul Jones
Tiger Conway, Jr. beat Blue Scorpion (sub for Ivan Koloff)
Tommy Seigler & Sandy Scott beat Mr. Hayashi & Frank Monte
Charlie Cook beat Ken Dillinger
Joe Furr beat Don Kernodle

2/7/75: Richmond, VA @ Coliseum
Gene & Ole Anderson no contest with Sonny King & Wahoo McDaniel
The Avenger draw Super Destroyer
Swede Hanson beat Ric Flair
Abe Jacobs & Kevin Sullivan beat Art Neilson & Mr. Fuji
Klondike Bill beat Cowboy Parker
Mike Stallings beat Frank Morrell
Tio Tio beat George Harris

2/8/75: Roanoke, VA @ Starland Arena
Wahoo McDaniel beat Super Destroyer by CO
Charlie Cook beat Frank Monte (sub for Blue Scorpion)
Charlie Cook (sub for Tio Tio) & Mike Stallings beat The Outlaws
Bobby Williams beat El Gaucho (sub for Tony Romano)

2/8/75: Spartanburg, SC @ Memorial Auditorium
Gene & Ole Anderson beat Tiger Conway, Jr. & Swede Hanson

198

MID-ATLANTIC WRESTLING 1975 YEARBOOK

Tommy Seigler beat Brute Bernard
Don Kernodle beat Frank Morrell
Terry Sawyer draw Mr. Hayashi (20:00)

2/8/75: Winston-Salem, NC @ Memorial Coliseum
Johnny Valentine DDQ Sonny King
Ric Flair beat Paul Jones to win the NWA Mid Atlantic Television Title
Sandy Scott & Kevin Sullivan beat Art Neilson & Mr. Fuji by DQ
Klondike Bill beat George Harris
Abe Jacobs beat Mike Paidousis
Johnny Heidman beat ??

2/10/75: Charlotte, NC @ Park Center
The Avenger beat Super Destroyer by DQ
Art Neilson & Mr. Fuji draw Tommy Seigler & Charlie Cook (45:00)
Klondike Bill beat Mike Paidousis
Kevin Sullivan beat Frank Morrell

2/10/75: Fayetteville, NC @ Cumberland County Memorial Auditorium
Johnny Valentine no contest with Sonny King
Ric Flair & Brute Bernard beat Sandy Scott & Abe Jacobs (subs for Charlie Cook & Tommy Seigler)
George Harris beat Bill Crouch (sub for Sandy Scott)
Joe Furr (sub for Tio Tio) beat Ken Dillinger

2/10/75: Greenville, SC @ Memorial Auditorium
Paul Jones & Wahoo McDaniel beat Gene & Ole Anderson
Tiger Conway, Jr. beat Blue Scorpion
Swede Hanson beat Cowboy Parker
Mike Stallings beat Mr. Hayashi
Frank Monte draw Don Kernodle

2/11/75: Raleigh, NC @ Dorton Arena
The Avenger beat Super Destroyer
Tiger Conway, Jr. beat Mr. Fuji
Brute Bernard & Art Neilson draw Charlie Cook & Abe Jacobs
Klondike Bill beat George Harris
Frank Monte draw Mike Stallings

2/11/75: Columbia, SC @ Township Auditorium
Sonny King & Paul Jones beat Gene & Ole Anderson
Ric Flair beat Sandy Scott
Kevin Sullivan beat Mike Paidousis
Cowboy Parker beat Mr. Hayashi (sub for Tio Tio)

2/12/75: Raleigh, NC @ WRAL Studios (TV)

2/13/75: Norfolk, VA @ Scope

2/14/75: Richmond, VA @ Coliseum
Johnny Valentine beat Paul Jones
Ric Flair beat Swede Hanson
Art Neilson & Blue Scorpion beat Kevin Sullivan & Tommy Seigler by DQ
Mike Stallings beat Ken Dillinger
Cowboy Parker beat Tio Tio

2/14/75: Charleston, SC @ County Hall
The Avenger & Tiger Conway, Jr. vs. Super Destroyer & Brute Bernard
Charlie Cook vs. Mr. Fuji
Sandy Scott vs. George Harris
Joe Furr vs. Mr. Hayashi
Don Kernodle vs. Frank Monte

2/14/75: Lynchburg, VA @ City Armory
Wahoo McDaniel & Sonny King beat Gene & Ole Anderson
Joyce Grable beat Donna Christianello
Frank Morrell beat Klondike Bill
Abe Jacobs beat Mike Paidousis

2/15/75: Spartanburg, SC @ Memorial Auditorium

2/15/75: Hampton, VA @ Coliseum
Wahoo McDaniel beat Johnny Valentine in an Indian strap match
The Avenger beat Super Destroyer
Charlie Cook & Tommy Seigler beat Art Neilson & Cowboy Parker
Joyce Grable beat Donna Christianello
Kevin Sullivan beat Frank Morrell
Tio Tio beat Ken Dillinger

2/15/75: Roanoke, VA @ Starland Arena
Gene & Ole Anderson beat Paul Jones & Tiger Conway, Jr.
Abe Jacobs beat Mr. Fuji
Mike Stallings vs. Frank Monte
Klondike Bill vs. Blue Scorpion
Don Kernodle vs. Mike Paidousis

2/16/75: Asheville, NC @ Civic Center
Wahoo McDaniel vs. Johnny Valentine in an Indian strap match
Gene & Ole Anderson & Ric Flair vs. Paul Jones, Tiger Conway, Jr. & Sonny King

199

Brute Bernard vs. Sandy Scott
Kevin Sullivan vs. George Harris
Blue Scorpion vs. Tommy Seigler

2/17/75: Charlotte, NC @ Park Center
Andre The Giant & Sonny King beat Johnny Valentine & Super Destroyer (25:00)
Charlie Cook beat Art Neilson by DQ
Sandy Scott beat Frank Monte
Ken Patera beat Cowboy Parker
Blue Scorpion beat Tio Tio

2/17/75: Greenville, SC @ Memorial Auditorium
Paul Jones & Wahoo McDaniel DDQ Gene & Ole Anderson
Ric Flair beat Swede Hanson
Tiger Conway, Jr. beat Mr. Fuji
Tommy Seigler beat Frank Morrell
Kevin Sullivan beat George Harris

2/18/75: Columbia, SC @ Township Auditorium
The Avenger & Sonny King beat Johnny Valentine & Super Destroyer
Tiger Conway, Jr. beat Mr. Fuji
Art Neilson draw Tommy Seigler
Klondike Bill beat Cowboy Parker
Abe Jacobs beat Ken Dillinger via pinfall

2/18/75: Raleigh, NC @ Dorton Arena
Paul Jones & Wahoo McDaniel beat Gene & Ole Anderson
Ken Patera beat Brute Bernard
Ric Flair beat Sandy Scott
Blue Scorpion beat Joe Furr
Mike Stallings beat Mr. Hayashi

2/19/75: Raleigh, NC @ WRAL Studios (TV)

2/20/75: Greensboro, NC @ Coliseum
NWA World Champion Jack Brisco beat Wahoo McDaniel no DQ match
Gene & Ole Anderson beat Tiger Conway, Jr. & Paul Jones (19:00) via pinfall to win NWA Mid Atlantic Tag Title
(Note: NWA Mid Atlantic Tag Titles were retired at this point)
Dusty Rhodes DCO with Ric Flair
Jerry Brisco beat Cowboy Parker
Ken Patera beat Art Neilson
Kevin Sullivan draw Tommy Seigler
Sandy Scott & Tio Tio beat Frank Monte & Frank Morrell

2/20/75: Charlotte, NC @ Park Center
Gene & Ole Anderson no contest with Paul Jones & Wahoo McDaniel
Harley Race beat Haystack Calhoun by DQ
Belle Starr & Fabulous Moolah beat Susan Green & Evelyn Stevens
Dusty Rhodes beat El Gaucho
Mike Stallings draw Don Kernodle (20:00)

2/21/75: Charleston, SC @ County Hall
Wahoo McDaniel beat Ole Anderson to win Russian Roulette battle royal
Ken Patera beat Frank Morrell
Paul Jones beat Kevin Sullivan
Gene Anderson beat Tommy Seigler
Bill Crouch draw Mike Stallings
El Gaucho draw Don Kernodle

2/20/75: Norfolk, VA @ Scope
Johnny Valentine & Super Destroyer beat Sonny King & Bearcat Wright by DQ
The Avenger & Swede Hanson b. Brute Bernard & Mr. Fuji
Abe Jacobs beat Blue Scorpion by DQ
Charlie Cook beat George Harris
Joe Furr & Klondike Bill beat Ken Dillinger & Mr. Hayashi

2/21/75: Charleston, SC @ County Hall
Wahoo McDaniel beat Ole Anderson to win 13-man Russian Roulette battle royal
Ken Patera beat Frank Morrell
Paul Jones beat Kevin Sullivan
Gene Anderson beat Tommy Seigler
Bill Crouch draw Mike Stallings
El Gaucho draw Don Kernodle

2/21/75: Lynchburg, VA @ City Armory
Ric Flair DDQ Tiger Conway, Jr.
Swede Hanson & Sandy Scott vs. Blue Scorpion & Cowboy Parker
Charlie Cook vs. Mr. Fuji
Bobby Williams vs. Mr. Hayashi

2/21/75: Tappahannock, VA @ Essex High School
Sonny King vs. Super Destroyer
Art Neilson & Brute Bernard vs. The Avenger & Abe Jacobs
Plus other matches

2/22/75: Conway, SC @ Williams-Brice Building
Wahoo McDaniel vs. Super Destroyer
Plus other matches

2/22/75: Roanoke, VA @ Starland Arena
Gene & Ole Anderson no contest with Paul Jones & Tiger Conway, Jr.
Charlie Cook beat Blue Scorpion by DQ
Kevin Sullivan draw Frank Morrell
Bill Crouch beat El Gaucho
Bobby Williams beat Ken Dillinger

2/22/75: Spartanburg, SC @ Memorial Auditorium
Johnny Valentine beat Sonny King
Tommy Seigler beat Ric Flair by DQ
Ken Patera beat George Harris
Mike Stallings beat Joe Furr
Klondike Bill & Abe Jacobs draw Cowboy Parker & Brute Bernard (20:00)

2/23/75: Greenville, SC @ Memorial Auditorium (Special Sunday Card)
The Avenger draw Super Destroyer (60:00)
Paul Jones beat Gene Anderson in a Texas death match
Ole Anderson & Ric Flair beat Tiger Conway, Jr. & Tommy Seigler
Ken Patera beat Cowboy Parker
Frank Monte beat Mike Stallings
Art Neilson draw Sandy Scott

2/24/75: Charlotte, NC @ Park Center
Paul Jones beat Johnny Valentine in a Texas death match
Tiger Conway, Jr. beat Ric Flair by DQ
Mr. Fuji & Brute Bernard beat Kevin Sullivan & Sandy Scott
Charlie Cook beat George Harris
Tio Tio beat Mr. Hayashi

2/24/75: Fayetteville, NC @ Cumberland County Memorial Auditorium
Wahoo McDaniel & Ken Patera beat Gene & Ole Anderson
The Avenger beat Cowboy Parker
Tommy Seigler beat Blue Scorpion
Abe Jacobs beat Frank Morrell
Klondike Bill beat Ken Dillinger

2/25/75: Columbia, SC @ Township Auditorium
The Avenger beat Super Destroyer by DQ
Gene & Ole Anderson beat Swede Hanson & Tiger Conway, Jr.
Ken Patera beat Frank Monte
Brute Bernard beat Klondike Bill
Mike Stallings beat Ken Dillinger

2/25/75: Smithfield, NC @ Smithfield-Selma High School Gym
Paul Jones & Wahoo McDaniel vs. Ric Flair & Johnny Valentine
Mr. Fuji vs. Tommy Seigler
Art Neilson vs. Charlie Cook
Blue Scorpion vs. Joe Furr

2/26/75: Raleigh, NC @ WRAL Studios (TV)

2/27/75: Marion, NC @ McDowell High School Gym
Wahoo McDaniel vs. Super Destroyer
Sandy Scott & Kevin Sullivan vs. Mr. Fuji & Art Neilson
Ken Patera vs. Cowboy Parker
Abe Jacobs vs. George Harris
Frank Morrell vs. Tommy Seigler

2/28/75: Charleston, SC @ County Hall
Gene & Ole Anderson DCO with Paul Jones & Sonny King
Ken Patera vs. Brute Bernard
The Avenger vs. Frank Monte
Klondike Bill vs. Frank Morrell
Joe Furr vs. Bill Crouch

2/28/75: Lynchburg, VA @ City Armory
Ric Flair vs. Tiger Conway, Jr.
Swede Hanson vs. Super Destroyer
Abe Jacobs & Kevin Sullivan vs. The Outlaws
Tio Tio vs. George Harris

2/28/75: Roanoke Rapids, NC
Wahoo McDaniel vs. Johnny Valentine
Plus other matches

MARCH

3/1/75: Camden, SC @ City Arena
Wahoo McDaniel vs. Ole Anderson
Ric Flair vs. Tiger Conway, Jr.
Charlie Cook & Swede Hanson vs. Mr. Fuji & Art Neilson
Mike Stallings vs. Ken Dillinger

3/1/75: Spartanburg, SC @ Memorial Auditorium
Johnny Valentine vs. Sonny King
Brute Bernard vs. Tommy Seigler
Tio Tio & Klondike Bill vs. George Harris & Frank Morrell
Joe Furr vs. Mr. Hayashi

3/1/75: Salem, VA @ Civic Center
Super Destroyer DCO with The Avenger
Paul Jones beat Gene Anderson
Ken Patera beat Blue Scorpion

MID-ATLANTIC WRESTLING 1975 YEARBOOK

Kevin Sullivan & Sandy Scott beat Cowboy Parker & Frank Morrell
Bobby Williams beat Bill Crouch
Don Kernodle beat Johnny Heidman

3/2/75: Asheville, NC @ Civic Center
Wahoo McDaniel vs. Johnny Valentine in a no time limit, no DQ match
Ric Flair vs. Paul Jones
Art Neilson & Mr. Fuji vs. Charlie Cook & Tommy Seigler
Ken Patera vs. Brute Bernard
Sandy Scott vs. Mr. Hayashi
Ken Dillinger vs. Tio Tio

3/3/75: Charlotte, NC @ Park Center
Johnny Valentine beat Paul Jones by CO
Ken Patera beat Ric Flair by DQ
Sandy Scott & Tommy Seigler beat Cowboy Parker & Art Neilson
Frank Morrell beat Mike Stallings
Bill Crouch beat Joe Furr

3/3/75: Fayetteville, NC @ Cumberland County Memorial Auditorium
The Avenger beat Super Destroyer by DQ
Tiger Conway, Jr. beat Mr. Fuji
Abe Jacobs & Kevin Sullivan beat Brute Bernard & Blue Scorpion
Klondike Bill beat Frank Monte
El Gaucho beat Don Kernodle

3/3/75: Greenville, SC @ Memorial Auditorium
Wahoo McDaniel & Sonny King beat Gene & Ole Anderson
Blackjack Mulligan beat Charlie Cook
Swede Hanson beat George Harris
Steve Keirn beat Mr. Hayashi
Tio Tio beat Ken Dillinger

3/4/75: Columbia, SC @ Township Auditorium
Wahoo McDaniel won a 13-man battle royal for $5,400
Wahoo McDaniel beat Ole Anderson by DQ
Ric Flair beat Tommy Seigler
Sonny King beat Mr. Fuji
Tiger Conway, Jr. draw Art Neilson
Sandy Scott draw Frank Morrell
Steve Keirn beat George Harris

3/4/75: Raleigh, NC @ Dorton Arena
Johnny Valentine won a Russian Roulette battle royal for $5,400

Johnny Valentine beat Paul Jones by CO
Klondike Bill beat Super Destroyer by DQ
Ken Patera beat Blue Scorpion
Blackjack Mulligan beat Tio Tio
The Avenger beat Frank Monte
Brute Bernard draw Swede Hanson

3/5/75: Raleigh, NC @ WRAL Studios (TV)

3/6/75: Asheboro, NC @ Southwestern Randolph Senior High School
Ric Flair vs. Paul Jones
Ken Patera & Sandy Scott vs. Brute Bernard & Art Neilson
Abe Jacobs vs. Cowboy Parker
Joe Furr vs. Mr. Hayashi
Charlie Cook vs. Frank Morrell

3/6/75: Anderson, SC @ Recreation Center
Wahoo McDaniel & Tiger Conway, Jr. vs. Johnny Valentine & Super Destroyer
Blackjack Mulligan vs. Kevin Sullivan
Tommy Seigler vs. Blue Scorpion
Steve Keirn vs. Ken Dillinger
Mike Stallings vs. Bill Crouch

3/6/75: Portsmouth, VA @ Woodrow Wilson High School
The Avenger & Sonny King vs. Gene & Ole Anderson
Swede Hanson vs. Mr. Fuji
Plus other matches

3/7/75: Charleston, SC @ County Hall
Paul Jones vs. Gene Anderson in a Texas death match
Tiger Conway, Jr. & Charlie Cook vs. Brute Bernard & Art Neilson
Kevin Sullivan vs. George Harris
Swede Hanson vs. Frank Morrell
Mr. Hayashi vs. Tio Tio

3/7/75: Richmond, VA @ Coliseum
Super Destroyer beat The Avenger in a no time limit, no DQ match
Sonny King & Wahoo McDaniel beat Ric Flair & Ole Anderson
Ken Patera beat Cowboy Parker
Blackjack Mulligan beat Abe Jacobs
Steve Keirn & Sandy Scott beat Frank Monte & Blue Scorpion
Tommy Seigler draw Mr. Fuji

3/8/75: Hampton, VA @ Coliseum
Gene & Ole Anderson beat Paul Jones & Wahoo McDaniel

by DQ
Ken Patera beat Super Destroyer
Blackjack Mulligan beat Don Kernodle
Sandy Scott & Tommy Seigler beat Mr. Fuji & Cowboy Parker
Steve Keirn beat Bill Crouch

3/8/75: Roanoke, VA @ Starland Arena
Sonny King beat Johnny Valentine by DQ
Art Neilson & Blue Scorpion beat Abe Jacobs & Kevin Sullivan
George Harris beat Joe Furr
Tio Tio beat Mr. Hayashi
Kevin Sullivan (sub for Mike Stallings) beat Ken Dillinger

3/8/75: Spindale, NC @ Spindale House
Ric Flair vs. Tiger Conway, Jr.
Brute Bernard & Frank Monte vs. Charlie Cook & The Avenger
Swede Hanson vs. El Gaucho
Klondike Bill vs. Frank Morrell

3/9/75: Charlotte, NC @ Park Center (Special Sunday Afternoon Card)
Paul Jones beat Johnny Valentine to win NWA Mid Atlantic Title in a fence match
Wahoo McDaniel & Dusty Rhodes beat Ric Flair & Billy Graham
Blackjack Mulligan beat Tio Tio
Darling Dagmar beat Diamond Lil
Tiger Conway, Jr. & Sonny King beat Mr. Fuji & Blue Scorpion

3/10/75: Lumberton, NC @ Recreation Center
Paul Jones & Wahoo McDaniel vs. Ric Flair & Johnny Valentine
Plus other matches

3/10/75: Greenville, SC @ Memorial Auditorium
Super Destroyer beat The Avenger
Ken Patera & Sandy Scott beat Mr. Fuji & Art Neilson
Blackjack Mulligan DDQ Sonny King
Klondike Bill draw Blue Scorpion
Steve Keirn beat Frank Morrell

3/11/75: Raleigh, NC @ Dorton Arena
Ken Patera & Paul Jones beat Super Destroyer & Johnny Valentine
Blackjack Mulligan beat Charlie Cook
Tommy Seigler beat Mr. Fuji by DQ
Frank Monte draw Kevin Sullivan

Steve Keirn beat Ken Dillinger

3/11/75: Columbia, SC @ Township Auditorium
Wahoo McDaniel & Sonny King beat Gene & Ole Anderson
Tiger Conway, Jr. beat Brute Bernard by DQ
Blue Scorpion vs. Tio Tio
Abe Jacobs draw Art Neilson
Cowboy Parker beat Mike Stallings

3/12/75: Raleigh, NC @ WRAL Studios (TV)

3/13/75: Greensboro, NC @ Coliseum
Wahoo McDaniel beat Johnny Valentine (17:00) in an Indian strap match
Dusty Rhodes beat Ric Flair
Super Destroyer beat The Avenger
Mr. Fuji & Blackjack Mulligan beat Charlie Cook & Swede Hanson
Tiger Conway, Jr. beat Frank Monte by DQ
Steve Keirn beat Mr. Hayashi

3/13/75: Norfolk, VA @ Scope
Paul Jones vs. Gene Anderson in a Texas death match
Sonny King vs. Ole Anderson in a no DQ match
Ken Patera vs. Art Neilson
Abe Jacobs & Kevin Sullivan vs. The Outlaws
Klondike Bill vs. Frank Morrell

3/14/75: Charleston, SC @ County Hall
Wahoo McDaniel beat Johnny Valentine
Sandy Scott & Tiger Conway, Jr. beat Brute Bernard & Mr. Fuji
Steve Keirn beat Mike Stallings
Tio Tio beat Bill Crouch

3/14/75: Richmond, VA @ Coliseum
After both men survived a 13-man battle royal, Sonny King beat Ole Anderson to win $5,400
Ken Patera beat Ric Flair by DQ
Gene Anderson beat Charlie Cook
Kevin Sullivan draw Art Neilson
Chris Taylor beat Klondike Bill
Abe Jacobs beat Ken Dillinger

3/15/75: Conway, SC @ Williams-Brice Building
Paul Jones & Wahoo McDaniel vs. Gene & Ole Anderson
Plus other matches

3/15/75: Roanoke, VA @ Starland Arena
Sonny King beat Johnny Valentine
Swede Hanson & Charlie Cook beat Art Neilson & Mr. Fuji

Don Kernodle beat Frank Morrell (sub for Abe Jacobs)
Frank Morrell beat Mike Stallings
Frank Monte draw Kevin Sullivan

3/15/75: Spartanburg, SC @ Memorial Auditorium
Super Destroyer & Ric Flair vs. Ken Patera & Tiger Conway, Jr.
Brute Bernard vs. The Avenger
Cowboy Parker vs. Klondike Bill
Tio Tio vs. Ken Dillinger
El Gaucho vs. Mr. Hayashi

3/16/75: Asheville, NC @ Civic Center
Russian Roulette battle royal featuring Wahoo McDaniel, Paul Jones, Ole Anderson, Gene Anderson, Ric Flair, Blackjack Mulligan, Steve Keirn, Super Destroyer, Ken Patera, Johnny Valentine, Tiger Conway, Jr., The Avenger & Blue Scorpion
Plus 7 other matches

3/17/75: Greenville, SC @ Memorial Auditorium

3/17/75: Charlotte, NC @ Park Center
Gene & Ole Anderson beat Wahoo McDaniel & Sonny King by DQ
Swede Hanson beat Blackjack Mulligan by DQ
Doug Gilbert draw Bob Bruggers
Sandy Scott beat Frank Morrell
Frank Monte beat Mike Stallings

3/17/75: Fayetteville, NC @ Cumberland County Memorial Auditorium
Super Destroyer beat The Avenger in a no time limit, no DQ, loser must unmask match
Ken Patera beat Ric Flair
Art Neilson & Mr. Fuji beat Charlie Cook & Tiger Conway, Jr.
Kevin Sullivan draw Steve Keirn
Klondike Bill beat Blue Scorpion by DQ

3/18/75: Columbia, SC @ Township Auditorium
Gene & Ole Anderson beat Wahoo McDaniel & Sonny King
Ken Patera beat Ric Flair
Brute Bernard & Art Neilson draw Abe Jacobs & Bob Bruggers
Blue Scorpion draw Charlie Cook

3/18/75: Raleigh, NC @ Dorton Arena
Paul Jones beat Johnny Valentine
Blackjack Mulligan & Mr. Fuji beat Tiger Conway, Jr. & Swede Hanson
Doug Gilbert draw Tommy Seigler
Bill Crouch beat Mr. Hayashi
Tio Tio beat Ken Dillinger

3/19/75: Raleigh, NC @ WRAL Studios (TV)
Announced that Paul Jones had been stripped of the NWA Mid Atlantic Title by NWA President Sam Muchnick and the belt has been awarded back to Johnny Valentine.

3/20/75: Danville, VA @ City Armory
Gene & Ole Anderson beat Paul Jones & Tiger Conway, Jr.
Swede Hanson beat Brute Bernard by CO
Klondike Bill beat Art Neilson by DQ
Tommy Seigler beat Frank Morrell
Sandy Scott draw Blue Scorpion (20:00)

3/20/75: Norfolk, VA @ Scope
Sonny King & Bearcat Wright beat Super Destroyer & Johnny Valentine no DQ
Ken Patera beat Ric Flair
Mr. Fuji & Blackjack Mulligan beat ??
Doug Gilbert beat ??
Steve Keirn beat ??
Bob Bruggers beat ??

3/21/75: Charleston, SC @ County Hall
Super Destroyer beat The Avenger no time limit, no DQ, loser must unmask
Ric Flair beat Paul Jones by DQ when Jones hit the referee
Swede Hanson & Charlie Cook beat Art Neilson & Blue Scorpion
Tommy Seigler beat Mr. Hayashi
Sandy Scott beat Brute Bernard

3/21/75: Richmond, VA @ Coliseum
Gene & Ole Anderson beat Wahoo McDaniel & Sonny King by DQ
Blackjack Mulligan beat Tiger Conway, Jr.
Ken Patera beat Mr. Fuji
Bob Bruggers beat Doug Gilbert by DQ
Abe Jacobs beat Frank Monte
Kevin Sullivan draw Steve Keirn

3/22/75: Winston-Salem, NC @ Memorial Coliseum
Bearcat Wright & Sonny King vs. Johnny Valentine & Super Destroyer
Ric Flair vs. Paul Jones
Ken Patera vs. Blackjack Mulligan
The Avenger & Bob Bruggers vs. Brute Bernard & Blue Scorpion
Steve Keirn vs. Ken Dillinger

MID-ATLANTIC WRESTLING 1975 YEARBOOK

Tio Tio vs. Frank Monte
Mr. Hayashi vs. Mike Stallings

3/22/75: Spartanburg, SC @ Memorial Auditorium
Gene & Ole Anderson beat Wahoo McDaniel & Tiger Conway, Jr.
Mr. Fuji & Art Neilson draw Charlie Cook & Tommy Seigler (30:00)
Sandy Scott beat Cowboy Parker
Doug Gilbert beat Tio Tio

3/24/75: Greenville, SC @ Memorial Auditorium
Wahoo McDaniel beat Johnny Valentine
Ken Patera & Sonny King beat Ric Flair & Mr. Fuji
Bob Bruggers beat Doug Gilbert
Tommy Seigler beat Frank Monte
Tio Tio beat Bill Crouch

3/24/75: Charlotte, NC @ Park Center
Paul Jones beat Super Destroyer by DQ
Blackjack Mulligan beat Swede Hanson
Tiger Conway, Jr. & Charlie Cook beat Art Neilson & Brute Bernard by DQ
Mr. Hayashi beat Mike Stallings
Kevin Sullivan draw Steve Keirn (20:00)

3/25/75: Raleigh, NC @ Dorton Arena
Gene & Ole Anderson beat Paul Jones & Wahoo McDaniel
Swede Hanson beat Blackjack Mulligan by DQ
Mr. Fuji beat Tiger Conway, Jr.
Steve Keirn beat Ken Dillinger

3/25/75: Camden, SC @ City Arena
Ric Flair & Johnny Valentine vs. Sonny King & Ken Patera
Brute Bernard vs. The Avenger
Art Neilson vs. Charlie Cook
Doug Gilbert vs. Sandy Scott
Masked Scorpion vs. Abe Jacobs

3/26/75: Raleigh, NC @ WRAL Studios (TV)

3/27/75: Anderson, SC @ Recreation Center
Paul Jones, Wahoo McDaniel & Sonny King vs. Ric Flair, Gene & Ole Anderson
Tommy Seigler vs. Brute Bernard
Frank Morrell vs. Abe Jacobs
Cowboy Parker vs. Mike Stallings

3/27/75: Norfolk, VA @ Scope
Super Destroyer beat The Avenger no time limit, no DQ, loser must unmask

Blackjack Mulligan beat Tiger Conway, Jr.
Bob Bruggers & Charlie Cook beat Art Neilson & Mr. Fuji
Doug Gilbert draw Sandy Scott
Kevin Sullivan draw Frank Monte

3/28/75: Charleston, SC @ County Hall
Wahoo McDaniel vs. Johnny Valentine
Swede Hanson vs. Blue Scorpion
Abe Jacobs & Tommy Seigler vs. Brute Bernard & Cowboy Parker
Steve Keirn vs. Frank Morrell
Mike Stallings vs. Ken Dillinger

3/28/75: Charlottesville, VA @ University Hall
Paul Jones & Ken Patera beat Gene & Ole Anderson by DQ
Blackjack Mulligan vs. Charlie Cook
Bob Bruggers vs. Art Neilson
Kevin Sullivan vs. Frank Monte
Mr. Hayashi vs. Tio Tio

3/28/75: Henderson, NC @ Vance High School Gym
Ric Flair & Super Destroyer vs. Sonny King & Tiger Conway, Jr.
Mr. Fuji vs. The Avenger
Doug Gilbert vs. Sandy Scott
Klondike Bill vs. Bill Crouch

3/29/75: Roanoke, VA @ Starland Arena
Ric Flair beat Paul Jones when Jones hit the referee
Swede Hanson beat Blackjack Mulligan
Abe Jacobs & Sandy Scott beat Cowboy Parker (sub for Doug Gilbert) & Blue Scorpion
Bobby Williams (sub for Mike Stallings) beat Mr. Hayashi

3/29/75: Laurinburg, NC
Wahoo McDaniel vs. Johnny Valentine
Plus other matches

3/29/75: Spartanburg, SC @ Memorial Auditorium
Ole Anderson beat Tiger Conway, Jr.
Gene Anderson DDQ The Avenger
Tommy Seigler & Charlie Cook beat Brute Bernard & Doug Gilbert by DQ
Don Kernodle draw Steve Keirn
Bob Bruggers beat Ken Dillinger

3/30/75: Greenville, SC @ Memorial Auditorium (Special Sunday Card)
Andre The Giant, Paul Jones & Sonny King beat Johnny Valentine, Gene & Ole Anderson
Blackjack Mulligan DCO with Swede Hanson
Klondike Bill beat Mr. Fuji

MID-ATLANTIC WRESTLING 1975 YEARBOOK

Sandy Scott draw Blue Scorpion
Bob Bruggers beat Mr. Hayashi

3/31/75: Fayetteville, NC @ Cumberland County Memorial Auditorium
Paul Jones & Ken Patera beat Ric Flair & Johnny Valentine
Sandy Scott beat Blue Scorpion by DQ
Blackjack Mulligan beat Charlie Cook
Kevin Sullivan draw Cowboy Parker
Don Kernodle beat Frank Monte

3/31/75: Charlotte, NC @ Park Center
Super Destroyer beat The Avenger in a no DQ match
Sonny King beat Ole Anderson by DQ
Bob Bruggers & Tommy Seigler beat Art Neilson & Mr. Fuji
Rufus R. Jones beat Frank Morrell
Doug Gilbert beat Tio Tio

APRIL

4/1/75: Raleigh, NC @ Dorton Arena
Johnny Valentine DDQ Paul Jones
Rufus R. Jones & Ken Patera beat Mr. Fuji & Art Neilson
Bob Bruggers beat Brute Bernard by DQ
Klondike Bill beat Frank Monte
Charlie Cook beat Ken Dillinger

4/1/75: Columbia, SC @ Township Auditorium
Gene & Ole Anderson beat Wahoo McDaniel & Sonny King
Ric Flair DCO with Swede Hanson
Doug Gilbert & Blue Scorpion beat Kevin Sullivan & Abe Jacobs
Sandy Scott beat Cowboy Parker

4/2/75: Raleigh, NC @ WRAL Studios (TV)

4/3/75: Greensboro, NC @ Coliseum
Gene & Ole Anderson no contest with Paul Jones & Wahoo McDaniel
Blackjack Mulligan beat Dusty Rhodes
Sonny King & Rufus R. Jones beat Mr. Fuji & Art Neilson
Billy Graham beat Abe Jacobs
Sandy Scott draw Doug Gilbert
Tommy Seigler & Bob Bruggers beat Cowboy Parker & Ken Dillinger

4/3/75: Norfolk, VA @ Scope
Ken Patera & Swede Hanson beat Ric Flair & Johnny Valentine by DQ

The Avenger beat Blue Scorpion
Charlie Cook beat Brute Bernard
Klondike Bill beat Frank Monte
Frank Morrell draw Tio Tio

4/4/75: Charleston, SC @ County Hall
Paul Jones beat Ric Flair by CO
Charlie Cook beat Mr. Fuji
Tommy Seigler & Bob Bruggers beat The Outlaws
Bill Crouch beat El Gaucho (sub for Don Kernodle)

4/4/75: Lynchburg, VA @ City Armory
Super Destroyer vs. The Avenger in a match with 2 referees
Brute Bernard & Art Neilson vs. Abe Jacobs & Kevin Sullivan
Bobby Williams vs. Frank Monte
Mr. Hayashi vs. El Gaucho

4/4/75: Richmond, VA @ Coliseum
Ken Patera & Sonny King beat Gene & Ole Anderson by DQ
Wahoo McDaniel beat Johnny Valentine
Blackjack Mulligan beat Swede Hanson by DQ
Rufus R. Jones beat Frank Morrell
Sandy Scott draw Doug Gilbert
Blue Scorpion beat Tio Tio

4/5/75: Spartanburg, SC @ Memorial Auditorium

4/5/75: Charlotte, NC @ Coliseum (Special Saturday Card)
NWA World Champion Jack Brisco draw Wahoo McDaniel (60:00)
Johnny Valentine DDQ Paul Jones
Gene & Ole Anderson beat Sandy Scott & Sonny King
Charlie Cook & Tommy Seigler beat Mr. Fuji & Doug Gilbert by DQ
Klondike Bill beat Cowboy Parker
Bob Bruggers beat Frank Morrell

4/5/75: Hampton, VA @ Coliseum
Super Destroyer beat Ken Patera by DQ
Rufus R. Jones & Swede Hanson beat Ric Flair & Blackjack Mulligan by DQ
The Avenger & Abe Jacobs beat Brute Bernard & Art Neilson
Blue Scorpion beat Kevin Sullivan
Tio Tio beat Mr. Hayashi
Frank Monte draw Don Kernodle

4/7/75: Fayetteville, NC @ Cumberland County Memorial Auditorium
Gene & Ole Anderson beat Wahoo McDaniel & Sonny

MID-ATLANTIC WRESTLING 1975 YEARBOOK

King by DQ
Rufus R. Jones beat Brute Bernard
Kevin Sullivan beat Art Neilson by DQ
Blue Scorpion draw Klondike Bill
Don Kernodle beat Frank Morrell

4/7/75: Greenville, SC @ Memorial Auditorium
Ken Patera beat Super Destroyer
Swede Hanson beat Blackjack Mulligan
Ric Flair & Doug Gilbert beat Sandy Scott & Bob Bruggers
Charlie Cook beat Mr. Fuji
Bill Crouch beat Tio Tio

4/8/75: Columbia, SC @ Township Auditorium
Sonny King & Wahoo McDaniel beat Gene & Ole Anderson in a Texas tornado match
Charlie Cook beat Mr. Fuji by DQ
Brute Bernard draw Tommy Seigler
Doug Gilbert beat Kevin Sullivan
Bob Bruggers beat Ken Dillinger

4/8/75: Raleigh, NC @ Dorton Arena
Rufus R. Jones & Ken Patera beat Ric Flair & Johnny Valentine
Swede Hanson DCO with Blackjack Mulligan
The Avenger beat Art Neilson by DQ
Frank Monte beat Tio Tio
Abe Jacobs draw Cowboy Parker

4/9/75: Raleigh, NC @ WRAL Studios (TV)

4/10/75: Asheboro, NC @ Southwestern Randolph Senior High School
Super Destroyer vs. Paul Jones
Art Neilson & Mr. Fuji vs. The Avenger & Charlie Cook
Dorothy Downs vs. Ann Casey
Don Kernodle vs. Bill Crouch

4/10/75: Martinsville, VA @ Junior High School
Blackjack Mulligan & Ric Flair vs. Ken Patera & Sonny King
Brute Bernard vs. Swede Hanson
plus 3 other matches

4/10/75: Norfolk, VA @ Scope
Gene & Ole Anderson beat Wahoo McDaniel & Rufus R. Jones
Sandy Scott & Bob Bruggers beat The Outlaws
Abe Jacobs beat Frank Morrell
Klondike Bill draw Blue Scorpion

4/11/75: Charleston, SC @ County Hall
Paul Jones beat Ric Flair in a lumberjack match
The Avenger & Charlie Cook beat Mr. Fuji & Art Neilson
L.D. Lewis beat Mr. Hayashi
Don Kernodle beat El Gaucho
Kevin Sullivan draw Frank Monte

4/11/75: Richmond, VA @ Coliseum
Wahoo McDaniel no contest with Super Destroyer
Swede Hanson beat Blackjack Mulligan
Rufus R. Jones beat Brute Bernard
Doug Gilbert beat Bob Bruggers
Abe Jacobs & Tio Tio beat The Outlaws

4/12/75: Roanoke, VA @ Starland Arena
Wahoo McDaniel beat Super Destroyer by DQ when Super Destroyer hit the referee
Mr. Fuji & Art Neilson beat Tommy Seigler & Sandy Scott
Rufus R. Jones beat Blue Scorpion
Klondike Bill beat Frank Monte
Frank Morrell beat Abe Jacobs

4/12/75: Spartanburg, SC @ Memorial Auditorium
Gene & Ole Anderson beat Ken Patera & Sonny King (25:00)
Charlie Cook DDQ Doug Gilbert
Bob Bruggers beat Cowboy Parker
Tio Tio beat Mr. Hayashi
Ann Casey beat Dottie Downs

4/14/75: Charlotte, NC @ Park Center
Ric Flair & Johnny Valentine beat Rufus R. Jones & Wahoo McDaniel
Doug Gilbert beat Charlie Cook
Brute Bernard beat Bob Bruggers
Sandy Scott beat Cowboy Parker
Frank Morrell draw L.D. Lewis 20:00

4/14/75: Greenville, SC @ Memorial Auditorium
Ken Patera & Swede Hanson beat Super Destroyer & Blackjack Mulligan
The Avenger beat Mr. Fuji by DQ
Klondike Bill beat Bill Crouch
Abe Jacobs draw Art Neilson
Tio Tio beat Ken Dillinger

4/14/75: Morgantown, NC @ Freedom High School
Gene & Ole Anderson vs. Paul Jones & Sonny King
Blue Scorpion vs. Tommy Seigler
Donna Christianello vs. Ann Casey
Mr. Hayashi vs. Don Kernodle

Kevin Sullivan vs. Frank Morrell

4/15/75: Columbia, SC @ Township Auditorium
Johnny Valentine DDQ Paul Jones
Blackjack Mulligan & Ric Flair beat Swede Hanson & Tommy Seigler
Frank Monte draw Abe Jacobs
Klondike Bill beat Cowboy Parker
L.D. Lewis beat Frank Morrell

4/15/75: Danville, VA @ City Armory
Sonny King & Ken Patera beat Gene & Ole Anderson (16:32) by DQ
The Avenger beat Mr. Fuji (11:05) via pinfall
Art Neilson draw Charlie Cook (20:00)
Bill Crouch beat Kevin Sullivan (12:06)
Tio Tio beat Ken Dillinger (8:55) by submission

4/15/75: Raleigh, NC @ Dorton Arena
Wahoo McDaniel beat Super Destroyer by DQ
Rufus R. Jones & Sandy Scott beat Brute Bernard & Doug Gilbert
Bob Bruggers beat Blue Scorpion
Don Kernodle beat Mr. Hayashi

4/16/75: Raleigh, NC @ WRAL Studios (TV)

4/17/75: Anderson, SC @ Recreation Center
Gene & Ole Anderson vs. Paul Jones & Sonny King
Blue Scorpion vs. Tommy Seigler
Art Neilson vs. Klondike Bill
El Gaucho vs. Tio Tio
Mr. Hayashi vs. Kevin Sullivan

4/17/75: Norfolk, VA @ Scope
Wahoo McDaniel beat Johnny Valentine to win 2000 Silver Dollars
The Avenger & Charlie Cook beat Doug Gilbert & Mr. Fuji
Don Kernodle beat Bill Crouch
Bob Bruggers beat Cowboy Parker
L.D. Lewis beat Ken Dillinger

4/18/75: Charleston, SC @ County Hall
Gene & Ole Anderson beat Sonny King & Paul Jones
Plus other matches

4/18/75: Lynchburg, VA @ City Armory
Ric Flair vs. Ken Patera
Haystacks Calhoun vs. Brute Bernard
Doug Gilbert & Cowboy Parker vs. Abe Jacobs & Charlie Cook

Frank Morrell vs. L.D. Lewis
Klondike Bill vs. Joe Wilson

4/18/75: Richmond, VA @ Coliseum
Wahoo McDaniel & Rufus R. Jones beat Super Destroyer & Blackjack Mulligan
The Avenger beat Mr. Fuji by DQ
Sandy Scott beat Frank Monte
Bob Bruggers beat Bill Crouch
Don Kernodle beat Ken Dillinger

4/19/75: Roanoke, VA @ Starland Arena
Wahoo McDaniel beat Johnny Valentine via pinfall to win 2000 Silver Dollars
Sandy Scott beat Mr. Fuji by DQ
Tommy Seigler & Kevin Sullivan beat The Outlaws
L.D. Lewis beat Johnny Heidman

4/19/75: Spartanburg, SC @ Memorial Auditorium
Ken Patera & Jerry Brisco beat Gene & Ole Anderson by DQ
Doug Gilbert beat Charlie Cook
Bob Bruggers beat Frank Monte
Don Kernodle beat Frank Morrell
Tio Tio beat El Gaucho

4/19/75: Winston-Salem, NC @ Memorial Coliseum
16-man over the top rope battle royal with $75.00 bonus to the winner featuring Super Destroyer, Paul Jones, Rufus R. Jones, Ric Flair, Blackjack Mulligan, Haystack Calhoun, Sonny King, Swede Hanson and The Avenger plus 7 others
Plus 8 other matches

4/20/75: Canton, NC @ Robertson Memorial YMCA
Ric Flair & Johnny Valentine vs. Paul Jones & Ken Patera
Haystack Calhoun vs. Blue Scorpion
Brute Bernard vs. Charlie Cook
Bob Bruggers vs. Cowboy Parker
L.D. Lewis vs. Frank Monte

4/21/75: Charlotte, NC @ Park Center
Wahoo McDaniel beat Johnny Valentine to win 2,000 Silver Dollars
Rufus R. Jones beat Brute Bernard
Tommy Seigler & Abe Jacobs beat Blue Scorpion & Art Neilson
Klondike Bill beat Frank Morrell

4/21/75: Fayetteville, NC @ Cumberland County Memorial Auditorium
Gene & Ole Anderson & Ric Flair vs. Sonny King, Paul Jones & The Avenger

also including Swede Hanson & Bob Bruggers

4/21/75: Greenville, SC @ Memorial Auditorium
Super Destroyer beat Ken Patera by DQ in a goal post match
Charlie Cook & Haystack Calhoun beat Doug Gilbert & Mr. Fuji
Don Kernodle draw Kevin Sullivan
Frank Monte beat L.D. Lewis

4/22/75: Columbia, SC @ Township Auditorium
Super Destroyer beat The Avenger no time limit, no DQ, loser must unmask
Rufus R. Jones & Charlie Cook vs. Ric Flair & Doug Gilbert
Brute Bernard vs. Klondike Bill
L.D. Lewis vs. Ken Dillinger

4/22/75: Raleigh, NC @ Dorton Arena
Gene & Ole Anderson beat Paul Jones & Wahoo McDaniel
Mr. Fuji & Art Neilson beat Bob Bruggers & Haystack Calhoun
Tommy Seigler beat Cowboy Parker
Frank Morrell beat Tio Tio

4/23/75: Raleigh, NC @ WRAL Studios (TV)

4/24/75: Greensboro, NC @ Coliseum
Johnny Valentine no contest with Paul Jones
Dusty Rhodes beat Blackjack Mulligan in a match with Haystack Calhoun as special referee
Wahoo McDaniel beat Super Destroyer via pinfall
Sonny King & Swede Hanson beat Ric Flair & Doug Gilbert
Klondike Bill & Bob Bruggers beat Brute Bernard & Cowboy Parker
Kevin Sullivan beat Bill Crouch
Tio Tio beat Frank Morrell

4/24/75: Norfolk, VA @ Scope
Ole Anderson won a 13-man Russian Roulette battle royal for $5,400
Ole Anderson beat Rufus R. Jones
Ken Patera beat Art Neilson
Mr. Fuji beat L.D. Lewis
Blue Scorpion draw Abe Jacobs
The Avenger beat Ken Dillinger
Tommy Seigler beat Frank Monte

4/25/75: Charleston, SC @ County Hall
Ken Patera & Rufus R. Jones beat Blackjack Mulligan & Super Destroyer
Swede Hanson beat Brute Bernard
Klondike Bill beat Bill Crouch
Kevin Sullivan beat Frank Morrell

4/25/75: Richmond, VA @ Coliseum
Johnny Valentine beat Paul Jones by DQ
Ric Flair & Doug Gilbert beat Haystack Calhoun & Charlie Cook
Tommy Seigler draw Art Neilson
Abe Jacobs beat Cowboy Parker
Tio Tio beat Ken Dillinger

4/26/75: Roanoke, VA @ Starland Arena
Gene & Ole Anderson no contest with Ken Patera & Sonny King
The Avenger beat Art Neilson
Charlie Cook beat Frank Monte
Abe Jacobs beat Cowboy Parker
L.D. Lewis beat Bill Crouch

4/26/75: Spartanburg, SC @ Memorial Auditorium
The Super Destroyer vs. Haystack Calhoun
Blackjack Mulligan vs. Rufus R. Jones
Doug Gilbert & Brute Bernard vs. Klondike Bill & Swede Hanson
Don Kernodle vs. Ken Dillinger
Kevin Sullivan vs. Johnny Heidman

4/27/75: Asheville, NC @ Civic Center
Gene & Ole Anderson vs. Paul Jones & Wahoo McDaniel
Ken Patera vs. Blackjack Mulligan
Rufus R. Jones vs. Mr. Fuji
Art Neilson vs. Bob Bruggers
L.D. Lewis vs. Frank Morrell

4/28/75: Charlotte, NC @ Park Center
Blackjack Mulligan beat Wahoo McDaniel by DQ
Ken Patera beat Ric Flair
Rufus R. Jones & Haystacks Calhoun beat Mr. Fuji & Art Neilson
Sandy Scott beat Larry Sharpe
Bob Bruggers beat Frank Monte

4/28/75: Greenville, SC @ Memorial Auditorium
Paul Jones DDQ Johnny Valentine
Super Destroyer & Brute Bernard beat Charlie Cook & Sonny King
Blue Scorpion beat The Avenger
Doug Gilbert draw Tommy Seigler
Jerry Blackwell beat Tio Tio

4/29/75: Columbia, SC @ Township Auditorium
Paul Jones beat Johnny Valentine by DQ in a match with

Haystack Calhoun as special referee
Sonny King beat Gene Anderson
Swede Hanson & Sandy Scott beat Brute Bernard & Art Neilson
Klondike Bill beat Frank Monte
Jerry Blackwell beat Tio Tio

4/29/75: Gretna, VA @ High School
Rufus R. Jones & Ken Patera vs. Blackjack Mulligan & Ric Flair
Blue Scorpion vs. The Avenger in a loser must unmask match
Kevin Sullivan vs. Don Kernodle
L.D. Lewis vs. Bill Crouch

4/29/75: Raleigh, NC @ Dorton Arena
Ole Anderson vs. Wahoo McDaniel
The Avenger vs. Super Destroyer (Avenger will unmask before the match)
Charlie Cook & Abe Jacobs vs. Mr. Fuji & Doug Gilbert
Tommy Seigler vs. Larry Sharpe
Bob Bruggers vs. Frank Morrell

4/30/75: Raleigh, NC @ WRAL Studios (TV)

MAY

5/1/75: Norfolk, VA @ Scope
Ken Patera beat Johnny Valentine by DQ
Rufus R. Jones beat Ole Anderson
Gene Anderson beat Tommy Seigler
Jerry Blackwell & Blue Scorpion beat Abe Jacobs & Klondike Bill
Blue Scorpion (sub for Frank Morrell) beat Kevin Sullivan

5/2/75: Richmond, VA @ Coliseum
Paul Jones beat Ric Flair by CO
Gene & Ole Anderson beat The Avenger & Sonny King
Klondike Bill beat Jerry Blackwell by DQ
Kevin Sullivan beat Frank Morrell

5/2/75: Charleston, SC @ County Hall
Ken Patera beat Super Destroyer by DQ
Rufus R. Jones beat Blackjack Mulligan
Charlie Cook beat Mr. Fuji
Frank Monte beat Tio Tio
Bill Crouch beat Don Kernodle

5/3/75: Hampton, VA @ Coliseum
Johnny Valentine DDQ Paul Jones

The Avenger, Swede Hanson & Tommy Seigler beat Doug Gilbert, Art Neilson & Blue Scorpion
Super Destroyer beat Ken Patera in a no DQ match
Frank Morrell beat L.D. Lewis
Jerry Blackwell draw Abe Jacobs

5/3/75: Roanoke, VA @ Starland Arena
Ole Anderson beat Sonny King
Gene Anderson beat Sandy Scott
Mr. Fuji & Frank Monte beat Don Kernodle & Charlie Cook
Larry Sharpe beat Tio Tio

5/3/75: Greenwood, SC
Ric Flair vs. Wahoo McDaniel
Plus other matches

5/5/75: Charlotte, NC @ Park Center
Wahoo McDaniel beat Blackjack Mulligan in a no DQ match
Gene & Ole Anderson beat Swede Hanson & Sonny King
Tommy Seigler beat Blue Scorpion by DQ
Abe Jacobs beat Bill Crouch
Terry Sawyer beat Mr. Hayashi

5/5/75: Fayetteville, NC @ Cumberland County Memorial Auditorium
Ken Patera beat Super Destroyer by CO
Rufus R. Jones & Sandy Scott beat Mr. Fuji & Art Neilson
Charlie Cook beat Larry Sharpe
Kevin Sullivan beat Frank Morrell
Tio Tio draw El Gaucho (20:00)

5/5/75: Greenville, SC @ Memorial Auditorium
Paul Jones beat Johnny Valentine by DQ
Ric Flair beat The Avenger
Bob Bruggers & Klondike Bill beat Doug Gilbert & Brute Bernard
Jerry Blackwell beat L.D. Lewis
Frank Monte draw Don Kernodle

5/6/75: Columbia, SC @ Township Auditorium
Johnny Valentine beat Paul Jones via pinfall
Doug Gilbert & Ric Flair beat Sandy Scott & Rufus R. Jones
Art Neilson draw Abe Jacobs
Blue Scorpion beat Kevin Sullivan via pinfall
Larry Sharpe beat L.D. Lewis

5/6/75: Danville, VA @ City Armory
Sonny King beat Super Destroyer (28:17) by DQ
Brute Bernard & Mr. Fuji beat Ken Patera & The Avenger

(21:33) via pinfall
Tommy Seigler beat Bill Crouch (16:16) via pinfall
Frank Morrell draw Tio Tio (20:00)

5/6/75: Raleigh, NC @ Dorton Arena
Wahoo McDaniel vs. Ole Anderson in an Indian strap match
Blackjack Mulligan vs. Swede Hanson in a no DQ, no CO
Bob Bruggers vs. Gene Anderson
Charlie Cook & Klondike Bill vs. Jerry Blackwell & Mr. Hayashi
Don Kernodle vs. El Gaucho

5/7/75: Raleigh, NC @ WRAL Studios (TV)

5/8/75: Marion, NC @ McDowell High School
Ric Flair & Johnny Valentine vs. Paul Jones & Wahoo McDaniel
Art Neilson vs. Swede Hanson
Brute Bernard vs. Bob Bruggers
Frank Morrell vs. Kevin Sullivan
Mr. Hayashi vs. Tio Tio

5/8/75: Goldsboro, NC @ Wayne County Boys Club
Blackjack Mulligan & Super Destroyer vs. The Avenger & Sonny King
Plus other matches

5/8/75: Norfolk, VA @ Scope
Rufus R. Jones & Ken Patera beat Gene & Ole Anderson in a Texas tornado match
Jerry Blackwell draw Klondike Bill
Doug Gilbert draw Charlie Cook
Sandy Scott beat Larry Sharpe
Blue Scorpion beat Don Kernodle

5/9/75: Charleston, SC @ County Hall
Super Destroyer vs. Ken Patera
Rufus R. Jones vs. Ric Flair
Abe Jacobs & The Avenger vs. Brute Bernard & Art Neilson
L.D. Lewis vs. Frank Monte
Tommy Seigler vs. Frank Morrell

5/9/75: Richmond, VA @ Coliseum
Johnny Valentine beat Paul Jones
Wahoo McDaniel beat Blackjack Mulligan
Sonny King beat Ole Anderson
Charlie Cook, Sandy Scott & Swede Hanson beat Mr. Fuji, Gene Anderson & Doug Gilbert

5/10/75: Durham, NC @ Civic Center
Sonny King & Ken Patera vs. Ric Flair & Super Destroyer
The Avenger vs. Mr. Fuji
Art Neilson vs. Tommy Seigler
Frank Monte vs. Tio Tio
Bill Crouch vs. Don Kernodle

5/10/75: Roanoke, VA @ Starland Arena
Johnny Valentine vs. Paul Jones
Jerry Blackwell & Doug Gilbert vs. Klondike Bill & Bob Bruggers
Larry Sharpe vs. Charlie Cook
L.D. Lewis vs. Mr. Hayashi

5/12/75: Greenville, SC @ Memorial Auditorium
Paul Jones beat Johnny Valentine in a Texas death match
Ken Patera & The Avenger beat Doug Gilbert & Ric Flair
Charlie Cook beat Frank Monte
Brute Bernard draw Sandy Scott
Klondike Bill DDQ Jerry Blackwell

5/12/75: Rockingham, NC
Blackjack Mulligan & Mr. Fuji vs. Swede Hanson & Tommy Seigler
Plus other matches

5/13/75: Columbia, SC @ Township Auditorium
Paul Jones & Rufus R. Jones beat Ric Flair & Johnny Valentine
The Avenger beat Mr. Fuji
Doug Gilbert draw Swede Hanson
Bob Bruggers beat Bill Crouch
Larry Sharpe beat Tio Tio

5/13/75: Raleigh, NC @ Dorton Arena
Gene & Ole Anderson vs. Ken Patera & Wahoo McDaniel in a Texas tornado match
Art Neilson vs. Charlie Cook
Klondike Bill vs. Jerry Blackwell
Blue Scorpion vs. Sandy Scott

5/14/75: Raleigh, NC @ WRAL Studios (TV)

5/15/75: Greensboro, NC @ Coliseum
Paul Jones & Wahoo McDaniel beat Gene & Ole Anderson (33:00) via pinfall to win the NWA World Tag Title Dusty Rhodes beat Blackjack Mulligan in a bullrope match
Ric Flair beat Ken Patera by DQ
Swede Hanson & Bob Bruggers beat Mr. Fuji & Art Neilson by DQ
Sandy Scott beat Frank Monte

MID-ATLANTIC WRESTLING 1975 YEARBOOK

Ox Baker beat Charlie Cook
Don Kernodle beat Bill Crouch

5/15/75: Norfolk, VA @ Scope
Rufus R. Jones beat Johnny Valentine by DQ
Sonny King beat Super Destroyer by DQ
Klondike Bill beat Jerry Blackwell in a no DQ match
Susan Green beat Paula Kaye
Doug Gilbert & Brute Bernard beat Abe Jacobs & Tommy Seigler
Kevin Sullivan beat Mr. Hayashi
Tio Tio beat Frank Morrel

5/16/75: Charleston, SC @ County Hall
Paul Jones & Rufus R. Jones beat Gene & Ole Anderson
Charlie Cook beat Art Neilson by DQ
Sandy Scott beat Blue Scorpion
Larry Sharpe beat El Gaucho
Don Kernodle draw Frank Monte (20:00)

5/16/75: Charlottesville, VA @ University Hall
Johnny Valentine vs. Wahoo McDaniel
Ken Patera vs. Super Destroyer
Paula Kaye vs. Susan Green
Brute Bernard & Doug Gilbert vs. Abe Jacobs & Tommy Seigler
Klondike Bill vs. Bill Crouch
Kevin Sullivan vs. Frank Morrell

5/16/75: Lynchburg, VA @ City Armory
Ric Flair beat Sonny King
Swede Hanson beat Blackjack Mulligan
Jerry Blackwell & Mr. Fuji beat Bob Bruggers & The Avenger
Tio Tio beat Mr. Hayashi

5/17/75: Charlotte, NC @ Park Center
Johnny Valentine beat Paul Jones
Wahoo McDaniel beat Blackjack Mulligan in an Indian strap match
Super Destroyer & Brute Bernard beat Sonny King & Swede Hanson
Ann Casey beat Peggy Patterson
Art Neilson & Blue Scorpion beat Bob Bruggers & Tommy Seigler
Klondike Bill beat Jerry Blackwell by DQ
Steve Keirn beat Bill Crouch
Larry Sharpe beat Tio Tio

5/17/75: Spartanburg, SC @ Memorial Auditorium
Gene & Ole Anderson & Ric Flair beat Ken Patera, Rufus R. Jones & Sandy Scott

Charlie Cook beat Mr. Fuji by DQ
Doug Gilbert draw Abe Jacobs
Kevin Sullivan beat Frank Morrell

5/18/75: Asheville, NC @ Civic Center
Paul Jones & Wahoo McDaniel vs. Gene & Ole Anderson
Ric Flair vs. Ken Patera
Mr. Fuji vs. Bob Bruggers
Sandy Scott vs. Larry Sharpe
Kevin Sullivan vs. Blue Scorpion

5/19/75: Fayetteville, NC @ Cumberland County Memorial Auditorium
Sonny King vs. Super Destroyer
Brute Bernard & Doug Gilbert vs. Bob Bruggers & Sandy Scott
Abe Jacobs vs. Charlie Fulton
Bill Crouch vs. Greg Peterson
Terry Sawyer vs. El Gaucho

5/19/75: Greenville, SC @ Memorial Auditorium
Wahoo McDaniel beat Blackjack Mulligan
Gene & Ole Anderson beat Rufus R. Jones & The Avenger
Klondike Bill beat Jerry Blackwell
Steve Keirn beat Larry Sharpe
Frank Monte beat Tio Tio

5/19/75: Salem, VA @ Roanoke Valley Civic Center
Johnny Valentine beat Paul Jones via pinfall
Ken Patera beat Ric Flair by DQ
Swede Hanson & Charlie Cook beat Art Neilson & Mr. Fuji
Vicki Williams & Honey Girl Paige beat Paula Kaye & Marie LeVeau
Kevin Sullivan beat Frank Morrell
Don Kernodle draw Blue Scorpion

5/20/75: Raleigh, NC @ Dorton Arena
Gene & Ole Anderson vs. Ken Patera & Wahoo McDaniel in a falls count anywhere match
Sonny King vs. Blackjack Mulligan
Klondike Bill vs. Jerry Blackwell in a no DQ match
Mr. Fuji vs. Kevin Sullivan
Steve Keirn vs. Frank Monte

5/20/75: Columbia, SC @ Township Auditorium

5/21/75: Raleigh, NC @ WRAL Studios (TV)

5/21/75: Rocky Mount, NC @ Ball Park
Paul Jones & Sonny King vs. Super Destroyer & Blackjack

Mulligan in an elimination match
Swede Hanson vs. Brute Bernard
Art Neilson vs. Abe Jacobs
Klondike Bill vs. Jerry Blackwell
Charlie Fulton vs. Tio Tio

5/22/75: Norfolk, VA @ Scope

5/22/75: Anderson, SC @ Recreation Center
Johnny Valentine vs. Ken Patera
Sonny King & Steve Keirn vs. Doug Gilbert & Brute Bernard
Jerry Blackwell vs. Abe Jacobs
Larry Sharpe vs. Tio Tio
Bob Bruggers vs. Frank Morrell

5/22/75: Elizabeth City, NC @ Northeastern High School
Wahoo McDaniel vs. Super Destroyer
Rufus R. Jones vs. Blackjack Mulligan
Also including The Avenger, Swede Hanson, Mr. Fuji, Art Neilson and others

5/23/75: Charleston, SC @ County Hall
Johnny Valentine DDQ Paul Jones
Ric Flair beat The Avenger
Abe Jacobs & Bob Bruggers beat Jerry Blackwell & Blue Scorpion
Steve Keirn beat Frank Morrell

5/23/75: Lynchburg, VA @ City Armory
Ken Patera & Rufus R. Jones beat Gene & Ole Anderson
Sandy Scott beat Chuck O'Connor (sub for Brute Bernard)
Larry Sharpe beat Greg Peterson
Don Kernodle beat George Harris
Tio Tio beat Bill Crouch

5/23/75: Richmond, VA @ Coliseum
Wahoo McDaniel beat Blackjack Mulligan
Super Destroyer beat Sonny King
Mr. Fuji & Art Neilson vs. Charlie Cook & Swede Hanson
Klondike Bill vs. Charlie Fulton
Frank Monte vs. Kevin Sullivan

5/24/75: Florence, SC @ Memorial Stadium
Gene & Ole Anderson vs. Wahoo McDaniel & Rufus R. Jones
Brute Bernard & Art Neilson vs. Abe Jacobs & The Avenger
Bob Bruggers vs. Blue Scorpion
Don Kernodle vs. Frank Morrell

5/24/75: Roanoke, VA @ Starland Arena
Super Destroyer beat Sonny King by DQ
Ken Patera beat Blackjack Mulligan
Swede Hanson & Kevin Sullivan beat Charlie Fulton & Frank Monte
Larry Sharpe beat Tio Tio

5/24/75: Spartanburg, SC @ Memorial Auditorium
Paul Jones & Andre The Giant beat Ric Flair & Johnny Valentine
Sandy Scott beat Mr. Fuji by DQ
Charlie Cook beat Jerry Blackwell
Klondike Bill beat Two Ton Harris
Greg Peterson beat Bill Crouch

5/26/75: Greenville, SC @ Memorial Auditorium

5/26/75: Winston-Salem, NC @ Dixie Fair Grandstand
Paul Jones, Rufus R. Jones & Wahoo McDaniel vs. Johnny Valentine, Super Destroyer & Ric Flair in an elimination match
Gene & Ole Anderson vs. Sonny King & Charlie Cook
Blackjack Mulligan vs. Ken Patera
Larry Sharpe vs. Steve Keirn
Swede Hanson vs. Chuck O'Connor
Frank Monte vs. Kevin Sullivan
Bill Crouch vs. Charlie Fulton

5/27/75: Raleigh, NC @ Dorton Arena
Johnny Valentine vs. Rufus R. Jones
Ric Flair vs. Paul Jones

5/27/75: Sumter, SC @ Riley Park
Sonny King vs. Super Destroyer
Wahoo McDaniel vs. Blackjack Mulligan in a no DQ match
Brute Bernard & The Scorpion vs. Charlie Cook & The Avenger
Sandy Scott vs. George Harris
Bob Bruggers vs. Bill Crouch

5/28/75: Raleigh, NC @ WRAL Studios (TV)

5/29/75: Norfolk, VA @ Scope
Paul Jones & Wahoo McDaniel DDQ Gene & Ole Anderson
Steve Keirn (sub for The Avenger) beat Mr. Fuji by DQ
Steve Keirn beat Greg Peterson
Larry Sharpe beat Tio Tio
Frank Monte draw Kevin Sullivan

5/29/75: Roxboro, NC @ Optimist Park
Ric Flair vs. Ken Patera
Blackjack Mulligan vs. Rufus R. Jones
Charlie Cook & Abe Jacobs vs. Art Neilson & Charlie Fulton
Jerry Blackwell vs. Bill Crouch

5/30/75: Charleston, SC @ County Hall
Brute Bernard & The Blue Scorpion vs. Charlie Cook & Abe Jacobs
Frank Morrell vs. Don Kernodle
Jerry Blackwell vs. Bob Bruggers
Sonny King vs. The Super Destroyer

5/30/75: Richmond, VA @ Coliseum
Wahoo McDaniel vs. Blackjack Mulligan in an Indian strap match
Gene & Ole Anderson vs. Swede Hanson & Rufus R. Jones
The Avenger vs. Charlie Fulton
Kevin Sullivan vs. Bill Crouch
Frank Monte vs. Tio Tio

5/31/75: Roanoke, VA @ Starland Arena
Sonny King beat Super Destroyer by DQ in a match with no referee
Ken Patera beat Jerry Blackwell
Swede Hanson & Steve Keirn beat Two Ton Harris & Blue Scorpion
Kevin Sullivan beat Bill Crouch

5/31/75: Spartanburg, SC @ Memorial Auditorium
Paul Jones beat Ric Flair by CO
Charlie Cook & Don Kernodle (sub for The Avenger) beat Brute Bernard & Charlie Fulton by DQ
Klondike Bill beat Frank Monte
Larry Sharpe beat Tio Tio
Don Kernodle draw Greg Peterson

JUNE

6/2/75: Charlotte, NC @ Park Center
Super Destroyer DDQ Sonny King (22:00)
Ric Flair & Mr. Fuji beat Ken Patera & Sandy Scott
Abe Jacobs beat Blue Scorpion by DQ
Steve Keirn beat Frank Monte
Larry Sharpe draw Kevin Sullivan

6/2/75: Fayetteville, NC @ Cumberland County Memorial Auditorium
Wahoo McDaniel & Rufus R. Jones vs. Gene & Ole Anderson
Swede Hanson vs. Jerry Blackwell
Charlie Fulton vs. Greg Peterson
Tio Tio vs. Frank Morrell

6/2/75: Greenville, SC @ Memorial Auditorium
Johnny Valentine beat Paul Jones
Boris Malenko beat Klondike Bill
Brute Bernard & Art Neilson beat Bob Bruggers & Charlie Cook
Don Kernodle draw George Harris
Joe Soto beat Bill Crouch

6/3/75: Columbia, SC @ Township Auditorium
Sonny King beat Super Destroyer in a match with 2 referees
Gene & Ole Anderson beat Charlie Cook & Ken Patera
Boris Malenko beat Sandy Scott
Bob Bruggers beat George Harris
Abe Jacobs draw Joe Soto

6/3/75: Raleigh, NC @ Dorton Arena
Rufus R. Jones beat Johnny Valentine
Paul Jones beat Ric Flair by CO
Brute Bernard & Art Neilson beat Steve Keirn & Kevin Sullivan
Greg Peterson beat Frank Morrell

6/4/75: Raleigh, NC @ WRAL Studios (TV)

6/5/75: Greensboro, NC @ Coliseum
Paul Jones & Wahoo McDaniel beat Jack Brisco & Jerry Brisco
Gene & Ole Anderson beat Swede Hanson & Sandy Scott
Boris Malenko beat Jose Lothario
Sonny King beat Super Destroyer by DQ
Brute Bernard beat Bill Crouch (sub for Danny Miller)
Klondike Bill DCO with Jerry Blackwell
Kevin Sullivan beat Greg Peterson
Steve Keirn beat Charlie Fulton

6/5/75: Norfolk, VA @ Scope
Ken Patera & Rufus R. Jones beat Ric Flair & Johnny Valentine
Mr. Fuji beat Charlie Cook
Art Neilson beat Bob Bruggers
Abe Jacobs beat Larry Sharpe by DQ
Frank Monte draw Joe Soto

6/6/75: Charleston, SC @ County Hall
Paul Jones & Wahoo McDaniel beat Gene & Ole Anderson
Steve Keirn beat Brute Bernard

Tio Tio beat Charlie Fulton
Greg Peterson & Kevin Sullivan b. George Harris & Jerry Blackwell

6/6/75: Richmond, VA @ Coliseum
Johnny Valentine vs. Ken Patera
Super Destroyer vs. Sonny King in a lumberjack match
Ric Flair & Boris Malenko vs. Rufus R. Jones & Swede Hanson

6/7/75: Hampton, VA @ Coliseum
Paul Jones & Wahoo McDaniel beat Gene & Ole Anderson
Johnny Valentine beat Rufus R. Jones by DQ
Boris Malenko beat Klondike Bill
Bob Bruggers & Sandy Scott beat Joe Soto & Blue Scorpion
Don Kernodle beat Bill Crouch

6/7/75: Roanoke, VA @ Victory Stadium
Ric Flair beat Ken Patera by DQ
Mr. Fuji & Art Neilson beat Abe Jacobs & Charlie Cook
Kevin Sullivan draw Larry Sharpe
Greg Peterson beat Frank Morrell
Bobby Williams beat Frank Monte

6/7/75: Spartanburg, SC @ Memorial Auditorium
Super Destroyer beat Sonny King by DQ
Swede Hanson & Steve Keirn beat Brute Bernard & Charlie Fulton
Jerry Blackwell beat Terry Sawyer
Steve Keirn (sub for Tio Tio) beat George Harris

6/9/75: Charlotte, NC @ Park Center
Ken Patera & Sonny King beat Ric Flair & Super Destroyer
Swede Hansen beat Brute Bernard
Jerry Blackwell DDQ Klondike Bill
Greg Peterson beat Charlie Fulton
Joe Soto beat Bill Crouch

6/9/75: Greenville, SC @ Memorial Auditorium
Paul Jones & Wahoo McDaniel beat Gene & Ole Anderson in a no time limit, no DQ, no CO match
Boris Malenko beat Sandy Scott
Charlie Cook beat Blue Scorpion
Ron Starr beat Frank Morrell
Frank Monte draw Don Serrano

6/10/75: Columbia, SC @ Township Auditorium
Sonny King vs. Super Destroyer
Boris Malenko vs. Klondike Bill
Swede Hanson & Steve Keirn vs. Brute Bernard & Art Neilson
Larry Sharpe vs. Kevin Sullivan
Greg Peterson vs. Joe Soto

6/10/75: Raleigh, NC @ Dorton Arena
Paul Jones beat Ric Flair in a lumberjack match
Gene & Ole Anderson vs. Ken Patera & Rufus R. Jones
Brute Bernard vs. Don Kernodle
Ron Starr vs. Charlie Fulton
Don Serrano vs. Frank Monte

6/11/75: Raleigh, NC @ WRAL Studios (TV)
Gene & Ole Anderson beat Paul Jones & Wahoo McDaniel to win the NWA World Tag Team Title

6/11/75: Rocky Mount, NC @ Municipal Stadium
Johnny Valentine vs. Wahoo McDaniel
Ric Flair vs. Rufus R. Jones
Brute Bernard & Mr. Fuji vs. Steve Keirn & Charlie Cook
Blue Scorpion vs. Sandy Scott
Klondike Bill vs. George Harris

6/12/75: Anderson, SC @ Recreation Center
Johnny Valentine beat Paul Jones by DQ
Ken Patera beat Ole Anderson via pinfall
Steve Keirn & Kevin Sullivan beat Art Neilson & Mr. Fuji
Larry Sharpe draw Don Kernodle

6/12/75: Norfolk, VA @ Scope
Sonny King vs. Super Destroyer
Boris Malenko vs. Sandy Scott
Jerry Blackwell & George Harris beat Klondike Bill & Abe Jacobs

6/13/75: Charleston, SC @ County Hall
Sonny King beat Super Destroyer by DQ
Art Neilson & Brute Bernard & Mr. Fuji beat Steve Keirn & Kevin Sullivan & Charlie Cook
Larry Sharpe vs. Greg Peterson
Joe Soto vs. Don Kernodle

6/13/75: Lynchburg, VA @ City Armory
Gene & Ole Anderson beat Paul Jones & Wahoo McDaniel by DQ
Boris Malenko beat Swede Hanson
Bobby Williams draw Blue Scorpion
Susan Green & Sheila Shepherd beat Leilani Kai & Fabulous Moolah

6/13/75: Richmond, VA @ Coliseum
Johnny Valentine vs. Rufus R. Jones
Ric Flair vs. Ken Patera
Don Serrano vs. Frank Morrell
Ron Starr vs. Charlie Fulton
Abe Jacobs vs. Frank Monte

MID-ATLANTIC WRESTLING 1975 YEARBOOK

Jerry Blackwell & George Harris vs. Klondike Bill & Sandy Scott

6/14/75: Roanoke, VA @ Victory Stadium
Sonny King beat Super Destroyer by DQ
Sandy Scott, Swede Hanson & Klondike Bill beat George Harris, Art Neilson & Jerry Blackwell
Ron Starr beat Larry Sharpe
Bill Crouch beat Bobby Williams

6/14/75: Spartanburg, SC @ Memorial Auditorium
Ric Flair & Boris Malenko beat Rufus R. Jones & Wahoo McDaniel by DQ
Abe Jacobs beat Frank Monte
Charlie Cook beat Joe Soto
Don Serrano beat Frank Morrell
Don Kernodle draw Buddy Porter 20:00

6/15/75: Asheville, NC @ Civic Center
Johnny Valentine vs. Wahoo McDaniel
Ric Flair vs. Paul Jones in a lumberjack match
Boris Malenko vs. Sandy Scott
Brute Bernard & Mr. Fuji vs. Klondike Bill & Steve Keirn
Greg Peterson vs. Don Serrano
Ron Starr vs. Larry Sharpe

6/16/75: Charlotte, NC @ Park Center
Gene & Ole Anderson beat Paul Jones & Wahoo McDaniel by DQ
Charlie Cook beat Art Neilson
Mr. Fuji draw Steve Keirn
Danny Miller beat Larry Sharpe
Ron Starr beat Charlie Fulton

6/16/75: Fayetteville, NC @ Cumberland County Memorial Auditorium
Johnny Valentine vs. Rufus R. Jones
Ken Patera vs. Brute Bernard
Also included Klondike Bill, Sandy Scott & Blue Scorpion

6/16/75: Greenville, SC @ Memorial Auditorium
Sonny King beat Super Destroyer
Ric Flair & Boris Malenko beat Swede Hansen & Abe Jacobs
Frank Monte draw Greg Peterson (sub for Bob Bruggers)
Bill Crouch beat Don Serrano
Kevin Sullivan beat Frank Morrell

6/17/75: Raleigh, NC @ Dorton Arena
NWA World Champion Jack Brisco vs. Paul Jones in a no time limit match
Sonny King vs. Super Destroyer
Boris Malenko vs. Bob Burns
Brute Bernard & Mr. Fuji vs. Danny Miller & Charlie Cook
Ron Starr vs. Frank Morrell

6/17/75: Sumter, SC @ Riley Park
Johnny Valentine vs. Wahoo McDaniel
Ric Flair vs. Swede Hanson
Jerry Blackwell & George Harris vs. Sandy Scott & Klondike Bill
Bob Bruggers vs. Frank Monte
Abe Jacobs vs. Blue Scorpion

6/18/75: Raleigh, NC @ WRAL Studios (TV)

6/19/75: Norfolk, VA @ Scope
NWA World Champion Jack Brisco beat Sonny King
Sandy Scott DDQ Boris Malenko
Kevin Sullivan & Steve Keirn beat Brute Bernard & Blue Scorpion
Charlie Fulton draw Don Kernodle
Joe Soto beat Bob Burns

6/20/75: Charleston, SC @ County Hall
Paul Jones & Wahoo McDaniel beat Ric Flair & Johnny Valentine via pinfall
Klondike Bill (sub for Bob Bruggers) beat Art Neilson
Danny Miller beat Mr. Fuji
Frank Monte beat Greg Peterson
Don Serrano beat Larry Sharpe

6/20/75: Richmond, VA @ Coliseum
Super Destroyer beat Sonny King
Ken Patera & Sandy Scott beat Boris Malenko & Brute Bernard
Steve Keirn beat Charlie Fulton in a fence match
Blue Scorpion beat Bob Burns
Don Kernodle beat Bill Crouch
Kevin Sullivan draw Joe Soto

6/21/75: Roanoke, VA @ Victory Stadium
Sonny King vs. Super Destroyer in a fence match
Sandy Scott vs. Boris Malenko
Steve Keirn & Kevin Sullivan vs. Mr. Fuji & Blue Scorpion
Bob Bruggers vs. Larry Sharpe
Ron Starr vs. Bill Crouch

6/21/75: Spartanburg, SC @ Memorial Auditorium
Wahoo McDaniel beat Ric Flair
Ken Patera & Charlie Cook beat Brute Bernard & Art Neilson by DQ
Jerry Blackwell beat Bob Burns

MID-ATLANTIC WRESTLING 1975 YEARBOOK

Danny Miller beat Frank Monte
Don Kernodle beat Frank Morrell

6/22/75: Burlington, NC @ Elon College Gym
Gene & Ole Anderson vs. Paul Jones & Wahoo McDaniel
Ric Flair vs. Swede Hanson
Ken Patera vs. Jerry Blackwell
Ron Starr vs. Boris Malenko
Don Kernodle vs. George Harris

6/23/75: Charlotte, NC @ Park Center
Wahoo McDaniel beat Ole Anderson
Ken Patera beat Johnny Valentine
Boris Malenko beat Abe Jacobs
Danny Miller & Charlie Cook beat Blue Scorpion & Frank Monte
Don Serrano beat Frank Morrell

6/23/75: Greenville, SC @ Memorial Auditorium
Sonny King beat Super Destroyer
Rufus R. Jones beat Gene Anderson
Art Neilson & Mr. Fuji beat Steve Keirn & Kevin Sullivan
Ron Starr beat Joe Soto
Larry Sharpe beat Bob Burns

6/23/75: Lenoir, NC @ Mack Cook Stadium
Ric Flair DDQ Paul Jones
Sandy Scott & Bob Bruggers beat Brute Bernard & Jerry Blackwell
Swede Hanson beat George Harris
Klondike Bill beat Bill Crouch
Greg Peterson draw Charlie Fulton

6/24/75: Columbia, SC @ Township Auditorium
Sonny King beat Super Destroyer in a boxing match
Ken Patera beat Mr. Fuji
Ron Starr & Steve Keirn beat Art Neilson & Blue Scorpion
Klondike Bill beat Jerry Blackwell
Greg Peterson beat Bill Crouch

6/24/75: Raleigh, NC @ Dorton Arena
Paul Jones, Rufus R. Jones & Wahoo McDaniel beat Ric Flair, Gene & Ole Anderson
Danny Miller vs. Brute Bernard
Charlie Cook vs. Boris Malenko
Bob Bruggers vs. Frank Morrell

6/25/75: Raleigh, NC @ WRAL Studios (TV)

6/26/75: Anderson, SC @ Recreation Center
Wahoo McDaniel & Sonny King vs. Ric Flair & Johnny Valentine
Swede Hanson vs. Brute Bernard
Blue Scorpion vs. Kevin Sullivan
Steve Keirn vs. Charlie Fulton
Joe Soto vs. Bob Burns

6/26/75: Norfolk, VA @ Scope
Gene & Ole Anderson beat Paul Jones & Rufus R. Jones
Danny Miller beat Jerry Blackwell by DQ
Bob Bruggers beat George Harris via pinfall
Sandy Scott beat Blue Scorpion
Don Serrano beat Bill Crouch

6/27/75: Charleston, SC @ County Hall
Super Destroyer beat Sonny King in a lumberjack match
Brute Bernard & Art Neilson vs. Steve Keirn & Ron Starr
Charlie Fulton vs. Kevin Sullivan
Frank Morrell vs. Greg Peterson

6/27/75: Lexington, VA @ VMI Field House
Gene & Ole Anderson vs. Paul Jones & Ken Patera
Mr. Fuji vs. Klondike Bill
Charlie Cook vs. Larry Sharpe
Danny Miller vs. Joe Soto
Don Serrano vs. Bill Crouch

6/27/75: Richmond, VA @ Coliseum
Wahoo McDaniel & Rufus R. Jones beat Ric Flair & Johnny Valentine
Boris Malenko beat Sandy Scott
Abe Jacobs (sub for Swede Hanson) beat Jerry Blackwell by DQ
Bob Bruggers draw Blue Scorpion
Abe Jacobs beat George Harris via pinfall

6/28/75: Roanoke, VA @ Victory Stadium
Gene & Ole Anderson no contest with Paul Jones & Rufus R. Jones
Mr. Fuji beat Danny Miller
Sandy Scott beat Joe Soto
Abe Jacobs beat Larry Sharpe
Bob Bruggers beat George Harris

6/28/75: Spartanburg, SC @ Memorial Auditorium
Ric Flair beat Wahoo McDaniel
Ron Starr & Steve Keirn beat Brute Bernard & Jerry Blackwell
Charlie Cook beat Buddy Porter
Greg Peterson draw Charlie Fulton
Don Serrano beat Frank Morrell

6/29/75: Asheville, NC @ Civic Center
Wahoo McDaniel beat Johnny Valentine to win the NWA Mid Atlantic Title in a o time limit, no DQ, no CO match with George Scott as special referee
Gene & Ole Anderson vs. Ken Patera & Rufus R. Jones
Art Neilson vs. Bob Bruggers
Klondike Bill vs. Jerry Blackwell
Sandy Scott vs. Frank Monte
Ron Starr vs. Larry Sharpe

6/30/75: Charlotte, NC @ Memorial Stadium
Andre The Giant beat Super Destroyer by DQ
Wahoo McDaniel beat Blackjack Mulligan in a Texas death match
Danny Miller & Steve Keirn beat Boris Malenko & Doug Gilbert
Fabulous Moolah beat Shelia Shepherd
Klondike Bill beat Ox Baker by DQ
Don Serrano beat Frank Valois
Ron Starr beat Frank Monte

6/30/75: Fayetteville, NC @ Cumberland County Memorial Auditorium
Ken Patera beat Johnny Valentine
Sonny King beat Ric Flair by DQ
Abe Jacobs & Bob Bruggers beat George Harris (sub for Jerry Blackwell) & Blue Scorpion
El Gaucho beat Terry Sawyer (sub for George Harris)
Greg Peterson beat Joe Soto

6/30/75: Greenville, SC @ Memorial Auditorium
Gene & Ole Anderson beat Paul Jones & Rufus R. Jones
Sandy Scott & Swede Hansen beat Art Neilson & Mr. Fuji
Susan Green beat Donna Christian
Charlie Fulton beat Kevin Sullivan
Larry Sharpe beat Bob Burns

JULY

7/1/75: Columbia, SC @ Township Auditorium
Andre The Giant & Wahoo McDaniel beat Ric Flair & Johnny Valentine
Sonny King & Steve Keirn beat Ox Baker & Doug Gilbert
Sandy Scott draw Blue Scorpion
Larry Sharpe beat Greg Peterson
George Harris beat Bob Burns

7/1/75: Raleigh, NC @ Dorton Arena
Gene & Ole Anderson beat Ken Patera & Rufus R. Jones
Swede Hanson beat Boris Malenko by DQ
Mr. Fuji beat Abe Jacobs
Art Neilson draw Bob Bruggers
Charlie Fulton beat Kevin Sullivan
7/2/75: Raleigh, NC @ WRAL Studios (TV)

7/2/75: Rocky Mount, NC @ Municipal Stadium
Andre The Giant, Paul Jones & Wahoo McDaniel vs. Ric Flair, Doug Gilbert & Johnny Valentine
Sonny King vs. Art Neilson
Mr. Fuji vs. Ron Starr
Steve Keirn vs. George Harris

7/3/75: Greensboro, NC @ Coliseum
Johnny Valentine beat Harley Race to win NWA United States Title
Gene & Ole Anderson beat Andre The Giant & Paul Jones
Rufus R. Jones won 20-man battle royal
Ken Patera beat Mr. Fuji
Rufus R. Jones beat El Goucho
Boris Malenko beat Abe Jacobs
Ox Baker draw Danny Miller (10:00)
Klondike Bill & Sandy Scott beat Frank Monte & George Harris
Steve Keirn beat Joe Soto
Ron Starr beat Don Serrano

7/3/75: Norfolk, VA @ Scope
Ric Flair beat Wahoo McDaniel
Sonny King beat Super Destroyer in a no DQ match
Swede Hanson & Bob Bruggers beat Doug Gilbert & Blue Scorpion
Charlie Fulton beat Greg Peterson
Larry Sharpe draw Kevin Sullivan

7/4/75: Marion, NC @ McDowell High School (Afternoon Card)
Andre The Giant & Ken Patera vs. Johnny Valentine & Boris Malenko
Toni Rose & Donna Christianello vs. Susan Green & Sheila Shepherd
El Gaucho vs. Bob Burns
Sandy Scott vs. Frank Valois

7/4/75: Charleston, SC @ County Hall (Evening Card)
Johnny Valentine vs. Ken Patera
Rufus R. Jones vs. Boris Malenko
Mr. Fuji & Jerry Blackwell vs. Ron Starr & Danny Miller
Plus other matches

7/4/75: Richmond, VA @ Coliseum (Evening Card)
Gene & Ole Anderson draw Paul Jones & Wahoo McDaniel (60:00)

MID-ATLANTIC WRESTLING 1975 YEARBOOK

Andre The Giant beat Super Destroyer by DQ
Swede Hanson & Sonny King beat Ric Flair & Doug Gilbert
Sandy Scott & Bob Bruggers beat Charlie Fulton & Blue Scorpion
Greg Peterson beat Larry Sharpe
Klondike Bill beat Joe Soto
Steve Keirn draw Art Neilson

7/5/75: Hampton, VA @ Coliseum
Johnny Valentine beat Rufus R. Jones
Ric Flair beat Paul Jones
Susan Green & Sheila Shepherd beat Toni Rose & Donna Christian
Bob Bruggers beat Johnny Heidman
Sandy Scott beat Charlie Fulton
Klondike Bill beat Art Neilson by DQ
Doug Gilbert draw Steve Keirn

7/5/75: Salem, VA @ Civic Center
Andre The Giant & Sonny King beat Super Destroyer & Boris Malenko
Danny Miller beat Mr. Fuji
Joe Soto beat Bob Burns
Abe Jacobs beat Blue Scorpion
Greg Peterson draw Larry Sharpe

7/5/75: Spartanburg, SC @ Memorial Auditorium
Gene & Ole Anderson DDQ Ken Patera & Wahoo McDaniel
Swede Hanson beat Jerry Blackwell
Ron Starr beat Frank Monte
George Harris draw Kevin Sullivan (20:00)
Don Serrano beat El Gaucho

7/6/75: Wilmington, NC @ Legion Stadium
Super Destroyer & Johnny Valentine vs. Andre The Giant & Wahoo McDaniel
Ric Flair vs. Rufus R. Jones
Plus other matches

7/7/75: Charlotte, NC @ Park Center
Ken Patera beat Johnny Valentine by DQ
Steve Keirn & Ron Starr beat Boris Malenko & Doug Gilbert
Charlie Cook beat Joe Soto
Abe Jacobs beat Charlie Fulton
Kevin Sullivan beat El Gaucho

7/7/75: Greenville, SC @ Memorial Auditorium
Andre The Giant, Paul Jones & Rufus R. Jones beat Gene & Ole Anderson & Super Destroyer

The Avenger beat Jerry Blackwell
Sandy Scott beat Frank Monte
Bob Bruggers beat Frank Valois
Don Serrano beat Greg Peterson

7/8/75: Columbia, SC @ Township Auditorium
Ken Patera, Rufus R. Jones & The Avenger beat Ric Flair, Super Destroyer & Johnny Valentine
Swede Hanson DCO with Boris Malenko
Bob Bruggers beat Mr. Fuji
Don Serrano beat Charlie Fulton

7/8/75: Raleigh, NC @ Dorton Arena
Gene & Ole Anderson draw Paul Jones & Wahoo McDaniel
Jerry Blackwell DDQ Sandy Scott
Doug Gilbert beat Steve Keirn
Larry Sharpe draw Greg Peterson
Charlie Cook beat Joe Soto

7/9/75: Raleigh, NC @ WRAL Studios (TV)

7/10/75: Anderson, SC @ Recreation Center
Wahoo McDaniel DDQ Ric Flair
Tony White (sub for Swede Hanson) & Bob Bruggers beat Art Neilson & Blue Scorpion
Swede Hanson (sub for Sonny King) beat Mr. Fuji via pinfall
Greg Peterson draw Frank Monte

7/10/75: Burlington, NC @ Fairchild Park
Johnny Valentine vs. Ken Patera
Steve Keirn & Ron Starr vs. Doug Gilbert & Boris Malenko
Don Serrano vs. El Gaucho
Klondike Bill vs. George Harris
Charlie Cook vs. Charlie Fulton

7/10/75: Norfolk, VA @ Scope
Paul Jones & Rufus R. Jones beat Gene & Ole Anderson
The Avenger beat Jerry Blackwell
Sandy Scott beat Joe Soto
Abe Jacobs draw Kevin Sullivan
Larry Sharpe beat Bob Burns

7/11/75: Charleston, SC @ County Hall
Rufus R. Jones (sub for Sonny King) vs. Super Destroyer
Bob Bruggers & Danny Miller vs. Doug Gilbert & Boris Malenko
Swede Hanson vs. Blue Scorpion
Klondike Bill vs. George Harris
Frank Monte vs. Don Serrano

MID-ATLANTIC WRESTLING 1975 YEARBOOK

7/11/75: Charlottesville, VA @ University Hall
Gene & Ole Anderson vs. Ken Patera & Wahoo McDaniel
The Avenger vs. Jerry Blackwell
Sandy Scott vs. Larry Sharpe
Abe Jacobs vs. Joe Soto
Kevin Sullivan vs. Bob Burns

7/12/75: Roanoke, VA @ Victory Stadium
Gene & Ole Anderson beat Steve Keirn (sub for The Avenger) & Ken Patera
Charlie Cook beat Art Neilson
Frank Monte beat Kevin Sullivan
Steve Keirn beat Joe Soto
Don Serrano beat Greg Peterson

7/12/75: Spartanburg, SC @ Memorial Auditorium
Wahoo McDaniel beat Ric Flair
The Avenger & Sandy Scott beat Doug Gilbert & Boris Malenko
Ron Starr beat George Harris
Klondike Bill beat Charlie Fulton
Larry Sharpe beat Bob Burns

7/14/75: Charlotte, NC @ Park Center
Johnny Valentine beat Ken Patera by DQ
Ric Flair & Boris Malenko beat Steve Keirn & Ron Starr
Charlie Cook beat Blue Scorpion
Frank Monte beat Greg Peterson
Charlie Fulton beat Tio Tio

7/14/75: Fayetteville, NC @ Cumberland County Memorial Auditorium
Rufus R. Jones beat Super Destroyer
Danny Miller & Sandy Scott beat Jerry Blackwell & George Harris
The Avenger beat Mr. Fuji
Bob Bruggers beat Larry Sharpe
Kevin Sullivan draw Don Serrano

7/14/75: Greenville, SC @ Memorial Auditorium
Gene & Ole Anderson draw Paul Jones & Wahoo McDaniel (60:00)
Rufus R. Jones vs. Art Neilson
Doug Gilbert vs. Swede Hanson
Abe Jacobs vs. Joe Soto
Klondike Bill vs. El Gaucho

7/15/75: Columbia, SC @ Township Auditorium
Super Destroyer beat Ken Patera
Ric Flair DDQ Rufus R. Jones
Art Neilson & Boris Malenko beat Swede Hanson & The Avenger
Danny Miller beat George Harris
Sandy Scott beat Charlie Fulton

7/15/75: Raleigh, NC @ Dorton Arena
Wahoo McDaniel beat Johnny Valentine
Steve Keirn & Ron Starr beat Doug Gilbert & Mr. Fuji
Charlie Cook beat Larry Sharpe
Klondike Bill beat Frank Monte
Greg Peterson beat El Gaucho

7/16/75: Raleigh, NC @ WRAL Studios (TV)

7/16/75: Rocky Mount, NC @ Ball Park
Gene & Ole Anderson vs. Paul Jones & Rufus R. Jones
Abe Jacobs vs. Doug Gilbert
Bob Bruggers vs. Art Neilson
Sandy Scott vs. Frank Monte
Kevin Sullivan vs. Joe Soto

7/17/75: Collinsville, VA @ Fieldale-Collinsville H.S.
Johnny Valentine vs. Rufus R. Jones
Ken Patera vs. Jerry Blackwell
Plus other matches

7/17/75: Norfolk, VA @ Scope
Wahoo McDaniel beat Ric Flair
Tony Atlas beat Mr. Fuji
Boris Malenko & Doug Gilbert beat Sandy Scott & Danny Miller
Frank Monte draw Bob Bruggers
Charlie Cook beat Larry Sharpe

7/18/75: Charleston, SC @ County Hall
Gene & Ole Anderson beat Ken Patera & Rufus R. Jones
Abe Jacobs beat Art Neilson
Jerry Blackwell beat Don Serrano
Charlie Fulton draw Tio Tio
Don Serrano beat Kevin Sullivan
Also advertised was Swede Hanson vs. Doug Gilbert

7/18/75: Richmond, VA @ Coliseum
Wahoo McDaniel beat Blackjack Mulligan in a Texas death match
Paul Jones beat Ric Flair by DQ in a lumberjack match
Super Destroyer & Boris Malenko beat The Avenger & Bob Bruggers
Tony Atlas beat Larry Sharpe
Danny Miller & Sandy Scott beat Mr. Fuji & Doug Gilbert
Charlie Cook beat Frank Monte
Joe Soto draw Greg Peterson

MID-ATLANTIC WRESTLING 1975 YEARBOOK

7/19/75: Roanoke, VA @ Victory Stadium
Wahoo McDaniel beat Ric Flair
Danny Miller & Sandy Scott beat Doug Gilbert & Jerry Blackwell
Charlie Cook beat Larry Sharpe
Don Serrano beat El Gaucho
Charlie Fulton beat Bob Bruggers

7/19/75: Spartanburg, SC @ Memorial Auditorium
Ole Anderson DDQ Paul Jones
Ken Patera beat Gene Anderson
Tony Atlas & The Avenger beat Mr. Fuji & Art Neilson
Greg Peterson beat Buddy Porter
Abe Jacobs draw Kevin Sullivan

7/20/75: Asheville, NC @ Civic Center
NWA World Champion Jack Brisco vs. Wahoo McDaniel
Ric Flair, Boris Malenko & Mr. Fuji vs. Rufus R. Jones, Paul Jones & The Avenger
Danny Miller, Charlie Fulton & Klondike Bill vs. Blue Scorpion, Steve Keirn & Larry Sharpe
Plus other matches

7/20/75: Burlington, NC @ Fairchild Stadium
Gene & Ole Anderson & Ric Flair vs. Ken Patera, Tony Atlas & Swede Hanson
Doug Gilbert vs. Charlie Cook
Art Neilson vs. Ron Starr
Charlie Fulton vs. Kevin Sullivan

7/21/75: Charlotte, NC @ Park Center
Johnny Valentine beat Ken Patera (31:00)
Sandy Scott & Danny Miller beat Frank Monte & Art Neilson
Tony Atlas beat Blue Scorpion (6:00)
Bob Bruggers beat George Harris
Cowboy Lang beat Little John

7/21/75: Greenville, SC @ Memorial Auditorium
Paul Jones & Wahoo McDaniel beat Gene & Ole Anderson by DQ
Boris Malenko & Missouri Mauler beat Abe Jacobs & Klondike Bill
Lord Littlebrook beat Little Love
Charlie Fulton draw Greg Peterson
Don Serrano beat John Smith (sub for Tio Tio)

7/21/75: Sumter, SC @ Riley Park
Ric Flair vs. Rufus R. Jones
Super Destroyer vs. The Avenger
Doug Gilbert & Jerry Blackwell vs. Ron Starr & Steve Keirn
Tony Atlas vs. Larry Sharpe
Kevin Sullivan vs. El Gaucho

7/22/75: Columbia, SC @ Township Auditorium
Ric Flair & Super Destroyer beat Ken Patera & The Avenger
Steve Keirn & Ron Starr beat Doug Gilbert & Boris Malenko
Swede Hanson vs. El Gaucho
Larry Sharpe beat Don Serrano

7/22/75: Raleigh, NC @ Dorton Arena
Gene & Ole Anderson draw Paul Jones & Wahoo McDaniel (60:00)
Missouri Mauler & Art Neilson beat Bob Bruggers & Abe Jacobs
Cowboy Lang beat Lord Littlebrook
Tony Atlas beat Charlie Fulton
Kevin Sullivan beat George Harris by DQ

7/23/75: Raleigh, NC @ WRAL Studios (TV)

7/24/75: Marion, NC @ McDowell High School Gym
Wahoo McDaniel vs. Super Destroyer
Lord Littlebrook vs. Cowboy Lang
Boris Malenko & Missouri Mauler vs. Danny Miller & Bob Bruggers
Steve Keirn vs. Frank Monte
Ron Starr vs. George Harris

7/24/75: Norfolk, VA @ Scope
Gene & Ole Anderson beat Paul Jones & Rufus R. Jones in a no DQ match
Ric Flair beat Swede Hanson
Sandy Scott beat Blue Scorpion
Abe Jacobs beat Joe Soto
Buddy Porter draw El Gaucho

7/25/75: Charleston, SC @ County Hall
Ole Anderson no contest with Rufus R. Jones
Danny Miller beat Gene Anderson by DQ
Little Louie beat Little John
Ron Starr & Steve Keirn beat Art Neilson & Doug Gilbert
Charlie Cook beat George Harris

7/25/75: Lynchburg, VA @ City Armory
Paul Jones beat Super Destroyer by DQ
Ric Flair beat Swede Hanson
Lord Littlebrook beat Cowboy Lang
Bob Bruggers & Abe Jacobs beat Frank Monte & Blue Scorpion
Kevin Sullivan beat El Gaucho

7/25/75: Richmond, VA @ Coliseum
Wahoo McDaniel beat Johnny Valentine
Boris Malenko & Missouri Mauler beat Klondike Bill & Sandy Scott
Ken Patera beat Jerry Blackwell
Tony Atlas beat Joe Soto
Greg Peterson beat Buddy Porter
Larry Sharpe draw Don Serrano

7/26/75: Greensboro, NC @ Coliseum
Johnny Valentine beat Harley Race (51:00)
Wahoo McDaniel beat Ric Flair (27:00) by CO
Steve Keirn & Ron Starr beat Boris Malenko & Missouri Mauler
Mr. Wrestling (Tim Woods) beat Jerry Blackwell
Doug Gilbert beat Klondike Bill
Greg Peterson draw Charlie Fulton (15:00)

7/26/75: Spartanburg, SC @ Memorial Auditorium
Ken Patera beat Super Destroyer by DQ
Fabulous Moolah beat Susan Green
Sandy Scott & Danny Miller beat Frank Monte & Blue Scorpion
Tony Atlas beat Larry Sharpe (1:30)
The Avenger beat Kevin Sullivan

7/28/75: Charlotte, NC @ Park Center
Gene & Ole Anderson beat Paul Jones & The Avenger
Ken Patera beat Jerry Blackwell
Tony Atlas beat Charlie Fulton
Little Louie beat Little John
Larry Sharpe beat Greg Peterson

7/28/75: Fayetteville, NC @ Cumberland County Memorial Auditorium
Rufus R. Jones vs. Super Destroyer
Boris Malenko & Missouri Mauler vs. Abe Jacobs & Klondike Bill
Kevin Sullivan vs. Art Neilson
Bob Bruggers vs. Blue Scorpion
Joe Soto vs. Don Serrano

7/28/75: Greenville, SC @ Memorial Auditorium
Wahoo McDaniel beat Johnny Valentine
Ron Starr & Steve Keirn beat Doug Gilbert & Frank Monte
Ric Flair beat Swede Hanson
Cowboy Lang beat Lord Littlebrook
Charlie Cook beat George Harris

7/29/75: Columbia, SC @ Township Auditorium
Wahoo McDaniel beat Johnny Valentine
The Avenger beat Super Destroyer
Steve Keirn & Ron Starr beat Boris Malenko & Missouri Mauler
Cowboy Lang beat Little John
Charlie Cook beat Blue Scorpion
Larry Sharpe draw Abe Jacobs

7/29/75: Durham, NC @ Athletic Park
Tony Atlas, Paul Jones & Rufus R. Jones beat Gene & Ole Anderson & Ric Flair
Doug Gilbert beat Bob Bruggers
Little Louie beat Lord Littlebrook
Klondike Bill beat Jerry Blackwell
Charlie Fulton draw Greg Peterson

7/30/75: Raleigh, NC @ WRAL Studios (TV)

7/31/75: Anderson, SC @ Recreation Center
Super Destroyer vs. Paul Jones
Boris Malenko & Missouri Mauler vs. Klondike Bill & Sandy Scott
The Avenger vs. Frank Monte
Charlie Cook vs. Larry Sharpe
El Gaucho vs. Greg Peterson

7/31/75: Norfolk, VA @ Scope
Wahoo McDaniel beat Ric Flair
Steve Keirn & Ron Starr beat Art Neilson & Doug Gilbert
Cowboy Lang beat Lord Littlebrook
Tony Atlas beat Blue Scorpion
Don Serrano draw Charlie Fulton

7/31/75: Orangeburg, SC
Gene & Ole Anderson vs. Rufus R. Jones & Ken Patera
Little Louie vs. Little Love
Jerry Blackwell vs. Swede Hanson
Abe Jacobs vs. Roberto Soto
Kevin Sullivan vs. George Harris

AUGUST

8/1/75: Charleston, SC @ County Hall
Rufus R. Jones beat Super Destroyer by DQ
Boris Malenko & Missouri Mauler beat Klondike Bill & Sandy Scott
The Avenger beat Jerry Blackwell
Swede Hanson beat Frank Monte
Abe Jacobs beat George Harris

MID-ATLANTIC WRESTLING 1975 YEARBOOK

8/1/75: Richmond, VA @ Coliseum
Gene & Ole Anderson draw Paul Jones & Wahoo McDaniel (90:00)
Johnny Valentine beat Ken Patera
Tony Atlas beat Ric Flair by DQ
Cowboy Lang & Little Louie beat Lord Littlebrook & Little John
Art Neilson & Doug Gilbert beat Don Serrano & Bob Bruggers
Ron Starr beat Blue Scorpion
Steve Keirn beat Charlie Fulton

8/2/75: Spartanburg, SC @ Memorial Auditorium

8/2/75: Roanoke, VA @ Civic Center
Gene & Ole Anderson draw Paul Jones & Wahoo McDaniel (60:00)
Ric Flair beat Swede Hanson
Tony White (aka Tony Atlas) beat Blue Scorpion
Missouri Mauler & Art Neilson beat Sandy Scott & The Avenger
Cowboy Lang beat Lord Littlebrook
Larry Sharpe draw Don Serrano

8/3/75: Wilmington, NC @ Legion Stadium
Gene & Ole Anderson vs. Paul Jones & Rufus R. Jones
Wahoo McDaniel vs. Johnny Valentine
Plus other matches

8/4/75: Greenville, SC @ Memorial Auditorium
Wahoo McDaniel beat Ric Flair
Ron Starr & Steve Keirn beat Boris Malenko & Missouri Mauler
Sandy Scott beat Charlie Fulton
Charlie Cook beat Joe Soto
El Gaucho beat Bob Burns

8/4/75: Charlotte, NC @ Park Center
Paul Jones & Ken Patera beat Gene & Ole Anderson by DQ
Tony Atlas beat Frank Monte
Abe Jacobs beat Larry Sharpe
Abe Jacobs draw Kevin Sullivan
Don Kernodle beat George Harris

8/4/75: Fayetteville, NC @ Cumberland County Memorial Auditorium
Johnny Valentine beat Rufus R. Jones by DQ
The Avenger beat Jerry Blackwell
Doug Gilbert & Art Neilson beat Swede Hanson & Bob Bruggers
Klondike Bill beat Buddy Porter

Don Serrano beat Greg Peterson

8/5/75: Raleigh, NC @ Dorton Arena
Paul Jones & Wahoo McDaniel beat Gene & Ole Anderson by DQ in a no time limit match
Steve Keirn & Ron Starr beat Boris Malenko & Missouri Mauler
Fabulous Moolah beat Sheila Shepherd
Tony Atlas beat Frank Monte
Greg Peterson draw Don Kernodle

8/5/75: Columbia, SC @ Township Auditorium
Rufus R. Jones beat Ric Flair
Doug Gilbert & Art Neilson beat Abe Jacobs & Swede Hanson
Danny Miller beat Charlie Fulton
Don Serrano beat Kevin Sullivan
Bob Bruggers beat Joe Soto

8/6/75: Raleigh, NC @ WRAL Studios (TV)

8/6/75: Rocky Mount, NC @ Ball Park
Ric Flair & Johnny Valentine vs. Paul Jones & Rufus R. Jones
Boris Malenko vs. Ken Patera
Missouri Mauler vs. Don Kernodle
The Avenger vs. Abe Jacobs
Greg Peterson vs. Don Serrano

8/7/75: Norfolk, VA @ Scope
Ole Anderson vs. Rufus R. Jones in a Texas death match
Johnny Valentine vs. Wahoo McDaniel
Boris Malenko & Missouri Mauler vs. Steve Keirn & Ron Starr
Mr. Wrestling vs. Frank Monte
Ken Patera vs. Jerry Blackwell
Bob Bruggers & Danny Miller vs. Joe Soto & Larry Sharpe

8/8/75: Charleston, SC @ County Hall
Wahoo McDaniel & Tony Atlas beat Gene & Ole Anderson by DQ
Swede Hanson beat Doug Gilbert
The Avenger beat Abe Jacobs
Charlie Cook beat Charlie Fulton
Greg Peterson draw Don Serrano

8/8/75: Lynchburg, VA @ City Stadium
Johnny Valentine DCO with Rufus R. Jones
Ken Patera beat Jerry Blackwell
Bob Bruggers & Ron Starr beat Art Neilson & Frank Monte
Klondike Bill beat Joe Soto

El Gaucho beat Bob Burns

8/8/75: Richmond, VA @ Coliseum
Paul Jones beat Ric Flair to win NWA Mid Atlantic Television Title
Boris Malenko & Missouri Mauler beat Danny Miller & Sandy Scott
Don Kernodle beat George Harris
Steve Keirn beat Larry Sharpe
Buddy Porter draw Kevin Sullivan (20:00)

8/9/75: Hampton, VA @ Coliseum
Gene & Ole Anderson draw Paul Jones & Wahoo McDaniel (60:00)
Ken Patera beat Ric Flair by DQ
Boris Malenko & Missouri Mauler beat Klondike Bill & Danny Miller
Mr. Wrestling beat Jerry Blackwell via pinfall
Don Kernodle draw Bob Bruggers
El Gaucho beat Bob Burns via pinfall

8/9/75: Spartanburg, SC @ Memorial Auditorium
Johnny Valentine beat Rufus R. Jones (32:00)
Ron Starr & Steve Keirn beat Doug Gilbert & Art Neilson by DQ
The Avenger beat Frank Monte
Sandy Scott beat Larry Sharpe
Abe Jacobs beat George Harris

8/9/75: Roanoke, VA @ Civic Center

8/11/75: Greenville, SC @ Memorial Auditorium
Wahoo McDaniel beat Ric Flair in an Indian strap match
Danny Miller & Tony Atlas beat Jerry Blackwell & George Harris
Missouri Mauler beat Ron Starr
Sandy Scott beat Doug Gilbert
Don Kernodle beat Kevin Sullivan

8/11/75: Charlotte, NC @ Park Center
Gene & Ole Anderson beat Paul Jones & Rufus R. Jones
Mr. Wrestling beat Art Neilson
Steve Keirn draw The Avenger
Bob Bruggers beat Joe Soto
Charlie Fulton draw Greg Peterson

8/12/75: Columbia, SC @ Township Auditorium
Gene & Ole Anderson draw Paul Jones & Sandy Scott (sub for Wahoo McDaniel)
Ken Patera beat Jerry Blackwell
Missouri Mauler beat Sandy Scott
Doug Gilbert beat Abe Jacobs
Tony Atlas beat Larry Sharpe
Greg Peterson beat George Harris

8/12/75: Greenville, NC @ Guy Smith Stadium
Ric Flair & Johnny Valentine vs. Rufus R. Jones & Mr. Wrestling
Charlie Cook vs. Boris Malenko
Danny Miller vs. Art Neilson
Steve Keirn vs. Bob Bruggers
Brute Bernard vs. Klondike Bill

8/12/75: Martinsville, VA @ Junior High School
Ken Patera & Rufus R. Jones beat Gene & Ole Anderson by DQ
The Avenger beat Doug Gilbert
Danny Miller beat Frank Monte
Swede Hanson beat Joe Soto
Klondike Bill beat Larry Sharpe (sub for George Harris)

8/13/75: Raleigh, NC @ WRAL Studios (TV)

8/14/75: Norfolk, VA @ Scope

8/14/75: Dillon, SC @ Memorial Stadium
Ric Flair vs. Rufus R. Jones
Boris Malenko & Missouri Mauler vs. Steve Keirn & Ron Starr
Brute Bernard vs. Abe Jacobs
Klondike Bill vs. Jerry Blackwell
Kevin Sullivan vs. Greg Peterson

8/14/75: Elizabeth City, NC @ Northeastern High School
Johnny Valentine vs. Paul Jones
Mr. Wrestling & Ken Patera vs. Art Neilson & Doug Gilbert
Also included Tony Atlas, The Avenger and others

8/15/75: Charleston, SC @ County Hall
Gene & Ole Anderson beat Wahoo McDaniel & Tony Atlas by CO
Ken Patera beat Missouri Mauler
Boris Malenko beat Klondike Bill
Steve Keirn beat Frank Monte
Ron Starr beat Don Serrano

8/15/75: Richmond, VA @ Coliseum
Ric Flair & a mystery partner vs. Paul Jones & Rufus R. Jones
Mr. Wrestling vs. Doug Gilbert
The Avenger vs. Charlie Fulton
Danny Miller vs. Art Neilson

Don Kernodle vs. Joe Soto

8/16/75: Roanoke, VA @ Civic Center
Wahoo McDaniel beat Ric Flair
Ken Patera beat Jerry Blackwell
Tony Atlas beat Art Neilson
Honey Girl Page & Princess Little Dove beat Diamond Lil & Marie LeVeau
Mr. Wrestling & Danny Miller beat Larry Sharpe & Frank Monte
Kevin Sullivan draw Don Serrano

8/16/75: Spartanburg, SC @ Memorial Auditorium
Paul Jones beat Missouri Mauler
Swede Hanson beat Brute Bernard by DQ
Steve Keirn & Ron Starr beat Abe Jacobs & The Avenger
John Smith draw Sandy Scott (20:00)

8/17/75: Asheville, NC @ Civic Center (Afternoon show)
Johnny Valentine vs. Wahoo McDaniel
Gene & Ole Anderson vs. Dusty Rhodes & Paul Jones
Ken Patera vs. Jerry Blackwell
Mr. Wrestling vs. Frank Monte
Steve Keirn vs. Bob Bruggers
Sandy Scott vs. Joe Soto

8/17/75: Greensboro, NC @ Coliseum
Gene & Ole Anderson DDQ Paul Jones & Wahoo McDaniel
Johnny Valentine beat Dusty Rhodes by CO
Rufus R. Jones beat Ric Flair
Mr. Wrestling beat Ron Starr
Boris Malenko & Missouri Mauler beat Swede Hanson & Klondike Bill
Tony Atlas beat Larry Sharpe
Don Kernodle beat Don Serrano
Note: The Sheik no showed his scheduled match against Kevin Sullivan.

8/18/75: Charlotte, NC @ Park Center
Ric Flair DDQ Dusty Rhodes
Boris Malenko & Missouri Mauler beat Steve Keirn & Ron Starr
Tony Atlas beat El Gaucho
Brute Bernard beat Kevin Sullivan
Bill Howard beat Greg Peterson

8/18/75: Fayetteville, NC @ Cumberland County Memorial Auditorium
Johnny Valentine beat Rufus R. Jones by CO in a match with 2 referees
Ken Patera & Danny Miller beat Art Neilson & Larry Sharpe (sub for Doug Gilbert)
The Avenger beat Buddy Porter (sub for Joe Soto)
Swede Hanson beat Lee Teal (sub for Larry Sharpe)
Don Kernodle beat Don Serrano

8/18/75: Greenville, SC @ Memorial Auditorium
Gene & Ole Anderson draw Paul Jones & Wahoo McDaniel (90:00)
Bob Bruggers beat Charlie Fulton
Charlie Cook beat Frank Monte
Jerry Blackwell beat Bearcat Brown (sub for Mr. Wrestling)
Klondike Bill beat Joe Soto

8/19/75: Columbia, SC @ Township Auditorium
Gene & Ole Anderson draw Paul Jones & Wahoo McDaniel (90:00)
Danny Miller & The Avenger beat Art Neilson & Doug Gilbert
Brute Bernard beat Charlie Cook
Charlie Fulton draw Greg Peterson (20:00)

8/19/75: Raleigh, NC @ Dorton Arena
Mr. Wrestling beat Johnny Valentine by DQ
Rufus R. Jones beat Ric Flair
Boris Malenko & Missouri Mauler beat Steve Keirn & Ron Starr
Ken Patera beat Jerry Blackwell
Tony Atlas beat Joe Soto
Klondike Bill draw Don Kernodle

8/20/75: Raleigh, NC @ WRAL Studios (TV)

8/20/75: Roxboro, NC @ Optimist Park
Paul Jones & Wahoo McDaniel beat Ric Flair & Johnny Valentine
Jerry Blackwell vs. Klondike Bill
Art Neilson & Doug Gilbert vs. Steve Keirn & Ron Starr
Bob Bruggers vs. Bill Howard

8/21/75: Anderson, SC @ Recreation Center
Gene & Ole Anderson vs. Ken Patera & Rufus R. Jones
Doug Gilbert vs. The Avenger
Danny Miller vs. Frank Monte
Bob Bruggers vs. Don Serrano
Kevin Sullivan vs. Joe Soto

8/21/75: Norfolk, VA @ Scope
Wahoo McDaniel beat Johnny Valentine by DQ in a match with 2 referees
Paul Jones beat Ric Flair

Boris Malenko & Missouri Mauler beat Steve Keirn & Ron Starr
Tony Atlas beat Brute Bernard
Mr. Wrestling beat Art Neilson
Swede Hanson beat Jerry Blackwell
Bill Howard draw Klondike Bill

8/22/75: Charleston, SC @ County Hall
Johnny Valentine vs. Rufus R. Jones
The Avenger vs. Doug Gilbert
Bob Bruggers & Kevin Sullivan vs. Joe Soto & Buddy Porter
Don Kernodle vs. Charlie Fulton

8/22/75: Lexington, VA @ Recreation Field
Ken Patera & Steve Keirn vs. Ric Flair & Boris Malenko
Swede Hanson vs. Jerry Blackwell
Susan Green vs. Vicki Williams
Terry Sawyer vs. Joe Soto

8/22/75: Richmond, VA @ Coliseum
Paul Jones & Wahoo McDaniel beat Gene & Ole Anderson by DQ
Ric Flair no contest with Mr. Wrestling
Tony Atlas, Danny Miller & Ron Starr beat Brute Bernard, Missouri Mauler & Art Neilson
Klondike Bill beat John Smith by DQ
Frank Monte draw Don Serrano
Bill Howard beat Greg Peterson

8/23/75: Durham, NC @ Athletic Park
Mr. Wrestling (sub for Wahoo McDaniel) beat Ole Anderson Indian strap match
Tiger Conway, Jr. & Steve Keirn beat Art Neilson & Doug Gilbert
Gene Anderson beat The Avenger
Swede Hanson beat Jerry Blackwell
Ron Starr beat El Gaucho
Don Kernodle beat Charlie Fulton

8/23/75: Lynchburg, VA @ City Armory
Paul Jones & Tony Atlas (sub for Mr. Wrestling) beat Ric Flair & Johnny Valentine by DQ
Fabulous Moolah beat Susan Green
Danny Miller (sub for Tony Atlas) beat Frank Monte
Danny Miller beat John Smith
Bobby Williams beat Don Serrano

8/25/75: Greenville, SC @ Memorial Auditorium
Gene & Ole Anderson beat Paul Jones & Wahoo McDaniel
Tony Atlas beat Larry Sharpe
Mr. Wrestling beat Jerry Blackwell

Charlie Cook beat Doug Gilbert
Bill Howard beat Kevin Sullivan
John Smith (sub for Brute Bernard) draw Klondike Bill

8/25/75: Sumter, NC @ Riley Park
Ric Flair & Johnny Valentine beat Rufus R. Jones & Ken Patera
Tiger Conway, Jr. beat Frank Monte
Bob Bruggers & Danny Miller beat Missouri Mauler & Boris Malenko
Don Kernodle beat Greg Peterson

8/26/75: Raleigh, NC @ Dorton Arena

8/26/75: Columbia, SC @ Township Auditorium
Paul Jones & Wahoo McDaniel beat Gene & Ole Anderson by DQ in a match with 2 referees
Fabulous Moolah (as Lillian Ellison) beat Ms. Masked Bolo
Mr. Wrestling beat Doug Gilbert
Tony Atlas beat Brute Bernard
The Avenger beat John Smith
Don Kernodle draw Kevin Sullivan
Greg Peterson beat Don Serrano

8/27/75: Raleigh, NC @ WRAL Studios (TV)
Ric Flair beat Abe Jacobs

8/28/75: Norfolk, VA @ Scope
Gene & Ole Anderson beat Ken Patera & Rufus R. Jones
Tiger Conway, Jr. beat Jerry Blackwell
Swede Hanson beat Doug Gilbert by DQ
Danny Miller beat Larry Sharpe
Kevin Sullivan draw Charlie Fulton

8/28/75: Waynesboro, VA @ East Side Speedway
Johnny Valentine vs. Paul Jones
Ric Flair vs. Mr. Wrestling
Steve Keirn & Ron Starr vs. Boris Malenko & Missouri Mauler
Tony Atlas vs. Art Neilson
Bill Howard vs. Bob Bruggers

8/29/75: Charleston, SC @ County Hall
Wahoo McDaniel beat Ole Anderson in an Indian strap match
Ken Patera beat Gene Anderson
Tiger Conway, Jr. beat Jerry Blackwell
Steve Keirn & Kevin Sullivan (sub for Ron Starr) beat John Smith & Bill Howard
Don Serrano beat El Gaucho (sub for Kevin Sullivan)

8/29/75: Richmond, VA @ Coliseum
Johnny Valentine beat Rufus R. Jones
Swede Hanson & Danny Miller vs. Boris Malenko & Missouri Mauler
Bob Bruggers vs. Art Neilson
Charlie Cook vs. Charlie Fulton
Larry Sharpe vs. Don Kernodle

8/30/75: Roanoke, VA @ Civic Center
Paul Jones & Wahoo McDaniel beat Gene & Ole Anderson when Gene Anderson was knocked unconscious and was unable to continue. The NWA World Tag Title did not change hands because the victory was not by pinfall or submission
Ken Patera & Tiger Conway beat Missouri Mauler & Boris Malenko by DQ
Tony White (aka Tony Atlas) beat Bill Howard (sub for Brute Bernard)
Klondike Bill beat Jerry Blackwell
Bill Howard beat Bobby Williams

8/30/75: Spartanburg, SC @ Memorial Auditorium
Mr. Wrestling beat Ric Flair by CO in a bounty match
Danny Miller & Swede Hanson beat Frank Monte & John Smith
Joe Soto beat Charlie Cook
Greg Peterson draw Charlie Fulton (20:00)
Don Kernodle beat Don Serrano

8/31/75: Asheville, NC @ Civic Center (Afternoon Card)
Wahoo McDaniel vs. Ric Flair
Paul Jones vs. Ole Anderson
Boris Malenko & Missouri Mauler vs. Ken Patera & Rufus R. Jones
Tiger Conway, Jr. vs. Doug Gilbert
Danny Miller vs. Frank Monte

8/31/75: Wilmington, NC @ Legion Stadium (Evening Card)
Gene & Ole Anderson vs. Paul Jones & Wahoo McDaniel
Ric Flair vs. Mr. Wrestling
Plus other matches

SEPTEMBER

9/1/75: Charlotte, NC @ Memorial Stadium
Gene & Ole Anderson beat Paul Jones & Wahoo McDaniel
Ken Patera beat Boris Malenko by DQ
Fabulous Moolah beat Susan Green
Tony Atlas beat Brute Bernard
Larry Sharpe beat Don Kernodle
Frank Monte draw Tony Rocco

9/1/75: Fayetteville, NC @ Cumberland County Memorial Auditorium
Mr. Wrestling beat Ric Flair by CO in a bounty match
Tiger Conway, Jr. & Steve Keirn beat Doug Gilbert & Bill Howard
Joyce Grable beat Toni Rose
Greg Peterson beat Buddy Porter
Bob Bruggers beat Joe Soto

9/1/75: Greenville, SC @ Memorial Auditorium
Johnny Valentine beat Rufus R. Jones
Ron Starr & Danny Miller beat Missouri Mauler & Art Neilson
Spoiler II (Paul 'Butcher' Vachon) beat Swede Hanson
Kevin Sullivan draw Don Serrano
Charlie Cook beat Charlie Fulton

9/2/75: Columbia, SC @ Township Auditorium
Ric Flair & Johnny Valentine beat Mr. Wrestling & Rufus R. Jones by DQ
Tiger Conway, Jr. & Steve Keirn beat Doug Gilbert & Art Neilson
Swede Hanson beat Jerry Blackwell
The Avenger draw Ron Starr
Tony Rocco beat Frank Monte

9/2/75: Raleigh, NC @ Dorton Arena
Gene & Ole Anderson beat Tony Atlas (sub for Paul Jones) & Wahoo McDaniel
Ken Patera & Danny Miller beat Boris Malenko & Missouri Mauler
Spoiler II beat Klondike Bill
Tony Atlas beat Brute Bernard
Bill Howard draw Don Kernodle

9/3/75: Rocky Mount, NC @ Ball Park
Ric Flair vs. Rufus R. Jones
Ken Patera vs. Boris Malenko
Brute Bernard & Missouri Mauler vs. Swede Hanson & Danny Miller
Bill Howard vs. Tony Rocco
Doug Gilbert vs. Charlie Cook

9/3/75: Raleigh, NC @ WRAL Studios (TV)
Ric Flair beat Greg Peterson

9/4/75: Anderson, SC @ Recreation Center
Ken Patera beat Boris Malenko by DQ
Tiger Conway, Jr. & Steve Keirn beat Missouri Mauler &

MID-ATLANTIC WRESTLING 1975 YEARBOOK

Brute Bernard
Vicki Williams beat Donna Christianello
Swede Hanson beat Jerry Blackwell
Klondike Bill beat Joe Soto

9/4/75: Danville, VA @ City Armory
Rufus R. Jones beat Ric Flair via pinfall
The Avenger & Ron Starr beat Art Neilson & Doug Gilbert by DQ
Larry Sharpe beat El Gaucho
John Smith beat Charlie Cook
Don Serrano draw Greg Peterson (20:00)

9/4/75: Norfolk, VA @ Scope
Johnny Valentine, Gene & Ole Anderson DDQ Mr. Wrestling, Tony Atlas & Danny Miller
Spoiler II beat Bob Bruggers
Tony Rocco beat Frank Monte
Bill Howard draw Kevin Sullivan
Don Kernodle beat Charlie Fulton

9/5/75: Charleston, SC @ County Hall
Gene & Ole Anderson draw Paul Jones & Wahoo McDaniel
Boris Malenko & Missouri Mauler vs. Tiger Conway, Jr. & Ron Starr
Steve Keirn vs. Joe Soto
Danny Miller vs. John Smith
The Avenger vs. Larry Sharpe

9/5/75: Richmond, VA @ Coliseum
Mr. Wrestling & Rufus R. Jones beat Ric Flair & Johnny Valentine by CO
Also included Spoiler II, Tony Rocco, Tony Atlas and others

9/6/75: Camden, SC @ City Arena
Johnny Valentine vs. Paul Jones
Plus other matches

9/6/75: Roanoke, VA @ Starland Arena
Mr. Wrestling vs. Ric Flair in a bounty match
Spoiler II vs. Bob Bruggers
Boris Malenko & Missouri Mauler vs. Danny Miller & Swede Hanson
Tony Atlas vs. Joe Soto

9/7/75: Greensboro, NC @ Coliseum
Dusty Rhodes beat Johnny Valentine by DQ
Wahoo McDaniel & Mr. Wrestling beat Gene & Ole Anderson in a Texas tornado match
Rufus R. Jones & Ken Patera beat Missouri Mauler & Boris Malenko
Mr. Wrestling beat Brute Bernard
Spoiler II beat Swede Hanson
Tiger Conway beat Doug Gilbert
Art Neilson draw Klondike Bill (15:00)
Greg Peterson & Tony Rocco beat Charlie Fulton & Bill Howard

9/8/75: Charlotte, NC @ Park Center
Rufus R. Jones beat Johnny Valentine by CO
Ken Patera beat Boris Malenko
The Avenger & Danny Miller beat Joe Soto & Michel Dubois
Bob Bruggers beat Bill Howard
Greg Peterson draw Kevin Sullivan

9/8/75: Fayetteville, NC @ Cumberland County Memorial Auditorium
Mr. Wrestling beat Ric Flair by CO in a no DQ, bounty match
Tiger Conway, Jr. & Steve Keirn beat Art Neilson & Missouri Mauler
Swede Hanson beat Jerry Blackwell
Ron Starr beat Charlie Fulton
Don Serrano beat El Gaucho

9/8/75: Greenville, SC @ Memorial Auditorium
Paul Jones & Wahoo McDaniel beat Gene & Ole Anderson by CO in a match with George Scott as special referee
Spoiler II beat Klondike Bill
Sandy Scott beat John Smith
Tony Rocco beat Larry Sharpe
Doug Gilbert beat Don Kernodle

9/9/75: Columbia, SC @ Township Auditorium
Gene & Ole Anderson beat Paul Jones & Wahoo McDaniel
Klondike Bill beat Jerry Blackwell
Danny Miller & Ken Patera beat Boris Malenko & Missouri Mauler
The Avenger beat Art Neilson
Michel Dubois beat Kevin Sullivan

9/9/75: Raleigh, NC @ Dorton Arena
Ric Flair & Johnny Valentine beat Mr. Wrestling & Rufus R. Jones by DQ
Tiger Conway, Jr. & Steve Keirn beat Doug Gilbert & Bill Howard
Spoiler II beat Ron Starr
Tony Rocco beat Joe Soto
Charlie Fulton draw Don Serrano

MID-ATLANTIC WRESTLING 1975 YEARBOOK

9/10/75: Raleigh, NC @ WRAL Studios (TV)

9/11/75: Norfolk, VA @ Scope
Mr. Wrestling beat Gene Anderson in a bounty match
Tiger Conway, Jr. & Steve Keirn beat Missouri Mauler & Doug Gilbert
Ken Patera beat Boris Malenko
Kevin Sullivan beat Don Serrano
Bob Bruggers draw Billy Howard

9/11/75: Sumter, SC @ Riley Park
Johnny Valentine vs. Wahoo McDaniel
Charlie Cook & Swede Hanson vs. Art Neilson & Jerry Blackwell
Plus 3 other matches

9/12/75: Charleston, SC @ County Hall
Rufus R. Jones beat Johnny Valentine by DQ
Spoiler II beat Klondike Bill (sub for Charlie Cook)
Swede Hanson & The Avenger beat Jerry Blackwell & Art Neilson
Ron Starr beat Michel Dubois
Greg Peterson beat John Smith

9/12/75: Richmond, VA @ Coliseum
Gene & Ole Anderson beat Paul Jones & Wahoo McDaniel
Mr. Wrestling beat Ric Flair in a bounty match
Danny Miller & Ken Patera beat Boris Malenko & Missouri Mauler
Tiger Conway, Jr. beat Doug Gilbert
Bob Bruggers beat Don Serrano
Bill Howard beat Kevin Sullivan
Steve Keirn beat Tony Rocco

9/13/75: Greenville, NC @ Minges Coliseum
Gene & Ole Anderson vs. Paul Jones & Wahoo McDaniel
Ric Flair vs. Ken Patera
Mr. Wrestling vs. Art Neilson
Tiger Conway, Jr. & Danny Miller vs. Jerry Blackwell & Michel Dubois
Tony Rocco vs. Charlie Fulton
Klondike Bill vs. Joe Soto

9/13/75: Roanoke, VA @ Civic Center
Mr. Wrestling beat Johnny Valentine
Ric Flair beat Tony Atlas
Tiger Conway, Jr. & Steve Keirn beat Art Neilson & Missouri Mauler
Spoiler II beat Klondike Bill
Michel Dubois beat Mark Starr
Tony Rocco beat Larry Sharpe

9/15/75: Charlotte, NC @ Park Center
Gene & Ole Anderson beat Paul Jones & Wahoo McDaniel
Spoiler II beat Klondike Bill
The Avenger beat Jerry Blackwell
Tony Rocco beat George Harris
Michel Dubois beat Don Serrano

9/15/75: Fayetteville, NC @ Cumberland County Memorial Auditorium
Ric Flair vs. Mr. Wrestling in a lumberjack, bounty match
Tiger Conway, Jr. & Steve Keirn vs. John Smith & Doug Gilbert
Swede Hanson vs. Art Neilson
Kevin Sullivan vs. Joe Soto
Greg Peterson vs. Charlie Fulton

9/15/75: Greenville, SC @ Memorial Auditorium
Johnny Valentine beat Rufus R. Jones by CO
Boris Malenko & Missouri Mauler beat Ken Patera & Danny Miller by DQ
Tony Atlas beat Bill Howard
Roberto Soto beat Larry Sharpe
Don Kernodle draw Bob Bruggers

9/16/75: Collinsville, VA @ Fieldale Collinsville High School
Wahoo McDaniel vs. Gene Anderson
Tony Atlas vs. Art Neilson
Tony Rocco & Klondike Bill vs. John Smith & Charlie Fulton
The Avenger vs. George Harris
Kevin Sullivan vs. Greg Peterson

9/16/75: Columbia, SC @ Township Auditorium
Mr. Wrestling beat Ric Flair by CO in a bounty match
Ken Patera beat Boris Malenko
Tiger Conway, Jr. & Steve Keirn beat Jerry Blackwell & Joe Soto
Spoiler II beat Swede Hanson via pinfall
Bill Howard beat Don Serrano

9/16/75: Durham, NC @ Athletic Park
Rufus R. Jones beat Johnny Valentine by DQ
Doug Gilbert & Missouri Mauler beat Ron Starr & Danny Miller
Michel Dubois beat Bob Bruggers
Roberto Soto beat Larry Sharpe
Don Kernodle beat Buddy Porter

9/17/75: Raleigh, NC @ WRAL Studios (TV)

229

9/18/75: Anderson, SC @ Recreation Center
Wahoo McDaniel vs. Gene Anderson
Tiger Conway, Jr. & Steve Keirn vs. Doug Gilbert & Art Neilson
Spoiler II vs. Bob Bruggers
Larry Sharpe vs. Greg Peterson
Ron Starr vs. John Smith

9/18/75: Norfolk, VA @ Scope
Mr. Wrestling beat Ric Flair by CO in a bounty match
Ken Patera beat Boris Malenko
Tony Atlas & Danny Miller beat Bill Howard & Missouri Mauler
Roberto Soto beat El Gaucho (sub for Greg Peterson)
Tony Rocco draw Michel Dubois

9/18/75: Camp Lejeune, NC
Paul Jones & Rufus R. Jones vs. Ole Anderson & Johnny Valentine
The Avenger & Swede Hanson vs. Jerry Blackwell & George Harris
Charlie Fulton vs. Klondike Bill
Don Serrano vs. Joe Soto

9/19/75: Charleston, SC @ County Hall
Rufus R. Jones & Mr. Wrestling beat Ric Flair & Johnny Valentine by DQ
Steve Keirn beat Doug Gilbert
Klondike Bill beat Joe Soto
Ron Starr draw The Avenger
Don Kernodle beat Larry Sharpe

9/19/75: Danville, VA @ City Armory
Paul Jones beat Gene Anderson
Tony Atlas & Ken Patera beat Jerry Blackwell & George Harris
Don Serrano beat Michel Dubois
Tony Rocco beat John Smith
Charlie Fulton draw Greg Peterson (20:00)

9/19/75: Richmond, VA @ Coliseum
Ole Anderson beat Wahoo McDaniel by DQ
Boris Malenko & Missouri Mauler beat Swede Hanson & Danny Miller
Bob Bruggers beat Spoiler II
Tiger Conway, Jr. beat Art Neilson
Roberto Soto beat Bill Howard

9/20/75: Hampton, VA @ Coliseum
Ric Flair beat Wahoo McDaniel to win NWA Mid Atlantic Title hair vs. title match
Johnny Valentine DDQ Mr. Wrestling
Swede Hanson & Danny Miller beat Spoiler II & Art Neilson
Bob Bruggers beat George Harris
Bill Howard draw Greg Peterson
Charlie Fulton beat Don Serrano

9/20/75: Lynchburg, VA @ City Armory
Paul Jones & Tiger Conway, Jr. beat Boris Malenko & Missouri Mauler
Tony Atlas beat Jerry Blackwell
Klondike Bill beat Michel Dubois by DQ
Roberto Soto beat Larry Sharpe
Kevin Sullivan beat El Gaucho

9/20/75: Spartanburg, SC @ Memorial Auditorium
Gene & Ole Anderson no contest with Ken Patera & Rufus R. Jones
Steve Keirn beat Doug Gilbert
The Avenger beat John Smith by DQ
Tony Rocco beat Joe Soto
Ron Starr draw Don Kernodle (20:00)

9/21/75: Asheville, NC @ Civic Center
Johnny Valentine vs. Wahoo McDaniel
Ric Flair vs. Mr. Wrestling in a bounty match
Boris Malenko & Missouri Mauler vs. Tiger Conway, Jr. & Steve Keirn
Art Neilson vs. Klondike Bill
Roberto Soto vs. Michel Dubois
Joe Soto vs. Tony Rocco

9/22/75: Charlotte, NC @ Park Center
Paul Jones beat Gene Anderson
Art Neilson & Missouri Mauler DCO with Tiger Conway, Jr. & Steve Keirn
Bob Bruggers beat Spoiler II
Tony Rocco beat Charlie Fulton by DQ
Greg Peterson draw Don Kernodle

9/22/75: Greenville, SC @ Memorial Auditorium
Johnny Valentine beat Rufus R. Jones
Mr. Wrestling beat Boris Malenko in a bounty match
Swede Hanson & The Avenger beat Jerry Blackwell & Billy Howard
Roberto Soto beat Don Serrano
Michel Dubois beat Kevin Sullivan

9/23/75: Columbia, SC @ Township Auditorium
Mr. Wrestling beat Ric Flair in a lumberjack, bounty match
Tiger Conway, Jr. & Steve Keirn b. Spoiler II & Doug Gilbert

MID-ATLANTIC WRESTLING 1975 YEARBOOK

Tony Rocco beat Michel Dubois by DQ
Bob Bruggers beat George Harris
Don Kernodle draw John Smith (20:00)

9/23/75: Raleigh, NC @ Dorton Arena
Johnny Valentine beat Ken Patera
Paul Jones beat Gene Anderson
Danny Miller & The Avenger beat Boris Malenko & Missouri Mauler
Tony Atlas beat Jerry Blackwell
Roberto Soto beat Larry Sharpe

9/24/75: Raleigh, NC @ WRAL Studios (TV)

9/24/75: Rocky Mount, NC @ Municipal Stadium
$5,400 Russian Roulette battle royal featuring Ric Flair, Rufus R. Jones, Ken Patera, Spoiler I (Doug Gilbert), Spoiler II (Butcher Vachon), Tiger Conway, Jr., Swede Hanson, Michel Dubois, Art Neilson, George Harris, Charlie Fulton, Klondike Bill, & Danny Miller
plus singles matches determined by order of elimination

9/25/75: Norfolk, VA @ Scope
Mr. Wrestling beat Ric Flair in a lumberjack, bounty match
Spoiler II beat Swede Hanson
Tony Atlas & Danny Miller beat Spoiler I (Doug Gilbert) & Art Neilson
Roberto Soto beat Jerry Blackwell
Ron Starr draw Tony Rocco

9/26/75: Charleston, SC @ County Hall
Gene & Ole Anderson vs. Paul Jones & Wahoo McDaniel
Rufus R. Jones vs. Missouri Mauler
Ken Patera vs. Boris Malenko
Tiger Conway, Jr. & Steve Keirn vs. Michel Dubois & Bill Howard
Bob Bruggers vs. Joe Soto

9/26/75: Charlottesville, VA @ University Hall
Johnny Valentine vs. Mr. Wrestling
Ric Flair & Spoiler II vs. The Avenger & Danny Miller
Tony Atlas vs. Art Neilson
Swede Hanson vs. Spoiler I
Tony Rocco vs. Ron Starr
Roberto Soto vs. Jerry Blackwell

9/27/75: Roanoke, VA @ Starland Arena
Gene & Ole Anderson beat Tiger Conway, Jr. & Steve Keirn
Tony Atlas vs. Boris Malenko
The Avenger vs. Michel Dubois
Larry Sharpe & Charlie Fulton vs. Greg Peterson & Kevin Sullivan

9/27/75: Spartanburg, SC @ Memorial Auditorium
Paul Jones beat Ric Flair by DQ
Spoiler I & Spoiler II beat Bob Bruggers & Ken Patera
Swede Hanson beat John Smith
Ron Starr beat Don Serrano
Bill Howard draw Tony Rocco (20:00)

9/28/75: Canton, NC @ Robertson Memorial YMCA (Afternoon Show)
Ric Flair vs. Dusty Rhodes
Rufus R. Jones vs. Spoiler I
Art Neilson & John Smith vs. Roberto Soto & Swede Hanson
Klondike Bill vs. Bill Howard
Tony Rocco vs. Don Serrano

9/28/75: Greensboro, NC @ Coliseum
Paul Jones & Dusty Rhodes beat Gene & Ole Anderson by CO
Johnny Valentine beat Wahoo McDaniel
Ray Stevens beat Mr. Wrestling by DQ in a bounty match
Ken Patera beat Boris Malenko
Spoiler II beat The Avenger
Tiger Conway, Jr. beat Ric Flair
Danny Miller & Steve Keirn beat Jerry Blackwell & Michel Dubois

9/29/75: Greenville, SC @ Memorial Auditorium
Paul Jones & Wahoo McDaniel beat Gene & Ole Anderson by DQ in a lumberjack match
Bob Bruggers & Tony Atlas beat Spoiler I & Jerry Blackwell
Ken Patera beat Missouri Mauler by DQ
Roberto Soto beat Charlie Fulton
Greg Peterson beat Don Serrano

9/29/75: Charlotte, NC @ Park Center
Ric Flair DCO with Mr. Wrestling (22:00) in a bounty match
Johnny Weaver & Tiger Conway, Jr. beat Michel Dubois & Art Neilson
Spoiler II beat Steve Keirn
Larry Sharpe beat Tony Rocco
Don Kernodle beat George Harris

9/30/75: Raleigh, NC @ Dorton Arena

9/30/75: Columbia, SC @ Township Auditorium
Gene & Ole Anderson beat Paul Jones & Rufus R. Jones
Spoiler I & Spoiler II DDQ Tiger Conway, Jr. & Steve Keirn
Johnny Weaver beat Bill Howard

Roberto Soto beat Larry Sharpe
Don Kernodle beat Tony Rocco

OCTOBER

10/1/75: Raleigh, NC @ WRAL Studios (TV)

10/2/75: Norfolk, VA @ Scope
Gene & Ole Anderson beat Tiger Conway, Jr. & Steve Keirn
Spoiler I & Spoiler II beat The Avenger & Swede Hanson
Johnny Weaver beat Bill Howard
Roberto Soto beat Charlie Fulton
Tony Rocco beat Jerry Blackwell

10/2/75: Waynesville, NC @ Tuscola Senior High School
Paul Jones & Ken Patera vs. Boris Malenko & Missouri Mauler
Jerry Blackwell vs. Danny Miller
Tony Atlas & Bob Bruggers vs. Art Neilson & Michel Dubois
Kevin Sullivan vs. Tony Rocco

10/3/75: Lynchburg, VA @ City Armory
Ric Flair DDQ Paul Jones
Rufus R. Jones beat Missouri Mauler
Swede Hanson & Ron Starr beat Joe Soto & Larry Sharpe (sub for John Smith)
Steve Keirn beat Charlie Fulton
Larry Sharpe beat Don Serrano

10/3/75: Charleston, SC @ County Hall
Johnny Valentine vs. Mr. Wrestling
Tony Rocco vs. Ron Starr
Plus other matches

10/3/75: Richmond, VA @ Coliseum
Wahoo McDaniel beat Ole Anderson in an Indian strap match
Tiger Conway, Jr. beat Gene Anderson
Spoiler I & Spoiler II beat Klondike Bill & The Avenger
Johnny Weaver beat George Harris
Roberto Soto beat Bill Howard

10/4/75: Roanoke, VA @ Starland Arena
Tiger Conway, Jr. & Steve Keirn beat Gene & Ole Anderson by DQ
Ken Patera vs. Michel Dubois
Johnny Weaver vs. Bill Howard
George Harris vs. Ron Starr
Tony Rocco vs. Greg Peterson

10/4/75: Kingstree, SC @ Tomlinson Gym
Paul Jones & Rufus R. Jones vs. Missouri Mauler & Boris Malenko
Plus other matches

10/4/75: Wilmington, SC @ Legion Stadium
Wahoo McDaniel won a battle royal for $5,000
Johnny Valentine vs. Mr. Wrestling
Ric Flair vs. Wahoo McDaniel
Note: The airplane crash involving Johnny Valentine, Ric Flair, Tim Woods, Bob Bruggers and David Crockett happened before this Wilmington card.
Also Note: The NWA United States Title was declared vacant with Valentine's injury.

10/5/75: Asheville, NC @ Civic Center
NWA World Champion Jack Brisco vs. Wahoo McDaniel
Ric Flair & Gene Anderson vs. Mr. Wrestling & Paul Jones
Ron Starr vs. John Smith
Tony Rocco vs. Larry Sharpe
Don Serrano vs. George Harris
Greg Peterson vs. Kevin Sullivan
Note: The plane crash changed this card from the listed lineup.

10/6/75: Charlotte, NC @ Park Center
NWA World Champion Jack Brisco beat Paul Jones by DQ in a 2 of 3 falls match
Ken Patera beat Gene Anderson (sub for Ric Flair)
Swede Hanson & Johnny Weaver beat Steve Strong & Art Neilson
Larry Sharpe & Joe Soto beat Kevin Sullivan & Roberto Soto
Tony Rocco beat Don Serrano

10/6/75: Fayetteville, NC @ Cumberland County Memorial Auditorium
Wahoo McDaniel (sub for Mr. Wrestling) beat Spoiler II
Tiger Conway, Jr. & Steve Keirn beat Missouri Mauler & Michel Dubois
Spoiler I beat The Avenger via pinfall
Danny Miller beat John Smith
Bill Howard beat Greg Peterson

10/6/75: Greenville, SC @ Memorial Auditorium

10/7/75: Columbia, SC @ Township Auditorium
Paul Jones, Tiger Conway, Jr. & Danny Miller (sub for Mr. Wrestling) beat Spoiler I (sub for Ric Flair), Spoiler II & Gene Anderson
Missouri Mauler beat Klondike Bill

MID-ATLANTIC WRESTLING 1975 YEARBOOK

Steve Keirn beat George Harris
Charlie Fulton draw Greg Peterson

10/7/75: Raleigh, NC @ Dorton Arena
NWA World Champion Jack Brisco beat Wahoo McDaniel
Ken Patera beat Boris Malenko
Johnny Weaver beat Bill Howard
Steve Strong beat Swede Hanson
Roberto Soto & Tony Rocco beat John Smith & Michel Dubois
Don Kernodle beat Joe Soto

10/8/75: Raleigh, NC @ WRAL Studios (TV)

10/9/75: Anderson, SC @ Recreation Center
Wahoo McDaniel beat Spoiler II via pinfall
Steve Strong beat The Avenger
Johnny Weaver & Danny Miller beat Art Neilson & Bill Howard
Tony Rocco beat John Smith
Ron Starr beat Charlie Fulton

10/9/75: Norfolk, VA @ Scope
NWA World Champion Jack Brisco vs. Paul Jones
Rufus R. Jones vs. Gene Anderson
Tiger Conway, Jr. & Steve Keirn vs. Michel Dubois & Steve Strong
Greg Peterson vs. Kevin Sullivan
Roberto Soto vs. Larry Sharpe

10/10/75: Charleston, SC @ County Hall
Wahoo McDaniel beat Gene Anderson in a Texas death match
Spoiler II beat The Avenger
Johnny Weaver & Danny Miller beat Michel Dubois & Steve Strong
Spoiler I vs. Don Kernodle
Klondike Bill vs. Larry Sharpe

10/10/75: Richmond, VA @ Coliseum

10/11/75: Spartanburg, SC @ Memorial Auditorium

10/11/75: Greensboro, NC @ Coliseum
NWA World Champion Jack Brisco beat Dory Funk, Jr (sub for Johnny Valentine)
Gene & Ole Anderson beat Paul Jones & Dusty Rhodes
Tiger Conway & Steve Keirn beat Michel Dubois & Bill Howard
Johnny Weaver & Roberto Soto beat Larry Sharpe & John Smith

Steve Strong beat Klondike Bill
Danny Miller beat Charlie Fulton
Mr. Wrestling beat Spoiler II

10/13/75: Charlotte, NC @ Park Center
Gene & Ole Anderson beat Tiger Conway, Jr. & Steve Keirn
Mr. Wrestling beat Missouri Mauler by CO
Johnny Weaver beat Art Neilson
Michel Dubois beat Ron Starr
Tony Rocco draw Don Kernodle (20:00)

10/13/75: Greenville, SC @ Memorial Auditorium
Wahoo McDaniel beat Billy Graham (sub for Ric Flair) by DQ
Rufus R. Jones DDQ Boris Malenko
Spoiler I & Spoiler II beat Ken Patera & The Avenger
Steve Strong beat Kevin Sullivan
Greg Peterson draw Charlie Fulton

10/14/75: Columbia, SC @ Township Auditorium
Paul Jones beat Spoiler II by DQ
Rufus R. Jones beat Spoiler I
Boris Malenko & Missouri Mauler beat Klondike Bill & Danny Miller
Roberto Soto beat Bill Howard via pinfall
Joe Soto beat Kevin Sullivan

10/14/75: Raleigh, NC @ Dorton Arena
Gene & Ole Anderson vs. Tiger Conway, Jr. & Steve Keirn
Steve Strong & Billy Graham vs. Johnny Weaver & Swede Hanson
Ron Starr vs. George Harris
Don Serrano vs. Larry Sharpe

10/15/75: Raleigh, NC @ WRAL Studios (TV)
Billy Graham & Steve Strong vs. Johnny Weaver & Don Kernodle
Billy Graham & Steve Strong vs. Kevin Sullivan & The Avenger

10/16/75: Norfolk, VA @ Scope
Rufus R. Jones beat Gene Anderson in a Texas death match
Mr. Wrestling beat Spoiler II via pinfall
Johnny Weaver & Roberto Soto beat Michel Dubois & Steve Strong by DQ
Tony Rocco beat Charlie Fulton
Bill Howard beat Greg Peterson

10/17/75: Charleston, SC @ County Hall
Paul Jones & Rufus R. Jones vs. Missouri Mauler & Boris Malenko

MID-ATLANTIC WRESTLING 1975 YEARBOOK

Ken Patera vs. Art Neilson
The Avenger vs. Larry Sharpe
Ron Starr vs. Joe Soto
Kevin Sullivan vs. George Harris

10/17/75: Richmond, VA @ Coliseum
Gene & Ole Anderson beat Tiger Conway, Jr. & Steve Keirn
Wahoo McDaniel beat Billy Graham (sub for Ric Flair)
Mr. Wrestling beat Steve Strong
Spoiler I & Spoiler II beat Swede Hanson & Johnny Weaver
Michel Dubois draw Danny Miller
Klondike Bill beat Bill Howard
Tony Rocco beat Charlie Fulton

10/18/75: Roanoke, VA @ Starland Arena
Tiger Conway, Jr. & Steve Keirn beat Gene & Ole Anderson by CO in a no DQ match
Steve Strong beat The Avenger
Tony Rocco & Ron Starr vs. Doug Somers & Joe Soto
Klondike Bill vs. Charlie Fulton

10/18/75: Spartanburg, SC @ Memorial Auditorium
Paul Jones & Rufus R. Jones beat Missouri Mauler & Boris Malenko by DQ
Bob Backlund & Danny Miller beat Larry Sharpe & Bill Howard
Sandy Scott beat Michel Dubois by DQ
Greg Peterson beat Buddy Porter

10/19/75: Asheville, NC @ Civic Center
Jack Brisco & Jerry Brisco vs. Paul Jones & Wahoo McDaniel
Roberto Soto & Tony Rocco vs. Missouri Mauler & Boris Malenko
Art Neilson vs. Steve Keirn
Billy Graham vs. Ron Starr
Greg Peterson vs. Don Serrano

10/20/75: Charlotte, NC @ Park Center
Paul Jones beat Billy Graham by DQ
Boris Malenko & Missouri Mauler beat Ken Patera & Danny Miller
Steve Strong beat Kevin Sullivan
Klondike Bill beat Charlie Fulton
Greg Peterson beat Buddy Porter by DQ

10/20/75: Fayetteville, NC @ Cumberland County Memorial Auditorium
Spoiler I & Spoiler II beat Wahoo McDaniel & Rufus R. Jones
Swede Hanson beat Larry Sharpe

Johnny Weaver beat Art Neilson (sub for Michel Dubois)
The Avenger & Ron Starr beat Doug Somers & Joe Soto

10/20/75: Greenville, SC @ Memorial Auditorium
Gene & Ole Anderson beat Tiger Conway, Jr. & Steve Keirn
Roberto Soto & Don Kernodle beat Billy Howard & George Harris
Michel Dubois beat Bob Backlund
Tony Rocco beat Don Serrano

10/21/75: Columbia, SC @ Township Auditorium
Gene & Ole Anderson beat Tiger Conway, Jr. & Steve Keirn
Danny Miller beat Boris Malenko
Johnny Weaver beat Art Neilson
Swede Hanson beat Joe Soto
Roberto Soto beat Doug Somers

10/21/75: Danville, VA @ City Armory
Paul Jones & Rufus R. Jones beat Spoiler I & Spoiler II by DQ
Missouri Mauler beat Ron Starr via pinfall
Klondike Bill beat George Harris via pinfall
Bill Howard beat Kevin Sullivan
Larry Sharpe draw Greg Peterson (20:00)

10/21/75: Henderson, NC @ Vance High School
Wahoo McDaniel & Ken Patera vs. Billy Graham & Steve Strong
The Avenger vs. Michel Dubois
Don Kernodle vs. Charlie Fulton
Tony Rocco vs. Don Serrano

10/22/75: Raleigh, NC @ WRAL Studios (TV)

10/23/75: Norfolk, VA @ Scope
Tiger Conway, Jr. & Steve Keirn beat Gene & Ole Anderson by DQ
Billy Graham beat Swede Hanson
Steve Strong beat Klondike Bill
Roberto Soto beat Art Neilson
Doug Somers beat Don Serrano (sub for Kevin Sullivan)

10/24/75: Charleston, SC @ County Hall
Rufus R. Jones beat Boris Malenko in a Russian chain match
Spoiler I & Spoiler II vs. Ron Starr & Steve Keirn
Swede Hanson vs. Michel Dubois
Bill Howard draw Don Kernodle
Tony Rocco vs. Charlie Fulton

234

10/24/75: Richmond, VA @ Coliseum
Gene & Ole Anderson vs. Paul Jones & Wahoo McDaniel in a lumberjack match
Billy Graham & Steve Strong vs. Ken Patera & Tiger Conway, Jr.
Mr. Wrestling vs. Missouri Mauler
Johnny Weaver vs. Art Neilson
Klondike Bill vs. Doug Somers
Kevin Sullivan vs. Don Serrano
The Avenger & Roberto Soto vs. Joe Soto & George Harris

10/25/75: Hampton, VA @ Coliseum
Paul Jones & Wahoo McDaniel beat Spoiler I & Spoiler II
Mr. Wrestling beat Steve Strong by DQ
The Avenger beat Missouri Mauler by DQ
Tony Rocco & Roberto Soto beat Charlie Fulton & Doug Somers
The Avenger beat Larry Sharpe

10/25/75: Roanoke, VA @ Starland Arena
Gene & Ole Anderson vs. Tiger Conway, Jr. & Steve Keirn lumberjack match
Johnny Weaver vs. Michel Dubois
Swede Hanson vs. Joe Soto
Don Serrano vs. Don Kernodle
Klondike Bill vs. Buddy Porter

10/25/75: Spartanburg, SC @ Memorial Auditorium
Rufus R. Jones beat Boris Malenko
Ken Patera beat Art Neilson
Ron Starr & Sandy Scott beat George Harris & Bill Howard
Bearcat Brown beat Masked Raider
Bill Howard (sub for Kevin Sullivan) beat Greg Peterson

10/26/75: Charlottesville, VA @ University Hall
Paul Jones & Wahoo McDaniel vs. Boris Malenko & Missouri Mauler
Spoiler II vs. Swede Hanson
Steve Strong vs. Klondike Bill
Michel Dubois vs. Ron Starr
Tony Rocco & Roberto Soto vs. Bill Howard & Doug Somers

10/27/75: Charlotte, NC @ Park Center
Paul Jones & Wahoo McDaniel beat Spoiler I & Spoiler II
Rufus R. Jones beat Boris Malenko by DQ
Michel Dubois & Steve Strong beat Ron Starr & Swede Hanson
Roberto Soto beat Doug Somers

10/27/75: Greenville, SC @ Memorial Auditorium
Gene & Ole Anderson beat Tiger Conway, Jr. & Steve Keirn in a Texas tornado match with 2 referees
Ken Patera beat Missouri Mauler by DQ
Johnny Weaver & Klondike Bill beat Art Neilson & Billy Howard
Tony Rocco beat Joe Soto
Greg Peterson draw Larry Sharpe

10/28/75: Columbia, SC @ Township Auditorium
Gene & Ole Anderson beat Tiger Conway, Jr. & Steve Keirn in a match with 2 referees
Boris Malenko & Missouri Mauler beat The Avenger & Johnny Weaver
Danny Miller beat Charlie Fulton
Larry Sharpe draw Don Kernodle

10/28/75: Raleigh, NC @ Dorton Arena
Paul Jones & Rufus R. Jones draw Spoiler I & Spoiler II
Ken Patera beat Michel Dubois
Steve Strong beat Klondike Bill or Ron Starr
Roberto Soto beat Art Neilson
Joe Soto draw Greg Peterson

10/29/75: Raleigh, NC @ WRAL Studios (TV)

10/30/75: Marion, NC @ McDowell High School Gym
Paul Jones & Ken Patera vs. Spoiler I & Spoiler II in a Texas tornado match
Mr. Wrestling & Sandy Scott vs. Charlie Fulton & Michel Dubois
Swede Hanson vs. Joe Soto
Plus other matches

10/30/75: Norfolk, VA @ Scope
Gene & Ole Anderson beat Tiger Conway, Jr. & Steve Keirn lumberjack match
Steve Strong beat The Avenger
Don Kernodle & Klondike Bill beat Larry Sharpe & Doug Somers
Roberto Soto beat Greg Peterson

10/31/75: Richmond, VA @ Coliseum

NOVEMBER

11/1/75: Roanoke, VA @ Starland Arena
Gene & Ole Anderson vs. Wahoo McDaniel & Ken Patera
Mr. Wrestling vs. Bill Howard
Plus other matches

235

MID-ATLANTIC WRESTLING 1975 YEARBOOK

11/1/75: Spartanburg, SC @ Memorial Auditorium
Boris Malenko won a 11-man battle royal for $4,500 by beating Steve Keirn
Others in the Battle Royal: Missouri Mauler, Tiger Conway, Jr., Doug Somers, Art Neilson, Klondike Bill, The Avenger, Sandy Scott, Pepe Lopez & Don Kernodle

11/2/75: Asheville, NC @ Civic Center (Afternoon Show)
Gene & Ole Anderson & Steve Strong vs. Wahoo McDaniel, Paul Jones & Rufus R. Jones
Ken Patera vs. Michel Dubois
Swede Hanson vs. Missouri Mauler
Johnny Weaver vs. Bill Howard
Danny Miller vs. Charlie Fulton

11/3/75: Charlotte, NC @ Park Center
Tiger Conway, Jr. & Steve Keirn beat Gene & Ole Anderson by DQ
Ken Patera & Roberto Soto beat Michel Dubois & Joe Soto
Klondike Bill beat Larry Sharpe
Tony Rocco beat Don Serrano

11/3/75: Fayetteville, NC @ Cumberland County Memorial Auditorium
Rufus R. Jones vs. Spoiler II
Boris Malenko & Missouri Mauler vs. The Avenger & Johnny Weaver
Donna Christianello vs. Sheila Shepherd
Danny Miller vs. Bill Howard
Pedro Lopez vs. Buddy Porter

11/3/75: Greenville, SC @ Memorial Auditorium
Billy Graham & Steve Strong beat Paul Jones & Wahoo McDaniel
Swede Hanson & Don Kernodle beat Charlie Fulton & Bill White
Sandy Scott (sub for Mr. Wrestling) beat Spoiler I by DQ
Greg Peterson beat Doug Somers

11/4/75: Columbia, SC @ Township Auditorium
Gene & Ole Anderson beat Paul Jones & Rufus R. Jones
Steve Strong beat Swede Hanson
Roberto Soto & Danny Miller beat Bill Howard & Michel Dubois
Klondike Bill beat Charlie Fulton

11/4/75: Danville, VA @ City Armory
Tiger Conway, Jr. & Steve Keirn DDQ Boris Malenko & Missouri Mauler
Donna Christianello beat Sheila Shepherd
Johnny Weaver & Don Kernodle b. Doug Somers & Joe Soto

Tony Rocco beat Don Serrano

11/4/75: Raleigh, NC @ Dorton Arena
Wahoo McDaniel vs. Billy Graham in an Indian strap match
The Avenger & Ken Patera vs. Spoiler I & Spoiler II
Mr. Wrestling vs. Bill White
Pedro Lopez vs. Larry Sharpe
Greg Peterson vs. Buddy Porter

11/5/75: Raleigh, NC @ WRAL Studios (TV)
Billy Graham & Steve Strong vs. The Avenger & Pepe Lopez

11/6/75: Kingstree, SC @ High School
Gene & Ole Anderson vs. Wahoo McDaniel & Paul Jones

11/6/75: Norfolk, VA @ Scope
Billy Graham & Steve Strong beat Ken Patera & Rufus R. Jones
Swede Hanson beat Boris Malenko by DQ
Tiger Conway, Jr. & Steve Keirn beat Spoiler I & Spoiler II
Bill White draw Pepe Lopez

11/7/75: Charleston, SC @ County Hall
Gene & Ole Anderson beat Ken Patera & Rufus R. Jones
Roberto Soto beat Michel Dubois
Tony Rocco beat Bill Howard
Klondike Bill beat Joe Soto
Larry Sharpe beat Don Serrano

11/7/75: Richmond, VA @ Coliseum
Billy Graham beat Wahoo McDaniel in a Texas death match
Paul Jones beat Spoiler II by forfeit
Steve Strong & Blackjack Mulligan beat Mr. Wrestling & Johnny Weaver
Missouri Mauler & Boris Malenko beat Tiger Conway, Jr. & Steve Keirn
Spoiler I beat Pepe Lopez
Swede Hanson beat Bill White by DQ
The Avenger beat Charlie Fulton

11/8/75: Roanoke, VA @ Starland Arena
Tiger Conway, Jr. & Steve Keirn vs. Spoiler I & Spoiler II
Boris Malenko & Missouri Mauler vs. Johnny Weaver & The Avenger
Plus other matches

11/8/75: Spartanburg, SC @ Memorial Auditorium
Ken Patera & Sandy Scott (sub for Mr. Wrestling) beat Gene & Ole Anderson by DQ
Wahoo McDaniel beat Terry Funk

Roberto Soto beat Bill White by DQ
Don Serrano beat Charlie Fulton
Greg Peterson beat Buddy Porter

11/8/75: Conway, SC @ Williams-Brice Building
Blackjack Mulligan vs. ??
Billy Graham & Steve Strong vs. Paul Jones & Rufus R. Jones
Plus other matches

11/9/75: Greensboro, NC @ Coliseum
NWA United States Title tournament
1st Round
Rufus R. Jones beat Steve Strong via pinfall
Terry Funk beat Red Bastien via pinfall
Blackjack Mulligan beat Ken Patera via pinfall
Dusty Rhodes beat Boris Malenko via pinfall
Wahoo McDaniel beat Billy Graham via pinfall
Harley Race beat Tiger Conway, Jr. via pinfall
Paul Jones beat Ole Anderson via pinfall
Johnny Weaver (sub for Ray Stevens) beat Gene Anderson by judge's decision

2nd Round
Terry Funk beat Rufus R. Jones via pinfall
Dusty Rhodes beat Blackjack Mulligan via pinfall
Harley Race beat Wahoo McDaniel by DQ
Paul Jones beat Johnny Weaver via pinfall

Semifinals
Terry Funk beat Dusty Rhodes by DQ
Paul Jones beat Harley Race via pinfall

Finals
Terry Funk beat Paul Jones via pinfall to win vacant NWA United States Title

11/10/75: Charlotte, NC @ Park Center
Tiger Conway, Jr. & Steve Keirn beat Gene & Ole Anderson by CO
Angelo Mosca beat Klondike Bill
Johnny Weaver & The Avenger beat Steve Strong & Michel Dubois
Bill White draw Don Kernodle (20:00)

11/10/75: Greenville, SC @ Memorial Auditorium
Wahoo McDaniel beat Billy Graham in an Indian strap match
Ken Patera & Rufus R. Jones beat Spoiler I & Spoiler II
Danny Miller beat Bill Howard
Roberto Soto beat Larry Sharpe

Pedro Lopez draw Charlie Fulton

11/11/75: Columbia, SC @ Township Auditorium
Gene & Ole Anderson beat Paul Jones & Rufus R. Jones
Spoiler I & Spoiler II beat Ken Patera & The Avenger
Angelo Mosca beat Don Serrano
Swede Hanson beat Bill White
Joe Soto draw Pepe Lopez (20:00)

11/11/75: Raleigh, NC @ Dorton Arena
Wahoo McDaniel & Tiger Conway, Jr. beat Boris Malenko & Missouri Mauler
Steve Strong & Michel Dubois beat Danny Miller & Don Kernodle
Roberto Soto beat Bill Howard
Tony Rocco beat George Harris

11/12/75: Raleigh, NC @ WRAL Studios (TV)

11/13/75: Norfolk, VA @ Scope
Paul Jones & Rufus R. Jones beat Gene & Ole Anderson by DQ
Angelo Mosca beat The Avenger
Klondike Bill beat Charlie Fulton
Tony Rocco & Roberto Soto beat Joe Soto & Bill Howard

11/13/75: Waynesville, NC @ Tuscola High School
Wahoo McDaniel vs. Spoiler II
Johnny Weaver & Sandy Scott vs. George Harris & Michel Dubois
Swede Hanson vs. Larry Sharpe
Spoiler I vs. Don Kernodle

11/14/75: Charleston, SC @ County Hall
Rufus R. Jones & Swede Hanson vs. Spoiler I & Spoiler II
Michel Dubois vs. Steve Keirn
Joe Turner vs. Greg Peterson
Larry Sharpe vs. Sandy Scott

11/14/75: Lynchburg, VA @ City Armory
Gene & Ole Anderson beat Tiger Conway, Jr. & Ken Patera
Johnny Weaver beat Bill White
Tony Rocco & Roberto Soto beat Joe Soto & Bill Howard
Tony Rocco draw Bill Howard

11/14/75: Richmond, VA @ Coliseum
Paul Jones & Wahoo McDaniel beat Boris Malenko & Missouri Mauler
Steve Strong beat The Avenger
Angelo Mosca beat Klondike Bill
Danny Miller beat George Harris

MID-ATLANTIC WRESTLING 1975 YEARBOOK

Charlie Fulton draw Don Serrano

11/15/75: Roanoke, VA @ Starland Arena
Boris Malenko & Missouri Mauler vs. Wahoo McDaniel & Rufus R. Jones
Angelo Mosca vs. Klondike Bill
Johnny Weaver vs. Roberto Soto
Plus other matches

11/15/75: Morgantown, NC @ Freedom High School
Ole Anderson vs. Paul Jones
Gene Anderson vs. The Avenger
Plus other matches

11/15/75: Spartanburg, SC @ Memorial Auditorium
Ken Patera DDQ Steve Strong
Tiger Conway, Jr. & Steve Keirn beat Spoiler I & Spoiler II
Swede Hanson beat Joe Turner
Don Kernodle beat Bill Howard by DQ
George Harris draw Pedro Lopez

11/17/75: Charlotte, NC @ Park Center
Gene & Ole Anderson beat Tiger Conway, Jr. & Steve Keirn
Angelo Mosca beat Swede Hanson
Larry Zbyszko beat Jerry Blackwell by DQ
Spoiler I draw Roberto Soto (20:00)
Larry Zbyszko (sub for Pepe Lopez) beat Joe Turner

11/17/75: Fayetteville, NC @ Cumberland County Memorial Auditorium
Rufus R. Jones beat Spoiler II in a Texas death match
Boris Malenko & Missouri Mauler beat The Avenger & Johnny Weaver
Sheila Shepherd beat Donna Christianello
Danny Miller beat Bill Howard
Pepe Lopez beat Buddy Porter

11/17/75: Martinsville, VA @ Junior High School
Ken Patera vs. Steve Strong
Danny Miller & Tony Atlas vs. Bill Howard & Bill White
The Avenger vs. Michel Dubois
Klondike Bill vs. Larry Sharpe
Don Serrano vs. Larry Sharpe

11/18/75: Columbia, SC @ Township Auditorium
Rufus R. Jones beat Ole Anderson by DQ
Wahoo McDaniel beat Spoiler II by CO
Missouri Mauler & Boris Malenko beat Roberto Soto & Tony Rocco
Angelo Mosca beat Don Kernodle
Klondike Bill beat George Harris

11/18/75: Henderson, NC @ Vance High School
Ken Patera vs. Steve Strong
Tiger Conway, Jr. & Steve Keirn vs. Bill White & Michel Dubois
Danny Miller vs. Bill Howard
Spoiler I vs. The Avenger
Larry Zbyszko vs. Larry Sharpe

11/19/75: Raleigh, NC @ WRAL Studios (TV)

11/20/75: Anderson, SC @ Recreation Center
Wahoo McDaniel & Johnny Weaver beat Missouri Mauler & Boris Malenko
Michel Dubois beat The Avenger
Larry Zbyszko beat Joe Soto
Sandy Scott (sub for Tony Atlas) beat Bill Howard
Danny Miller beat Bill White

11/20/75: Danville, VA @ City Armory
Paul Jones beat Ole Anderson
Rufus R. Jones beat Gene Anderson
Swede Hanson & Don Kernodle beat Jerry Blackwell & Joe Turner
George Harris draw Tony Rocco

11/20/75: Elizabeth City, NC @ Northeastern High School
Steve Strong vs. Ken Patera
Tiger Conway, Jr. & Steve Keirn vs. Spoiler I & Spoiler II
Plus other matches

11/21/75: Charleston, SC @ City Armory
Rufus R. Jones beat Spoiler II
Johnny Weaver & Danny Miller beat Jerry Blackwell & Bill White
Klondike Bill beat Joe Soto
Tony Rocco beat Don Serrano
Pepe Gomez draw George Harris

11/21/75: Richmond, VA @ Coliseum
Wahoo McDaniel beat Boris Malenko
Michel Dubois & Steve Strong beat Tiger Conway, Jr. & Steve Keirn
Angelo Mosca DDQ Swede Hanson
Missouri Mauler draw Roberto Soto
Larry Sharpe beat Greg Peterson

11/22/75: Roanoke, VA @ Starland Arena
Rufus R. Jones vs. Missouri Mauler
Spoiler I & Spoiler II vs. Roberto Soto & The Avenger

238

MID-ATLANTIC WRESTLING 1975 YEARBOOK

plus 3 other matches

11/22/75: Spartanburg, SC @ Memorial Auditorium
Ken Patera beat Steve Strong
Tiger Conway, Jr. & Steve Keirn beat Michel Dubois & Jerry Blackwell
Johnny Weaver beat Bill White
Larry Zbyszko beat Joe Soto
Charlie Fulton beat Tony Rocco via pinfall

11/24/75: Charlotte, NC @ Park Center
Wahoo McDaniel beat Boris Malenko
Rufus R. Jones & Ken Patera beat Steve Strong & Michel Dubois
Mr. Wrestling beat Jerry Blackwell
Tony Atlas beat Larry Sharpe
Roberto Soto beat Joe Soto

11/24/75: Greenville, SC @ Memorial Auditorium
NWA World Champion Jack Brisco beat Paul Jones by DQ
Andre The Giant & Tiger Conway, Jr. beat Gene & Ole Anderson by DQ
Danny Miller & Steve Keirn beat Spoiler I & Spoiler II
Angelo Mosca beat Klondike Bill
Larry Zbyszko beat Billy Howard
Tony Rocco draw George Harris

11/25/75: Columbia, SC @ Carolina Coliseum
Wahoo McDaniel beat NWA World Champion Jack Brisco by DQ
Gene & Ole Anderson DCO with Andre The Giant & Rufus R. Jones
Angelo Mosca beat The Avenger
Danny Miller & Johnny Weaver beat Jerry Blackwell & George Harris
Klondike Bill beat Joe Turner
Pepe Lopez draw Charlie Fulton

11/25/75: Raleigh, NC @ Dorton Arena
Boris Malenko, Missouri Mauler & Steve Strong vs. Paul Jones, Mr. Wrestling & Ken Patera
Tony Atlas vs. Bill Howard
Tiger Conway, Jr. vs. Michel Dubois
Swede Hanson vs. Bill White

11/26/75: Raleigh, NC @ WRAL Studios (TV)

11/27/75: Greensboro, NC @ Coliseum
Wahoo McDaniel beat NWA World Champion Jack Brisco by CO
Paul Jones beat Terry Funk to win NWA United States Title
Blackjack Mulligan no contest with Mr. Wrestling
Tiger Conway, Jr. & Steve Keirn beat Boris Malenko & Missouri Mauler
Swede Hanson & Larry Zbyszko beat Spoiler I & Spoiler II
Angelo Mosca beat The Avenger
Bill White beat Pepe Lopez
Klondike Bill beat George Harris

11/27/75: Norfolk, VA @ Scope
Andre the Giant, Rufus R. Jones & Ken Patera beat Gene & Ole Anderson & Billy Graham
Andre the Giant beat Billy Graham in an arm wrestling match
Danny Miller & Johnny Weaver beat Michel Dubois & Steve Strong
Tony Rocco & Roberto Soto beat Bill Howard & Larry Sharpe
Tony Atlas beat Jerry Blackwell
Don Kernodle beat Joe Soto
Joe Turner beat Don Serrano

11/28/75: Charleston, SC @ County Hall
NWA World Champion Jack Brisco beat Rufus R. Jones by DQ
Gene & Ole Anderson vs. Tiger Conway, Jr. & Steve Keirn
Swede Hanson vs. Joe Turner
Pepe Lopez vs. Larry Sharpe
Don Kernodle vs. Charlie Fulton

11/28/75: Richmond, VA @ Coliseum
Wahoo McDaniel beat Billy Graham in an Indian strap match
Paul Jones & Andre The Giant beat Blackjack Mulligan & Steve Strong by DQ
Boris Malenko & Missouri Mauler beat Tony Rocco & Roberto Soto
Angelo Mosca beat The Avenger
Johnny Weaver & Danny Miller beat Jerry Blackwell & Bill White
Tony Atlas beat Bill Howard
Klondike Bill draw Michel Dubois
Joe Soto beat Don Serrano

11/29/75: Spartanburg, SC @ Memorial Auditorium
Paul Jones & Wahoo McDaniel beat Boris Malenko & Missouri Mauler
Spoiler II beat Steve Keirn
Pepe Lopez draw Joe Soto (20:00)
Klondike Bill beat Larry Sharpe
Larry Zbyszko beat Charlie Fulton

11/29/75: Salem, VA @ Civic Center
Andre The Giant, Mr. Wrestling & Rufus R. Jones vs. Gene & Ole Anderson & Steve Strong
Ken Patera vs. Jerry Blackwell
Angelo Mosca vs. Swede Hanson
Johnny Weaver & Tony Atlas vs. Michel Dubois & Bill White
Tony Rocco vs. Don Serrano

11/30/75: Charlottesville, VA @ University Hall
Ken Patera & Wahoo McDaniel vs. Billy Graham & Steve Strong
Spoiler I & Spoiler II vs. Larry Zbyszko & Johnny Weaver
Angelo Mosca vs. Danny Miller
Charlie Fulton vs. Don Serrano
Tony Atlas vs. Joe Soto

11/30/75: Asheville, NC @ Civic Center
Andre The Giant, Mr. Wrestling & Paul Jones vs. Gene & Ole Anderson & Blackjack Mulligan
Tiger Conway, Jr. vs. Boris Malenko
Missouri Mauler vs. Klondike Bill
Michel Dubois vs. Roberto Soto
Don Kernodle vs. Joe Turner

DECEMBER

12/1/75: Fayetteville, NC @ Cumberland County Memorial Auditorium
Gene & Ole Anderson vs. Paul Jones & Rufus R. Jones
Spoiler I vs. Johnny Weaver
Larry Zbyszko vs. Bill Howard
Tony Rocco vs. Joe Soto
Klondike Bill vs. Charlie Fulton

12/1/75: Charlotte, NC @ Park Center
Ken Patera & Andre The Giant beat Steve Strong & Blackjack Mulligan
Danny Miller & Tony Atlas beat Michel Dubois & Bill White by DQ
Angelo Mosca beat Pepe Lopez
Roberto Soto beat Joe Turner
Greg Peterson beat Don Serrano

12/1/75: Greenville, SC @ Memorial Auditorium
Wahoo McDaniel beat Billy Graham in a Texas death match
Tiger Conway, Jr. & Steve Keirn beat Boris Malenko & Missouri Mauler by DQ
Mr. Wrestling beat Jerry Blackwell
Swede Hanson beat George Harris
Larry Sharpe draw Klondike Bill

12/2/75: Winston-Salem, NC @ Coliseum
Gene & Ole Anderson vs. Paul Jones & Rufus R. Jones
Blackjack Mulligan vs. Tony Atlas
Spoiler I vs. Mr. Wrestling
Spoiler II vs. Tony Rocco
Michel Dubois vs. Roberto Soto
Pepe Lopez vs. Don Serrano
Steve Keirn vs. Joe Turner

12/2/75: Columbia, SC @ Township Auditorium
Wahoo McDaniel beat Boris Malenko
Ken Patera beat Steve Strong via pinfall
Angelo Mosca & Missouri Mauler beat Johnny Weaver & Danny Miller
Tiger Conway, Jr. beat Jerry Blackwell
Larry Zbyszko draw Bill White

12/3/75: Raleigh, NC @ WRAL Studios (TV)
Note: Paul Jones vacates the NWA Mid Atlantic Television Title in order to defend the NWA United States Title.

12/4/75: Danville, VA @ City Armory
Ken Patera & Rufus R. Jones DDQ Blackjack Mulligan & Steve Strong
Johnny Weaver beat Michel Dubois by DQ
Danny Miller beat Bill White
Klondike Bill beat Joe Soto
Greg Peterson draw Larry Sharpe

12/4/75: Norfolk, VA @ Scope
Wahoo McDaniel beat Boris Malenko
Missouri Mauler & Angelo Mosca beat Tiger Conway, Jr. & Steve Keirn
Spoiler II beat Don Kernodle
Swede Hanson beat Jerry Blackwell
Larry Zbyszko beat Charlie Fulton

12/4/75: Camden, SC @ Camden City Arena
Paul Jones & Tony Atlas vs. Gene & Ole Anderson
Don Serrano vs. Joe Turner
Roberto Soto vs. Bill Howard
Tony Rocca vs. George Harris

12/5/75: Charleston, SC @ County Hall
Tiger Conway, Jr. & Steve Keirn beat Gene & Ole Anderson by DQ
Tony Atlas beat George Harris
Klondike Bill beat Michel Dubois

MID-ATLANTIC WRESTLING 1975 YEARBOOK

Roberto Soto beat Bill Howard
Bill White beat Greg Peterson

12/5/75: Richmond, VA @ Coliseum
Ken Patera & Wahoo McDaniel vs. Blackjack Mulligan & Steve Strong
Angelo Mosca vs. Swede Hanson in a no DQ match
Johnny Weaver & Danny Miller vs. Missouri Mauler & Boris Malenko
Larry Zbyszko vs. Jerry Blackwell
Don Kernodle vs. Charlie Fulton

12/6/75: Roanoke, VA @ Starland Arena
Ken Patera vs. Steve Strong in a no DQ match
Ole Anderson vs. Rufus R. Jones
Plus 3 more matches

12/6/75: Spartanburg, SC @ Memorial Auditorium
Wahoo McDaniel beat Boris Malenko
Blackjack Mulligan beat Larry Zbyszko
Johnny Weaver & Roberto Soto beat Spoiler I & Bill White
Pepe Lopez draw Joe Turner
Tony Rocco beat Larry Sharpe

12/8/75: Greenville, SC @ Memorial Auditorium

12/8/75: Charlotte, NC @ Park Center
Blackjack Mulligan beat Ken Patera
Tiger Conway, Jr. & Steve Keirn beat Spoiler I & Spoiler II
Steve Strong beat Tony Rocco
Michel Dubois beat Roberto Soto (20:00)
Charlie Fulton draw Rick McGraw

12/8/75: Fayetteville, NC @ Cumberland County Memorial Auditorium
Gene & Ole Anderson vs. Paul Jones & Rufus R. Jones in a lumberjack match
Angelo Mosca vs. Klondike Bill
Johnny Weaver vs. Missouri Mauler
Larry Zbyszko vs. Larry Sharpe
Don Kernodle vs. Greg Peterson

12/9/75: Raleigh, NC @ Dorton Arena
Paul Jones vs. Blackjack Mulligan
Steve Strong & Michel Dubois vs. Johnny Weaver & Danny Miller
Angelo Mosca vs. Swede Hanson
Tony Atlas vs. Jerry Blackwell
Pepe Lopez vs. Charlie Fulton

12/9/75: Columbia, SC @ Township Auditorium

Wahoo McDaniel beat Boris Malenko in a Russian chain match
Tiger Conway, Jr. & Steve Keirn beat Spoiler I & Spoiler II
Klondike Bill beat George Harris via pinfall
Roberto Soto beat Bill Howard
Don Kernodle draw Greg Peterson

12/10/75: Raleigh, NC @ WRAL Studios (TV)
12/11/75: Marion, NC @ McDowell High School
12-man battle royal for $4,800 featuring Paul Jones, Boris Malenko, Johnny Weaver, Steve Strong, Swede Hanson, Klondike Bill, Jerry Blackwell, Don Kernodle, Greg Peterson, Joe Turner, Larry Sharpe and Charlie Fulton
Plus other matches

12/11/75: Anderson, SC @ Recreation Center
Gene & Ole Anderson beat Tiger Conway, Jr. & Steve Keirn in a Texas death match
Angelo Mosca beat Tony Atlas
Danny Miller beat Michel Dubois
Rick McGraw draw Joe Soto
George Harris beat Don Serrano

12/11/75: Norfolk, VA @ Scope
Rufus R. Jones beat Missouri Mauler
Blackjack Mulligan vs. Ken Patera
Spoiler I & Spoiler II vs. Tony Rocco & Larry Zbyszko
Plus other matches

12/12/75: Charleston, SC @ County Hall
Gene & Ole Anderson beat Tiger Conway, Jr. & Steve Keirn
Angelo Mosca beat Klondike Bill
Swede Hanson beat Steve Strong
Don Kernodle beat Joe Turner

12/12/75: Richmond, VA @ Coliseum
Paul Jones beat Blackjack Mulligan
Johnny Weaver & Roberto Soto (sub for Mr. Wrestling) beat Spoiler I & Spoiler II by DQ
Tony Atlas beat Bill White
Bill Howard beat Don Serrano (sub for Roberto Soto)
George Harris beat Pepe Lopez

12/12/75: Lynchburg, VA @ City Armory
Boris Malenko & Missouri Mauler vs. Ken Patera & Rufus R. Jones
Danny Miller & Larry Zbyszko vs. Jerry Blackwell & Joe Soto
Michel Dubois vs. Tony Rocco
Greg Peterson vs. Larry Sharpe

241

MID-ATLANTIC WRESTLING 1975 YEARBOOK

12/13/75: Spartanburg, SC @ Memorial Auditorium
Gene & Ole Anderson beat Paul Jones & Tony Atlas
Johnny Weaver DCO with Spoiler I
Swede Hanson beat Bill White
Larry Sharpe beat Pepe Lopez
Klondike Bill beat Joe Soto

12/13/75: Roanoke, VA @ Starland Arena
Ken Patera & Mr. Wrestling vs. Blackjack Mulligan & Steve Strong
Roberto Soto vs. Michel Dubois
Larry Zbyszko vs. Bill Howard

12/14/75:-12/24/75: No Wrestling
Annual Two-Weeks off Before Christmas

12/25/75: Charlotte, NC @ Park Center
Gene & Ole Anderson draw Mr. Wrestling & Johnny Weaver
Haiti Kid & Vicky Williams beat Little Tokyo & Leilani Kai
Tiger Conway, Jr. beat Spoiler I
Steve Keirn beat Jerry Blackwell

12/25/75: Greenville, SC @ Memorial Auditorium
Paul Jones beat Blackjack Mulligan
Danny Miller & Swede Hanson beat Steve Strong & Missouri Mauler
Angelo Mosca beat Ken Patera
Tony Atlas beat Billy Howard
Charlie Fulton beat Don Serrano
Sheila Shepherd beat Donna Christianello

12/25/75: Norfolk, VA @ Scope
Wahoo McDaniel vs. Boris Malenko in a Russian chain match
Rufus R. Jones vs. Spoiler II in a no time limit, no CO, no DQ match
Cowboy Lang vs. Sonny Boy Hayes
Roberto Soto & El Rayo vs. Michel Dubois & Bill White
Larry Zbyszko vs. George Harris
Joe Turner vs. Johnny Heidman

12/26/75: Charleston, SC @ County Hall
Tiger Conway, Jr. & Steve Keirn beat Boris Malenko & Missouri Mauler
Johnny Weaver beat Jerry Blackwell
Donna Christianello vs. Shirley Sheppard
Tony Atlas beat Joe Soto
Greg Peterson draw Don Kernodle

12/26/75: Greensboro, NC @ Coliseum
Paul Jones beat Spoiler II
Mr. Wrestling beat Blackjack Mulligan
Roberto Soto & El Rayo beat Michel Dubois & Spoiler I
Larry Zbyszko beat Bill Howard
Swede Hanson draw Bill White (20:00)

12/26/75: Richmond, VA @ Coliseum
Gene & Ole Anderson beat Ken Patera & Rufus R. Jones
Wahoo McDaniel no contest Angelo Mosca
Danny Miller beat Steve Strong by DQ
Charlie Fulton beat Johnny Heidman
George Harris beat Joe Turner
Haiti Kid & Vicki Williams vs. Little Tokyo & Leilani Kai

12/27/75: Hampton, VA @ Coliseum
Paul Jones beat Blackjack Mulligan
Angelo Mosca beat Ken Patera
Roberto Soto & El Rayo beat Steve Strong & Michel Dubois
Danny Miller beat George Harris

12/27/75: Roanoke, VA @ Starland Arena
Wahoo McDaniel vs. Spoiler II
Boris Malenko & Missouri Mauler vs. Swede Hanson & Tony Atlas
Plus 3 more matches

12/27/75: Spartanburg, SC @ Memorial Auditorium
Gene & Ole Anderson DDQ Mr. Wrestling & Rufus R. Jones
Haiti Kid beat Tokyo Joe
Tiger Conway, Jr. & Steve Keirn beat Spoiler I & Bill White
Don Kernodle beat Larry Sharpe (sub for Joe Soto)

12/28/75: Asheville, NC @ Civic Center
Mr. Wrestling & Wahoo McDaniel vs. Blackjack Mulligan & Billy Graham
Steve Strong vs. Rufus R. Jones
Johnny Weaver vs. Bill White
Larry Zbyszko vs. George Harris

12/29/75: Fayetteville, NC @ Cumberland County Memorial Auditorium
Wahoo McDaniel beat Billy Graham
Danny Miller beat Steve Strong
Roberto Soto & El Rayo beat Michel Dubois & Bill White
Haiti Kid beat Sonny Boy Hayes
Larry Zbyszko draw Jack Evans

12/30/75: Columbia, SC @ Township Auditorium
Ric Flair in Graham and Mulligan's corner
Mr. Wrestling & Rufus R. Jones beat Billy Graham &

Blackjack Mulligan
Steve Keirn (sub for Swede Hanson) beat Steve Strong by DQ
Roberto Soto & El Rayo beat Michel Dubois & Bill White
Cowboy Lang beat Sonny Boy Hayes
Steve Keirn beat Larry Sharpe

12/30/75: Raleigh, NC @ Dorton Arena
Paul Jones vs. Gene Anderson
Wahoo McDaniel vs. Angelo Mosca
Spoiler I & Spoiler II vs. Johnny Weaver & Swede Hanson
Little Tokyo vs. Haiti Kid
Jerry Blackwell vs. Danny Miller
Greg Peterson vs. Jack Evans

12/31/75: Raleigh, NC @ WRAL Studios (TV)

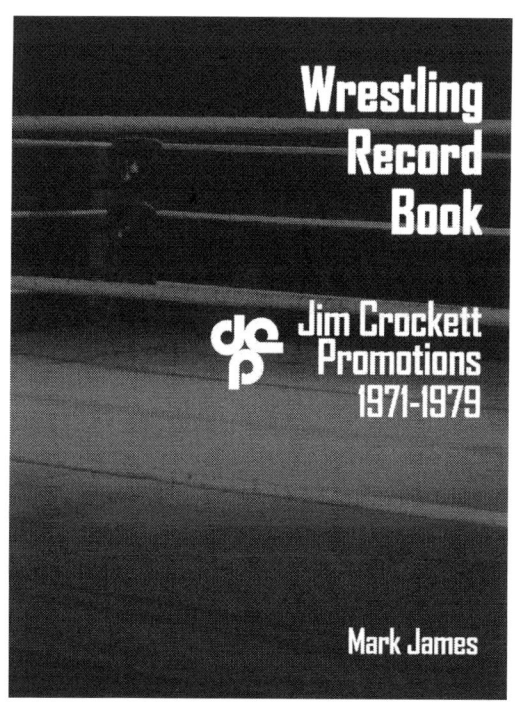

Mid-Atlantic Wrestling record rook content is from "Wrestling Record Book: Jim Crockett Promotions 1970-1979" a collection by Mark James. For more information visit MemphisWrestlingHistory.com

MID-ATLANTIC WRESTLING 1975 YEARBOOK

Check out these great books from
The Mid-Atlantic Gateway

Available Online at
www.MidAtlanticGateway.com